THE SANSKRIT EPICS' REPRESENTATION OF VEDIC MYTHS

The Sanskrit Epics' Representation of Vedic Myths

DANIELLE FELLER

MOTILAL BANARSIDASS PUBLISHERS
PRIVATE LIMITED • DELHI

First Edition: Delhi, 2004

ISBN: 978-81-208-2008-8

MOTILAL BANARSIDASS
41 U.A. Bungalow Road, Jawahar Nagar, Delhi 110 007
8 Mahalaxmi Chamber, 22 Bhulabhai Desai Road, Mumbai 400 026
120 Royapettah High Road, Mylapore, Chennai 600 004
236, 9th Main III Block, Jayanagar, Bengalore 560 011
8 Camac Street, Kolkata 700 017
Ashok Rajpath, Patna 800 004
Chowk, Varanasi 221 001

Printed in India

BY JAINENDRA PRAKASH JAIN AT SHRI JAINENDRA PRESS
A-45, NARAINA, PHASE-I, NEW DELHI 110 028
AND PUBLISHED BY NARENDRA PRAKASH JAIN FOR
MOTILAL BANARSIDASS PUBLISHERS PRIVATE LIMITED,
BUNGALOW ROAD, DELHI 110 007

ná vā́ u etán mriyase ná riṣyasi
devā́m íd eṣi pathíbhiḥ sugébhiḥ

Ṛgveda 1.162.21

Contents

Acknowledgments

This book is the slightly modified version of my Ph.D. thesis defended at the University of Lausanne, Switzerland, in June 2001. A Ph.D. thesis is not just the work of one person, but also the sum total of the investment made by others, in the form of advice, discussion, criticism, computer help or moral support.

My thanks go first of all to Prof. Johannes Bronkhorst, who directed this thesis, and who never withdrew his support, even when progress was slow and the outcome seemed doubtful. Secondly to Prof. Alf Hiltebeitel and Prof. Peter Schreiner, who were members of the jury. My debt to these three scholars is beyond words to express. Each one of them could have written a much better book than this one, and I owe them all my gratitude for letting me go my own way, in spite of all my shortcomings, for which I am of course entirely responsible.

In the course of writing my thesis, I received great help in the form of stimulating discussion from Dr. Andreas Bigger, who very generously devoted much time thinking over some of the problems raised in this study. Dr. Katja Kupfer very kindly helped me get the Vedic accents right. Dr. Sibylle Walther gave me an invaluable outsider's view on my writing. Mr. Raymond Conus provided sorely needed help with the final computer formatting and with the index. My gratitude goes to my colleagues, doctoral students of the Section de langues et civilisations orientales of the University of Lausanne, for providing a congenial environment of friendly discussion. My warmest thanks are due to the scholars of the Sanskrit Department of the University of Poona, especially to Prof. Ganesh U. Thite who initiated me into Vedic studies. While writing this thesis, I have immensely benefited from being able to attend some of the Dubrovnik International Conferences on the Sanskrit Epics and Purāṇas, and I here wish to express my heart-felt thanks to Prof. Mislav Jezic, and Mrs. Klara Gönc Moacanin, the kind organisers of these conferences. In the course of my investigations, I made use of the electronic versions of the Mahābhārata that we owe to Profs. Muneo Tokunaga and John Smith, and I wish to take this opportunity to thank them.

Two chapters of this book are revised versions of articles which were published previously. I here wish to express all my gratitude to Dr. Mary Brockington and Prof. Peter Schreiner, and to Prof. Jan Houben and Karel R. van Kooij, the editors of the two collections of articles in which these two chapters were published, and who helped me in many ways to get my thoughts straight and also to improve my English. My thanks are also due to the editors of these two collections, Brill in Leiden, and the Croatian Academy of Sciences and Arts, for granting me permission to publish again these two articles here.

This study was made possible by various grants. My thanks go to the University of Lausanne and the University of Poona, to the Indian Council for Cultural Relations, and to the Swiss National Science Foundation.

Finally, I wish to express my gratitude to the Editor, Motilal Banarsidass, and especially to Mr. N.P. Jain, for accepting to publish this book in their valuable collection.

November 2003 —DANIELLE FELLER
Lausanne

Abbreviations

AB	:	Aitareyabrāhmaṇa
ĀpŚS	:	Āpastambaśrautasūtra
ĀśvŚS	:	Āśvalāyanaśrautasūtra
AV	:	Atharvaveda Saṃhitā
BĀU	:	Bṛhadāraṇyaka Upaniṣad
BaudhŚS	:	Baudhāyanaśrautasūtra
BD	:	Bṛhaddevatā
BhG	:	Bhagavadgītā
ChU	:	Chāndogya Upaniṣad
DrāhŚS	:	Drāhyāyanaśrautasūtra
GobhGS	:	Gobhilagṛhyasūtra
JB	:	Jaiminīyabrāhmaṇa
KapS	:	Kapiṣṭhala Kaṭha Saṃhitā
KauṣB	:	Kauṣītakibrāhmaṇa
KS	:	Kāṭhaka Saṃhitā
KŚS	:	Kātyāyanaśrautasūtra
LāṭŚS	:	Lāṭyāyanaśrautasūtra
MBh	:	Mahābhārata
MS	:	Maitrāyaṇī Saṃhitā
MSmṛ	:	Manusmṛti
MW	:	Monier-Williams Dictionary
Nir	:	Nirukta
R	:	Rāmāyaṇa
ṚV	:	Ṛgveda Saṃhitā
ṢaḍvB	:	Ṣaḍviṃśabrāhmaṇa

ŚB	:	Śatapathabrāhmaṇa
Sup	:	Suparṇākhyāna
TB	:	Taittirīyabrāhmaṇa
TMB	:	Tāṇḍyamahābrāhmaṇa
TS	:	Taittirīya Saṃhitā
VS	:	Vājasaneyi Saṃhitā

1. Introduction

As the title of this study, "The Sanskrit Epics' Representation of Vedic Myths", suggests, my aim is to examine the way in which certain myths which first appear (as far as India is concerned) in the Vedas, and more specifically in the Ṛgveda, are retold in the Sanskrit Epics, the Mahābhārata and the Rāmāyaṇa,[1] and to examine in what way the Epics re-use the mythological material earlier used in the Vedas.[2] Before proceeding any further, I shall first give a brief summary of the nature, contents and dates of the texts mentioned above.

The texts

The oldest stratum of Sanskrit literature is called the Veda, a term which (originally at least) was roughly synonymous with *mantra* or *brahman* and meant 'sacred utterance'.[3] The Veda is also called the *śruti* 'that which has been heard', or the 'revelation', and is, according to the later Indian tradition – especially according to the Mīmāṃsā, a school of Vedic exegesis – eternal and authorless, and was 'revealed' to the Vedic *ṛṣi*s or seers.[4] The Veda is divided into several layers of texts: first come the Saṃhitās or 'collections'. There are four Saṃhitās:

[1] Unless mentioned otherwise, reference will be given throughout to the critical editions of these two texts. The critical editions were mainly used for the sake of convenience. As SULLIVAN (1990:18) remarks: "Because variant readings are listed in the notes for each verse, and episodes which appear in only a small proportion of the textual tradition have been put in Appendices, the critical edition is, in a sense, the most complete edition of the text, and certainly the most convenient one to use." The critical editions of the Epics do not, however, enjoy universal support. One of the staunchest critics of the critical editions is Madeleine Biardeau, according to whom the Epics, although they have one original author, are the products of a long subsequent oral tradition, and who thinks that there is no 'archetype', no written text from which all the manuscripts derive, but that each manuscript simply represents a written version of the story. See e.g. BIARDEAU (1997:85-86), (1999:LIII-LIV), and (2002:18-19).

[2] Some of the myths studied are also found in the literatures of other Indo-European languages. But in this work I will mostly limit myself to the Indian material.

[3] See BRONKHORST (1989 [1990]: 132).

[4] Only the youngest stratum of Vedic literature, especially the Vedāṅgas, are not considered as *śruti*.

the oldest is the Ṛgveda Saṃhitā, or the 'collection of verses', (dated circa 1500-1000 B.C.E.),[5] composed in ten *maṇḍala*s or books. Out of these, the tenth *maṇḍala* is usually considered to be younger than the rest of the collection. The Ṛgveda consists of hymns attributed to certain families of seers, mainly containing prayers and praise addressed to different gods. In these hymns, the poets frequently mention and describe the mythical deeds of these gods. The Ṛgveda Saṃhitā is thus of paramount importance for our study. The Sāmaveda Saṃhitā, or the 'collection of melodies', mainly consists of verses taken over from the Ṛgveda.[6] But the Sāmaveda adds musical annotations to these verses, which were meant for the use of the *udgātṛ*-priest who had to sing these parts in the ritual. The Yajurveda Saṃhitā, or the 'collection of sacrificial formulae', whose oldest text goes back to about 800 B.C.E., is not unitary, unlike the other collections. It is first subdivided into 'white' (*śukla*) and 'black' (*kṛṣṇa*) Yajurveda, and consists of five texts, namely: the Vājasaneyi Saṃhitā belonging to the White Yajurveda; and the Kaṭha (or Kāṭhaka) Saṃhitā, the Kapiṣṭhala Kaṭha Saṃhitā, the Maitrāyaṇī Saṃhitā and the Taittirīya Saṃhitā belonging to the Black Yajurveda. Although these five Saṃhitā are said to be recensions (*śākhā*s), they are too different to go back to a single, original Ur-Yajurveda, or at least to allow such a text to be reconstructed. (See MYLIUS (1988:53)). The Yajurveda Saṃhitā, as its name shows, is mainly concerned with the sacrificial ritual. But, and this point is important for our study, it also narrates many myths, mainly in order to justify or explain certain aspects of the ritual. Finally, the

5 The dates of the Vedic texts are very hypothetical. The absolute chronology is especially problematic. Thus the dates of the Ṛgveda Saṃhitā can vary by thousands of years according to different authors. The relative chronology of these texts, on the other hand, is a little more certain. On the whole, it seems that the bulk of Vedic literature, except the younger Upaniṣads and the Vedāṅgas, is pre-Buddhist. (See GONDA (1975:20) and MYLIUS (1988:33)).

6 For this reason, we shall rarely refer to the Sāmaveda in the course of this study, for it hardly contains anything which is not already there in the Ṛgveda.

Atharvaveda Saṃhitā derives its name from the fire-priest Atharvan. According to MYLIUS (1988:32), it is as old as the tenth book of the Ṛgveda Saṃhitā, but it was accepted as part of the Veda (which is often called the *trayī vidyā* or 'triple knowledge') only late, and was never quite considered as the equal of the other Samhitās. This Saṃhitā consists for the greatest part of magical formulae or charms, and is of little relevance for the solemn ritual. It contains some speculative hymns, but, as GONDA (1975:294) remarks: "These poets are [...] less inclined to make the traditional mythological figures an element of their speculations."

The remaining Vedic texts are necessarily attached to one of the four Saṃhitās. We can distinguish several different groups of texts, which were roughly composed in the following chronological order, though there are some overlaps: the Brāhmaṇas, the Āraṇyakas, the Upaniṣads and the Vedāṅgas.[7] The Brāhmaṇas are prose compositions mainly dealing with the sacrifice, composed for the Brahmins. By their subject-matter, they continue the line of the Yajurveda Saṃhitā. They give precise descriptions and explanations of the sacrificial ritual, but also contain dogmatic commentaries, philosophical speculations, and are a real treasure-trove of legends and myths, a point which makes them highly relevant for our study. (See MYLIUS (1998:63)). The Āraṇyakas derive their name from the term *araṇya*, 'forest'. They probably received this appellation due to the fact that, as secret texts, they had to be studied in the wilderness. MYLIUS (1988:72) notes that the Āraṇyakas still mainly concern the sacrificial ritual, but not in a concrete sense: they give the ritual a mystical-allegorical interpretation leading to meta-ritualistic ideas. The Upaniṣads mark a break in the Vedic literature. While retaining a connection with the sacrifice, they

[7] However, GONDA (1975:22) draws our attention to the fact that "the ideas of chronological succession of 'literary genres' and of corresponding forms of religious interest can no longer be maintained."

are also philosophical texts, recording, for instance, the emergence of the theory of *saṃsāra* (cyclical reincarnation), the identification of *ātman* and *brahman*, etc. Finally, the Vedāṅgas, or auxiliary texts of the Veda, contain treatises on the ritual, phonetics, grammar, etymology, metrics and astronomy. They are all composed in the very terse *sūtra*-style. Of these, only the auxiliary texts concerning the ritual, or Kalpasūtras (subdivided into *śrautasūtra*s, concerning the solemn ritual, and *gṛhyasūtra*s, concerning the domestic ritual) are of some limited relevance for us. In the course of this study, and mainly for the sake of convenience, we shall principally distinguish between the Ṛgveda Saṃhitā, due to its greater antiquity, and the rest of the Vedic texts, which will be grouped together under the denomination of 'the later Veda'.

As for the two Sanskrit Epics, the Mahābhārata and the Rāmāyaṇa, let us first note that although we distinguish them by the appellation 'Epics', the Indian tradition itself does not generally consider that they belong to the same literary genre. The MBh is usually classified as *itihāsa* (history), a genre to which also belong, most importantly, the Purāṇas, whereas the R is considered as a *kāvya*, even as the *ādi-kāvya*, the 'first poem', because of its more refined form, and also because it marks the beginning of a long line of poetry. However, the tradition is not unanimous in this respect; the MBh sometimes refers to itself as *kāvya* and the R is also classified by certain writers on *alaṃkāraśāstra* as *itihāsa*.[8] These two works, however, present enough overall similarities to justify their common designation as 'Epics'. The MBh and the R are voluminous works: in their unabridged form, they contain respectively about 100'000 and 25'000 verses (*śloka*s), somewhat less in the critical editions.[9] Their dates are the subject of

---

[8] See GOLDMAN (1984:16, note 10).

[9] As far as the MBh is concerned, the total of 100'000 verses can only be obtained if the Harivaṃśa is included. On this topic, SULLIVAN (1990:3) notes: "However, in view

much dispute, and no real consensus has been reached on this score. The broad spectrum of dates which is often and for somewhat mysterious reasons given for these texts is 400 B.C.E. to 400 C.E., but this is valid only if we accept that they were composed in successive stages.[10] Concerning the relative priority of these two texts, no consensus has been reached either, and it seems indeed that it is impossible to determine with any certainty which one of them is older. We shall therefore consider them to be roughly contemporary. The authorship of the MBh is attributed to the sage Kṛṣṇa Dvaipāyana, also called Vyāsa, and that of the R to the sage Vālmīki. Both authors appear as characters in their own works. The MBh is composed in 18 books (*parvan*s),[11] and describes the fratricidal war which opposes two sets of cousins, the Kauravas and the Pāṇḍavas, who fight over the inheritance of the kingdom of Hastināpura. The R is composed in 7 books (*kāṇḍa*s) and describes the exile of Rāma, prince of Ayodhyā, and his subsequent war with the demon Rāvaṇa who has kidnapped his wife Sītā.[12] Apart from these central events, both Epics contain digressions on various topics. This trait is much more prominent in the MBh, which contains also much didactic material similar in content to that of treatises of law (*dharmaśāstra*s), and less so in the R, where these digressions are limited to the first and last books.

---

of the fact that the *Harivaṃśa* is not part of the MBh proper, it would be best to regard the 100,000 verses as a 'round figure'."

[10] Concerning this span of eight hundred years, BIARDEAU (2002:16-17) exclaims: "pourquoi ces huit cents ans, je ne l'ai jamais compris". For a more precise discussion of the dates of the MBh, see e.g. SULLIVAN (1990:3-5); for the R, see GOLDMAN (1984:14-23).

[11] The number 18 is very significant throughout the MBh: the Bhagavadgītā is also composed in 18 books, the great war lasts for 18 days, there are 18 army-divisions fighting in the war, etc. According to Śaṅkara, as BIARDEAU (2002:757-8) notes, this number has a sacrificial significance: it represents the 16 priests who officiate in the solemn ritual, plus the sacrificer and his wife. These 18 main *parvan*s are further subdivided into another set of *parvan*s, which I will call sub-*parvan*s for the sake of clarity.

[12] For summaries of the mains events of the MBh and R, see respectively VAN BUITENEN (1973:XIII-XVI) and GOLDMAN (1984:6-13).

The first part of this research consisted in reading the Ṛgveda and the two great Epics, and listing the mythological narratives which appear in the ṚV on the one hand, and in one or both Epics on the other. The later Vedic texts were of course also taken into consideration, but the references to these texts were obtained from secondary sources (their sheer bulk making their complete reading a daunting task). The second step consisted in choosing a few of these narratives, for dealing with all of them was beyond the scope of this work.[13] Out of all the mythological narratives obtained, the following were retained for our investigation, and will be treated in this order in the different chapters of this study:

Agni's hiding
Ṛgveda: 1.65.1-4; 1.67.3-8; 1.72.2-6; 1.98.2; 1.146.4; 2.4.2; 3.1.9; 3.5.10; 3.9.2 & 4-6 & 9; 5.2.8; 5.11.6; 5.15.5; 6.1.2-4; 6.8.4; 6.9.7; 7.4.3; 7.49.4; 8.84.2; 8.102.4-6; 10.5.5; 10.32.6-8; 10.46.2-9; 10.51-53; 10.79.3; 10.115.4.
The later Veda: *Taittirīya Saṃhitā*: 1.5.1; 2.6.6; 5.1.4.3-4; 6.2.8.4-6; *Maitrāyaṇī Saṃhitā*: 1.7.2; 3.8.6; *Kāṭhaka Saṃhitā*: 8.15; 25.7; *Kapiṣṭhala Kaṭha Saṃhitā*: 8.3; 39.5; *Śatapathabrāhmaṇa*: 1.2.3.1; 1.3.3.13-17; 2.2.3.1-11; 7.3.2.14-15; *Kauṣītakibrāhmaṇa*: 1.3.1-30; *Jaiminīyabrāhmaṇa*: 2.41; *Taittirīyabrāhmaṇa*: 1.1.3.9.
Mahābhārata: 1.5-7; 3.207; 3.212.6-19; 9.46.12-20; 13.83-84.

Indra and Ahalyā
Ṛgveda: (Indra as a ram): 1.51.1; 1.52.1; 8.2.40; 8.97.12.
The later Veda: *Maitrāyaṇī Saṃhitā*: 2.5.5; *Kāṭhaka Saṃhitā*: 13.5; *Śatapathabrāhmaṇa*: 3.3.4.17-19; *Taittirīyāraṇyaka*: 1.12.3; *Ṣaḍviṃ-*

[13] This study is not intended to function as a sort of compendium of MACDONELL's *Vedic Mythology* and HOPKINS' *Epic Mythology*. These two detailed works, which are of course very helpful as works of reference, are rather descriptive in nature, whereas this study aims at being more interpretive. Besides, this study does not aim at representing all the available material.

śabrāhmaṇa: 1.1.14-25; *Jaiminīyabrāhmaṇa*: 1.228; 2.79; 3.199-200; 3.234; *Bāṣkalamantra Upaniṣad*.
Mahābhārata: 5.12.6; 12.329.14.i-ii; 13.41.21; 13.138.6.
Rāmāyaṇa: 1.47.11-1.48; 7.30.15-42.

The theft of the soma
Ṛgveda: 1.80.2; 1.93.6; 3.43.7; 4.18.13; 4.26-27; 6.20.6; 8.82.9; 8.100.8; 9.48.3-4; 9.68.6; 9.77.2; 9.89.2; 10.11.4; 10.144.3-5.
The later Veda: *Taittirīya Saṃhitā*: 3.5.7; 6.1.6; *Maitrāyaṇī Saṃhitā*: 3.7.3; 4.1.1; *Kāṭhaka Saṃhitā*: 23.10; 34.3; *Śatapathabrāhmaṇa*: 1.7.1.1; 3.2.4.1-7; 11.7.2.8; *Aitareyabrāhmaṇa*: 3.25-26; *Tāṇḍyamahābrāhmaṇa*: 8.4.1; *Taittirīyabrāhmaṇa*: 1.1.3.10; 3.2.1.1-2.
Suparṇākhyāna.
Mahābhārata: 1.14-30; Anuśāsanaparvan, Appendix IA.
Rāmāyaṇa: 3.33.27-35.

The Aśvins rescue blind and buried people
Ṛgveda: 1.112.4-6 & 8; 1.116.11 & 14 & 16 & 24; 1.117.5 & 12 & 17-18; 1.118.6-7; 1.119.6-7; 8.5.23; 8.8.20; 10.39.3 & 8-9.
Jaiminīyabrāhmaṇa: 3.72-73; *Chāndogya Upaniṣad*: 4.4-9; 4.10-14.
Mahābhārata (Upamanyu falls into a hole due to his blindness and is rescued by the Aśvins): 1.3.19-82; 13.14; (the closely related story of Uttaṅka): 1.3.83-176 and 14.52-57.[14]

[14] Other mythical narratives are as follows (this list makes no claim to be exhaustive, at least as far as the Ṛgvedic passages are concerned):
Indra kills Vṛtra. ṚV: 1.16.8; 1.23.9; 1.32; 1.33.13; 1.51.4; 1.52; 1.54.10; 1.56.5-6; 1.61.6-12; 1.63.4; 1.80; 1.81.1; 1.84.3; 1.85.9; 1.100.2; 1.103.2 & 7-8; 1.106.6; 1.108.3; 1.121.11; 1.130.4; 1.165.6-8; 1.174.2; 1.187.1 & 6; 2.11.2 & 5 & 9 & 18; 2.12.3 & 11; 2.13.5; 2.14.2; 2.15.1; 2.19.2-4; 2.20.7; 2.22 (?); 2.30.1-3; 3.31.11 & 13-14 & 18 & 21; 3.32.4 & 6 & 11-12; 3.33.6-7; 3.34.3; 3.36.8; 3.37.5-6; 3.45.2; 3.47.3-4; 3.51.8-9; 3.54.15; 4.16.7; 4.17.1 & 3 & 7-8; 4.18.7 & 11; 4.19; 4.22.5; 4.28.1; 4.30.1; 4.42.7-9; 5.29.2-8; 5.30.6; 5.31.4 & 7; 5.32; 6.17.1 & 9-11; 6.18.14; 6.20.2; 6.22.6; 6.25.8; 6.30.4; 6.36.2; 6.44.15; 6.45.5; 6.47.2; 6.61.5; 6.68.3; 6.72.3; 7.19.5; 7.20.2; 7.21.3 & 6; 7.93.1 & 4; 8.1.14; 8.2.26 & 32 & 36; 8.3.19-20; 8.4.11; 8.6.6 & 13 & 16-17 & 40; 8.7.23-24 & 31; 8.12.22 & 26; 8.13.15; 8.21.12; 8.24.2 & 8; 8.27.8; 8.29.4; 8.32.11 & 25-26; 8.33.1 & 14; 8.37.1; 8.38.2; 8.45.4 & 25; 8.46.13; 8.54.5; 8.61.15; 8.62.8 & 11; 8.64.9; 8.66.3 & 10-11; 8.70.1; 8.76.2-3; 8.77.3; 8.78.7; 8.82.1; 8.89.3-5; 8.90.1; 8.92.24; 8.93.2 & 4 & 7 & 14-15

My choice of dealing with the myths of Agni's hiding, Indra's seduction of Ahalyā, the theft of the Soma and Upamanyu's salvation by the Aśvins was motivated by the fact that these myths deal with the four principal divinities in the Ṛgveda: Agni, Indra, Soma and the Aśvins, and I felt that it would be particularly interesting to examine the treatment that these major Vedic gods receive in the Epics. Moreover, these four myths are perfect illustrations of the various ways in which the Epics can represent Vedic myths. I also chose to deal with myths which are fairly well represented in both Vedic and epic literature.[15] Perhaps the R is rather under-represented in this study, but it seems to be true that the R contains far less Vedic material than the MBh. As BIARDEAU (1997:87) says: "Personally, I was struck [...] that the links with Vedic literature were looser in the R than in the MBh though both epics had some connection with it."[16] While the god Indra retains a fair amount of importance in the R, Agni's role is

& 18 & 20 & 23; 8.96.5 & 7 & 19-21; 8.97.4; 8.99.6; 8.100.2 & 7 & 12; 9.113.1; 10.23.2; 10.42.5; 10.49.6; 10.50.2; 10.65.2; 10.66.8; 10.67.12; 10.73.5; 10.74.6; 10.89.7; 10.99.1-2; 10.103.10; 10.104.9-10; 10.111.6 & 9; 10.113; 10.124.6 & 8; 10.138.5-6; 10.147.1-2; 10.152.2-3; 10.153.3. MBh: 3.38.12; 3.98-99; 3.135.2; 3.168.19; 5.9.40-5.17; 7.69.49-67; 12.329.27.iv; 14.11.6-20. R: 1.23.17-23; 7.75-77.

Indra kills Namuci. ṚV: 1.53.7; 5.30.7-9; 6.20.6; 7.19.5; 8.14.13; 10.73.6-7. MBh: 9.42.27-37.

Indra kills Triśiras (Viśvarūpa). ṚV: 10.8.8-9; 10.99.6. MBh: 5.9.1-39; 12.329.21-27.

Indra clips the wings of the mountains. ṚV: 4.19.4; 8.41.4. R: 5.1.108-112.

Cyavana's rejuvenation by the Aśvins. ṚV: 1.51.12; 1.116.10; 1.117.13; 5.74.5; 5.75.5; 7.68.6; 7.71.5; 10.39.4; 10.61.2. MBh: 3.121.20-3.125.10; 13.141.15-30.

Agastya and Lopāmudrā. ṚV: 1.179. MBh: 3.94-96.

Purūravas and Urvaśī. ṚV: 1.31.4; 4.2.18; 10.95. MBh: 1.70.16-21. R: Appendix I, no. 8, 165-170 (Crit. Ed.); 7.56 (Gorakhpur ed.).

The story of Śunaḥśepa. ṚV: 1.24.12-13; 5.2.7. R: 1.60-61.

Trita thrown into a well. ṚV: 1.105; 10.8.7. MBh: 9.35.

The birth of the Maruts. ṚV: 6.66; 7.56.1-4; 7.58.2. MBh: 9.37.29-32. R: 1.45-46.

The story of Naciketas. ṚV: 10.135. MBh: 13.70.

The story of Dīrghatamas. ṚV: 1.158 4-6. MBh: 1.98.

Puruṣasūkta. ṚV: 10.90. MBh: 12.175.11-21. R: 3.13.29-30.

15 I could incur the reproach of not dealing with the myth of Indra slaying Vṛtra, which is indeed extremely well represented in all three works (see preceding footnote). But this myth is so voluminous and complex that it would deserve to be treated by itself. Besides, a huge amount of secondary literature has already been dedicated to this subject.

16 See also RENOU (1960:14): "Le Rāmāyaṇa se sert des choses védiques comme d'une sorte d'élément décoratif." And BROCKINGTON (1998:14-15).

very limited, the Aśvins' practically non-existent, and the myth of the theft of the *soma* is only very briefly and allusively narrated in this text. Finally, the topic of the sixth chapter of this study: '*Raṇa-yajña*: the Mahābhārata war as a sacrifice', does not, it is true, concern a myth. It primarily concerns the sacrifice, but the connection between myth and sacrifice is often (though not always) quite prominent. In the cases which concern us here, the myths of Agni's hiding, the theft of the *soma* and Indra's seduction of Ahalyā clearly have a lot to say about the sacrificial ritual. However, the chapter on *raṇa-yajña* does not deal with the way myth talks about sacrifice, but on the contrary with the way in which the paramount Vedic category, or indeed world-view, that of sacrifice, is in turn 'mythified' in the MBh.

According to the nature of the material, I was led to proceed in different ways. In the case of the myths of Agni's hiding and the theft of the *soma*, which appear in the ṚV in a cluster of hymns which have the form of a dialogue (*saṃvāda* hymns), and which describe the mythical event fairly coherently and exhaustively,[17] I first deal with the ṚV, then the later Veda and finally the Epics, in the chronological order. These two cases can be traced back to a definite cluster of Ṛgvedic hymns. On the other hand, the myths of Indra and Ahalyā and Upamanyu's salvation cannot be traced back to one single systematic and comprehensive Ṛgvedic narration. In the case of Indra's seduction of Ahalyā, a few scattered elements of the myth (but not all of them) occur separately in the ṚV and seem to have merged with each other, and with other elements, under the influence of a later text, the Śatapathabrāhmaṇa. In the case of Upamanyu's salvation too, there is no single Ṛgvedic model, but this MBh episode seems to be a

[17] In both cases, these myths are also mentioned elsewhere in the ṚV, but in a more allusive form. The fact that these two myths first appear in Ṛgvedic *saṃvāda* hymns is interesting, because scholars often claim that the epic genre itself derives not only from the *itihāsas* or *ākhyānas* narrated in the Brāhmaṇas, but that the precursors of the Epics can also be found in the *saṃvāda* hymns. (See e.g. MYLIUS 1988:91).

conglomeration of several (but content-wise similar) Ṛgvedic themes, which are however much more substantially represented in the ṚV than the scattered elements of the story of Indra and Ahalyā. In these two cases, I first deal with the Epic narratives and then trace back their Vedic antecedents. This is one of the reasons why I claim that these chosen myths are particularly interesting, precisely because they show that the transmission of myths can occur under various forms, and that there is no one preferred Ṛgvedic form which was particularly suited for a long posterity.

Vedic versus epic

Why choose specifically these two poles: Vedic and epic, and not some others? For many of the myths studied here also reappear in the subsequent literature. The Epics are particularly interesting in that they mark a turning point in the religious history of brahmanical India. As BIARDEAU remarks:

> "The two Sanskrit epics announce the end of what can be called the Vedic religion and in a way build, though they are mainly narrative poems, the ideological base of classical Brahmanism and of what will be its more widely spread form: the Hindu *bhakti* as the religion of devotion." (1997:73).

Furthermore, she says:

> "Ces épopées marquent un tournant dans l'histoire de la culture brahmanique [...]. Le brahmanisme y prend en effet un tour nouveau et marque une véritable cassure, sans que pour autant nous sortions de la culture brahmanique. A elles deux, les épopées constituent une véritable charte du brahmanisme classique d'où est sorti progressivement ce qu'on appelle maintenant 'hindouisme' avec ses ramifications à tous les niveaux sociaux, hautes et basses castes réunies – un fait socio-culturel 'total' en quelque sorte." (1999:X-XI).

Thus the Epics are an end and a beginning at the same time: the end of Vedism and the beginning of Hinduism. Therefore the myths narrated in these texts should prove particularly interesting, since they contain within themselves the remnants of the old times and the seeds of the new. But how do the Epics represent themselves? Do they situate themselves in the line of the Vedic tradition, or, on the contrary, do they claim to break new ground? Not much can be gleaned on that score from the R. The 'ouverture' of this text (1.2) shows us the sage Vālmīki, who, under Brahmā's inspiration, 'invents' a new verse, the *śloka* (1.2.14), and is subsequently advised by Brahmā to compose Rāma's story in that verse. While the divine inspiration received by the *ṛṣi* from a god definitely continues the line of the Vedic *ṛṣi*s who are said to receive the divine 'revelation' of the Veda,[18] the use of a new verse on that occasion rather seems to point to a change of direction, to an opening up of new horizons towards *kāvya*. However, this should be taken as a mere hypothesis on my part, and, although it would seem to be verified by the fact that the R contains little Vedic material, it is never stated in so many words by the R itself. This text simply does not adopt a outspoken stance on this topic.

The MBh's stance, on the contrary, is quite clear, if not emphatic: for the MBh does not merely claim to follow the Vedic tradition, it even claims to be a Veda itself.[19] The MBh's equivalence with the Veda is repeatedly stressed at the very beginning of the text, as if to

[18] Brahmā's role in this scene, however, is typically epico-purāṇic.

[19] For this topic in general, see FITZGERALD (1991). Not only the MBh, but the Itihāsapurāṇa as a whole is frequently called the fifth Veda, both in Brahmanical (for the first time in ChU 7.1.2; 7.1.4; 7.2.1; 7.7.1) and non-Brahmanical texts. See BRONKHORST (1989 [1990]) and SULLIVAN (1990:88). Furthermore, the MBh is frequently said to be the Veda for *śūdras* and women. However, the MBh itself merely states that it is fit to be recited to all four *varṇas* (12.314.45). (But according to MBh 18.5.43 only to three *varṇas*, *śūdras* presumably being excluded). The specific mention of *śūdras* and women is found in a later text, the Bhāgavatapurāṇa 1.4.25 & 29 (*circa* 9th century C.E.). For the connection between the MBh and *śūdras*, see SHARMA (2000).

establish this concept once for all as the foundational building-block of the whole edifice. Usually, the MBh calls itself an *ākhyāna* (legend) or an *itihāsa* (history),[20] but in 1.1.205 and 1.56.17, it calls itself the *kārṣṇa veda*: the Veda of Kṛṣṇa, from the name of its composer, Kṛṣṇa Dvaipāyana,[21] also called Vyāsa. Not only is the MBh explicitly said to be a Veda, moreover the text says that its author Vyāsa also compiled the Vedas themselves. Thus in 1.57.72-73, we read that Vyāsa, knowing that *dharma* becomes weaker in each successive eon, divided the Veda (into four, in order to make it more easily accessible),[22] and in 1.57.74, that "he taught the Vedas with the MBh as the fifth": *vedān adhyāpayāmāsa mahābhāratapañcamān*. Vyāsa is generally described by the MBh as a *ṛṣi,* a Vedic seer endowed with preternatural and visionary powers. (See FITZGERALD 1991:160). Although Vyāsa himself is not said to be the author of any Vedic hymns, he is the great-grand-son of the *ṛṣi* Vasiṣṭha, to whose family is attributed the seventh *maṇḍala* of the Ṛgveda. In 1.53.31, the MBh is again kept on par with the Veda, for there we read that during the breaks in Janamejaya's *sarpa-sattra*, Brahmins recited tales based on the Vedas, but Vyāsa recited the great and eternal tale of the Bhāratas:

> *karmāntareṣv akathayan dvijā vedāśrayāḥ kathāḥ /*
> *vyāsas tv akathayan nityam ākhyānam bhāratam mahat //*[23]

---

[20] In this quality, the MBh, unlike the Vedas, is usually included in the category of *smṛti*, and not *śruti*. As FITZGERALD (1991:168) notes: "Generally, when he quoted it in the course of arguments, Śaṅkara would simply refer to the *MBh* with a confident '*smṛteḥ*', 'from authoritative tradition'."

[21] But perhaps a pun on Kṛṣṇa (which can designate Kṛṣṇa Dvaipāyana the composer, but also of course Kṛṣṇa Vāsudeva, Viṣṇu's *avatāra* in the MBh), is not ruled out. For a study of the personage of Vyāsa in the MBh, see SULLIVAN (1990).

[22] Verse 1.57.73 c-d contains an etymology of the name Vyāsa:
vivyāsa vedān yasmāc ca tasmād vyāsa iti smṛtaḥ /
Because he divided the Vedas he is known as the Divider.
We also read that Vyāsa divided the one and eternal Veda in 1.1.52 and 1.54.5.

[23] However, this statement at the same time implies that the MBh is inherently different from the Vedas.

Verses 1.1.208-9 go a step further and claim that the MBh is (literally) weightier than all the Vedas together, hence its name, *mahā-bhārata*: 'which has a great weight':

> *catvāra ekato vedā bhārataṃ caikam ekataḥ /*
> *samāgataiḥ surarṣibhis tulām āropitaṃ purā /*
> *mahattve ca gurutve ca ghriyamāṇaṃ tato 'dhikam //*
> *mahattvād bhāravattvāc ca mahābhāratam ucyate /*
> Once the divine seers foregathered, and on one scale they hung the four *Vedas* in the balance, and on the other scale *The Bhārata*; and both in size and in weight it was the heavier. Therefore, because of its size and its weight, it is called *The Mahābhārata*. (Transl. VAN BUITENEN 1973).[24]

A comparable train of thought is pursued in 1.2.235, where we read that "a Brahmin who knows the four Vedas, along with the auxiliary texts and the Upaniṣads, but who does not know this tale (the Mahābhārata), has no learning":

> *yo vidyāc caturo vedān sāṅgopaniṣadān dvijaḥ /*
> *na cākhyānam idaṃ vidyān naiva sa syād vicakṣaṇaḥ //*

Thus the Mahābhārata does not only claim to be a Veda (the fifth), and to have been composed by Vyāsa, the compiler of the Vedas, but also to be weightier than all the Vedas taken together.[25] How should

[24] As HILTEBEITEL (2001:101) notes, this verse suggests "a written book".

[25] In fact, the MBh claims to be a sort of compendium of all the existing literary genres. Apart from being a Veda and an *itihāsa* or *ākhyāna*, it is also said to be an Upaniṣad in 1.1.191, and verses 1.2.236-7 even claim that it is the highest form of poetry and an inspiration for future poets:

> *śrutvā tv idam upākhyānam śrāvyam anyan na rocate /*
> *puṃskokilarutaṃ śrutvā rūkṣā dhvāṅkṣasya vāg iva //*
> *itihāsottamād asmāj jāyante kavibuddhayaḥ /*
> "Once one has heard this story so worthy of being heard no other story will please him: it will sound harsh as the crow sounds to one after hearing the cuckoo sing. From this supreme epic rise the inspirations of the poets". (Transl. VAN BUITENEN 1973).

The first part of this verse may raise reasonable doubt. The MBh, unlike the R which is designated as the *ādi-kāvya*, is not usually listed under the category of *kāvya* or poetry,

we interpret this statement? Is this mere lip-service? For as RENOU (1960:2) remarks: "Même dans les domaines les plus orthodoxes, il arrive que la révérence au Veda soit un simple 'coup de chapeau', donné en passant à une idole dont on entend ne plus s'encombrer par la suite." Furthermore, the same author (1960:14) states: "L'Epopée, le plus souvent, se borne à révérer de loin la *śruti*, faisant allusion, en passant, aux sacrifices, aux récitations." On this score, the problem of the incomprehensibility of the Vedic language is often evoked. Thus BIARDEAU (1997:162):

> "At a certain point [...] the *śruti* texts were set apart as an intangible revelation, the authority of which could not be questioned. More than that, the normative criterion which placed the *śruti* in this position was probably mainly its unintelligibility. The language of the hymns had never belonged to daily language, given its intricate prosody and ways of chanting. But the rest of the *śruti* is hardly more intelligible, the differences between the daily language and the Vedic idiom increasing more and more. Even the spoken Sanskrit of the *brahmans* was remote from the text they had to know by heart and recite everyday."[26]

Commenting on the MBh's claim to be a Veda, FITZGERALD (1991:159-160) remarks:

or at least this seems to have happened only late in the tradition. (See TUBB 1991:175, note 7). (For instance, the MBh is called three times a *kāvya* in a passage kept in Appendix I.1.1 (lines 13 & 34-35), which a certain number of manuscripts insert at the very beginning of the text, and which contains the scene where Vyāsa, having mentally composed his work, turns to Brahmā for advice and help.) But the second part of the verse sounds quasi-prophetic, for it is a fact that later Sanskrit poetry, especially Mahākāvyas, borrowed their subject-matter from the Epics.

26 This incomprehensibility of the Vedic Sanskrit may perhaps account for the fact that we find few purely linguistic correspondances between the Vedic and the epic occurrences of one and the same myth. The Vedic language was perhaps considered too alien to allow for this, except in cases of direct quotes or in conscious and deliberate imitations of the Vedic style. As RENOU (1960:13) remarks: "Avec cette fidélité au fond contraste la désaffection pour la forme."

> "As [...] a new 'Veda', it was obvious that the *Great Bhārata* was a Veda only metaphorically. The *Great Bhārata* was a very different sort of text from the Veda in many more ways than the two were substantively similar. But the *Great Bhārata* was intended to function in Indian culture in the same imposing and authoritative way the ancient Vedas had, and the formulators of this *Great Bhārata* developed their metaphor with some care."

Furthermore, BROCKINGTON (1998:5, note 11) notes that: "it may well be that the emphasis on the epic as a fifth Veda and comparisons with them in reality testifies to a break between the Vedas and the Mahābhārata". In his review article, HILTEBEITEL (2000:163) comments on this as follows:

> "The notion of 'a break' between Veda and epic is thus worth pursuing. One might consider a break that would allow for a reclamation of Veda by poets for whom it remained of utmost importance, poets who knew their Veda well, who could now compose something new while making use of all kinds of Vedic allusions".

Continuing Hiltebeitel's line of thinking, the basic assumption of this study, since it deals with the Epics' representation of Vedic mythological material, is that the epic authors knew (and understood) the Vedas.[27] I believe that the references to the Veda involve much more than mere lip-service, and that a great part of the epic redactors' effort went into reworking the Vedic material to fit it into the Epics, at least as far as the Mahābhārata is concerned. The representation of Vedic mythological narratives on the one hand, and the representation

---

27. HOPKINS (1920:chapt.1) lists the works which were certainly known to the author(s) of the MBh. Either because they are named (this includes the three or four Vedas, the Brāhmaṇas (only the Śatapatha is mentioned by name), the Āraṇyakas and Upaniṣads, or because they are cited. RENOU (1960:11, note 1) gives a further bibliography of works listing Vedic quotes in the Epics. See also GOPAL (1982) and especially BROCKINGTON (1998:7-15).

of the Mahābhārata war as a sacrifice on the other, are part of this effort. And here again, we notice a deliberate attempt to make this clear at the very beginning of the text. For we find in Ādiparvan 1.3-1.53.26 (i.e., after the two summaries of the main events of the MBh (1.1 & 1.2), and before the beginning of the narration of the central epic events) a veritable cluster of myths which have immediately perceptible Vedic antecedents: Upamanyu's salvation by the Aśvins, Agni's hiding, and the theft of the Soma.[28] What is more, these mythical narratives are interspersed with accounts of various sacrificial performances: Śaunaka's twelve-year *sattra* (1.1 and 1.4); Janamejaya's *aśvamedha* or horse-sacrifice (1.3);[29] and, most importantly, Janamejaya's *sarpa-sattra* or snake-sacrifice (1.13.48 and 1.47-53).[30] What is more, these various *sattra*s provide the frame-stories in which the narrations of myths are embedded, and the occasion on which the myths are told.[31] On the whole, concerning the function of such depictions of sacrifices in the epics, I would tend to agree with HILTEBEITEL (2001:119) when he remarks: "Rather than looking at Vedic sacrifices as prior forms or schemas by which the epic poets "ritualize," "transpose" or indeed *allegorize* an older story into another register, I argue that they make knowing *allusion* to Veda, its rituals included, within the primary texture of their composition." Thus the beginning of the MBh sets a truly Vedic programme: establishing the text's identity as a Veda, containing narrations of Vedic mythological material and descriptions

---

[28] The myths of Upamanyu's salvation and Agni's hiding are subsequently narrated again in the MBh.

[29] Janamejaya Pārikṣita's *aśvamedha* is already mentioned in ŚB 13.5.4.1-3. In this text, just as in the MBh, Janamejaya is said to perform this sacrifice with his three brothers, Bhīmasena, Śrutasena and Ugrasena. In the MBh, Indra's bitch Saramā is moreover said to intervene in the sacrifice. Saramā is well-known in Vedic literature, from the ṚV onwards, where she is said to find Indra's cows, but this is the only place in the Epic where she appears in a story, not just in lists enumerating the names of gods (2.11.29) or of foetus-eating demons (2.219.33).

[30] The *sarpa-sattra* is also a Vedic rite, and a rather explicit prefiguration or at least a 'double' of the war-sacrifice itself.

[31] See MINKOWSKI (1989).

of Vedic sacrifices. This contributes to laying a Vedic foundation for the whole narration, giving a mythical and ritual flavour to the whole 'ouverture' of the epic narrative, as if this text's major concern had been to "anchor" firmly the great epic vessel in Vedic ground, before letting it float off. Whether this was planned from the start or the fruit of a subsequent addition ultimately matters little. Subsequently, as the main epic narration starts unfolding, this Vedic programme merges into the background mythical structure, and sporadically emerges in the form of a mythological narration having Vedic sources.

Secondary literature

What is the place of this research in the landscape of epic studies? I shall not attempt to pass in review all the existing secondary literature on this topic, for the history of Rāmāyaṇa, and especially Mahābhārata, criticism is nearly as colourful and eventful, though not as old, as that of the Epics themselves.[32] The reader is especially referred to the very comprehensive survey of epic studies which can be found in BROCKINGTON (1998:chapt. 2), which gives detailed and rather fair-minded summaries of the works and theories of all the major scholars who wrote on the Epics, right from the beginning of Indological studies.[33] However, though I shall refrain from rewriting a history of epic studies, (since this has been done abundantly before), I will very briefly discuss the current trends in epic studies, and my more immediate models.

Broadly speaking, we may distinguish nowadays two major trends in epic studies: namely, the text-historical school, and the structural school. The text-historical school, as its name shows, has tried to

---

[32] The secondary literature which is directly relevant for each one of my chosen topics will of course be mentioned and commented in the course of this study.

[33] See also SULLIVAN (1990:13-25).

establish a history of the development of the epic texts, attempting to distinguish, according to various criteria (stylistic, religious, etc.), the chronological layers of composition of these texts. For according to this view, the Epics were composed by successive accretion over the course of many centuries. The structural school, which serves as my model for reasons which will be discussed further on in the course of this introduction, takes a more holistic and ahistorical view of these texts. In this regard, we may quote LAINE (1989:23), who describes the endeavors of the scholars belonging to this school as follows:

> "Recent Mahābhārata-criticism has concentrated on developing literary analysis of the deeper symbolic structure of the extant epic. These theories suggest there is an underlying unity in the epic which scholars of a previous generation branded as a disorderly conglomeration."

The main representatives of this view are scholars such as Georges Dumézil, Madeleine Biardeau and Alf Hiltebeitel, who have attempted to relate the epic narration to a mythic superstructure, to find out the mythic symbolism behind the core of the epic narration. Dumézil's work concentrates mainly on the Epics' correlation with Indo-European myth. His main contribution to the topic is his 'trifunctional' theory, which we will have occasion to discuss, especially in the chapter on Indra and Ahalyā. While Dumézil looks backward, so to say, to the correlation between the epic and Indo-European material, Biardeau on the contrary looks forward and tries to correlate the Epics with the more recent religious developments in Hinduism. Thus Biardeau, in her masterful studies of the Epics, unravels the symbolism and the various levels of interpretation underlying these texts (especially the MBh), relating them to a 'universe of *bhakti*'. HILTEBEITEL, as he himself states (1976:41), seeks to find out the "epic continuations" of "mythic models", an effort which he continued in several subsequent articles and books. While my work, it is hoped, continues this effort of connecting Epic and myth, my method is the reverse: I am planning to deal with the myths themselves as they are represented in the Epics, that is, with 'peripheral' mythological narratives, and more particularly those having Vedic 'sources', and see what use they have on the background of the epic narration, what they mean and what exemplary value they have.

Myth

Since my chosen topic is the representation of myths in the Epics, this is perhaps the place to define what I mean by the term 'myth'. Unfortunately, though not surprisingly, this proves no easy task. Myth is a deceptively simple word: we all think that we know what a myth is, but when it comes to defining the term more precisely, the difficulties begin. In order to clarify the subject-matter to a certain extent, we may first quote what might be considered nowadays as a 'classical' definition of myth, (and one with which I chiefly agree), namely the one given by a distinguished scholar of myth, especially Indian myths, Wendy DONIGER (1998:2):

> "[A] myth is not a lie or a false statement to be contrasted with truth or reality or fact or history, though this usage is, perhaps, the most common meaning of myth in casual parlance today. But in the history of religions, the term *myth* has far more often been used to mean 'truth.' What makes this ambiguity possible is that a myth is above all a story that is *believed*, believed to be true, and that people continue to believe despite sometimes massive evidence that it is, in fact, a lie. [...] In its positive and enduring sense, what a myth *is* is a story that is sacred to and shared by a group of people who find their most important meanings in it; it is a story believed to have been composed in the past about an event in the past, or, more rarely, in the future, an event that continues to have meaning

> in the present because it is remembered; it is a story that is part of a larger group of stories."[34]

But quoting merely one definition of myth given by one scholar would be skirting the issue. For in no other field of inquiry, perhaps, do we find such a bewildering variety of opinions and definitions. STRENSKI (1987:1) describes the situation in apt and vivid terms:

> "Myth is everything and nothing at the same time. It is *the* true story or a false one, revelation or deception, sacred or vulgar, real or fictional, symbol or tool, archetype or stereotype. It is either strongly structured and logical or emotional and pre-logical, traditional and primitive or part of contemporary ideology. Myth is about the gods, but often also the ancestors and sometimes certain men. [...] It is charter, recurring theme, character type, received idea, half-truth, tale or just a plain lie."

Indeed, in his book, Strenski, investigating the theories of myth of four major thinkers of the 20th century (Cassirer, Malinowski, Eliade and Léṿi-Strauss), shows not only how these thinkers' theories differ so widely from each other as to have almost no common denominator at all, but also how the life-situations of these authors had a very profound influence on the particular way they came to think about myths. Without further discussing how the political situation of their times influenced these thinkers (for which subject the reader is referred to Strenski's book),[35] we shall give here brief summaries of Eliade and Lévi-Strauss's theories of myth, not only to exemplify the dissimilarity of their theories, but also because we shall sometimes refer to these important thinkers in the course of our inquiry.

---

[34] See also DONIGER (1998:80).

[35] However, this subject is important, for it eminently shows the subjectivity of these thinkers' views.

While discussing Eliade, STRENSKI (1987:72) first briefly quotes that thinker's own definition of myth: "Eliade defines 'myth' in a deceptively simple way: 'myth is, before everything else, a tale. [...] It has no other function than to reveal *how something came into being* [...], how worlds are born and what happened afterward'."[36] In a more detailed fashion, he further enumerates what he considers as the three main points of Eliade's definition of myth:

> "1 [Myths] are stories about origins, beginnings, creations.
> 2 They function to provide men with an existential, ontological orientation by narrating the sacred, external events of their own origins, beginnings or creations.
> 3 They originate in the human experience of a yearning for such a fundamental orientation. To satisfy the yearning is to achieve a real appropriation of timelessness in the midst of history." (STRENSKI 1987:72).

Discussing Lévi-Strauss' theory of myth, STRENSKI (1987:130) notes that for Lévi-Strauss, "'myth' is a strongly structured, important story." He then proceeds to quote Lévi-Strauss' own definition of myth (STRENSKI 1987:132):

> "[Myths] teach us a great deal about the societies from which they originate, they help us lay bare their inner workings and clarify the *raison d'être* of beliefs, customs and institutions, the organization of which was at first slightly incomprehensible; lastly, and most importantly, they make it possible to discover operational modes of the human mind, which have remained so constant over the centuries, and are so widespread [...] that we can assume them to be fundamental". (LEVI-STRAUSS 1981:639).

36 Quoted from Mircea Eliade. *No Souvenirs*. (p. 16). New York: Harper and Row, 1977.

Continuing on this point the line of the Durkheimians, Lévi-Strauss thinks that "myth is an autonomous mode of representation." (STRENSKI 1987:156). "For Lévi-Strauss, myth does not exemplify a distinctly religious mode of knowing [...]. Myth exemplifies formal or purely logical (oppositional) thinking." (STRENSKI 1987:156). "Although Lévi-Strauss affirms the reference of his studies of myth to concrete societies, he eventually resists founding myths on collectivities. Despite a 'determinism [...] from the infrastructure', myth has its own entelechy. In the end, 'myth' is explained by nothing except 'myth'."[37] (STRENSKI 1987:158). Finally, STRENSKI (1987:165-66) gives a 6-point summary of Lévi-Strauss' structural theory of myth:

> "1 *'Strong structure' entails analysis.* If structuralism stands for anything, it stands for the ability to analyse individual myths into constituent units, to connect myths by rules of *logical* transformation.
> 2 *Myth before social ritual; nature and thought before man.* [...] especially in *The Naked Man* Lévi-Strauss takes pains to dissociate myth from ritual and collective foundations, and to associate it with the natural teleology of the mind.
> 3 *Contemplation before action.* Myths are interesting not for their uses in political propaganda, but as demonstrations of how the mind thinks itself in myth.
> 4 *Scientific knowledge, not interference.* The structural study of myth is hostile to using myth to legitimate action, because action destroys the authority of myth by demonstrating the relativity of the variation of mythic structures.
> 5 *Secular.* Myths reveal no religious truths and deploy no supernatural power."
> [6 Myth is autonomous.]

---

[37] Quoted from LEVI-STRAUSS (1981:628).

As can be seen from the above, these two definitions of myth are very unlike, and differ in fundamental ways (and those of Cassirer and Malinowski, which we have not discussed here, show even more dissimilarities.) Out of all this confusion and all these irreconcilable opinions, STRENSKI concludes that myth is a "twentieth-century artifact" (1987:194), and that it has no reality of its own, but is a mere projection (1987:1):

> "Such confusion indicates graphically enough that there is no such 'thing' as myth. There may be the word 'myth', but the word names numerous and conflicting 'objects' of inquiry, not a 'thing' with its name written on it. 'Myth' names a reality that we 'cut out', not one that 'stands out'. It is the camel in the cloud, the profile in the Rorschach test, the duck or rabbit in the 'duck-rabbit'."

However, in spite of the many apparently insurmountable differences of opinion about myth, and in spite of Strenski's 'deconstruction' of myth,[38] people continue to discuss myth. And they continue to hold very dissimilar ideas about myth. This is for instance clearly revealed in a fairly recent publication, *Myth and Method* (1996), which contains a series of articles written by authorities in the field of myth (including Strenski himself). We may quote some examples of dissent concerning two topics which are standard subjects of dispute: the relationship between myth and ritual, and the distinctions between myth, legend, folktale and history. While many authors of these articles do not even mention the word 'ritual', others, like DOUGLAS (1996:29-51), continuing in this the line of Robertson Smith and the Durkheimians, insist on the primacy of ritual over myth, and the impossibility of understanding myth without reference to the

[38] Strenski is of course not the first 'deconstructionist' of myth. This title rightfully belongs to Plato (~428-348 B.C.E.), who "felt the need to demolish the authority of narrative discourse in order to establish that of syllogistic argumentation." (LINCOLN 1996:167), and from whom we have probably inherited the notion that myth = lie.

underlying ritual.[39] On the other hand, DOUGLAS does not seem to make any distinction between myths, legends and folktales (since she analyzes together and compares Biblical mythological narratives and the story of Little Red Riding Hood), while in the same volume, DUNDES (1996:147) insists upon this classical distinction and is indeed dismayed by the lack of respect some other scholars show for it:

> "Even in volumes purportedly treating 'myth and method' one will find essays treating folktales and legends, rather than myths. There is, of course, nothing inherently wrong with analyzing folktales and legends, or short stories or poems for that matter, but it is truly dismaying to folklorists to see such analyses wantonly labeled discussions of 'myth'.
>
> The generic distinctions between myth, folktale, and legend have been standard among folklorists for at least two centuries, going back to the publications of the brothers Grimm, who published separate works on each of these genres. For the folklorist, a myth is a sacred narrative explaining how the world and mankind came to be in their present form. Myths and legends (narratives told as true and set in the postcreation era) are different from folktales, which are narratives understood to be fictional, often introduced as such by an opening formula such as 'Once upon a time'."[40]

To further exemplify the problems inherent in any study of myth, in any attempt to explain myth, we shall examine how different theoreticians of myth explain the so-called 'universality', or at least 'cross-culturality'[41] of certain myths.[42] While this problem may not

---

[39] We may quote here Henri Hubert's famous image: "The mythological imagination dances on the threshing floor trodden by rituals, and it is there that one might grasp it." (Quoted by STRENSKI 1996:67).

[40] See also LINCOLN (1989:25) for the differences between these categories of narratives. This author distinguishes fable, legend, history and myth according to three criteria: truth-claims, credibility and authority. Only myth has all three of them.

[41] See DONIGER (1998:59) for this important distinction.

[42] Though for some, like DUNDES (1996:149) who understands 'universal' in the literal sense of the term, this is admittedly not a problem: "*no motif is universal.* To my

seem directly relevant for the topic of this research, which is after all restricted to the study of myth within one and the same civilisation, I nevertheless think that it can also be useful to explain the persistence of certain myths within one and the same culture over centuries, if not millennia, in spite of considerable religious and social changes. One way of solving the problem of the universality of myth is to invoke the 'diffusionist theory', whose major proponent is Joseph Campbell (see especially *The Masks of God*[43]) who argues extensively that myths were actually transmitted, not only over time, but over vast geographical distances as well. While this theory may seem fairly convincing in certain instances, as in the case of Indo-European myths, it is much more problematic in some others, where it would involve extensive overseas travels. A radically different theory which seeks to explain the universality of myths is that of Carl G. Jung: according to Jung, myths represent archetypes, which belong to the 'collective unconscious'. As SEGAL (1996:97) explains:

> "For Jung, myth functions to reveal the existence of the unconscious: 'Myths are original revelations of the preconscious [i.e., collective] psyche, involuntary statements about unconscious psychic happenings. [...] Modern psychology treats the products of unconscious fantasy-activity as self-portraits of what is going on in the unconscious, or as statements of the unconscious psyche about itself.'[44] Whoever takes myth literally thinks that it is revealing the existence of something external like the godhead and immaterial world, but in fact it is revealing the workings of the unconscious."

knowledge, there is not one single myth that is universal, 'universal' meaning that it is found among every single people on the face of the earth, past and present." But of course this summary dismissal does not help to explain the cross-culturality of myth.

43 Joseph Campbell. *The Masks of God*. 4 vols. Reed. London: Arkana, 1991.

44 Quoted from C.G. Jung. "The Psychology of the Child Archetype." In *The Archetypes and the Collective Unconscious*. (pp. 154-55). Collected Works, vol. 9, pt. 1, 2d ed. Edited by Sir Herbert Read and others. Translated by R.F.C. Hull and others. Princeton: Princeton University Press, 1968, 151-81.

Other scholars have proposed other ways of explaining why similar myths appear all over the world. According to Lévi-Strauss, this is due to "a basic need for order in the human mind and since, after all, the human mind is only part of the universe, the need probably exists because there is some order in the universe and the universe is not a chaos." (Quoted by DONIGER 1996:111).[45] DONIGER herself, instead of considering the universality of myth as the result of a given and unchangeable 'disposition' of the human mind, prefers to explain it as the result of common human experiences:

> "I would argue that, although there are few universals (for there are exceptions to almost everything), there are many human experiences that occur in many different cultures, particularly experiences connected with the body, experiences that we might call quasi-universal. Underlying these myths are certain wide-spread, if not universal` experiences: the realization that I am separate from my parents, the discovery that I am one sex and not the other, the knowledge that I will die. My own rather cumbersome definition of a myth is: a narrative in which a group finds, over an extended period of time, a shared meaning in certain questions about human life, to which the various proposed answers are usually unsatisfactory in one way or another. These would be questions such as, Why are we here? What happens to us when we die? Is there a God? Stories about these themes, though inevitably mediated by culture, must needs have something in common." (1996:112).[46]

The foregoing discussion shows that there is hardly any consensus in the scholarly world as to the nature, function or purpose of myth, and indeed, (at least in Strenski's work), the very existence of myth as

---

[45] From C. Lévi-Strauss. *Myth and Meaning*. New York: Schocken Books, 1979. Repr. with a new foreword by W. Doniger, 1995 (p. 11). See also DONIGER (1998:59).

[46] See also DONIGER (1998:54).

an object of inquiry is questioned. Yet in spite of all the difficulties one meets while trying to define myth, I nevertheless believe that there is such a thing as myth, which makes a myth different from any other story. As DONIGER (1998:2) succinctly puts it: "all myths are stories, but not all stories are myths." And, as LINCOLN (1996:165) says: "Myths, I would suggest [...] are the stories that everyone knows and the stories that everyone has heard before." The basic distinction, in my view, is that I can invent a story, but I cannot create a myth. However, I am not planning to add my own definition of myth to the long list of definitions which I have given above (and the many more which I have not even touched upon), nor indeed do I have such a definition to produce at instant notice. Instead of trying to give a minimalist (in the sense of all-including, most general) definition of myth,[47] I prefer to keep in mind the above-delineated approaches, believing that each one of them can contribute to our understanding of myth, and that, according to the content and the nature of the chosen narratives, one should choose the appropriate tools to tackle them. This is rather in the lines of the 'toolbox approach' first described by DONIGER O'FLAHERTY (1976/1980:9-10), by means of a culinary metaphor and a rather self-deprecating simile:

> "I have [...] used a tool that would do the job – a bit of philology, a measure of theology, lashings of comparative religion, a soupçon of anthropology, even a dash of psychoanalysis – rather like a

[47] For whenever one tries to give a definition of myth, immediately numerous instances of myths which do not neatly fit into this definition come to our minds: if I say that myth is a true story, then one might object that some cultures call their myths lies (see DONIGER 1998:2). If I say that a myth is about the past, about the creation of the world, then one might object that there are eschatological myths, concerning the future. If I say that a myth is fundamentally religious, then one might say that there are myths about the origins of food, about the origins of society, of institutions. If I say that a myth is a collective, anonymous story, then hard-core folklorists might object that fairy-tales, which should according to them be distinguished from myths, also fit the definition, which is therefore too inclusive. And so on, and so forth.

> monkey piling up complex scientific gadgets into a miscellaneous heap in order to pluck the banana from the top of the cage."

She further defends this approach in (1980:4-5):

> "But since myths are about so many things – about life and art and the universe and the imagination – almost everything in the realms of the natural sciences, humanities, and social sciences is relevant to the study of myths. A myth is like a palimpsest on which generation after generation has engraved its own layer of messages, and we must decipher each layer with a different code book. The different aspects of myths pose different problems, requiring different methods of approach. [...] This is the toolbox approach to the study of myth: carry about with you as wide a range of tools as possible, and reach for the right one at the right time."[48]

Thus on the whole, and before venturing to draw more ample conclusions as to the function of myths, I prefer to see myth 'in action', to observe how myth operates in concrete cases. For my immediate purpose, I will call 'myths' the stories narrating the deeds of certain gods which are found in the Vedas and are again narrated in the Epics.[49] While the detailed analysis of each myth will have to wait for the relevant chapters, we shall presently examine how the MBh and the R deal with some broader issues concerning myth.

---

48 DONIGER O'FLAHERTY further expounds on the same theoretical approach in (1984:7-8).

49 This does not mean that other non-Vedic stories related in the Epics are not myths. I also do not insist on the rigid distinction between myth and legend: indeed, according to the definition of myth proposed by DUNDES (1996:147) and quoted above, a myth is specifically "a sacred narrative explaining how the world and mankind came to be in their present form", whereas legends are "narratives told as true and set in the postcreation era". Following these definitions, it is in fact doubtful whether any of our chosen narratives would really fit the definition of myth: certainly none of them explains how the world came into being. (As a matter of fact, according to this definition, only cosmological narratives would fit into the category of myth.) In practice, it soon becomes evident that the boundaries between the two sorts of narratives thus defined are often fuzzy, and the lines of distinction are blurred more often than not. See also DONIGER O'FLAHERTY (1985a:10-11) who argues against the distinction between myth and folktale in her study of the Jaiminīyabrāhmaṇa.

Myth in the Epics

The first question we should ask is whether it is legitimate to use the term myth, which is derived from Greek *mûthos*, and therefore represents a Western category, while dealing with Sanskrit texts. Would it not be preferable to use a Sanskrit term? Do the Epics themselves designate the mythical narratives with a special term, or designation, which would immediately make the listener or reader attentive to their peculiar nature, and which would serve to distinguish such narratives from the central events of the Epics? The answer seems to be no. First of all, we must note that the narrators of the mythical tales which concern us here do not always specifically state that they are presently going to tell a story. And when this does happen, the designations are varied: out of the three common terms used to designate a tale or story, (*itihāsa, kathā* and *ākhyāna*), two of them are used in the cases which concern us here: *itihāsa* and *kathā*. *Itihāsa* occurs twice in the standard expression *itihāsaṃ purātanam*, in the context of the myth of Agni's hiding: once as a prelude to the story of Agni and Aṅgiras (MBh 3.207.6), and once as a prelude to the story of Pārvatī's curse (MBh 13.83.29). We find the term *kathā* three times in the prelude to the story of Bhṛgu's curse (MBh 1.5.2, 3, 6) and once in the conclusion of the story of the *soma*-theft (MBh 1.30.22). Now, GOPAL (1982:233) notes that "[a]ccording to Vedic commentators, a legend relating to Vedic gods is known as *Itihāsa* in Vedic literature." The term *itihāsa* literally means "thus indeed it was": *iti ha āsa*, and therefore seems to designate, like the term myth, a 'true story which took place in ancient times'[50] (the perfect tense being used to refer to

[50] See e.g. DONIGER (1998:2) quoted above.

the remotest past).[51] The term *kathā* on the other hand is a more general term designating any 'story', more specifically a work of fiction. But the MBh does not seem to use these terms distinctively.[52] At least in the examples which concern us here, *itihāsa* and *kathā* are used rather indiscriminately, and *kathā* certainly does not have the implication of an 'imaginary story'.[53] Therefore, since there is no Sanskrit term which fits exactly the object in view, we shall continue to use the word 'myth'.

As we have seen,[54] an important point in the definition of myths, except in the case of eschatological myths, which do not concern us here, is that they pertain to events which happened in the remote past. Now, the Epics often (though not always) give time references when a mythical tale is introduced, and the reference is necessarily to the past. In most cases, the terms which are used are *purā* or *pūrvam*: 'formerly, in ancient times, previously'.[55] Twice, a more precise time reference is

---

51 However, the term *itihāsa* is also translated in the dictionaries as "history". Thus it appears that the Sanskrit makes no difference between factual, historical truth, and mythical truth.

52 And indeed, this was the case long before the Epics. PATTON (1996:197-198) notes that the distinction between the terms *itihāsa* and *ākhyāna* is unclear in the Brāhmaṇas, and that Yāska and Śaunaka, the authors of the Nirukta and Bṛhaddevatā respectively, "use *itihāsa* and *ākhyāna* without being explicit as to the distinction between them." Furthermore (1996:198, note 11), she remarks that the commentators Ṣaḍguruśiṣya and Sāyaṇa indiscriminately use a variety of terms, and that sometimes one and the same narrative is called by different designations by different commentators.

53 This is especially true as far as the story of Bhṛgu's curse is concerned, which is designated as a *kathā* three times. Yet the story is told in the context of the genealogy of the Bhārgavas, which is narrated to Śaunaka, a Bhārgava himself. Therefore, in the MBh's view, it would rather belong to the category of historical narratives, certainly not to that of works of fiction.

54 E.g. in Eliade (quoted in STRENSKI 1987:72), DONIGER (1998:2), DUNDES (1996:147), all quoted above.

55 This discussion is restricted to the passages studied here. Thus, when Vasiṣṭha narrates to Rāma Jāmadagnya the story of Skanda 's birth and Agni's hiding, he says that he heard the story *pūrvaṃ purāṇe*: "formerly, in a story of olden times" (MBh 13.83.39), as told by Prajāpati to Manu (with the implication that the events forming the subject-matter of the tale are themselves even older). Viśvāmitra, telling Rāma the story of Ahalyā's seduction, says that these events happened *purā* (R 1.47.16) and *pūrvam* (R 1.47.15); in the second R version of Ahalyā's seduction, Brahmā, reminding Indra of his past misdeed, uses the word *purā* (R 7.30.17). Similarly, Nahuṣa, referring to the same

given: *purā devayuge* (MBh 1.14.5), introducing the story of the *soma*-theft, and *purā kṛtayuge* (MBh 13.14.75), introducing the story of Upamanyu. Thus, in most cases, the Epics do make a time distinction between the main events of the Epics and the mythical tales which are occasionally narrated therein, implying that the events narrated in the mythical tales happened in the distant past.

These time distinctions are important, precisely because they allow us to distinguish between the central epic events and the mythical narratives. Yet at the same time the Epics often take care to attach these mythical narratives to the temporality of the epic narration: in the first R version of the story of Indra and Ahalyā, Ahalyā is released from her curse by Rāma himself, the hero of the Rāmāyaṇa. The second version attaches the story to that of Rāvaṇa, the 'villain' of the Rāmāyaṇa, who has recently been slain by Rāma. In the first version of Agni's hiding, the story is attached to the history of the Bhārgavas, especially Bhṛgu and Cyavana, who are the direct ancestors of Śaunaka, to whom the story is told. The myth of the theft of the *soma* is causally linked with the story of the *sarpa-sattra* of Janamejaya, the great-grand-son of Arjuna: the snake-sacrifice (which takes place long after the great Mahābhārata war) happens because the snakes were cursed by their mother, the circumstances of the curse being narrated in the story of the *soma*-theft, which occurred in the Kṛtayuga. In the second versions of the stories of Upamanyu and Uttaṅka, both of them meet Kṛṣṇa. In all these cases, it is true that the events of the mythical tales are purported to have taken place long ago, in the most distant past, but at the same time either their *dénouement* takes place in the temporality of the Epics, or they have results which take effect in the temporality of the Epics, or else the epic characters to whom they are told have a direct

events, says that they took place *pūrvam* (MBh 5.12.6). In the second story of Upamanyu, Upamanyu, relating to Kṛṣṇa events pertaining to his own (very distant) youth, repeatedly uses the terms *purā* (MBh 13.14.72 & 73 & 75) and *pūrvam* (MBh 13.14.74).

affiliation or even acquaintance with the characters of the tales. In one instance we even find a tree which endures from ancient mythical times up to the time of the main events of the Epics: in R 3.33.27-35, Rāvaṇa sees the banyan whose branch Garuḍa broke before flying to heaven to steal the *amṛta*. Thus on the whole, the Epics to a certain extent erase the distinctions between the two levels of narration, and events, personages or objects of the most distant mythical past are made coterminous with the epic events themselves.

The only instance (as far as our topics are concerned) of a mythical tale having clear Vedic antecedents, which is *not* said to happen in the distant past, is the first version of the story of Upamanyu's salvation by the Aśvins in the MBh.[56] This version, which relates events pertaining to Upamanyu's and also Uttaṅka's youth, is temporally situated around the time of Janamejaya,[57] that is, long after the main events of the MBh. In this case, the Mahābhārata confuses the issue by retelling these stories in the Anuśāsana- and Āśvamedhikaparvans, where the two protagonists Upamanyu and Uttaṅka, well advanced in age, meet Kṛṣṇa, before and immediately after the great war, but at the same time projecting their youth into the most distant, 'mythical' past. How can we explain this time inversion? If we adopt a text-historical view, we could say that the Pauṣya-sub-parvan version is the result of a 'later' insertion, precisely motivated by the efforts of some redactors to transfer events pertaining to the deepest past into the temporality of the Epic. However, even according to the text-historical perspective, it is

[56] However, some caution is in order here: although the story has clear Vedic antecedents and is highly reminiscent of the salvation of certain personages in the Ṛgveda, Upamanyu himself is never mentioned in the ṚV, which perhaps allows the Epic a certain freedom when it comes to situating him in time.

[57] At least, this can be said with certainty about the story of Uttaṅka, since the latter meets king Janamejaya and advises him to perform the *sarpa-sattra* (MBh 1.3.177-195). Upamanyu, who is said to be the co-student of Uttaṅka's master Veda, never meets Janamejaya, nor is Janamejaya mentioned in connection with his story. But the beginning of the Pauṣya-sub-parvan first mentions the horse-sacrifice performed by Janamejaya, before introducing the story of Upamanyu with the words *etasminn antare*: "in the meanwhile", which seems to indicate that the two events are contemporary.

not at all clear whether the Pauṣya-sub-parvan is really late or not.[58] WILHELM does not deal with the Anuśāsanaparvan version of Upamanyu's story, but he thinks that the Āśvamedhikaparvan version of Uttaṅka's story is younger than the version of the Pauṣya-sub-parvan, because Kṛṣṇa in his divine form appears in it, and generally the passages where Kṛṣṇa appears in his divine form are considered to be late (1965:30).[59] Moreover, it would indeed be tempting to say that version of the Pauṣya-sub-parvan is older, simply because it advocates the worship of the Vedic gods. Yet all these arguments lose some of their value if we consider that even if the MBh was composed over an extended period of time and by different groups of people, there may have existed at the same time groups advocating the new trend of *bhakti* (which itself probably has Vedic origins[60]), and others advocating old Vedic beliefs. And they lose even more value if we think that the MBh was composed as a concerted effort from the start. On the other hand, if we consider the problem solely from the point of view of the sequence of the text, we could say that the MBh was fooled by its own flash-back technique, and that, due to the overall mythical 'flavour' of the beginning of the narration, events which happen long after the central epic events depicted in the MBh were reinterpreted as having happened in the most distant past by subsequent portions of the Epic. However, this time inversion between the different versions of these stories remains enigmatic, and would deserve further investigation. On the whole, it is perhaps due to the epic redactors' very effort to link as closely as possible events which happened in the distant past with the temporality of the Epics that the two time-planes occasionally get confused.

---

[58] See chapter 5, footnote 28.

[59] This is already VOGEL's opinion (1926:64-65).

[60] See BIARDEAU (1999:XVIII).

What about the 'truth' of myths? A recurring point in definitions of myth (see e.g. DONIGER (1998:2) and DUNDES (1996:147) cited above), is that myths are stories which are believed to be true. How should we take this statement? Are myths supposed to be 'literally' true, or only true in a rather vague metaphorical sense? Reading the secondary literature on myth, it occurs to us that the question seems to be avoided more often than confronted. Most authors refer with predilection to the Greek civilization, where myths were from an early date the object of deconstruction, with Plato and Euhemerus, who no longer took myth literally, but sought to explain it more 'rationally': for instance, according to Euhemerus (~3rd-4th c. B.C.E.), gods are deified kings. The problem is obviously compounded by the fact that we can only imagine with the greatest difficulty how anybody could ever give credence to stories which, to us, seem highly improbable. Myths, however unconsciously we may formulate this in our minds, are always 'other peoples' myths'. However, BRONKHORST (2002:91) shows that in the Indian tradition, even in the philosophical tradition of the Vaiśeṣika,[61] certain myths are cited as true "not in any metaphorical, but in a most literal manner." We may therefore assume that if myths were believed to be literally true by certain philosophical schools,[62] the same holds also *a fortiori* for the Epics, which are precisely "books of stories and myths". Yet the Epics never make explicit truth-claims with regard to the tales they narrate (as far as this can be affirmed with any certainty of such voluminous texts). Not, however, because these were assumed to be fictitious, but rather

---

[61] Thus "the Padārthadharmasaṃgraha is no book of stories and myths, and nor is it meant to be read as literature. Quite on the contrary, it is a [...] treatise about the constitution of reality, of which it presents a coherent and systematic explanation." (2001:91).

[62] The Mīmāṃsakas, however, probably due to the attacks of Buddhists who ridiculed the Brahmanical beliefs in certain myths, held the position that none of the Vedic myths should be taken literally: they are all either *arthavāda* or *mantra*. See BRONKHORST (2001:91, ff.).

because everything narrated in the Epics is implicitly true. The idea that any narrative could be fictitious never occurs at all. What better way of explaining this could the Epics figure out than making their authors protagonists of their own tales? These authors are thus in the position of witnesses of the events they retell, and absolute warrants of the truth of their own narratives. And we have already commented upon the way in which the Epics make events happening in the mythical tales coterminous with, and even causally affecting, the main events of the Epics themselves. Thus there is no solution of continuity between past and present, which would invalidate the authors' authority and knowledge of past events.

The problem in believing that myths are believed is intensified by the fact that myths are continuously fluctuating narratives. Indeed, the one thing which firmly impresses itself on the reader's mind while reading Lévi-Strauss' *Mythologiques* is the ever-changing nature of mythical narratives. How are belief and change compatible? How can we still believe a story to be true when it is told in a dozen different ways? Are the two not irreconcilable? On the level of the oral tradition of so-called 'primitive' societies, it is unclear how far, in fact, people know (or knew) of the existence of other versions of a particular myth. The anthropologist is in a privileged position, in that he can collect myths from different peoples and thus gets a bird's-eye view. But on 'ground-level', it is probable that story-telling sessions take place within the group, on which occasion only the version known to the group is narrated. Yet there must be occasional confrontations, as when people belonging to different groups meet and tell each other stories. And the changes introduced in the myths probably arise precisely from such occasional confrontations.

The situation is different in India, however. It is true that the tradition was also oral, but the Vedas were remembered. The Brahmins' chief task precisely consisted in memorizing and transmitting the Vedas. Thus they knew their Vedas by heart, and therefore presumably knew that these texts contained different versions of the myths (differences among the Vedic texts themselves, and differences between the Vedic texts and the Epics). Ignorance of the other versions is therefore probably not an explanation in the case of the redactors of the Epics.[63] It is true that in the Epics we sometimes notice a resistance against accepting other versions of a myth; this is for instance shown by the way in which some redactors can try to superpose the version of a myth known to them on a different version. This shows that when two versions of a myth are confronted, the reaction of the 'myth-makers' is not to suppress the alien version, but to produce a new version reconciling and compiling both versions.[64] How, then, is belief in the literal truth of myths compatible with the knowledge of different versions of the same myth? It seems to me (and I formulate this as a hypothesis) that since the idea of a decline in the *yuga*s is omnipresent in the Epic cosmogonic representations, along with the idea that in the present Kaliyuga people can no longer understand the *śruti*, (which is why Vyāsa had to divide it into four Vedas and compose the MBh as the fifth, in order to make it accessible to each and everyone), then the changing myths could also be logically accounted for, within the Indian paradigm itself, by the fact that they are versions of the one and eternal *śruti* adapted to the needs of the people of the present age.

[63] Here we are confronted with the question of who composed the Epics. But according to most theories, the Brahmins had a hand in it: either because they composed the Epics from the start, or because they composed certain later portions. (See below). Even if we assume that the Epics were (at least partly) composed by Brahmins, did they understand the Vedas they learnt by heart? We have seen above (BIARDEAU (1997:162)) that the Vedic language is thought to have become incomprehensible at an early date. These problems are of course difficult to answer. Personally, I feel that the gulf between Vedic and classical (or epic) Sanskrit is not so insuperable, and that among the group of people who exclusively dedicated themselves to learning the Vedic texts, some of them at least must have bothered to understand their meaning, even if it was not the majority.

[64] LINCOLN (1996:167 & 171-2) also nicely illustrates this resistance to change in the process of myth-making, and the way changes are nevertheless introduced and ratified by the group.

We have noted above (footnote 62) that the Mīmāṃsakas, constrained as they were to argue rationally with the Buddhists, adopted the view that myths are not to be taken literally. If BIARDEAU's contention should be true, namely, that the Epics were composed as a "'riposte' au bouddhisme impérial" (1999:XXIV), or in stronger terms as a "'riposte' à la menace bouddhique" (2002:136), then we could fathom how different the Epics' position was from that of the Mīmāṃsakas: instead of retorting to Buddhist attacks on the level of 'rational' argumentation, the Epics' answer (if it is really an answer) would resolutely place itself on the mythical plane, providing a massive compendium of past and present Brahmanical mythical representations of the world, and letting it stand and speak for itself, as it were.

The general contention that myths are considered to be not only true, but also 'sacred' narratives,[65] can perhaps best be verified in the Epics by examining the contexts in which myths are told, and the identity of the narrators and the audience of mythical tales.[66] As far as the MBh is concerned, a cluster of myths are narrated by the *sūta* Ugraśravas, the son of Lomaharṣaṇa, to Śaunaka, the grand-son of Bhṛgu, and other Brahmins, on the occasion of Śaunaka's twelve-year *sattra* which takes place in the Naimiṣa forest.[67] A few mythical narratives are directly told by Vaiśampāyana, the disciple of Vyāsa, to Arjuna's grand-son Janamejaya, on the occasion of the latter's *sarpa-sattra*.[68] Two myths are told by the sage Mārkaṇḍeya, a Bhārgava, to

[65] See above the definitions of myth given by DONIGER (1998:2); Eliade (defined in STRENSKI (1987:72)); DUNDES (1996:147).

[66] The following observations are restricted to the myths which are the object of our study.

[67] Namely, Upamanyu's salvation by the Aśvins (MBh 1.3); Agni's hiding due to Bhṛgu's curse (MBh 1.5-7); the theft of the *soma* (MBh 1.14-30).

[68] These are: Agni's hiding at a place which has now become the Agni-*tīrtha*, in the context of the description of Balarāma's *tīrthayātrā* (MBh 9.46.12-20). The story of Uttaṅka who meets Kṛṣṇa in a desert when the latter is returning home after the war, including the narration of Uttaṅka's adventures in his youth (MBh 14.52-57). These two

the Pāṇḍavas while they are sojourning in exile in the Kāmyakavana.[69] Two tales are told near Bhīṣma's death-'bed' in the Anuśāsanaparvan: one by Bhīṣma himself, the other one by Kṛṣṇa.[70] Concerning the R, we can make the following observations: the story of Indra and Ahalyā in the first *kāṇḍa* is narrated by the sage Viśvāmitra to Rāma, in Gautama's abandoned hermitage, in the wilderness. In the seventh *kāṇḍa*, it is told by the sage Agastya to Rāma in his court. The story of the theft of the *soma* (R 3.33.27-35) is part of the main events: Rāvaṇa sees the tree whose branch was broken by Garuḍa; and in this connection, the main points of the *soma*-theft are narrated.

What can we conclude out of these observations? As story-tellers, we find in the MBh the *sūta* Ugraśravas; Vyāsa's disciple Vaiśampāyana (who retells the MBh as he learnt it from Vyāsa); the sage Mārkaṇḍeya; Bhīṣma (who retells a story from Vasiṣṭha, who himself retold it from Prajāpati); and Kṛṣṇa (reporting the sage Upamanyu's words); in the R, the sages Viśvāmitra and Agastya. The least we can say about all these people is that they are persons of authority. To whom are the myths told? To Śaunaka and his assembly of Brahmins, to Janamejaya, to the Pāṇḍavas, to Rāma. In the main, to people who are the protagonists of the central events of the Epics. On what occasion and where are they told? On the occasion of sacrifices: Śaunaka's twelve-year *sattra*; Janamejaya's *sarpa-sattra*; Rāma

episodes are told by the main and first narrator of the MBh, Vaiśampāyana, who indeed recites the whole MBh (except the parts subsequently told by Ugraśravas which occur at the beginning of the Ādiparvan). We can thus note that both stories are told as part of the main events of the MBh, not as part of a story-telling session reported on a 'second-hand' basis by Vaiśampāyana. Both narrations are prompted by events occurring in the main story.

[69] Namely: the stories of Agni and Aṅgiras (MBh 3.207), and of Agni and Atharvan (MBh 3.212.6-19).

[70] Namely: Agni's hiding in connection with Pārvatī's curse (MBh 13.83-84). This story is reported by Bhīṣma to Yudhiṣṭhira, as told by Vasiṣṭha to Rāma Jāmadagnya, after the latter's *aśvamedha*, as it had been told previously by Prajāpati to Manu. On Bhīṣma's request, the story of Upamanyu (MBh 13.14) is narrated by Kṛṣṇa, who reports what Upamanyu told him in his hermitage of the Himālaya.

Jāmadagnya's *aśvamedha*; in connection with a pilgrimage-description; near Bhīṣma's death-place; in the forest.[71] On the whole, in places or on occasions endowed with an inherent sanctity. The choice of these settings is certainly not haphazard, and neither is the narration of myths on such occasions a mere pastime for people who have nothing better to do. On the contrary, such settings show that myths can only be told in surroundings which induce a meditative and concentrated frame of mind. On the whole, we see that the telling of myths is a serious matter, and that myths should only be told by persons of authority to a select audience, on sacred occasions,[72] and that myths have an exemplary value: they are often told to the main protagonists of the epic tales, so that they can learn from those myths in order to live their own lives in a more satisfactory manner.

Another thorny problem which is often raised in connection with the study of myth, as we have noted above, is that of the relation between myth and ritual. While this relation is often explicitly stated in the texts of the Yajur Veda and in the Brāhmaṇas, which tell myths in order to illustrate and justify a certain point of the sacrificial performance (a ritual action, the choice of certain *soma* substitutes, of certain types of wood to be used, etc.), this relation is far from being so explicit in the ṚV on the one hand, and in the Epics on the other. While there is a dispute on this point as far as the ṚV is concerned,[73] as far as the Epics are concerned it seems that we can safely rule out any such ritual connection, for these texts were not used for such a

[71] In the case of Śaunaka's *sattra*, two elements are combined: the sacrifice takes place in the forest.

[72] Only one narrative constitutes an exception to this rule, namely the story of Indra and Ahalyā, in the seventh *kāṇḍa* of the R: there the story is told to Rāma who is comfortably settled in his court, his time of trial being over. In this case, it would appear that listening to stories is a mere pastime for Rāma.

[73] Certain authors, like KRICK (1982) or HEESTERMAN (1983 & 1993) argue that all Ṛgvedic hymns were used at sacrifices, whereas according to VON SCHROEDER (1908), RENOU & FILLIOZAT (1985:I, § 521) and GONDA (1978), this was not necessarily the case.

purpose. In MBh 1.53.31, (quoted above), it is said that Vyāsa recited the MBh during the *breaks* in Janamejaya's sacrifice: *karmāntareṣu*. Not during the sacrificial ritual itself, like Vedic hymns. Similarly, the *sūta* narrates the MBh to Śaunaka and other Brahmins during their spare time in-between ritual acts, and Kuśa and Lava, Rāma's sons, recite the R on the occasion of Rāma's *aśvamedha*. Thus the Epics were probably considered to be auspicious and recited on festive and solemn occasions, but unlike the Vedas they did not have a *mantra*-like quality which would render their recitation effective in the sacrificial ritual.[74] However, as we shall see in the course of this study, this does not mean that the myths related in the Epics do not mention or concern certain aspects of the sacrificial ritual.

Methodology

Since my task concerns the representation of Vedic myths in the Epics, my focus could be of two different kinds: 'historicizing' or 'ahistorical'. Following the method of the historicizing discourse, the myths could either be viewed as undergoing a gradual development and growth from their 'infancy' in the Ṛgvedic allusions, to a fully mature state in the Epics, through all the intermediary stages in the later Vedas, Brāhmaṇas, Āraṇyakas, etc. Or, on the contrary, as deriving from an 'archetypal', 'original' Ṛgvedic narration, the subsequent

[74] The situation has changed again nowadays: due to the catastrophe of cosmic dimensions it describes, the MBh as a whole (though not certain parts of it, like the Bhagavadgītā), is usually considered to be inauspicious, and some people fear to keep copies of the book in their house. (DONIGER O'FLAHERTY 1988:62). The R on the contrary is considered to be highly auspicious. I have witnessed myself certain people going on private solemn Rāmāyaṇa recitation courses in order to obtain various worldly advantages, such as job-transfers and the like (apparently with positive results, or so they claimed). Thus it would appear that nowadays the two Sanskrit Epics are not only recited solemnly, but are even believed to have the *mantra*-like power of influencing worldly events.

retellings being understood as more or less spurious, artificial versions, sometimes based on a misunderstanding of the original.[75]

The present work, however, is not meant to be a sort of 'Ṛgvedic legends through the ages', taking one myth from the Veda and following its various avatars throughout Sanskrit literature, though concretely, I have often first dealt with the Ṛgveda, then with the later Veda, and finally with the Epics, following the chronological order. Rather, since my aim is to compare the two poles: Vedic and epic, following a type of 'ahistorical' correlation, I plan to view one particular mythical motif as belonging to the general background of a particular culture and being used in various ways and contexts by the different layers and genres of the literature belonging to that culture, in order to serve different ideological and cosmological aims. On this score, let me clarify that I do not consider that the Vedas contain the 'origins' of these myths, for the origins of myths are lost in the mists of time. As PATTON (1996:38) rightly notes:

> "[S]uch concerns with origins frequently prevent mythologists from paying sufficient attention to the context in which the myths are being told. The origin of the myth becomes the sole explanatory principle in the study of mythology. Moreover, such a view perpetuates the illusion that there can be a 'first myth' of which all other myths are simple 'variants' or 'versions'."

Furthermore (1996:206-207), she remarks that "it is useless to assume that there ever was a 'first telling' of any narrative, narratives are always in a state of response and transition to conditions and themes around them." Therefore we shall not attempt to trace the 'origins' of the particular myths we are dealing with here, but rather to examine how

[75] There are two trends in indological studies concerning this topic: some (like Geldner or Sieg) believed in an unbroken *itihāsa*-tradition. Others, like Tokunaga for instance, believe that the subsequent retellings of Vedic myths are more or less artificial. See PATTON (1996:203-206).

two different literary corpora in India at different times in the religious evolution represented the same myths,[76] and more precisely, to understand what motivated the epic redactors to narrate the Vedic myths in their poems.

This means that, though the redactors of the later versions of the myth would almost certainly be aware of the older versions,[77] they did not necessarily build on what had been done so far, in a type of linear development, but appear to have discarded certain old traits, reused certain even older ones, and changed or innovated on some others, to suit their particular needs. This was done, as we shall see, in order to fit a given mythological narrative in the larger framework of the text as a whole, whenever such a framework exists. Usually, enough common traits – be they deeds, objects or characters – exist in the different versions to make the myth immediately recognizable. But at other times, one particular version of a myth can be changed beyond recognition, unless we take into account the process of inversion – a process which is especially highlighted by Lévi-Strauss's structural theory – which is indeed frequent in myths; sometimes, a lexical element, remaining common throughout all the versions, alerts us to the actual identity of a particular mythical tale. Yet at other times, a myth can grow by accretion: that is, a simple motif can conglomerate with others to result into a more complex myth.

---

[76] What I mean by 'same myth' is explained below.

[77] If they were Brahmins they would know the versions which were consigned in 'their' Veda(s). But myths were certainly also transmitted by other means than the Vedic tradition. Unfortunately for us, (at least for the earliest period), this is all we have now and all we can judge by, but we should keep in mind that this is by no means all that ever existed. As KNIPE (1966-67:349) rightly observes: "Indeed, few ethnologists could accept the flat declaration: 'The borrowing of ideas is usually attested by texts.' What is in fact the case is that when we are fortunate enough to find texts preserved we are aware that they record a minute fraction of that constant flow of human experience and expression that occurs on the level of oral tradition." See also PATTON (1996:209): "The *Rg Veda* is, of course prior [...]. Yet [...] it cannot act as the sole *fons et origo*, and therefore the explanatory principle behind all subsequent mythological narratives."

While examining the epic mythological narratives and comparing them with the Vedic ones, there can therefore be no question of establishing one-to-one correspondences between them. Moreover, the Ṛgvedic narratives are often ambiguous, due to their allusiveness and scattered nature, and also due to the (for us) sometimes obscure meaning of certain terms and expressions. Besides, in the ṚV, similar epithets and hence the mythical deeds themselves tend to be attributed to more than one divinity. This situation hardly arises in the Epics, where the Sanskrit is seldom obscure, the narrative is exhaustive and the mythical deeds are rather clearly differentiated and attributed to definite personages. But this last point does not rule out the hypothesis that certain epic characters have inherited the Vedic multivalence. Therefore, while dealing with a deed, an object of a personage figuring in a myth, we shall always keep in mind the most directly relevant multivalences of those acts, objects or personages, for they are what makes possible the variations of a myth, to a large extent.

This leads us to one of the main problems we are confronted with while attempting to interpret myth. Myths do not talk in a straightforward manner: they often say one thing and mean another. How then, should we interpret them? Or more precisely: how do we know that one interpretation is correct, and another perhaps wrong? There are many ways of interpreting myths, and certainly not only one way is the right one. And there are, especially, many levels of interpretation: one and the same myth may have an astronomical meaning, a ritual meaning, a social meaning, and so on. But the way of deciding whether one particular interpretation is meaningful, if not correct, is not by referring to any external, 'rational' or 'objective' reality, but by seeing if this particular interpretation is consistent with the internal framework of a text, on the one hand, and on the other hand with the system of multivalence or correspondence mentioned above. Myths, I would suggest, have an internal coherence rather than an external one.

As I have made it clear above, I rather tend to have a leniency towards a type of 'structural' analysis, over a 'text-historical' one. However, this statement should be qualified to a certain extent. My method could indeed be called 'text-historical', for the simple reason that it is mainly based on the study of texts, and because I see these texts in a historical sequence (however vaguely defined it is), considering that the Saṃhitās, the Brāhmaṇas, and other Vedic texts antedate the Epics. Thus I respect the basic chronology of the texts. But within one and the same text, like the Epics for instance, I usually refrain from making text-historical comments, because the history of the composition of these texts remains to a great extent mysterious, and because, due to the previous point, such text-historical comments are often based on subjective views. On the other hand, the term 'structural' should not be taken in the strictest sense either. The reader should not expect to find in this study pure structural analyses '*à la* Lévi-Strauss', complete with diagrams, etc. The reasons for the differences are of course obvious enough. Lévi-Strauss mainly based his studies of myth on the oral, so-called 'ahistorical' traditions of the American Indians, whereas the present study is based on texts which were composed millennia ago. Nor do I think, like Lévi-Strauss, that myths reveal only the functioning of the human mind, and nothing about the religion and the ideologies of the society from which they emanate. On the contrary, in my view, many transformations that myths undergo over sometimes extended periods of time can be explained by corresponding ideological, religious, or social changes.

However, the structural method can be very useful in that it shows that a particular version of a myth is often elucidated by comparing it with other versions:[78] one element which is obscure in one version

[78] This would correspond to point 1 of Lévi-Strauss' six-point definition of myth given by STRENSKI (1987:165-66) and quoted above.

might be made clear and explicit in another. As LEVI-STRAUSS (1964:21) remarks:

> "Lors donc qu'un aspect d'un mythe particulier apparaît inintelligible, une méthode légitime consiste à le traiter, de manière hypothétique et préliminaire, comme une transformation de l'aspect homologue d'un autre mythe, rattaché pour les besoins de la cause au même groupe et qui se prête mieux à l'interprétation. [...] [La méthode] implique seulement que chaque mythe pris en particulier existe comme application restreinte d'un schème que les rapports d'intelligibilité réciproque, perçus entre plusieurs mythes, aident progressivement à dégager."

A myth is a type of fluctuating story: it is made out of certain elements which (usually) make it immediately recognizable, but these elements can rearrange themselves according to different patterns, accommodate others, drop out altogether, etc. As LEVI-STRAUSS (1971:576) says: "*conter* n'est jamais que *conte redire*, qui s'écrit aussi *contredire*". In cases such as these, where the material itself is by nature and essence unstable and shifting, we can perhaps pin-point text-historical developments, but, at least within one and the same text, these do not necessarily imply parallel historical developments. It is true that I shall make here and there text-historical comments: for instance in the case of the version of the myth of Agni's hiding which appears in MBh 13.83-84. But not with the basic aim of proving that 'this is earlier than that', but rather to show precisely the options available to the author(s) while narrating a particular myth. At times, a mythical narrative may become incoherent and even self-contradictory, precisely because the redactor (or perhaps several subsequent redactors) wished to accommodate somehow in one single narrative as many versions of the myth as he/they knew of, even at the cost of consistency. In cases such as these, the text-historical method may indeed demonstrate that 'version 1' was composed first and 'version 2' superposed on it, but this obviously does not prove that 'version 1' is older, in the sense that at the particular time when it was composed, 'version 2' was yet unknown, and is therefore a later innovation. Just because a myth, or a particular version of a myth, does not appear in one text does not yet prove conclusively that it was unknown at that time.[79]

In any case, the dating of early, 'anonymous'[80] Indian Sanskrit texts, and their absolute chronology, is usually so inaccurate as to mean almost nothing at all, and the texts themselves rarely, if ever, refer to historical events which would allow us to date them more precisely.[81] Here moreover we meet with the problem of the composition of the Epics. The view which has long been, and still is, commonly held, is that the Epics were first transmitted orally, by bards or *sūta*s who freely improvised on a basic given topic; in this manner, continual additions were made to them over the course of centuries, from a *kṣatriya* epic core, describing the central epic events, to brahmanical didactic layers exemplifying various points of *dharma*. Against this view, HILTEBEITEL (2000:168-9) notes with some pertinence that both Epics claim to have been composed by Brahmins and subsequently transmitted by bards, which is in flat contradiction with the theory summarized above. He also holds that the Epics were not orally transmitted, but were "*written* by Brahmans over a much shorter period than is usually advanced." (1999:155).[82] This means

[79] The critical editions are useful in this respect, for they show (in passages kept in the critical apparatus) how certain redactors, who knew a different version of a myth, tried with various degrees of skill to incorporate elements of the version known to them into another rather incompatible version. See some of my remarks to this effect especially in the chapter entitled "Indra, the Lover of Ahalyā".

[80] I keep 'anonymous' in quotes, because the Indian tradition itself considers that some of these texts, like the Epics for instance, have one established author.

[81] See BIARDEAU (1999:XXII): "l'Inde, si indifférente aux faits – qu'elle omet de rapporter –". But in (1999:LI-LII), BIARDEAU tentatively dates the MBh to the second century B.C.E.. and the R to the first century B.C.E.

[82] The texts themselves, however, do not support the idea that they were written. Both the MBh and R say that they were (mentally) composed by the *ṛṣi*s Vyāsa and Vālmīki, recited and heard. It is only in the apocryphal story of Gaṇeśa taking dictation from Vyāsa that the idea of writing occurs. But this story, though it is nowadays very popular,

that there are no layers representing *kṣatriya* versus brahmanical worldviews, nor layers representative of *bhakti* or sectarian tendencies. These problems are obviously important, but perhaps not so much for my work, or at least not in the way I wrote it. Since I am not planning here to concentrate specifically on these topics, I have mostly chosen to side-step them, though this often proves difficult. Even unconsciously, one may formulate sentences in a biased way, and at times the feeling is rather like that of walking in a mine-field, where one's smallest step should be watched.

is only poorly attested in the manuscript tradition, and is kept in the notes to Appendix I.1.1 of the MBh.

2. When Agni Goes Hiding

Introductory

The present chapter deals with Agni, the god of fire, in connection with the myth of what can be termed 'Agni's hiding'. This myth is narrated in the Ṛgveda, then in certain texts of the later Vedic literature, and in the Mahābhārata. To my knowledge, it is not found in the Rāmāyaṇa.

This myth is important from various points of view: generally speaking, it can be classified among the myths which deal with obtaining the fire. Such myths can be found in most mythologies all over the world.[1] As far as the Ṛgveda is concerned, in spite of this text's scanty references to this myth, the importance of the myth of Agni's hiding lies in the fact that it deals with one of the very few mythical deeds which are peculiar to Agni alone. For otherwise, this god is mostly mentioned in connection with his ritual and household functions, though a few mythical exploits which are primarily Indra's are at times attributed to him.[2] As far as the Mahābhārata is concerned, it is noteworthy that this myth is narrated not less than five times in a developed form in this text. There are considerable differences among these versions. Why this myth concerning Agni, a relatively 'minor'[3] god in epic times, finds such frequent mention in the MBh is a question we shall try to answer in this study.

The structure of this particular mythical narrative shows such considerable variation from one version to the other that even the

---

[1] FRAZER's *Myths of the Origin of Fire* (1930) offers a comprehensive survey of this type of myths.

[2] This is due to his close connection with this god. See MACDONELL (1898:95 & 98). According to OLDENBERG (1894:105) and MACDONELL (1898:91), the myths about Agni say little about his deeds because his anthropomorphism is scarcely developed. We shall have occasion to return to the question of Agni's anthropomorphism below.

[3] Minor as compared to the position of primacy he enjoyed in Vedic hymns and as compared to the more important position enjoyed by Viṣṇu and Śiva in the Epic.

following concise summary may not apply to all of them: Agni, who is for a variety of reasons either scared or angry, vanishes from the world and goes into hiding, mostly in the waters or in the plants, to the great dismay of gods and *ṛṣis*. After great searching, and sometimes after being 'tipped off' by various animals, they manage to find him and coax him to come back to his (mostly sacrificial) duties.

This myth of Agni's disappearance, or of his hiding, has mostly been explained as a reminiscence of the dawn of humanity, when the fire was not yet a secure possession and mankind had to make its difficult acquisition, the even more difficult apprenticeship of its preservation, and subsequently of its production. (See HOLTZMANN 1878:12). In all likelihood, the prehistoric people must have learned how to use the fire long before they learned how to produce it. Hence the preservation of fire was the object of much care, for should it get extinguished, getting a new fire involved much hardship. (See STAAL 1983:78-79). Fire remained an unstable possession even after man had learned how to kindle it. According to HEESTERMAN, the myth of Agni's hiding reflects first and foremost the fire's unreliability, instability, impermanence (1983:77 & 86; 1993:117). Fire is "fickle and ephemeral" (1983:77). "Indeed, the central theme of the cult and its imagery is not so much the security given by the fire as the fact that it constantly tends to withdraw from men and gods and to go into hiding". (1983:77). Thus the relationship between man and fire is fraught with uncertainty: "Man needs the fire in order to keep up the circulation of the goods of life, and the fire needs man in order to be resuscitated again and again. But [...] the weight of cult and mythology goes to show that at best the relationship is one of compromise and mutual manipulation." (1983:78). Concretely, HEESTERMAN (1993:104) also explains the disappearance of the sacrificial fire, who is afraid of death in the myth, as being attributable to the type of oblations poured into the fire: with a distinction between fatty oblations, like ghee, which stimulate the fire, and damping ones which tend to extinguish it.[4]

Perhaps it should be made clear that this fire, Agni, who disappears, is not just any fire: it is always the sacrificial fire, in all the texts in which the myth appears, including the MBh. This may partly account for the persistence of this mythological motif even in the last-mentioned text. For although certain new ideological trends (for instance *bhakti*) appear in the MBh, it remains nonetheless clear from the descriptions of the numerous *sattra*s, *yajña*s, etc. which are found therein, that the society depicted in the MBh followed the Vedic ritualistic world-view. Hence Agni, though perhaps less important as a personal god, must have continued to be prominent on account of his position in the sacrificial ritual, which necessarily involved oblations poured into the fire.

The Ṛgveda

As far as the representation of this myth in the ṚV is concerned, we are faced with a very similar situation as the one we shall encounter in connection with the myth of the theft of the *soma*: namely, we find the myth narrated in full detail and circumstantially in a cluster of hymns which form a whole, containing a dialogue between the gods and Agni (10.51-53).[5] Otherwise we find only scattered and incomplete allusions

[4] Even an excess of fatty oblations can also make the fire sick, as is shown in the preliminary story (discarded by the Critical Edition to Appendix I, no 118-120-121) to the episode of the burning of the Khāṇḍava forest in Mahābhārata 1.214 ff. (for this topic, see HILTEBEITEL 1976/1982), in which the Fire is said to have been saturated with ghee during an interminable sacrifice organized by king Śvetaki, and then wishes to purge himself by eating 'wild food', i.e. the forest.

[5] Indirectly bearing on the interpretation of this myth are various theories concerning the so-called *saṃvāda*-hymns, or dialogical hymns. According to OLDENBERG's *ākhyāna*-theory, these dialogical hymns used to be accompanied by explanatory prose passages which were subsequently lost. This would explain why these hymns seem at times fragmentary and unclear. (See OLDENBERG 1883 & 1885). For the episode of Agni's hiding, see (1885:71-72). At the beginning of the 20th century, controversies

to it in other hymns of the corpus, mostly in hymns dedicated to Agni. The dialogical hymns of the 10th *maṇḍala* probably had no application in the ritual liṭurgy.[6] The fact that the detailed mythical account appears in the tenth book does not necessarily imply its relative lateness as compared to the allusions found scattered in the other books. As RENOU (1956a:3) shows, not all the hymns of the tenth *maṇḍala* are of a late date.[7]

To get a clearer idea of our topic, we shall first summarize the three above-mentioned hymns (10.51-53) and then turn to the other passages which mention this myth. Hymns 10.51-53, the so-called 'Agni Saucīka'[8] hymns, have the form of a dialogue. Fortunately, these hymns (especially 51 and 52 which are more immediately important for our topic) are couched in a relatively straightforward language and do not present major syntactical or grammatical obscurities. The first hymn, which is particularly relevant for the understanding of the myth, relates the dialogue which takes place between Agni and the gods' spokesman, Varuṇa, when the gods find him in his hiding-place. According to the tradition transmitted by the Anukramaṇikā, Varuṇa speaks the uneven, and Agni the even stanzas. Here we learn that Agni was hiding in the waters, enveloped in a thick *ulba* (embryonic membrane) (1). Thanks to his great effulgence, the gods, especially Yama, espied him although he was hiding in the waters and plants (3).

raged around this *ākhyāna*-theory. For a 'history' of these controversies, see PATTON (1996:199-203). The other theory (see VON SCHROEDER 1908, following LEVI 1890) is that these hymns were the object of dramatic representations.

[6] See VON SCHROEDER (1908:1; 35-36; 68). PATTON (1996:197) remarks that: "Yāska, Śaunaka, and Sāyaṇa did not give a ritual application (*viniyoga*) for these hymns, but preferred to tell a story in order to interpret them." KRICK on the other hand maintains that hymns 10.51-53 were used in connection with an existing ritual, that of the installation of the new *hotṛ* (1982:546; 551).

[7] See also GONDA (1978:5), who opines that the difference in genre between certain hymns of the 10th *maṇḍala* and the rest of the Ṛgvedic corpus might be due to their origin from a different milieu rather than to their later date of composition.

[8] The name is somewhat mysterious. According to VON SCHROEDER (1908:220), it derives from *sūcī* "needle", and means "son of the needle".

Agni explains that he ran away and hid, because he was afraid of performing the sacrificial duties incumbent on him as the *hotṛ*.[9] He doesn't even want to think about this business any longer (4), for his elder brothers came to harm plying the same task (6). The gods coax him to resume his sacrificial function, explaining that Manu (or man) wants to perform a sacrifice (5), and promising him long life (7). Agni agrees to return, on the condition that the major and best parts of the sacrifice will be his (8) and the gods grant him his wish (9).

In the following hymn (10.52), all the stanzas excepting the last one are spoken by Agni. Agni requests the gods to instruct him in his task (1) and declares himself ready to perform his duties as the *hotṛ* (2). He undertakes to help the gods in situations of distress (5). The last stanza (6), spoken by the poet, states that the gods honoured Agni, anointed him with ghee, strew the *barhis*-grass for him and instituted him as their *hotṛ*. The third hymn of the series is not directly relevant for our present investigation. It moves away from the mythical events and is more like an ordinary "Opferlied", to quote GELDNER's words.[10] We shall therefore not summarize it here, but we shall allude to some of its relevant points below, in the course of our study.

We shall now turn to the other scattered Ṛgvedic passages which contain allusions to this myth. As a preliminary, let us note that while some of them contain pretty straightforward and unambiguous statements, in the case of some others it is doubtful whether they really refer to this myth at all, and the outcome depends on the interpretation one chooses to give them, a situation which is of course only too

---

9 The *hotṛ* is the most important of the seven priests who accomplished the ritual in Ṛgvedic times. His main duty is to recite the Ṛgvedic verses. His name is variously interpreted as meaning the "pourer" of the oblations, or the "caller" of the gods, inviting them to the sacrifice. See RENOU & FILLIOZAT (1947/1985:§ 705). See also KEITH (1925:294-95).

10 All the references to GELDNER are to his translation of the Ṛgveda (1951).

common in the case of Ṛgvedic studies. The passages which concern us are the following:

1.65.1-4; 1.67.3-8; 1.72.2-6; 1.98.2; 1.146.4.
2.4.2.
3.1.9; 3.5.10; 3.9.2 & 4-6 & 9.
5.2.8; 5.11.6; 5.15.5.
6.1.2-4; 6.8.4; 6.9.7.
7.4.3; 7.49.4.
8.84.2; 8.102.4-6.
10.5.5; 10.32.6-8; 10.46.2-9; 10.79.3; 10.115.4.

These passages contain one or more verses which allude to the episode of Agni's hiding, mostly found in hymns dedicated to Agni which otherwise deal with other aspects of the god. By their very nature, these allusions are necessarily fragmentary and evoke only some points of the episode of Agni's flight, unlike hymns 10.51-53, which give us a more complete picture of this event. Rather than attempting to translate or summarize each passage separately, we shall give a general summary of all the points they contain, so as to form a clear picture of the mythical events related therein.

Agni went away in anger: *hṛṇīyámānaḥ* (5.2.8); he was hidden: *tiróhitam* (3.9.5); residing or moving in a secret place: *gúhā cátantam* (1.65.1; 10.56.2), *gúhā niṣī́dan* (1.67.3), *gúhā bhávantam* (1.67.7), *gúhā cárantam* (3.1.9); *gúhā hitám* (5.11.6). He was residing in the waters, or in the womb of the waters, which are sometimes called his mothers and which make him grow: *várdhantīm ā́paḥ panvā́ súśiśvim [...] gárbhe sújātam*: the waters make him grow by their praise, the beautifully grown one, who is born in their womb (1.65.4); *apā́m upásthe víbhṛto yád ā́ vasad*: when he lived in a differentiated state in the lap of the waters (1.144.2); *apā́ṃ sadhásthe*: in the abode of the waters (2.4.2; 10.46.2); *yán mātṝ́r ájagann apáḥ*: when you entered your mothers, the waters (3.9.2); *vaiśvānaró yā́su agníḥ práviṣṭas*: [the waters] in which Agni Vaiśvānara entered (7.49.4); *ánv īm avindan [...] apsú*: they found him in the waters (3.9.4); *apā́m upásthe*: in the lap of the waters (6.8.4); *samudrávāsasam*: clothed in the ocean (8.102.6);[11] *ápagūḷham apsú*: hidden in the waters (10.32.6). While hiding, he also resides in darkness: *támasi taṣṭhivā́ṃsam* (6.9.7);[12] or in every wood: *śiśriyāṇáṃ váne vane* (5.11.6), or on the head of a cow: *mūrdhány ághnyāyāḥ* (10.46.3). 'Desired' (i.e. looked for) in the sky, on the earth, he entered into all the plants: *pṛṣṭó diví pṛṣṭó agníḥ pṛthivyā́m pṛṣṭó víśvā óṣadhīr ā́ viveśa* (1.98.2).[13]

Due to Agni's flight, the gods are frightened: *bhiyānā́ḥ* (6.9.7). He kept them in fear: *áme devā́n dhāt*, because he is taking away all the riches/oblations with him: *háste dádhāno nṛmṇā́ víśvāni* (1.67.3). Following his foot-steps: *padaír ánu gman* (1.65.2; 10.46.2); *padavyáḥ* (1.72.2); *padáṃ devásya [...] vyántaḥ* (6.1.4), various personages or groups of personages find the hidden Agni: the gods: 1.65.2 & 3; 1.67.4 (*náraḥ*); 1.72.2; 3.9.4; 6.9.7; 6.8.4[14]; the gods

---

[11] According to GELDNER, stanzas 8.102.4-6 refer to Agni's hiding, but the case is not quite clear. According to Sāyaṇa, they refer to the submarine fire (*samudramadhyavartinaṃ vāḍavam*). Yet it is doubtful whether the concept of the submarine fire already existed in Vedic literature. At least the term *vaḍavāgni*, or *vāḍavāgni* does not appear therein. The motif seems to be epico-purāṇic. (See below note 52 for the origins of the submarine fire from Aurva.) We should probably not confuse Agni when he is hiding in the waters, or being born from them, with the submarine fire. For Agni, when he resides in the waters, is a creative principle, the germ of life, whereas the submarine fire as it is represented in the later literature is unmistakably a destructive principle: this fire continuously devours the waters and it will rise at the end of the *kalpa* to destroy the whole world.

[12] In this respect, we can mention here hymn 10.124, in which Agni is besought by Indra to join the gods, "having dwelt in darkness for a long time" (1). But, according to GELDNER, this hymn probably deals with another myth relating to the change of power between Asuras and Devas, in which Agni, who previously belonged to the Asuras' camp, joins the Devas'. On the other hand, OLDENBERG (1884:68), HILLEBRANDT (1927-29/1980:92), and VON SCHROEDER (1908:181; 196-203) consider that this hymn is related to the episode of Agni's hiding.

[13] 1.98.2a is practically identical with 7.5.2a: *pṛṣṭó diví dhā́yi agníḥ pṛthivyā́ṃ*; but 7.5.2 does not mention the fact that Agni hides anywhere.

[14] Here called *mahiṣā́ḥ*: buffaloes. According to Sāyaṇa, *mahiṣā́ḥ = mahānto marutāḥ*, but this term might also designate the gods in general or a group of *ṛṣis*.

with their wives: *pátnīvantaḥ* (1.72.5); Indra saw him as he was hiding (5.2.8; 10.32.6); a man or mortal(s) found him: *mártaḥ* (1.72.4); *mártāḥ* (3.9.6); *náraḥ* (6.1.2); *mártāsaḥ* (7.4.3); he was found by seers: *kaváyaḥ* (1.146.4); by the Bhṛgus (2.4.2; 10.42.2; 10.46.9);[15] by the Uśij (10.46.2; 10.46.4); by the Aṅgiras (5.11.6); by Mātariśvan (3.5.10; 3.9.5; 6.8.4; 10.46.9);[16] by Trita (10.46.3; 10.79.3; 10.115.4).

A number of stanzas indicate that the ones who looked for Agni and found him, whether they were gods or seers, approached him with respect and homage, praising him and contemplating him in their minds (1.72.2; 1.72.5; 1.146.4; 2.4.2; 6.1.4; 6.8.4; 6.9.7; 10.46.2; 10.46.4). In 1.67.4, the gods find him thanks to the recitation of the *mantras* they had composed in their hearts.

After being found, Agni is taken hold of for the sake of sacrifice (3.9.6).The Uśij make him the *hotṛ*, the leader of the sacrifice (10.46.4). The gods anoint him as their *hotṛ* (3.9.9 = 10.52.6) and keep him among mortals (8.84.2[17]). Agni promises riches to the one who found him (1.67.7-8).

Thus the major differences between the account of the myth given in the cluster of hymns 10.51-53, and the scattered allusions found elsewhere, are that in 10.51-53, only the gods, especially Yama, find the hidden Agni, whereas in the other passages, not only the gods, but also various individual seers, or groups of seers, or mortals, find him.

---

[15] But in 3.5.10, if GELDNER's interpretation is correct, he is said to hide from the Bhṛgus. The verse is not quite clear and admits of several interpretations: *yádī bhṛ́gubhyaḥ pári mātaríśvā gúhā sántaṃ havyavā́haṃ samīdhé*. GELDNER (1951:342) translates as follows: "wenn Mātaríśvan ihn, der sich vor den Bhṛgu's verborgen hielt, as den Opferfahrer entzündeṭ hat." But KUHN (1859:6) renders it as "von den Bhṛgu her entzündet".

[16] Mātariśvan is often said to bring Agni "from afar": *parāvátaḥ*. Cf. also verse 1.128.2, which does not mention that Agni was hiding. For the significance of the term *parāvátaḥ*, see BODEWITZ (2000).

[17] According to GELDNER, this verse refers to what happens after Agni's flight and restoration, but the reference is not quite clear.

Also, the cause of Agni's flight is hardly touched upon in the scattered allusions to this myth: only verse 5.2.8 mentions that Agni went away in anger, without further dwelling on the cause of his anger. Whereas in 10.51.4, Agni declares: *hotrā́d ahám varuṇa bíbhyad āyam néd evá mā yunájann átra devā́ḥ*: "I came (away) afraid of the *hotṛ* function, o Varuṇa, so that the gods would not yoke me to it." And in verse 6, he adds that his elder brothers (*pū́rve bhrā́taro*) used to fulfill this office, and due to fear of that he came far away: *tásmād bhiyā́ varuṇa dūrám āyam*. Neither Agni's fear, nor his elder brothers are ever mentioned in the other books of the Ṛgveda. Nor, for that matter, do they mention the bargain he strikes with the gods before accepting to return.

If we now try to define more clearly the precise identity of the Agni who goes hiding, we can make the following remarks: in most instances, Agni is simply called Agni, which is the most common and probably least 'specialized' appellation of the fire. He is called Jā́tavedas only in hymn 10.51, but there the epithet occurs three times: 1, 3 & 7. Finally he is called Agni Vaiśvānará in 1.98.2, 6.8.4 and 7.49.4. Now, as HAYAKAWA (2000:236) shows, Agni Jā́tavedas and Agni Vaiśvānará have different functions: Jā́tavedas is the "ritualistic" fire and "is often invoked as a priest or a oblation-carrier", whereas Vaiśvānará is the "cosmic" fire and the sun (2000:231). We understand why Agni is repeatedly addressed by the name Jā́tavedas in hymn 10.51, which is mainly concerned with the sacrificial fire: Agni should return in order to carry the oblations and resume his role in the sacrificial performance. The case is less clear as far as the use of the term Vaiśvānará in this myth is concerned: verse 1.98.2 states that Agni Vaiśvānará was "desired" (i.e. looked for and hence probably hidden) in the sky (*diví*), which would indeed be appropriate for the sun, but also on earth (*pṛthivyā́m*) and in the plants (*óṣadhīr*). Verse 7.49.4 states that Agni Vaiśvānará is hiding in the waters. Verse 6.8.4 contains the example which would suit the sun best, stating that "Mātariśvan brought Agni Vaiśvānará from afar": *ā́ [...] abharad [...]*

vaiśvānarám mātaríśvā parāvátaḥ. On the whole, the use of different names of the fire in this myth shows that the Agni who goes hiding is not restricted to any particular function, and is rather the fire in general than any particular fire.

Who finds Agni?

If we now look in general at all the persons who find Agni in the myth, we notice a curious thing, already remarked upon, but not further developed, by KUHN (1859:5-9): most of them are forms of Agni, or bear names which are also Agni's. We shall presently examine in detail the identity of all those who find the hidden Agni, hoping that this will throw some further light on the nature of this mythological narrative.

Mātariśvan, "the one who grows in his mother(s)", later became a denomination of the wind (this is how Sāyaṇa regularly interprets this name),[18] but in the Ṛgveda, he is either Agni himself, who grows in his mothers the *araṇis*, the kindling-sticks, or the personage who brings the fire from the sky. Since he brings the fire from the sky onto the earth, Mātariśvan has often been considered to be the personification of a natural phenomenon, the lightning (see e.g. KEITH 1925:156). Since the beginnings of indological studies (KUHN (1859:18), OLDENBERG (1894:122), HILLEBRANDT (1927-29/1980:97), VON SCHROEDER (1908:215), CARNOY (1931:321), FRAZER (1931:241-43), etc.), Mātariśvan has been called the "Indian Prometheus".[19] The first to emit serious doubts and objections against

[18] HILLEBRANDT (1927-29/1980:98) also opines that this is Mātariśvan's original nature: the wind activates the fire, hence it can be credited with bringing the fire.

[19] For an exhaustive list of the different scholars who compared Mātariśvan with Prometheus, and quotes of the passages, see KUIPER (1971:85-86; 91-93). Such comparisons between Indian material and other Indo-European material (especially Greek), was a trend at the beginning of Indological studies. These comparisons were often based on phonological resemblances: thus Mātariśvan was thought to derive from *pramātha-* or *pramantha*, which makes it similar to Prometheus. GONDA (1975:121)

such an identification was KUIPER (1971). While I agree with his final conclusion that Mātariśvan is not to be equated with Prometheus, I cannot quite agree with the path he took to reach such a conclusion, which, in my opinion, too heavily relies on a comparison between the descent of fire and the theft of the *soma*. Besides, as OBERLIES (1998:384, note 225) remarks:

> "Dagegen [i.e., against the Mātariśvan-Prometheus equivalence] hat KUIPER (1971) einwendungen vorgetragen. [...] Allerdings sind KUIPERS Ausführungen allein aus dem Grunde nicht schlüssig, dass er nicht alle Textstellen, die vom Gewinn des Feuers durch den Menschen sprechen, berücksichtigt und besprochen hat. Das Problem bedürfte dringend einer erneuten Untersuchung."

Without claiming any exhaustiveness myself concerning this topic, I would like to make the following few observations. Usually, Mātariśvan's deed of bringing the fire "from afar" or "from the sky" is not considered on par with the gods' or seers' finding the hidden Agni in the waters or plants, but as an altogether different myth relating the original descent of fire onto the earth.[20] However, in my opinion, Mātariśvan is but one of the many personages who find the hidden Agni. Indeed, this is stated in ṚV 3.5.10; 3.9.5; 6.8.4; 10.46.9. It is true that it is nowhere stated that Mātariśvan "brought the hidden Agni from the sky", but both propositions "hidden" and "from the sky" appear separately in a number of passages.[21] Moreover, verse 10.5.5 says: *antár yeme antárikṣe purājā́ icchán vavrím avidat pūṣaṇásya*: "The one who exists from old (= Agni) stopped in the air (intermediary

cautions us against such hasty comparisons and especially emits doubts concerning the Mātariśvan-Prometheus equivalence.

20 See e.g. OLDENBERG (1894:123). FRAZER, in his very short chapter on the origin of fire in ancient India (1931:241-43) restricts his discussion to the few Ṛgvedic verses mentioning Mātariśvan.

21 Concerning the Bhṛgus, there are also many passages which state that the Bhṛgus installed Agni among men, without saying that they first found him hiding in the waters and brought him back. See KUHN (1859:6). But this is certainly implied.

space), desiring a hiding-place, he found that of Pūṣan". The allusion to Pūṣan is obscure, but this verse clearly states that Agni was looking for a hiding-place in the *antárikṣa*. Indeed, we can notice that Agni's hiding-places are as a rule not different from his birth-places. His birth-places are variously listed, the most common ones being his birth from the waters, from the sky and from the wood or plants.[22] Thus he commonly has an aquatic, celestial and terrestrial birth. (See MACDONELL 1898:91-93). It would therefore not be surprising, but on the contrary even expected of him, to hide in the sky, besides hiding in the waters and the plants.

One of the verses which must have been responsible for the common view that Mātariśvan's deed of bringing Agni from the sky refers to a different myth altogether, is 3.9.5, which states that Mātariśvan brought Agni from afar, *for* or *from* the gods: the term *devébhyaḥ* can be either an ablative or a dative plural. Most of the translators render it as "from the gods",[23] but I think that KUIPER (1971:95) is right to note that it can just as well mean "for the gods". We may also note that Sāyaṇa interprets it as *devārtham*: for the sake of the gods, i.e., to the gods. And indeed, we know that Agni has been hiding from everyone, gods and mortals alike. The gods are thus not in the superior position of possessors of the fire, as opposed to men who must get it from them. In short, I see in the usual interpretation that Mātariśvan brings the fire from the gods a clear influence of studies on Greek mythology, where Prometheus steals the fire from the gods to bring it to mankind. In Indian thought, there is no such dichotomy between gods and mortals: on the contrary, both are at a loss without Agni, and both strive to bring him back. This is of course for the sake of the sacrifice, without which neither the gods (who need the

---

[22] Sometimes he is also said to be born from us (*asmád*) (ṚV 10.45.1). On the topic of Agni's three births, see HAYAKAWA (2001).

[23] The different translations are listed and quoted by KUIPER (1971:96-97).

sacrificial food) nor the men (who need to propitiate the gods) can survive. This is very well illustrated by a story told in TS 1.5.3.4; MS 1.7.5; KS 9.3: the Ādityas or gods went to heaven, taking everything with them including the fire. But, starving and thirsty, they promptly had to reinstate it on the earth, since they could not live without the sacrificial oblations offered in the fire. (See HEESTERMAN 1983:76).

Similarly linked with the model of the Prometheus myth is, in my opinion, the terminology which is sometimes used in connection with the myth of Agni's hiding, designating it as a *theft* of the fire.[24] Now, unlike the *soma*, the fire cannot by any stretch of imagination be said to have been stolen from its hiding place, and, generally speaking, it seems to me that too much emphasis is laid on the parallelism between the two myths.[25] There is indeed an element of theft involved in the myth of Agni's hiding, but not on the part of those who find Agni, as we shall see below. No verbs implying the idea of stealing are used, only verbs such as 'finding' or 'seeing'. And mostly, the persons who discover Agni approach him with respect: the Bhṛgus serve him in the waters, the gods go to him on their knees, even once with their wives as additional supplicants. According to hymns 10.51-53, we might say that Agni was bribed or hired back, but certainly not stolen. This is undoubtedly so due to the fact that Agni, though his outward appearance is never clearly described in the passages which concern us

---

24 E.g. KUIPER (1971: *passim*) who systematically mistranslates the verb *mathāyati*, which means "to churn, to kindle by means of friction", as "to steal". Also HEESTERMAN (1983:79). In a totally different context, namely the psychoanalytical analysis of the myth of Prometheus, FREUD (1932:4-5) also notes that the fire is constantly won through stealing and cheating, not only in the Greek myth, but in myths belonging to peoples scattered all over the world. Freud makes no mention of the Indian material, which was perhaps unknown to him. (He does not give any reference to Frazer).

25 Thus both KUHN (1859) and KUIPER (1971) deal with them together in their respective studies. ṚV 1.93.6 may be indirectly responsible for this representation, for this verse mentions together the bringing of fire and of *soma*: the one was brought from the sky (Agni), the other from the mountain (*soma*).

here, always appears as a *person* in this myth, and not as an object.[26] The gods and *ṛṣis* follow Agni's footsteps (one of the most persistent details of the description).[27] He speaks, bargains, has to be soothed and propitiated. In brief, unlike in many other mythologies, the bringing of the fire in Indian mythology consistently deals with the personified fire, and not with fire as an object. In my opinion, therefore, Indian mythology does not know of an original descent or theft of the fire: Agni's births (from various origins) are a favourite topic of his descriptions in the Ṛgveda, but there is no one single event of his first appearance among men: and indeed fire is continuously lighted anew. But on the other hand, there is one single myth of the fire's hiding and subsequent reinstatement at the sacrifice, which seems to be a more important event. In India, the fire's definite installation as the deity presiding over the sacrifice is viewed as more significant than its first appearance on earth for perhaps more mundane uses such as cooking food or warming oneself (which is what other myths of the origin of fire are mostly concerned with).

After this lengthy discussion on Mātariśvan, we shall now turn to the other seers who discover Agni. Aṅgiras, or the Aṅgiras, a seer or family of seers, is a name which Agni frequently bears. When it appears in the singular, this term mostly designates Agni himself, but also, occasionally, the ancient seer Aṅgiras. Thus in 5.11.6, the Aṅgiras find Agni, and Agni himself is called Aṅgiras. According to MACDONELL (1898:143), "the Aṅgirases were originally conceived [...] as attendants of Agni, who is so often described as a messenger between heaven and earth. [...] They may possibly have been personifications of the flames of fire as messengers to heaven."

[26] The *soma* on the other hand is more like an object and can therefore be stolen by the eagle. However, SCHNEIDER (1971) on the contrary extensively argues that Soma is also a person.

[27] The term *pada*, which is always used to designate Agni's footsteps, rules out the hypothesis that Agni's tracks might be the blackened burnt trail left by the fire.

OBERLIES (1998:205, note 275) observes that they are also considered to be Agni's descendants.

A number of possible etymologies for the name Bhṛgu or the Bhṛgus are provided in various Indian texts and also in modern studies.[28] These two sorts of etymologies are of course different. Indian etymologies are synchronic: they show that at one particular period in ancient India, a certain term was considered to have one particular meaning. Western etymologies are diachronic: they seek the (mostly) Indo-European roots and meanings of certain terms. But what is remarkable in the case of the term *bhṛgu* is that, while we find variations in the different sorts of etymologies proposed in Indian texts and modern studies, all of them ultimately concur in linking this term with some aspect, function or manifestation of the fire. In Yāska's Nirukta (3.17), based on AB 3.34, the word Bhṛgu is connected with the verb *bhṛjjati*, to roast, and according to this text, Bhṛgu was born from the flames. BD 5.97-103 relates the story of how Bhṛgu was born from the flames and Aṅgiras from the coals (*aṅgāra*) after Ka's and Varuṇa's semen was spilt in the fire. (See PATTON 1996:264-65). SIEG notes that according to MBh 3.85.105,[29] the word comes from the root *bhṛg-* and designates the crackling of the fire. According to MW, *bhṛg* is also an onomatopoeia used to express the crackling sound of fire. This is probably why DANIELOU (1992:487) translates the name Bhṛgu (without quoting any sources) as "le craquement du feu". According to MACDONELL (1898:140), it probably derives from the root *bhrāj-*, to illuminate (see also MW). According to BERGAIGNE (quoted by KUHN), Bhṛgu designates the fire, and KUHN (1859:8-10), thinks that it designates the lightning flash. Thus all the possible interpretations of this term intimately connect it with the fire.

---

[28] SIEG enumerates them in his article on "Bhṛgu" (1909/1991c:320).

[29] Unfortunately, he does not specify which edition of the text he uses.

The name of the Uśij, another family of rather shadowy seers who find Agni is said to mean "fire" by the Uṇādisūtras (cf. MW).

Trita, "the third", sometimes also called Trita Āptya is a rather shadowy personage whose name appears some 40 times in the ṚV. MACDONELL rather tentatively suggests that he was originally a god of lightning, the aerial form of fire, who was gradually ousted from this position by Indra (1898:69). The most salient story pertaining to him is that he fell into a well or pit and prayed to the gods for deliverance (ṚV 5.17; 10.8.7), a theme which is subsequently reused in the Brāhmaṇas and in the MBh, where his two wicked brothers Ekata and Dvita leave him to his fate. In the ṚV, Trita is intimately connected with Agni and at times identified with him (MACDONELL 1898:67). Thus in 10.46.3, Trita is said to find Agni, and in verse 6 of the same hymn, Agni himself is called Trita.

Likewise, the gods Indra, Varuṇa and Yama are closely connected with Agni, even at times identified with him (e.g. ṚV 1.164.46). Indra always has a close connection with Agni (cf. KEITH 1925:154), and is almost the only god with whose name that of Agni appears, more than 50 times, in the *dvandva*-compound *indrāgnī* (MACDONELL 1898:95; VARENNE 1977-78:376). And VARENNE (1977-78:377-78) adds: "The Indra-Agni solidarity is so strong that in many occurrences the poets do not hesitate to exchange one god's attributes with those of the other." HILLEBRANDT (1927-29/1980:44-47) notes that Varuṇa and Agni are sometimes equated with each other, Varuṇa being a manifestation of Agni, or vice versa. (See also MACDONELL 1898:95). According to OBERLIES (1998:358-59), Agni's intimate connection both with Indra and Varuṇa is due to the fact that, like these two gods, he fulfills the functions of kingship, but a type of kingship which fluctuates between and 'indraic' and a 'varuṇic' one:

> "Wie Varuṇa wacht auch er über das Einhalten von Vorschriften und Obligationen und über das Verhalten der Haus- und Viś-Bewohner,

> wie Varuṇa ist er Richter; doch anders als der *nicht-kämpfende* Friedenskönig Varuṇa ist er ein Gott, der auch kämpft: Er schützt das Haus, die Viś bei Angriffen."

As for Yama, the god of the dead or of the manes (*pitṛ*s), he is said to designate the lightning in Nir 12.10. KUHN (1859:208) considers him to be equivalent with the fire. MACDONELL (1898:171) notes that Yama is a close friend of "Agni, who as conductor of the dead would naturally be in close relations with him." FINDLY (1981:357, note 39) makes the following remark: "as the first mortal [...] and therefore one of the first of those to perform the ritual [...] Yama has a stake in the ritual continuity. Yama, moreover, since he is the god of the dead, is especially able to see those who have gone." VON SCHROEDER (1908:188) further notes that the *pitṛ*s, whose overlord is Yama, are especially credited with the winning of light and of hidden treasures. According to KRICK (1982:553, note 1502), Yama is enabled to see and find Agni hiding in the waters, because the waters are his own domain.

Thus we can observe a strong common thread linking all the persons who find the hidden Agni: they are all in some way or other aspects, forms, manifestations of the fire-god himself, or at least intimately connected with him through some of their activities or characteristics. Here we see at work the motif of equivalences, which is indeed very common in Vedic literature. The identification of Agni with those who find him is greatly facilitated by the equivalences which are not rarely established between the various gods in the ṚV. To adduce one example among many, in ṚV 1.164.46 we can read:

> *índram mitrám váruṇam agním āhur*
> *átho divyáḥ sá suparṇó garútmān |*
> *ékaṃ sád víprā bahudhā́ vadanti*
> *agním yamám mātaríśvānam āhuḥ ||*

> They call it Indra, Mitra, Varuṇa, Agni, and it is the divine bird Garutmat. Being one, the sages called it by many names. They call it Agni, Yama, Mātariśvan.[30]

Furthermore, we can note that some of the personages who discover Agni become his sons in the later literature. We have already mentioned how Bhṛgu, though he is basically (and usually considered to be) the son of Varuṇa, is born out of the flames of the sacrificial fire, and how Aṅgiras is born out of the coals. The theme of Aṅgiras' affiliation with Agni is even more unequivocally stressed in MBh 3.207, where Aṅgiras becomes Agni's son. (See below.) ŚB 1.2.3.1 relates how Trita Āptya and his two brothers are born when Agni spits into the waters (hence their name Āptya = of the water). In this connection we may perhaps quote CARNOY (1931:329) who makes the following very pertinent comment:

> "Les duplications de héros ou de divinités sont un phénomène courant en mythologie, les divers surnoms d'un dieu devenant autant de personalités. Dans la suite, souvent ces personnages concurrents deviennent père, frère ou fils de celui en qui s'incarne principalement la conception."

Wild versus tame fire

HEESTERMAN (1993:23-24) makes us attentive to the fact that the Vedic texts often speak of the fire as if it were a domestic animal. Indeed, the fire, just like cattle, is domesticated. But, "however tame, cattle are prone to run away, which is also a standard motif in the mythology of the fire." (HEESTERMAN 1993:25). Thus the set of opposites wild/tame plays a great role in this myth, and it is rather

[30] Translation according to GELDNER (1951). According to the commentators, the subject of this verse is Agni. In which case, the translation would run along the following lines: they say that Agni is Indra, Mitra, etc. But it is grammatically more likely that the subject is the *ékaṃ sád*, which bears the names of many gods.

strikingly reflected in the various comparisons and metaphors which occur in the Ṛgvedic passages concerning Agni's flight. The subject of comparison is Agni and the objects of comparison are mostly certain animals. This is where the bipolarity wild/domesticated emerges most clearly. 1.65.1: *paśvā́ ná tāyúṃ gúhā cátantaṃ*: like a thief moving in secret with a domestic animal; 1.72.2: *asmé vatsáṃ pári ṣántaṃ ná vindann*: not finding our calf which was moving about; 3.9.4: *apsú siṃhám iva śritám*: like a lion who has entered the waters; 5.15.5: *padáṃ ná tāyúr gúhā dádhāno*: like a thief keeping his foot in a secret place; 10.46.2: *paśúṃ ná naṣṭáṃ:* like a lost / escaped / perished cattle; in 10.51.6 Agni himself is speaking:

> *agnéḥ pū́rve bhrā́taro ártham etáṃ*
> *rathī́vā́dhvānam ánv ā́varīvuḥ* /
> *tásmād bhiyā́ varuṇa dūrám āyaṃ*
> *gauró ná kṣepnór avije jyā́yāḥ* //
> "Agni's previous brothers moved along on this job like a cart-horse on the path; out of fear of that, o Varuṇa, I came far away; like a white-buffalo, I recoiled from the flying of the bow-string."

There are two different sets of comparisons: Agni is either likened to a calf (*vatsa*) and domestic animal (*paśu*), or to a robber (*tāyu*), a lion (*siṃha*), and a species of wild buffalo, the "white-buffalo" (Bos Gaurus; *gaura*).[31] The essential distinction is that between domestic and wild. Further distinctions might be between harmless and dangerous, and sacrificial and non-sacrificial, an extension of the first category, for only domestic cattle are fit for sacrifice.[32] Verse 10.51.6 offers a double set of comparisons: Agni's previous brothers who used to fulfill the *hotṛ* function are here likened to *rathin*s, whereas Agni

[31] The Bos Gaurus is a species of wild bovine, a heavy, humped animal which roams on the lower slopes of the Himalaya. Somewhat surprisingly, given its name *gaura* (white), it is said to be dark-brown or black.

[32] See SMITH (1994:249-253).

himself, who does not want to perform the same work, compares himself to a *gaura*. Following GELDNER's translation of *rathin* as *Wagenross*, I have here translated this word as "cart-horse". As a matter of fact, *rathin* means "who has a chariot" and can thus designate charioteer, chariot-rider or chariot-horse. Keeping in mind the usual imagery of the fire as the charioteer of the gods, conveying the oblations to them, most translators have chosen charioteer here. Nevertheless, I think Geldner was right in his choice for the following reasons: firstly, comparing the fire to a horse, even though here they are the previous fires, not Agni himself, is not an unusual image: one of the fire's theriomorphic forms is precisely that of a white horse. Besides, respecting the parallelism of the two comparisons which occur in this verse, since Agni compares himself to a *gaura*, it is to be expected that his brothers are compared to another animal. And indeed, horse and *gaura* present us with the expected bipolarity of tame / wild, since Agni's elder brothers were tame fires plying the *hotṛ* function and Agni on the contrary refuses to be caught to fulfill the same office and runs away like a wild animal. But even more than that: it turns out that the *gaura* is the exact counterpart of the horse among wild animals. SMITH (1991:536) makes us attentive to a passage of AB 2.8, which describes how the sacrificial quality (*medha*) passed from one animal to the other, starting with man. After the *medha* has departed from each animal in turn, that animal becomes the equivalent wild animal. Thus man, deprived of his *medha*, becomes the *kimpuruṣa*, the horse becomes the *gaura*, the cow the gayal, etc. "These *paśu*s whose sacrificial quality had passed out of them became unfit for sacrifice. Therefore one should not eat them"[33] concludes the passage. Thus, by

---

33 This last assertion about the impropriety of eating these wild animals seems doubtful in the case of the *gaura*, since in Agni's words it is being hunted, most likely with a view to eating it. But perhaps it is understood that eating it would be possible if not likely for those people who were beyond the pale of Vedic Aryan society.

comparing himself to a *gaura*, Agni clearly puts himself outside the sphere of any sacrificial activity, unlike his tame horse-brothers.

On the whole, the comparisons which occur in these passages are very ambiguous: Agni is both wild and tame, he is the robber[34] and the stolen calf, he is a *paśu,* as well as a *gaura* and a lion. This is of course in keeping with Agni's generally ambiguous nature: beneficent sacrificial fire, versus 'rudraic', wild, destructive fire. It also expresses most effectively Agni's wavering on the brink of two worlds, that of the sacrifice and that of the wilderness. Most interesting in this respect is verse 1.65.1, for here, in the same sentence, Agni is both the thief and the stolen *paśu*, as if the wild personified fire was carrying away the domestic object fire. If we now remember what we noticed in the preceding section, concerning the identity of the various personages who find the hidden Agni, who all turn out to be in some way aspects or forms of Agni himself, we realize that Agni is the thief, the stolen object, and the finder, all rolled into one. Or, to use a more metaphysical expression, Agni is the seer, the seen, and the vision, he is the revealer, the revealed and the revelation. Thus Agni's 'Trinitarian' nature,[35] which is so evident in the case of this god in the Veda as far as various aspects and functions of his are concerned (births, dwellings, hiding-places, forms, sacrificial fires, etc.) is also revealed in the myth of his hiding. Besides, it gives us a good idea of the omnipotence of Agni, who can steal himself away, and find himself again, keeping the whole world in disarray.

---

[34] The comparison with the robber might at first appear somewhat outside the range of the rest of the comparisons which refer to animals. But the robber is in a way a 'wild' man, operating in the jungle and not belonging to the village. Often, robbers are put on par with wild beasts of prey, as for instance in the following passage (TB 3.9.1.2-4, quoted by SMITH (1991:535)), which warns against the evil consequences of sacrificing wild animals: "If he (the priest) were to perform the sacrifice with the jungle animals, [...] ravenous beasts, man-tigers, thieves, murderers, and robbers would arise in the jungles."

[35] Thus MACDONELL (1898:93) notes that Agni presents us with the earliest Indian trinity.

How Agni became a god

Most authors dealing with this myth have interpreted it as reflecting a cyclical phenomenon. In this, many of them have also drawn from the later Vedic occurrences of the myth. This is the case for KRICK (1982) (see below in the section on late Veda) and also for HEESTERMAN (1993:116-17) who makes the following remark:

> "[T]here can be no doubt about the cyclic periodicity of the fire cult. This involves a ritual paradigm that brings into play dimensions other than only renewal. It can perhaps best be described in terms of interlocking sets of oppositions – controlled and wild fire, integration and dispersal, manifest presence and disappearance, permanence and intermittence, stability and mobility. [...] In mythological terms, this is the theme of Agni's flight or withdrawal as against his retrieval and reinstatement ".

But to my knowledge, the first who dwelt at some length on the topic of Agni's hiding is HILLEBRANDT (1891-1902 / 1927-1929 / 1980:90-96). His contention is that the episode of Agni's flight refers to the transition between the two divisions of the year: the Dakṣiṇāyana or southern course of the sun, which leads to the ancestors: *pitṛyāna*, and the Uttarāyana or northern course of the sun, which leads to the gods: *devayāna*. At the end of the *pitṛyāna*, the sacrificial fires are put out and new ones must be kindled for the *devayāna*. This is referred to in 10.51.5, where Varuṇa tells Agni: "You live in darkness, Agni. Make the paths passable, which serve the gods (*sugā́n patháḥ kṛṇuhi devayā́nān*)."[36] Agni lives in darkness, that is, in the period when the fires are extinguished. At the beginning of the *devayāna* half-year, he should take up his duties, bringing the sacrifices to the gods. HILLEBRANDT (1927-29/1980:91) further remarks: "It does not take a

[36] Acc. to SARMA's translation of HILLEBRANDT (1927-29/1980:91).

keen intellect to see that the three brothers[37] of Agni who disappeared are the three sacrificial fires which were extinguished and that the Agni searched for by the gods is the sacrificial fire which should serve them anew." According to HILLEBRANDT, the Agni who hides in the waters is nothing but the form of Agni which is the sun (Agni Vaiśvānara). The sun is often said to hide in the ocean. The idea that Agni dwells in darkness might also refer to the sun as it is hidden in the rainy downpour of the monsoon, or might even be a reminiscence of the winter solstice, "a memory of older times under a different sky". (1927-29/1980:96).[38]

I would like to argue that this myth, before being used in the later Veda as a kind of justification for various rituals involving extinguishing and relighting the fire, is a myth about how Agni became a god. In the later Veda the number of his elder brothers who came to harm is fixed as three: they are the three sticks kept around the sacrificial fire. But in the Ṛgveda itself, their number is nowhere specified. Indeed, Agni may not only have had *three* elder brothers, but

---

[37] Here Hillebrandt bases himself on the late Veda (TS 2,6.6.1 & 6.2.8.4) which specifies that the number of Agni's elder brothers is three, the minimum number implied by the plural *bhrātaraḥ*, and deduces from it that the three brothers are the three previous sacrificial fires which were extinguished. The ṚV itself nowhere mentions the actual number of Agni's elder brothers.

[38] VON SCHROEDER (1908:184-86) fully concurs with Hillebrandt, but according to KEITH (1925:160), Hillebrandt's "conjecture unhappily lacks any verisimilitude: the picture of the bringing of Agni to work seems no more than the conception of an individual poet of the constant theme of the mode, in which Agni comes to be employed as the sacrificer on earth." Attributing this mythical episode to "the conception of an individual poet" appears to be erroneous, since this theme appears in many other hymns besides hymns 10.51-53, although it is fully developed only in these three.

FINDLY proposes the following interpretation of the myth. According to this author, "reflecting the first phase of a tradition growing old, hymns such as RV. X. 51 (and the related RV. X.52, 53) were composed out of the fear that ritual power was, or soon would be, waning, and as a portrayal of the attempt to revitalize the tradition by winning back its essence, i.e. Jātavedas." (1981:357). For FINDLY, the main issue tackled in this myth is that of authority. The priests have become too high-handed in their skillful machinations, but they are forced to realize that religion has a will and power of its own, symbolized by the flight of Agni Jātavedas. "The lesson is that if ritual is misused, its essence will depart; if, however, it is treated with respect and honor it will return." (1981:358).

a myriad of elder brothers, who, being extinguished after performing their role in the previous sacrificial performances, died, the way a fire which is put out dies. Wishing to avoid this fate, afraid of death, Agni, the next chosen fire, makes a kind of 'regression' and becomes a foetus again, hiding in the original waters, his mothers, out of which he was born in the first place. The foetal imagery is very strong throughout: he is a *garbha* (foetus) enveloped in an *ulba* (embryonic membrane). His mothers the waters grow him in their lap, etc. What does not emerge quite clearly is whether this Agni had already started fulfilling his functions as the sacrificial fire, more specifically the *hotṛ* function, or not. For he is at times called a *vatsa*, 'our' *vatsa* or a *paśu*, terms implying his domesticated nature, but at other times he is wild, a *gaura*, lion, thief, who has no place on the sacrificial ground. Besides, in hymn 10.52, after accepting to function as the *hotṛ*, Agni requests the gods to instruct him in his sacrificial duties. This seems to imply that he has never performed them before.

In any case, Agni stages his disappearance and also his come-back. The gods promise him a long life to lure him back: *kurmás ta ā́yur ajáraṃ yád agne yáthā yuktó jātavedo ná ríṣyāḥ*: "we make for you a life devoid of old age, so that, Agni, once you are yoked (to the sacrificial duties) you will not die, o Jātavedas!" (10.51.7). But Agni is not satisfied with this alone; he wants his share in the sacrifice:

> *prayājā́n me anuyājā́ṃś ca kévalān*
> *ū́rjasvantaṃ havíṣo datta bhāgám* /
> *ghṛtáṃ cāpā́ṃ púruṣaṃ caúṣadhīnām*
> *agnéś ca dīrghám ā́yur astu devāḥ* // 10.51.8 //
> "Give me the fore-offerings and the after-offerings exclusively as my own, and the juicy part of the oblations; and the ghee of the waters and the '*puruṣa*' of the plants, and let there be long life for Agni, o Gods!"

The expression *púruṣaṃ [...] oṣadhīnām*, literally: "the man of the plants", has given rise to many interpretations.[39] HERTEL (1938:34, note 6) gives the most convincing explanation: the plants or herbs have feminine names in Sanskrit (*vīrudh* and *oṣadhi*), whereas the *soma* is masculine. Hence it can be called the "man of the plants". Now, as OLDENBERG (1894:104), HILLEBRANDT (1927-29/1980:49) and OBERLIES (1998:241, 287) note, Agni, at least originally, hardly seems to have gotten any share of the *soma* offerings. Hence perhaps his insistence to drink *soma*, which would give him divine status. FINDLY (1981:358) opines that "the Jātavedas of this hymn is childishly willful and petulant". To this we must object that his very life is at stake. He can become an immortal only if he gets a share of the oblations. Then he will be able to transcend his mere existence as one particular fire, and live on eternally in all the fires, unlike his dead brothers who had no share, who were mere cart-horses, ploughing the sacrificial field without ever tasting its crops, and dying after fulfilling their function. Thus Agni is the first fire who manages to break the vicious circle and escape alive.

Hymns 10.51-53 illustrate how Agni gradually comes over to the gods' side. In 51 and 52, Agni and the gods respectively still form two clearly separate, even opposed groups.[40] Thus in 10.51, Agni speaks the even, and the gods, or rather their spokesman Varuṇa, the uneven stanzas. Likewise, in his speech in 10.52, Agni posits himself as the one *hotṛ* as opposed to all the gods, whom he addresses. For instance in 10.52.1: *víśve devāḥ śāstána mā*: "you all the gods, instruct me"; 10.52.2: *ahám hótā nyásīdam yájīyān víśve devā́ marúto mā junanti*:

[39] GELDNER keeps the literal translation of man (Mensch). KRICK (1982:545, note 1479) thinks that the first meaning is man (Mensch) and the metaphorical meaning is *soma*. HILLEBRANDT (1927-29/1980:91) renders it as "the pith of the plants".

[40] But, to undermine somewhat my own argument, it must be admitted that this is frequently the case with Agni. He is often kept apart and opposed to the compact mass of the gods, holding a separate position. See OLDENBERG (1894:104).

"I, the excellently sacrificing *hotṛ*, have taken my seat, all the gods (and) the Maruts are instigating me", etc. On the other hand, in the third hymn of the series, after being anointed as the gods' *hotṛ*, Agni now identifies himself with the gods and considers himself as one of them: *tád adyá vācáḥ prathamám̐ masīya yénā́surām̐ abhí devā́ ásāma*: "I shall now first think of that speech by which *we the gods* may defeat the Asuras." (10.53.4). Indeed, Agni would not be the only god whose divinity was won by some effort, and was not acquired as a birth-right. The same mythological motif of the acquisition of divine status is found in connection with the Aśvins and the Ṛbhus.[41] OLDENBERG (1894:104) and KEITH (1925:154) draw our attention to the somewhat lowly status of the fire-god which is noticeable at times. His existence on earth among men makes him of a lower order than the other gods.

The late Veda

In her monumental work, *Das Ritual der Feuergründung* (*agnyādheya*) (1982), KRICK dedicates a lengthy discussion to the myth of Agni's hiding. (See chapter VIII, esp. pp. 538-62.) Krick, like Hillebrandt, takes the ritual texts as the starting point of her analysis and explains the myth in connection with the ritual practice. More specifically, she shows how these later Vedic texts make use of the myth of Agni's hiding to exemplify the *punarādheya* ceremony: the reinstatement of the fire. According to the *sūtra*s, this ceremony is prescribed in certain cases when the instatement of the fire (*agnyādheya*) has not produced the desired results. (KRICK 1982:514-536). In KRICK's opinion, this ritual became optional (*kāmyeṣṭi*) only at a late date, after the

[41] The Aśvins had a lowly status due to their physician's profession, which made them move on earth among men. Besides, their descent seems to have been half-human on their mother's side (see ZELLER 1990: chapt. 2). ŚB 4.1.5.1 ff. and MBh 3.121-125 relate the story of how the Aśvins got a share in the sacrifice, and were allowed to drink *soma*, thanks to Cyavāna's intervention. As for the Ṛbhus, ṚV 1.110.4 states that they are mortals who gained the status of immortals. They earned their divine status thanks to their wondrous manual skills.

population had become sedentary. But originally, *agnyādheya* and *punarādheya* must have taken place yearly, at the spring and autumn solstices. These dates coincided with the beginning and end of the period of raids respectively (1982:534). Before its reinstatement, the fire is extinguished for a certain period of time, which in the myth is represented by Agni's hiding. Thus, underlying this interpretation, we find the concept of a cyclical phenomenon, reflecting the natural rhythm of the seasons, of the vegetation. A latent, sleeping period followed by an active one, whose beginning was marked by a renewal festival (1982:516, note 1401). The myth of Agni's hiding is also used in the late Vedic texts to explain the origin of the three sticks which surround the sacrificial fire: they are said to be Agni's three elder brothers who came to harm while plying the *hotṛ* function. According to KRICK, the fact that Agni, in the myth, is afraid of the *hotṛ* function shows that in the pre-classical situation, this function was temporary and the new *hotṛ* had to fight and kill his predecessor in a ritual fight perhaps involving a chariot-race (we remember that in the ṚV Agni calls his brothers *rathins*, which can also be translated as charioteer). Hence Agni's fear of dying, just like his elder brothers, the preceding *hotṛ*s. (See KRICK 1982:548, note 1490; 552; 561-2).

TS 1.5.1, MS 1.7.2, KS 8.15, KapS 8.3, ŚB 2.2.3.1-11, KauṣB 1.3.1-30, tell a roughly similar story, which seems to be a variant of the myth of Agni's flight and hiding, but, the KauṣB excepted, contain no direct reference to the Ṛgvedic version. Here the myth is invoked to explain the *punarādheya* ritual, that is, the reinstatement of the fire. The basic story is as follows: the gods are about to depart to wage war with the Asuras. They put all their forms or riches in Agni, for safekeeping, but Agni, out of greediness, runs away with them, sometimes hiding in the seasons. After their victory, the gods have to perform the *punarādheya* ritual to win their goods back. Agni's hiding in the seasons gives rise to a discussion on the proper season in which the ritual should be performed, which is usually said to be the monsoon.

More directly linked with the Ṛgvedic story of Agni's flight from the *hotṛ* function due to the death of his elder brothers, and his own fear of death, are the following passages: TS 2.6.6; 5.1.4.3-4; 6.2.8.4-6; MS 3.8.6; KS 25.7; KapS 39.5; ŚB 1.2.3.1; 1.3.3.13-17; 7.3.2.14-15; JB 2.41; TB 1.1.3.9. Since most of these texts are translated and commented upon by Krick, we shall only indicate here the main motifs which appear therein, in conformity with, or as new developments from, the Ṛgveda. Most of them use the myth to explain the origin and function of the three enclosing-sticks (*paridhis*), which are kept around the sacrificial fire and represent Agni's dead brothers.

The story is as follows: Agni had three elder brothers, who are sometimes given the names of Bhūpati, Bhuvanapati and Bhūtānāṃ Pati (TS 2.6.6; MS 3.8.6; KS 25.7; JB 2.41; ŚB 1.2.3.1 (Bhuvapati)), while the present Agni is called Bhūti (MS 3.8.6; JB 2.41) or Bhūta (KS 25.6). These brothers died while fulfilling their sacrificial duties. Sometimes it is said that they were struck down by the *vaṣaṭ*-call (MS 3.8.6; ŚB 1.3.3.13-17; JB 2.41).[42] Afraid of undergoing the same fate, Agni runs away and hides in the waters (TS 2.6.6; ŚB 1.2.3.1), in the ocean, and then in the reeds (KS 25.6), in the Pūtudru-tree for one night (out of which the surrounding sticks are manufactured), in the Sugandhitejana the second night, and between the horns of a ram the third night (TS 6.2.8.4-6). In TS 2.6.6, KS 25.7.111.7-19 and KapS 39.5, a fish denounces Agni to the gods, and Agni curses the fish: since it betrayed him, people would kill it whenever they wished. In the last two mentioned texts, a horse subsequently discovers him

---

42 PATTON (1996:383, note 32) defines this term as follows: "An exclamation by the *hotṛ* at the end of a verse that signals the *adhvaryu* priest to offer the oblation into the fire; also personified as a deity." The *vaṣaṭ*-call is notoriously dangerous. KRICK (1982:555, note 1504) remarks: "Der Vaṣaṭ-Ruf ist eine Blitzwaffe; ein Hotar [...], der beim Vaṣaṭ-Ruf an seinen Feind denkt, erschlägt ihn damit."

hiding in the reeds. The gods find him, and tell him to resume his *hotṛ* functions. Agni accepts to return on the condition that whatever of the poured oblation would fall outside the three surrounding sticks should be his dead brothers' share (TS 2.6.6; 6.2.8.4-6; MS 3.8.6; KS 25.7.111.7-19; KapS 39.5; ŚB 1.3.3.13-17; JB 2.41). For these surrounding sticks are indeed his brothers (KS 25.7.111.7-19; KapS 39.5; ŚB 1.3.3.13-17). This is a means of ensuring that no part of the oblation is really lost, since even that which falls on the ground will be somebody's share. TS 6.2.8.4-6 and MS 3.8.6 present a further development: Agni decides to shake off his bones (the sign of his mortality) because his brothers had bones and died due to them. Agni's shaken off bones (sometimes his flesh) become the surrounding sticks. But these actually represent his brothers,[43] who henceforth protect Agni. ŚB 1.3.3.13-17 and JB 2.41 present the following variant: the dead brothers' substance or blood entered the earth, that is why the oblation spilt on the ground (outside the fire) becomes their share.

ŚB 1.2.3.1 and TB 1.1.3.9 use the myth for different, but also etiologic, purposes: the ŚB explains thereby the origin of the Āptya deities: the gods find Agni hiding in the waters after his brothers' death, and make him return. Agni then spits on the waters, as an unsafe place of refuge, and hence spring the Āptya deities, Trita, Dvita and Ekata. TB invokes the myth of Agni's hiding to explain why the *aśvattha* tree is one of the seven types of wood which can be used as *saṃbhāra* (materials required in a sacrifice): Agni hid from the gods. Taking the form of a horse, he resided in an *aśvattha* for one year. Hence the name of the tree became *aśvattha* = *aśva-stha* (that in which the horse resided) and it can be used as a *saṃbhāra*, since it contained fire. TS 5.1.4.3-4 and ŚB 7.3.2.14-15 relate how Agni was found by Atharvan or Prajāpati as he was hiding in a lotus leaf. HILLEBRANDT

---

[43] See KRICK (1982:554-5) for a discussion on the various text-levels superimposed here.

(1927-29/1980:59) compares the lotus leaf to the womb of the waters in which Agni hides in the ṚV.

On the whole, the later Veda retains the sequentiality of the myth as it appeared in the Ṛgveda: Agni is afraid of assuming the office of *hotṛ* and runs away to hide. When he is found by the gods, he accepts to return on certain conditions.[44] But, although the general framework remains unchanged,[45] several details do change. First, the number of Agni's brothers is invariably fixed at three, and they are given names. This is important, since the aim of telling the myth is in most versions to explain the origin of the three surrounding sticks. The additional information that they were struck down by the *vaṣaṭ*-call is also an innovation of the late Veda. Agni's hiding places remain essentially the same, namely the waters and the plants, but the late Veda gives more importance to the plants as hiding place than the ṚV, which emphasized mostly the waters. Certain varieties of plants or trees are specified, and the *aśvattha* reappears in the MBh. Even the variant adopted by TS 2.8.4-6, in which Agni is said to spend his third night of hiding between the horns of a ram, might have its source in ṚV 10.46.3 wherein Trita finds Agni on the head of a cow (*mūrdhány ághnyāyāḥ*).[46] The motif of the animal (here a fish) which betrays Agni, has a further development in two versions of the myth in the MBh. This motif, as far as we can tell, is also an innovation of the late Veda, as well as the curse Agni inflicts upon the traitor. In the ṚV Agni reveals his presence by his own foot-steps and effulgence. On the other hand, the late Veda abandons the option that the *ṛṣi*s find the lost Agni (excepting Atharvan). Here the gods, who are interested in finding

44 In ŚB 1.3.3.13-17, Agni does not run away, but explains to the gods why he cannot accept the *hotṛ* function.

45 Except perhaps in TB which does not mention Agni's fear of the *hotṛ* function and his subsequent restoration to it after being found by the gods.

46 However, according to Sāyaṇa, this means *bhūmyāṁ*: in the earth.

him and making him return, are only mentioned as an undifferentiated group.[47] Agni's conditions for returning are different too: in the ṚV he asks favours for himself: immortality and a share in the sacrifice. Whereas in the late Veda he asks for a share for his brothers. But in some versions, this turns out to his own advantage, since his brothers, as the surrounding-sticks, undertake to protect him against a fate similar to their own. Agni's disintegration in certain versions of the myth, after accepting to perform the *hotṛ* function, is already hinted at in ṚV 1.144.2: *apā́m upásthe víbhṛto yád ā́vasad,* and 10.51.3: *bahudhā́ [...] právişṭam [...] apsú óṣadhīṣu*. But in the ṚV Agni undergoes a disintegration while hiding in various places, not after assuming the *hotṛ* function. This theme of Agni's disintegration is further developed in the Bṛhaddevatā (MACDONELL 1904:7.61-81; TOKUNAGA 1997:7.45-61) where different parts of Agni's body become various plants and metals, a passage which, according to TOKUNAGA (1997:273), is borrowed from MBh 3.212.12-14.[48]

The Mahābhārata

The MBh relates not less than five times the story of Agni's hiding. The places where the myth occurs are the following: 1.5-7; 3.207-212 (two occurrences of the myth); 9.46.12-20; 13.83-84. We shall first give a brief summary of each one of these five versions before turning to certain general themes which are present in the MBh's versions of this myth.

---

[47] Only KauṣB 1.3.1-30, which contains a different version of the myth, mentions in conformity with the ṚV that Yama and Varuṇa espy the hidden Agni.

[48] According to TOKUNAGA (1997:XXVII-XXX) some parts of the Bṛhaddevatā are much younger than MACDONELL assumed (dating up to about 500 C.E.) and borrow much from the MBh. The Bṛhaddevatā, while commenting here on ṚV 10.51-53, has also incorporated various themes of the late Veda and of the MBh. TOKUNAGA (1997:272) notes that the BD mentions five elder brothers of Agni, just like MBh 3.209.1f. But whether Agni is really one of the six fires mentioned in this MBh verse seems dubious, for these are said to be the sons of Bṛhaspati, who has himself just become Agni's own son.

Bhṛgu's curse: 1.5-7

The story is first told in the Ādiparvan (1.5-7), in the Pauloma-subparvan. That is to say, at the beginning, or rather, to be more precise, at the second beginning of the MBh. The first beginning of the MBh (1.1) relates how the bard Ugraśravas, son of Lomaharṣaṇa, arrives at the Naimiṣa forest, where the Bhārgava Śaunaka is holding a twelve-year *sattra*. Ugraśravas tells the assembled sages how he heard the MBh story recited by Vaiśampāyana at king Janamejaya's snake-sacrifice, and then proceeds (among other things) to give them a summary of the main events which take place in the Epic. In 1.4, that is, at the second beginning, we find once again the narration of Ugraśravas' arrival in the Naimiṣa forest, among the company of sages performing Śaunaka's *sattra*. But this time, Śaunaka requests the bard to entertain him with the account of the descent of his (Śaunaka's) own clan, the Bhṛgus (1.5.3). After Ugraśravas has recited their genealogy, ending with Śaunaka himself, Śaunaka wants to know more about Cyavana, the son of Bhṛgu, and how he came about his name (1.5.10). Now starts the actual story which concerns us here.

1.5.11-26: The sage Bhṛgu, says Ugraśravas, had a wife named Pulomā. She was pregnant with Bhṛgu's seed when Bhṛgu had to leave his hermitage to attend a royal consecration. Meanwhile, a *rakṣas* named Puloman arrived at the hermitage, and Pulomā[49] received him with all the due rites of hospitality. Seeing her, the *rakṣas* was filled with passion and also with doubt: he started suspecting that she was the girl who had been promised to him, who had been 'chosen' by him to be his wife, but was instead given to Bhṛgu by her father. Seeing a

[49] The MBh never clearly says so, but Pulomā, as her name shows, is most likely a *rākṣasī* herself, Puloman being a common name for *rākṣasas*. That Bhṛgu, a Brahmin sage, should marry a *rākṣasī* is not too surprising, for his clan had a general tendency to marry outside the Brahmin community. Many Bhārgavas have *kṣatriya* wives, or *apsaras* wives. Devayānī, the daughter of the Bhārgava Śukra, even enters into a *pratiloma* marriage with a *kṣatriya*, king Yayāti. For this topic, see GOLDMAN (1977:5; 98-99).

fire burning in the fire-house, he repeatedly pressed Agni to tell him in truth her identity: whose wife was she? If she was indeed Bhṛgu's, he would at once carry her off with him. Agni hesitates, "afraid of untruth as well as of a curse" (1.5.26). Caught in this double-bind, he prefers the curse, and answers that she is Bhṛgu's wife.

1.6. At once, the *rakṣas*, assuming the form of a boar,[50] carried her away. But the foetus she was bearing, enraged at this indignity, fell out of his mother's womb. Hence his name, Cyavana, the "falling one":[51] *roṣān mātuś cyutaḥ kukṣeś cyavanas tena so 'bhavat* (1.6.2).[52] When the *rakṣas* saw that baby who was shining like the sun: *ādityavarcasam* (1.6.3) he was instantly reduced to ashes.[53] Pulomā

---

[50] The form of a boar: *varāha-rūpeṇa* (1.6.1) seems to imply principally a lustful form. Certain Purāṇic versions of the myth of the *varāhāvatāra* relate how Viṣṇu, in his boar-form, was overcome by lust and remained united with the Earth whom he had rescued from the bottom of the ocean, fathering many children on her. Śiva ultimately had to kill him to force him to resume his normal duties. See DONIGER O'FLAHERTY (1973:41; 282-3). See also the description of the Asura Mūka, who, in the form of a boar, attacks Arjuna who is doing *tapas* on the mountain to obtain divine weapons. Before launching his attack, he rubs himself on the earth (MBh 3.163.18). (Cf. SCHEUER 1982:214). Thus the scene evoked here is ambiguous, as is Puloman's position anyway: on the one hand we are strongly reminded of another famous kidnapping, that of Sītā by Rāvaṇa, from her forest hermitage, a very negative comparison. On the other hand, in a more positive fashion, we are also reminded of Viṣṇu in his boar-form carrying the Earth, saving her. Indeed, Puloman, though he is acting unlawfully here, seems to have been genuinely wronged in being deprived of Pulomā whom he had 'chosen'. He twice refers to Bhṛgu as *anṛtakārin* "wrong-doer", in this passage (1.5.19 & 24). That Puloman and Pulomā might genuinely have been destined for each other is also made likely by their identical names: this trait reminds us of the two Jaratkārus (MBh 1.41 ff.). (See SCHNEIDER (1959:7-8) who explains why the ascetic Jaratkāru wants to marry a girl who has the same name as himself.)

[51] The Epic systematically has Cyavana, whereas the Vedic texts have Cyavāna.

[52] We find nearly the same formulation in 1.60.44: *yaḥ sa roṣāc cyuto garbhān mātuḥ mokṣāya*, which adds that his aim was to rescue his mother.

[53] This scene is reminiscent of another Bhārgava episode, related in MBh 1.169-171, that of the Bhārgava Aurva who blinds, as soon as he is born (from his mother's thigh which he pierces, hence his name Aurva, from *ūru*, the thigh) the *kṣatriyas* who have been persecuting his clan. Thus Aurva, like Cyavana, gets his name from his mode of birth. He is moreover described in very similar terms as Cyavana: *muṣṇan [...] madhyāhna iva bhāskaraḥ*: blinding like the midday sun (1.169.21). Thus both boys share the same native fierceness, or rather fieriness. They are both explicitly compared to the sun, but we must not forget that the sun has been considered as a form of the fire since Vedic times. (See OLDENBERG 1894:108). According to GOLDMAN (1977:97), Aurva is even said to be Cyavana's son in certain passages of the MBh. But whereas

picked up her son and ran away, weeping so much that her tears formed a river following her. Seeing her, Brahmā himself consoled her and named the river Vadhūsarā, "the Run-of-the-Bride."[54] Bhṛgu then saw his son and wife, and questioned her angrily: who had revealed her identity to that *rakṣas*? He could not possibly have known her for sure by himself! Pulomā reveals that it was Agni's doing, and Bhṛgu, enraged, curses the fire: *sarvabhakṣo bhaviṣyasi*: "you will become omnivorous!" (1.6.13).

1.7. Agni is incensed at the curse and rebukes Bhṛgu: how dare he curse him, who was only doing his duty as a witness? He could curse him in turn but will desist, since Brahmins are to be respected. Agni then proceeds to give Bhṛgu a very detailed description of his sacrificial duties. Most importantly, he is the *mouth* of the gods and ancestors, who eat the offered oblations through him. This being the case, how could he possibly become omnivorous? Then Agni disappears from all the sacrificial grounds. The gods and *ṛṣi*s, in great distress, repair to Brahmā and relate their plight. Brahmā summons Agni. He praises him as the maker of the worlds, and pacifies him: he will not become omnivorous with all his body, he says, but only with certain flames. Besides, whatever he burns or 'eats' will automatically be purified. Hence he should not hesitate to resume his sacrificial duties. Agni is satisfied with this and goes back to his duties. The whole world rejoices.[55]

Cyavana's anger seems to be exhausted by reducing the *rakṣas* to ashes, Aurva's cannot be quenched, and finally he is advised to throw it into the ocean where it becomes the submarine fire.

54 VAN BUITENEN's translation (1973:58).

55 For subsequent developments and transformations of this particular version of the myth in Purāṇic literature, see DONIGER O'FLAHERTY (1980:304).

Agni and Aṅgiras: 3.207

The second and third occurrences of our myth are found in the Āraṇyakaparvan (3.207-212), in the Āṅgirasa portion of the Mārkaṇḍeyasamāsyā-sub-parvan. We have here two quite different versions of the myth closely following each other. The first in 3.207 and the second in 3.212.6-19. The context is the following: the sage Mārkaṇḍeya, a Bhārgava, who is said to be several thousands of years old (cf. 3.180. 5 & 39 & 40), and who is reputed to know all kinds of tales, is telling stories to the Pāṇḍavas during their exile in the forest, while they are residing in the Kāmyakavana. In a previous story he had alluded to Agni's hiding and Skanda 's birth. Consequently, Yudhiṣṭhira requests him to tell him more about these two events (3.207.1-5). Mārkaṇḍeya starts with the story of Agni's hiding, referring to it as an *itihāsaṃ purātanam*: "an ancient tale", which indeed it is. Once upon a time, Agni, angry (*kruddha*), went to the forest to perform austerities. The sage Aṅgiras became Agni in his stead. Dwelling in his hermitage, heating and illuminating the world, he surpassed Agni. Agni saw him and became very frustrated, thinking that Brahmā had appointed another fire in his stead, since his own fieriness had vanished due to his penance. He wondered how he could again become the fire. Afraid, he slowly crept up to Aṅgiras' hermitage. The sage saw him and hailed him. He requested him to take up his duties again. First Agni refused, saying that he had lost his renown in the world. Let Aṅgiras be the first fire, and he himself would be content with a secondary position, that of the Prājāpatyaka-fire (3.207.15). But Aṅgiras insisted, and requested Agni to make him his own son. Agni finally agreed. Aṅgiras had a son named Prajāpati, who became the first-born son of Agni.[56] The gods ratified this decision.

Agni and Atharvan: 3.212.6-19

A list of fires which are Aṅgiras' progeny is enumerated till 3.212. Then the story of Agni's hiding is introduced again. The fire who goes hiding is probably the Bharata fire, who burns corpses and is mentioned in 6 a-b, though the case is somewhat confused.[57] In any case, the fire takes fright during an *agniṣṭoma* sacrifice, seeing the Niyata, "the greatest rite of the multitude": *kratuśreṣṭho bharasya*,[58] coming (6). He hides three times in three different places: first in the *arṇava* (sea), then in the earth, in which he dissolves, then in the *mahārṇava* (ocean). The watery hiding-place is well-known from the ṚV onwards, and the earth, especially the motif of the dissolution in the earth, from certain late Vedic versions. Agni's presence is revealed or brought forth by three different means in each case. When he hides in the sea, the gods cannot find him, although they look for him. The fire then sees the sage Atharvan, and requests him to carry the oblations in his stead (8). Then the fire goes to some other place, but the fish betray him, and he curses them thus: "You shall be the food of creatures in your various modes of being":[59] *bhakṣyā vai vividhair bhāvair bhaviṣyatha śarīriṇām* (10). Then the fire again requests

[56] The text is somewhat contradictory here. In verse 16, Aṅgiras himself is supposed to become Agni's son, whereas in 17-18, it is Aṅgiras' son who becomes Agni's first-born son.

[57] In this long list of fires, it is at times difficult to ascertain which are the proper names of the fires, and which are mere descriptive epithets. According to SCHREINER (1999:128, note 46), the Bharata fire is meant here. In any case, as soon as the story of Agni's hiding begins, all such distinctions between the different fires are erased, and the hiding fire is simply called Agni.

[58] Translation according to VAN BUITENEN (1975:645). I am not quite sure of what is meant here. According to HOPKINS (1915:101), the Niyata Kratu is the fire that burns the dead.

[59] Transl. according to VAN BUITENEN (1975:645).

Atharvan to carry the oblations for him. Atharvan tries to persuade him to resume his duties, but Agni refuses and abandons his body. He enters the earth, thereby producing various metals and precious stones out of different parts of his discarded body (13-14). There he remains fixed in the highest penance, but is again roused by the combined austerities of Bhṛgu, Aṅgiras and other seers, and bursts into flames. Seeing the sages, he takes fright once more, and hides in the ocean, where he disappears. The whole world is afraid and turns to Atharvan for help. Atharvan sees the fire, and creates the worlds. Then he churns the great ocean and the fire reappears from the water, and henceforth always carries the oblations (19). In the next chapter starts a lengthy description of Skanda's birth, which Yudhiṣṭhira had also inquired about.

The Agni-tīrtha: 9.46.12-20

The fourth occurrence of our myth is found in MBh 9.46.12-20, in the Śalyaparvan. Here the story is told in the context of Balarāma's *tīrthayātrā* or pilgrimage of holy places. Balarāma, unable to take sides in the war due to his equal affection for both parties, goes on a *tīrthayātrā* while the battle of Kurukṣetra is being fought. At the moment when the final and decisive mace-fight between Bhīma and Duryodhana is about to take place, he reappears on the scene to watch his two pupils fight (9.33). At this moment, Janamejaya requests Vaiśaṃpāyana to tell him more about Balarāma's travels. Accordingly, Vaiśaṃpāyana describes Balarāma's *tīrthayātrā* on the Sarasvatī river (9.34-53), after which he resumes the description of the mace-fight between Bhīma and Duryodhana. Like other such descriptions of tours of holy places,[60] Balarāma's lengthy *tīrthayātrā-varṇana* is a pretext to

[60] The most important are Arjuna's in 1.205-209, during his exile from the other Pāṇḍavas, and especially the Pāṇḍavas' in 3.91-139, while Arjuna sojourns in Indra's heaven (preceded from 3.80 onwards by descriptions of other *tīrthas*). For the topic of *tīrthayātrās*, see BIGGER (2001).

narrate many legends pertaining to the deeds of gods and *ṛṣis* in the hoary past, due to which certain places where these deeds took place (mostly near rivers) became sanctified, and the pilgrim gains great merit and various worldly advantages by performing ablutions there.

Just before coming to the Agni-*tīrtha*, in connection with which the story of Agni's hiding is told, Balarāma visits a *tīrtha* where Skanda was consecrated *senāpati* of the gods' army (in connection with which his birth and subsequent exploits are narrated) (9.43-45), and another *tīrtha* where Varuṇa was anointed king of the ocean and rivers (9.46). From there, Balarāma reaches the Agni-*tīrtha*, whereupon follows a very brief evocation of the myth of Agni's hiding (9.46.12-20): this *tīrtha* deserves its name because it is the place where Agni hid in a *śamī-garbha*[61] (and not, as we might expect since it is near a river, where Agni hid in the waters). Janamejaya wants to know more about the story, and Vaiśaṃpāyana gives him the gist of the main events: Agni, afraid of Bhṛgu's curse, went to hide in the *śamī-garbha* and vanished from the world. The gods, afraid that the whole world would perish, asked Brahmā for help. Then they set out to find Agni, along with Indra and with Bṛhaspati at their head. They found Agni in the *śamī-garbha*, felt happy and then went back the way they came. Henceforth, Agni was *sarvabhakṣa*.

---

[61] The term *śamī-garbha*, at least in the context of this myth, should not be taken in the sense of "inside a *śamī*-tree". In its technical sense, which is how we should understand it here, a *śamī-garbha* is an *aśvattha*-tree (Ficus religiosa) which has taken root on a *śamī*-tree (Acacia suma). Hence its name *śamī-garbha*, "whose womb is a *śamī*-tree". The *aśvattha*-trees, and many trees belonging to the ficus species in general, have a peculiar manner of growth: when birds leave these trees' seeds in the fork of another tree's branches, these seeds germinate, and then send down long aerial roots, which take root in the ground at the foot of the tree. Then these aerial roots grow tendrils which surround the trunk of the "mother-tree". Ultimately, these tendrils completely overgrow the first tree's trunk, and in the long run, the original tree is suffocated and dies, leaving the *aśvattha*-tree standing in its place. For a drawing of the mode of growth of the ficus species, see BOSCH (1960/1994:71, Fig. 10). *Śamīgarbha* is also a name of Agni himself, since fire can be produced by the friction of *śamī*-wood, and hence originates in a *śamī*. (See KUHN 1859:42).

This evocation of the myth is very sketchy, and only aims at mentioning the main episodes. This type of narration is not unusual in the context of descriptions of holy places. Bhṛgu's curse and Agni's subsequent *sarvabhakṣatva* correspond to the Ādiparvan version. Agni's hiding in a *śamī-garbha* and the gods' patient search for him are found in a more developed form in the Anuśāsanaparvan. On the whole, this version of the myth does not relate anything that is not found in a more developed fashion elsewhere in the MBh.

Pārvatī's curse: 13.83-84

The Anuśāsanaparvan (13.83-84) undoubtedly presents us with one of the richest and most interesting versions of the myth of Agni's hiding in the MBh. The story is told in the Dānadharma-sub-parvan, which enumerates the relative merits acquired by giving away various gifts. Once upon a time, Bhīṣma tells Yudhiṣṭhira, Rāma Jāmadagnya, having performed an *aśvamedha*, asked the assembled gods and *ṛṣis* to tell him what was the most purifying gift. Undoubtedly, replies Vasiṣṭha, it is gold. For gold is a form of Agni, and Agni is all the gods: *agnir hi devatāḥ sarvāḥ*.[62] Therefore who gifts gold gifts all the gods (13.83.36-37). To explain this further, he then proceeds to tell the following story: when the marriage of Śiva and Pārvatī took place, all the gods became afraid, thinking of the awesome power their future progeny would have, and therefore begged Śiva to desist from producing any offspring. He agreed to this, and became *ūrdhvaretas* (13.83.47). But Pārvatī was understandably furious and cursed all the gods: since they had deprived her of her progeny, they would not be able to have any either (13.83.49-50). Only Agni was not there at the time of the curse, and was consequently not affected by it. One day, a little of Śiva's semen was spilt on the earth, and from there it fell into the fire, where it grew. At that time, the Asura Tāraka became very

62 This is already a Vedic theme. Cf. e.g. AB 2.3: *agniḥ sarvā devatāḥ*.

powerful and started oppressing the gods and *ṛṣis*. They asked for Brahmā's help, since he had given the Asura the boon of quasi-invincibility (13.84.1-2). Brahmā told them that Agni, who was not there at the time of the curse (he was *naṣṭa*), and who was bearing Śiva's seed, would generate a very powerful son in the Gaṅgā, who would destroy Tāraka. He therefore advised them to find Agni. All the gods and *ṛṣis* accordingly set out to look for him, but could not find him. A frog betrayed Agni to the gods, as he was hiding in the waters. Agni cursed the frogs and went to hide in an *aśvattha*-tree. There an elephant revealed his hiding-place. Agni cursed the elephants and hid in a *śamī-garbha*. For this reason, fire can now be produced by friction out of this tree. This time a parrot revealed his hiding-place. Agni cursed him in turn. There the gods, who had compensated the three animals for their curse, finally cornered him and told him what they wanted of him. Agni agreed. He went to the Gaṅgā and became mixed with her (13.84.53) and produced a foetus in her.[63] Then follows the description of the birth of Skanda. Where he was born, everything became golden and this was the origin of gold. Therefore gold is the supreme purifier.

Agni's reasons for hiding

By and large in the MBh, the cause for Agni's disappearance is no longer his fear of sacrificial duties like in the Veda, but it is either attributed to Bhṛgu's curse (first and fourth versions) or not mentioned at all (second and fifth versions). Only the third version (3.212.6-19) maintains the Vedic motif of Agni's fear of the sacrifice. There he flees before the Niyata (literally "restrained") rite, which replaces the *vaṣaṭ*-call or the *hotṛ* function in the role of frightening the fire.

[63] How the Gaṅgā can have offspring, although she too is a goddess, is somewhat indirectly explained in other versions of the myth (e.g. R 1.36.8) by the fact that she is the sister of Pārvatī, who will therefore not object. In the R, the story of Skanda 's birth is not linked with that of Agni's hiding.

The motif of the curse is not new in connection with this myth: in the TS and KS, Agni also curses the fish which betrayed him. But in the Ādiparvan, Agni himself is cursed to start with. Here, as compared to some earlier Vedic versions we have examined, Agni's position is to begin with fundamentally reversed. Instead of being the one who is in hiding and who curses those who betray him to those who are looking for him, he becomes the one who betrays a hiding person to the one who is looking for her. For Pulomā is hidden, *rahogatā*, as Puloman expresses it in 1.5.20. One might wonder what is the connection between Agni's wrong-doing (if we may call it that) and the curse he is punished with. The case is not entirely clear, but one general observation is that Agni gets a curse affecting the organ whereby he has 'sinned', that is to say, his mouth. Though arguably, the misdeed and the curse are connected with two different functions of the mouth: that of speaking and that of eating.

The curse given by Bhṛgu: *sarvabhakṣo bhaviṣyasi*, is apparently an innovation of the Epic. This entails another important change: though Agni goes into hiding just like in all the previous versions we have dealt with, here his reasons for doing so are radically different, if not opposite. In Vedic literature Agni hides because he is afraid of performing his sacrificial functions, since he might come to harm – die – just like his elder brothers before him. But the Ādiparvan version on the contrary depicts an Agni who is completely immersed in these same duties, and in full agreement with them: he describes them in detail to Bhṛgu in 1.7.6-11. Being cursed to be omnivorous, his first reaction is to get angry (*kruddhaḥ*: 1.7.1), not to be afraid.[64] Being the mouth of the gods and ancestors, he cannot possibly become an all-eater, since they would become polluted by the impure things they

64 In the ṚV too, there is one verse (5.2.8), which says that Agni went away in anger: *hṛṇīyámānaḥ*, but no further explanation for the cause of is anger is available in that text.

would have to eat through his mouth.[65] For Agni himself, being the prototypical divine Brahmin, being omnivorous is bad enough. But he does not worry about himself, only about those he feeds though his mouth, the gods and ancestors. This is his duty since Vedic times (see WEBER-BROSAMMER 1988:112-13; SCHNEIDER 1971:73.) Thus Agni retires from his sacrificial duties not out of fear for his own life, but out of fear not to be able to perform them correctly, that is to say, with due purity.

But what does Agni's *sarvabhakṣatva* actually involve? Brahmā atones for the curse in the following way:

> *na tvaṃ sarvaśarīreṇa sarvabhakṣatvam eṣyasi /*
> *upādāne 'rciṣo yās te sarvaṃ dhakṣyanti tāḥ śikhin /*
> *yathā sūryāṃśubhiḥ spṛṣṭaṃ sarvaṃ śuci bhaviṣyati* // 1.7.20 //
> You will not become omnivorous with all your body. Those flames of yours which are (used) in *upādāna*, they will burn everything, o crested one, and everything you touch will become pure, just like that which is touched by the sun's rays.

The atonement which is immediately clear is that whatever the fire burns becomes reduced to ashes, and is therefore purified. But what exactly is meant by *upādāne 'rciṣaḥ*? HOPKINS's translation: "hinder rays" (1915:100) is not very clear. DONIGER O'FLAHERTY (1980:304) renders it simply as flames: only Agni's flames will be impure, not Agni himself. VAN BUITENEN (1973:59) translates this expression in the following way: "only those flames that are for acceptance", commenting in the notes (1973:441): "i.e. fires that are already at hand, not especially lighted for the purpose,"[66] adding: "I am not sure of

[65] Curiously, HOLTZMANN (1878:6) interprets Agni's denomination as 'mouth of the gods' from the point of view of speech, not from the point of view that he 'eats' the oblations for them: being the priest of the gods, Agni speaks the sacrificial formulae and generally acts as the gods' spokesman, that is why he is called the mouth of the gods.

[66] Of sacrifice?

this." Indeed, the expression is not quite clear. But translating *upādāna* as "acceptance" does not seem very illuminating. The first meaning of this term is: "the act of taking for one's self, appropriating for one's self". Thus we might translate *upādāne 'rciṣaḥ* as: "the flames used in the act of appropriating for yourself", or, with a slight extension of meaning, "in the act of *eating* for yourself". Thus these might be the flames Agni uses when he eats for himself, not when he acts as the mouth of gods and ancestors in the sacrifice.[67] And indeed, this might atone for Agni's main, unselfish fear, that of defiling the gods and ancestors. Another interpretation would be to apply these terms not to Agni himself, but to all the creatures in general. In this sense, these "flames used in the act of appropriating for one's self (i.e. eating)" would be the flames of the digestive fire, present in all beings.[68] And indeed, the digestive fire is called *viśvabhuj* (= *sarvabhakṣa*) in 3.209.17. Adding another dimension to the *sarvabhakṣa* problem, manuscript N adds a half-verse after 1.7.20: *kravyādā ca tanur yā te sā sarvaṃ bhakṣayiṣyati*: "that form of yours which eats corpses, that one will eat everything." Indeed, the Agni *kravyād*[69] or the fire of the funeral pyre, has always posed certain problems, being considered as a decidedly lower, impure form of the fire, which is feared and allowed to grow cold after performing its office, after which a new fire is lighted in the house. (See HOLTZMANN (1878:10-11), KEITH (1925:160), OBERLIES (1998:302-304)). On the whole, the function of

[67] It is interesting to note that in Pāli *upādāna* can mean "fuel". Fuel is precisely what the fire eats for itself, as opposed to the sacrificial oblations it eats for the gods.

[68] This is how SIEG (1909/1991c:319) interprets it. For a description of the way in which the digestive fire was thought to function, see SCHREINER (1999:139, note 79).

[69] GEIB (1976) convincingly shows that at the time of the Ṛgveda and Atharvaveda, Agni *kravyád* did not designate the cremation fire, but a fire of sickness, which eats the flesh (the literal meaning of *kravyád*) not of corpses, but of living men and cattle. But the meaning of cremation fire seems to have become wide-spread from the ŚB onwards (see GEIB 1976:199), and we can therefore assume that this is what is meant here in the MBh.

the myth here is obviously to explain why the fire, though it is omnivorous, is pure at the same time.

But, we might ask, how could there be a fire at all which is not *sarvabhakṣa*, since everything can burn, given sufficient heat? Indeed, the fire's greediness, its all-devouring appetite is one of this element's most striking characteristics. Already in the ṚV Agni is described in such terms: he is an all-eater (*viśvād*), his appetite is insatiable, indeed he even eats his own mothers or parents (the *araṇis* or kindling-sticks) as soon as he is born (see WEBER-BROSAMER 1988:11-113). But here it appears as if the fire had first and foremost been only a sacrificial fire,[70] and that its omnivorousness (including more mundane and impure tasks) had been imposed upon it subsequently by a curse. Ultimately, in this light, Bhṛgu's curse might be viewed as a blessing in disguise, for a fire which is not *sarvabhakṣa*, which eats only oblations for the gods in the sacrifices, would have very limited day-to-day utility. Perhaps, then, Bhṛgu's innovation in this case does not pertain to the sacrifice (like VAN BUITENEN (1973:441) suggests in his notes) but on the contrary in instituting a fire which has more *laukika* functions. Should this really be the case, then here again the myth would make an attempt to conciliate the two functions of the fire: its sacrificial functions and its *sarvabhakṣa* functions, the domestic fire and the wild fire. But indeed, in Brahmanical thought, most of the fire's functions have been subsumed under the category of sacrifice: the burning corpse is offered as a sacrifice, the food one eats is offered as a sacrifice into one's internal fires. As HEESTERMAN (1993:86, quoting BURKERT[71]) says: "Sacrifices without fire are rare [...] and conversely there is rarely a fire without sacrifice."

---

[70] The primordial importance of the sacrificial fire, over the ordinary fire, was seen already in the Vedic versions of Agni's hiding, which stress only the distress caused to sacrificers. And this is the case here too.

[71] W. BURKERT, *Greek Religion*. Oxford 1985, p. 61.

If, in the Ādiparvan (and also in the Śalyaparvan), Agni himself receives a curse, in other MBh versions of the myth, which in this follow the late Vedic pattern, he is the one who curses others. In 3.212.6-19, like in the TS and KS, the fish betray him when he hides in the *arṇava*. Here Agni curses them to be eaten (*bhakṣyāḥ*), not simply to be killed like in the late Vedic versions. Thus the curse pertains to food, as when Agni himself is cursed by Bhṛgu. The same theme of Agni's curse to certain animals is also found in the Anuśāsanaparvan. Now, the curses given by Agni, like the one he himself receives for betraying Pulomā to Puloman, all concern the mouth of these animals, more precisely their tongue, hence their power of speech and also that of taking food.

In the case of these three animals, the frog, the elephant and the parrot, we are dealing with etiologic myths which could be classified under the heading: "how animals lost human speech." The frog, *maṇḍūka*, reveals to the gods that Agni is asleep at the bottom of the waters, and heating up everything around him, which is why the frog betrays his presence there (13.84.22-26). Agni, who somehow comes to know of the frog's calumny (*paiśunam*) curses him thus: *na rasān vetsyasi* (you will not know the *rasas*) (13.84.27). Now, this curse can be interpreted variously, due to the many meanings of the term *rasa*: *rasa* can mean taste, tongue, water, or any liquid. The gods, when they make amends to the frogs, at first sight seem to interpret *rasa* in the sense of tongue-taste:

> *agniśāpād ajihvāpi*[72] *rasajñānabahiṣkṛtāḥ* /
> *sarasvatīṃ bahuvidhāṃ yūyam uccārayiṣyatha* // 13.84.30 //

---

[72] *ajihvāpi* = *ajihvā api*, which would be the correct *saṃdhi* for *ajihvāḥ api*. This is a case of 'double' *saṃdhi* which sometimes occurs in epic Sanskrit. See HOLTZMANN (1884:4).

> Though you are tongue-less due to Agni's curse, and deprived of the knowledge of taste, (nevertheless) you will utter speech of various kinds.

But the gods are not fooled by Agni's *śleṣa* or *double entendre*, and they outwit him by giving their words a double meaning too: for verse 30 b-d can also mean: "though you are deprived of the knowledge of water (*rasa*), you will cause a manifold river (*sarasvatī*) to spring forth". The term *sarasvatī* is certainly not randomly chosen here, for a much more common term to designate speech, but without the punning effect, is *vāc*. And the next verse also tends to show that the gods take into account the eventuality that the frogs might be deprived of water:

> *bilavāsagatāṃś caiva nirādānān acetasaḥ /*
> *gatāsūn api vaḥ śuṣkān bhūmiḥ saṃdhārayiṣyati /*
> *tamogatāyām api ca niśāyāṃ vicariṣyatha* // 13.84.31 //
> And the earth will support you even when you have gone to live in holes, taking no food, unconscious, and also when your breath has departed and you are dried up. And you will move about at night when it has become dark.

These two verses deal with a series of etiologic myths which account for various characteristic traits of frogs.[73] First of all, their power of producing speech of various kinds, though they do not have a tongue. Now, frogs are not actually tongue-less: their tongue is hidden at the base of their mouth, and can be whipped out with lightning speed to catch flying insects which remain stuck to it.[74] But it is noteworthy that frogs do not use their mouth or tongue when they croak. The noise is produced by an internal system of air circulation, and air-bags blown up on their cheeks or neck, and their mouth and nostrils remain firmly

---

[73] For scientific literature on anurans (frogs and toads) consult the bibliography given by JAMISON (1991-92:137, note 1).

[74] See PARKER & BELLAIRS (1971:99).

shut when they 'sing'.[75] The *sarasvatī bahuvidhā* probably refers to the veritable choruses of croaking they produce, characteristically in their mating season. As a matter of fact, each species of frogs has its own characteristic 'song', but since many different species often happen to mate at the same time near a pond, the overall effect is certainly that of various kinds of speeches. Verse 31 refers to the frogs' estivation during the hot season, when they are deprived of water: living in holes, dried up,[76] without taking food. Their habitually nocturnal habits (cf. JAMISON 1991-92:141) are also explained by their wish to avoid drying up in the sun. On the whole, the passage is meant to explain why frogs became amphibians. First the frog seems to live exclusively in the water: it comes from the *rasātalatala*: the "bottom of the nether world", which is often imagined as a watery world. But, after being "deprived of the knowledge of water", it has to become a partly terrestrial animal as well.

This whole passage dealing with the frogs' curse and the atonement offered by the gods is strongly reminiscent of the famous frog-hymn (ṚV 7.103). There too the frog during the hot season is described as "lying like a dried leather bag in the pond": *dṛ́tiṃ ná śúṣkaṃ sarasí śáyānam* (2). More importantly, the Vedic hymn also places great emphasis on the speech of the frogs: their chorus of croaking is likened to the Brahmins' chanting the Veda around the *soma*, and just like the Brahmins' chants, the frogs' song announces the rainy season. More than that, in magico-mythical thinking, the frogs' song is even thought to have the power to produce rain, and the hymn has been interpreted as a magico-religious rain-charm. (See VON SCHROEDER (1908:398) and GONDA (1975:143)). It is in this sense that we can explain the second

[75] See PARKER & BELLAIRS (1971:115).

[76] JAMISON (1991-92:143, note 12) mentions that the Indian bullfrog (Rana tigerina), a very common species in India, becomes totally shriveled up and dry if deprived of water for a few days, but when again kept in the water, it quickly becomes hydrated and recovers at once.

possible meaning of *sarasvatīm [...] uccārayiṣyatha*: you will cause a river to spring forth. By their croaking, the frogs have the magical power to produce rain, which in turn swells the rivers. Thus the gods' atonement to the frogs is actually more generous than it appears at first sight: though their speech is no longer understandable, they are gifted with a magical rain-producing speech, which moreover has certain brahmanical *mantra*-like qualities, as the comparison with the Ṛgvedic hymn shows.

The curses of the elephant and parrot are somewhat less theatrical. Since an elephant reveals Agni's presence in the *aśvattha*-tree, all the elephants are cursed by Agni as follows: *pratīpā bhavatāṃ jihvā bhavitrī* (13.84.34): "your tongue will be twisted back." The gods make the elephants the following amends:

> *pratīpayā jihvayāpi sarvāhārān kariṣyatha /*
> *vācaṃ coccārayiṣyadhvaṃ uccair avyañjitākṣaram* // 13.84.37 //
> Even with your tongue twisted back, you will be able to take all kinds of food. And you will utter a high-pitched indistinct cry.

What this passage exactly means by saying that the elephants have a tongue which is twisted back is not quite clear, but apparently the gods repair this disorder, since the elephants will be able to eat and utter sounds. But they will not be able to speak any longer. Undoubtedly the elephant is the least well-served of all three animals. The parrot, which betrays Agni as he is hiding in the *śamī-garbha*[77] is cursed thus: *vāgvihīno bhaviṣyasi*: "you will be deprived of speech", and the text adds: *jihvāṃ cāvartayāmāsa tasyāpi hutabhuk tadā*: "and then the eater of oblations twisted his tongue as well." (13.84.39). But the

[77] It would also be interesting to see what is the connection, if any, between the elephant and the *aśvattha* and the parrot and the *śamī-garbha*. I have not come across any convincing explanation. However, one of the aśvattha's by-names is *dviradāśana*: elephant's food. Perhaps elephants are really fond of *aśvattha*-leaves, which would explain why this particular elephant finds Agni in the *aśvattha*.

gods, apparently having more pity on the parrot than on the elephant, restore his power of speech, only adding that it would be somewhat indistinct and faulty, like that of a child. (13.84.41). Thus the parrot is the only one who retains a measure of the human speech, which apparently used to be common to all these animals. We may note in passing that among many societies of the world, it is a very common trait in myths relating to the discovery of fire, or the arrival of fire among men, to find animals of various kinds which bring the fire. And very often they are marked by the fire, burned most frequently, which is meant to explain why they have, for instance, a red beak or red tail, or some other peculiar physical characteristics. (Cf. FRAZER 1930).

By means of the motif of the curse, two important functions of Agni are revealed in the myth: his mastery over food, and his mastery over speech. Let us first turn to the theme of food: already in the ṚV Agni asks for certain sacrificial oblations in exchange for performing the *hotṛ* duties. Due to his greediness, and also due to the fact that he is in general the gods' mouth, Agni is the "lord of food": *ánnapati*, and as such he is frequently invoked in the Vedic ritual texts to "give us food". (See WEBER-BROSAMER 1988:121). In the MBh too, Agni turns out to be the master of food. Being himself cursed to be *sarvabhakṣa*, he manages to turn the curse into a blessing, transcending by his own purifying qualities all pollution attached to it. Thus he is enabled to eat everything without becoming impure,[78] which is far from being the case for men. He then in turn becomes the appointer and distributor of food. This mastery, as far as our myth is concerned, manifests itself mainly negatively (entailing dire consequences for the recipients of the curse) and pertains only to animals. The fish in the Āraṇyakaparvan are cursed to be eaten by everybody, while the frog, elephant and parrot of the Anuśāsanaparvan would have been doomed

---

[78] The *āgnika-dharma*, as HOPKINS (1915:106) notes, precisely gives the right to eat all things.

to starvation by Agni's curse (their tongues being either removed,[79] or twisted backwards), had the gods not made amends to them.

But these animals are not only cursed to starve: they also partly or fully lose their ability to speak. As the editor of the Crit. Ed. remarks (note *ad* 13.84.39): "It may be noted that the curses pronounced by Agni on frogs, elephants, and parrots relate to the tongue (and speech). This is so, presumably because Agni is the presiding deity of speech (cf. [...] *Ait. Up.* 2.4)." As far as Agni's relationship with speech is concerned, COOMARASWAMY (1977:160, note 5) notes that "Agni is the principle of speech (Vāc); to which she is reduced when freed from her natural mortality (BĀU 1.3.8)". Thus it would appear that the fire is the eternal power of speech, which exists beyond its transient manifestations. KNIPE (1975:96) notes that "from the RV [...] through the upaniṣads, there are constant connections established between fire and speech."[80] That fire and speech, Agni and Vāc, are two manifestations of one and the same principle, is also revealed by the story of Vāc's hiding, which is strikingly similar to that of Agni's hiding as it is told in the Anuśāsanaparvan: Vāc left the gods and hid in the waters. The waters gave her up and received as a boon from the gods to be free from pollution. Then Vāc entered into the trees, which refused to give her up. The gods cursed the trees to be slain with their own handle (i.e. the axe's wooden handle). Then the trees distributed Vāc in drums, lutes, axles and reed pipes. (Cf. TMB 6.5.10-13; TS 6.1.4.1; MS 3.6.8; KS 23.4; see DONIGER O'FLAHERTY (1980:145)).

---

[79] This would spell doom for the frog, for those animals, as we have already noted, catch their prey with their tongue.

[80] In the ṚV Agni appears as the master of speech, as the bestower of poetic inspiration. As KUIPER (1983:182) remarks: "The well-known hymn RS. VI. 9 depicts how the poet, by devout concentration upon the god, experiences this inspiration as an ecstasy. Hence Agni is called 'the inventor of resplendent speech' (*tvám śukrásya vácaso manótā* II. 9.4), 'bringing the light of inspired speech' (*vipā́ṃ jyótīṃṣi bíbhrate* III. 10.5)."

The similarities between both stories are so striking that they hardly need any comments: Vāc's hiding places are the same as Agni's (waters and trees), the motif of the curse and retribution (though differently distributed) also figure here. Most strikingly, the idea that Vāc – sound – is present in certain musical instruments because Vāc once resided in the trees out of whose wood these instruments are made, is very similar to the idea that fire can be produced by friction from the wood of certain trees, because Agni once hid in those trees.

DONIGER O'FLAHERTY deals with these two myths under the paradigm of the "Transfer of Evil" (1980:141-45). The general concept is that the gods, or one particular god, gets rid of the sin, pollution or death afflicting him (or her) by redistributing it further among other beings or substances. This is certainly true as far as the general pattern of this myth in the MBh as a whole is concerned: thus Agni, cursed to be *sarvabhakṣa*, in turn curses others, by means of an 'inverted' curse, to be eaten or not to be able to eat. But if we have a closer look at each version of the myth in the MBh separately, we notice the following thing: Agni is either cursed or cursing, but never both within the same context. This trait is especially noticeable in the Anuśāsanaparvan, where Agni is the only god who is explicitly not cursed by Pārvatī, and subsequently abundantly curses the creatures who betray him. Of course, the general background of all the versions of Agni's hiding might very well be Bhṛgu's curse (except in the third version). But the very fact that Agni's motive for hiding, which is after all a very important element of the story, is sometimes not mentioned, is in itself revealing. Thus the general pattern is that when Agni is cursed in the first place, he cannot curse others in turn. Apparently he can do so only when he has not been cursed himself. The general conception underlying this is probably that a curse implies a weakening of the one who is affected by it; and conversely, that in order to give a curse, all one's powers should be intact.

The identification of Agni with those who find him

After examining in the Epic Agni's reasons for going into hiding, and the various consequences and implications of his deed, we shall now turn to a point to which we dedicated considerable attention as far as the Ṛgvedic occurrences of this myth are concerned, namely, the identity of the various persons (or creatures) who find the hidden Agni. In the MBh just like in the ṚV, but quite unlike in the later Veda, the *ṛṣi*s play a prominent role in this myth. Why the *ṛṣi*s' role is nearly completely abandoned in the late Vedic versions of this myth should be examined from the point of view of the general role they play in the later Vedic literature. Perhaps the *ṛṣi*s – quite unlike in the ṚV where they are the seers of the hymns, and in the Epic, where, as the divine prototypical Brahmins, they have a power which often surpasses that of the gods themselves – do not have a great importance in the late Veda? In the MBh, they are not only credited with helping the gods to find Agni (Anuśāsanaparvan), they also curse him so that he vanishes (like Bhṛgu in the Ādiparvan), churn him out of the ocean when he is hiding (like Atharvan in the Āraṇyakaparvan), and even replace him in his duties while he is away (like Aṅgiras in the Āraṇyakaparvan). This shows that the basic identity in nature between the seers and the Fire, which was rather allusively hinted at in the ṚV, was fully understood and carried out in the mythological representations of the Epic. We shall presently examine in detail the *ṛṣi*s' function in each version of the myth in the MBh.

Though both gods and *ṛṣi*s play a role in the Ādiparvan version, they do not attempt to find Agni themselves, after he has vanished due to Bhṛgu's curse, but report to Brahmā: in the Epics, this is a common procedure in times of trouble,[81] which explains the innovation of this version of the myth on this point. As for Brahmā, he does not have to

[81] See SULLIVAN (1990:82).

launch a painstaking search for Agni: apparently he has the power to make him reappear by a mere wish, a power which the Vedic gods did not share. In this, the Ādiparvan version differs from the Anuśāsanaparvan, where the gods and *ṛṣis* together look for the lost Agni. Their painstaking search, their deep desire to find him, their concentrated attention and the way their mind is fixed on him in a nearly meditative way, conveyed by verses 13.84.19-22, are strongly reminiscent of the ṚV. Thus in a way the Ādiparvan gives less importance to Agni's disappearance (since he can easily be recalled) and underscores on the other hand the reason for his disappearance, namely Bhṛgu's curse, and Bhṛgu's role in general.

How did the myth of Agni's hiding come to be associated with the story of the Bhārgava family? Obviously, the 'Bhṛgu connection' is not new: already in the ṚV Bhṛgu or the Bhṛgus find the hidden Agni. But in the ṚV the Bhṛgus' activity was beneficent,[82] whereas here in the MBh he acts in a deliberately hostile way towards Agni. He does not help to retrieve the hidden Agni, but on the contrary, due to his curse, he is the cause of his disappearance. Besides, the age-old myth is here used in connection with new, truly epic events, namely the story of Cyavana's birth, explaining the origin of his name. More generally speaking, it is inserted into the history of the Bhārgava family, the Brahmin clan whose legends are tightly interwoven with those of the Kauravas in many places of the MBh. (See SUKTHANKAR 1936 and GOLDMAN 1972).[83] Now we must note the following: the fact that Bhṛgu should curse Agni, even if it is not in keeping with his Vedic character, is on the other hand very consistent with his epic character. Not only Bhṛgu himself, but the Bhārgava sages in general are

[82] Except in one verse, ṚV 3.5.10, where Agni is perhaps said to hide from the Bhṛgus.

[83] A good illustration of this can precisely be seen in the two beginnings of the MBh: whereas the first deals with the central epic events pertaining to the Kaurava family, the second pointedly deals with legends pertaining to the Bhārgava family.

aggressive and their hostility is not rarely directed against the gods themselves.[84] To quote only the more noteworthy examples: Cyavana, whose birth is here described, goes, in his old age, against Indra's order not to offer *soma* to the Aśvins, and he defeats that god in a contest of their powers (MBh 3.121-125). Jamadagni, the father of Rāma Jāmadagnya, threatens the sun-god Sūrya with his bow and arrows (MBh 13.97-98). Kavi Uśanas, or Śukra, is even the *purohita* of the gods' enemies, the Asuras. In this context, it is not surprising that Bhṛgu should dare to take on the Fire god himself, and indeed, he does so with impunity: Agni does not retaliate and even Brahmā implores Agni to make the sage's curse come true: *taṃ śāpaṃ kuru satyam ṛṣer* (1.7.22). Since the relationship between Bhṛgu and Agni is here basically a hostile one, how can we claim in this case to discern an identification of the two characters? The answer is that Bhṛgu here 'replaces' Agni in that he assumes Agni's own customary role, that of cursing, which he has in some late Vedic versions and also in some MBh versions.

In the first version of the Āraṇyakaparvan, the sage Aṅgiras replaces Agni when the latter gives up his duties. Aṅgiras is one of the old Vedic sages who find Agni when he is hiding, and the name Aṅgiras is also a common designation of Agni himself. Here the identical nature of the fire and whoever finds him is realized to the fullest extent, for Aṅgiras *becomes* the fire.[85] This version of the myth shows many

[84] See GOLDMAN (1977:114-121).

[85] According to HOLTZMANN (1878:29-30) this substitution shows that in epic times, Agni, the old fire-god, was losing popularity and might, and was in the process of being replaced by Aṅgiras, the fire-lighter. According to him, the MBh tries to conciliate both trends by making Aṅgiras Agni's son. However, apart from the fact that (to my knowledge) there is no trace in the Epic of Aṅgiras' increasing popularity, moreover HOLTZMANN was apparently not aware of the Vedic antecedents of the myth of Agni's hiding, and hence of Agni's age-old identification with those who find him: "Wie diese Berichte jetzt vorliegen, sind sie freilich sämmtlich ziemlich jungen Ursprungs, aber die zu Grunde liegende Sage selbst [...] ist vielleicht uralt, wenn sich auch in ihrer jetzigen Fassung die Erinnerung and die ursprüngliche Idee verloren hat." (1878:12). For the next version of the myth in MBh 3.212.6-19, he assumes some Purāṇic model (1878:13),

peculiar traits which are decided innovations on the old material. The first is that the angry Agni does not go into hiding properly speaking (though Yudhiṣṭhira refers to him as *naṣṭa* in verse 3.207.2), but goes to do *tapas* in the forest. The expression *tapas taptum* first appears somewhat amusing when applied to Agni, because producing heat (*tapas*) seems to be the fire's natural activity! We do not know why Agni is angry (whether this is due to Bhṛgu's or to some other reason is not explained here), but it is a common reaction in the case of many epic personages to undertake a great penance after being submitted to some affront or else being frustrated in some endeavour, thereby to gain supernatural power and take revenge or redress the situation. But the strange thing in Agni's case is that, far from gaining power through his penance, he becomes weakened. He is terribly wearied: *bhṛṣaṃ glānaḥ* (9); he says that he has lost his renown in the world: *naṣṭakīrtir ahaṃ loke* (14); he is afraid (*bhītaḥ*) of Aṅgiras (12) and is tortured by the latter's effulgence: *saṃtaptas tasya tejasā* (9). In short, he is no longer shining. This is very unusual: ascetics are usually described as glowing with the might of their penance. But if we reflect that *tapas* necessarily and essentially involves abstaining from food,[86] we immediately understand why Agni has lost his lustre: the fire cannot possibly survive without continuously consuming fuel. Viewed from this perspective, practising *tapas*, far from being the fire's natural activity, is on the contrary injurious to its very existence. Agni's weakened position here is moreover quite unlike his state when he goes into hiding in the waters, plants, etc.: then, all his powers, especially the power of cursing, usually remain intact, even when he is described as *naṣṭa*.

whereas it is perhaps the MBh version which preserves the greatest number of Vedic traits.

86 This makes it likely that Agni's reason for retiring to the forest is after all Bhṛgu's curse, for his natural reaction, being cursed to be *sarvabhakṣa*, would be to stop eating altogether. Another instance when Agni retires to the forest with the aim of abandoning his life is when he is frustrated in his love for the *ṛṣis*' wives (cf. MBh 3.213).

The consequence is that Agni comes to Aṅgiras, he himself willingly goes back: Aṅgiras' shine attracts him, just as Agni's shine in the ṚV attracts the gods and seers looking for him. This is quite unlike the other versions of the myth, where Agni does everything in his power to escape retrieval. Of course, nowhere else is Agni replaced in such a callous manner in his office, and he is clearly suffering from pangs of jealousy. His behaviour is quite chastened and humble, unlike his usual self. The story is typical of the Epic, in that supernatural powers are attributed to the *ṛṣis*, who are shown to be equal, if not superior to the gods in many episodes.[87] But we do not know how far Aṅgiras' power actually goes. For although he is described as heating and illuminating the worlds during his 'Agni-tenure', even surpassing Agni in that (7-8 & 11), he is never said to perform the sacrificial activity of carrying oblations, which is so essential to cosmic welfare. And on the contrary, Agni, even when he is weakened and doing *tapas* in the forest, is consistently called *hutavaha* (6), *havyavāha* (8), *havyavāhana* (10) (carrier of oblations) and *hutabhuk* (9) (eater of oblations). Only when the two address each other, we observe a curious reversal of the situation: Aṅgiras calls Agni *timirāpaha* and *tamonuda* (destroyer of darkness) (13) and Agni calls Aṅgiras *hutāśana* (eater of oblations) (14). Thus they probably attribute to each other the tasks that they were principally and most importantly performing themselves.

The question arises whether this particular version of the myth of Agni's hiding is not to some extent the 'multiform' of another myth, that of the slaying of Triśiras by Indra, as it is related in MBh 5.9-17. After killing Triśiras, Indra is affected by the sin incurred due to

[87] Agni suffers a similar humiliation in another episode of the MBh, namely in 14.9: there the sage Saṃvarta, Bṛhaspati's brother, threatens to burn (!) Agni, and the latter seems to be genuinely afraid, although Indra points out to him the inconsistency of the threat: how can the fire be burnt? Nevertheless, Agni concludes the discussion by saying that one should always beware of the Brahmins' *tejas*.

slaying a Brahmin, the *brahmahatyā* (5.10.42). He becomes minute, powerless and hides in a lotus-stalk. Meanwhile another Indra, the human king Nahuṣa, is appointed in his stead, but his overbearing behaviour soon makes it desirable to get rid of him, and to find and reinstate Indra in his kingly duties. Agni himself is sent on that task and, crossing the water, he manages to find Indra: here, as compared to the myth where he himself goes hiding, his role has undergone a basic reversal. From being the one who is hidden and looked for, he becomes the one who looks for the hidden Indra.[88] The motif of a god who disappears, weakened, and is replaced in his functions by a *ṛṣi* (Nahuṣa is a *rājarṣi*) occurs in both cases.[89] But Aṅgiras behaves more chivalrously than Nahuṣa, gladly giving back his office to Agni. Perhaps because he was unable to perform the sacrificial duties incumbent on the fire? As a compensation, either Aṅgiras or his son Bṛhaspati becomes the eldest son of Agni. We have noted above that in mythical thinking it is a common procedure to make two distinct personages out of one who bears different names, often making one the son of the other.

The figure of Atharvan,[90] another hoary Vedic sage, plays the main role in the second version of the Āraṇyakaparvan. Though he is not clearly credited with finding the hidden Agni in the ṚV, he is said to rub forth the fire in 6.15.17, "leading it out of darkness", and ṚV

---

[88] This reversal (which in this respect is perhaps specifically a reversal from the version where he denounces Pulomā to the *rākṣasa*) is so complete that Agni even assumes "a marvellous woman's form": *strīveṣam adbhutaṃ kṛtvā* (5.15.27). HILTEBEITEL's translation, see (2001:190). See *ibid.* for the *abhicāra* (black magic) implications of this transformation.

[89] It appears as if the myth of Indra's demission and hiding underwent the influence of the myth of Agni's hiding in the first place, and then in turn influenced this particular version of the myth of Agni's hiding, at least as far as the motifs of the weakening and the replacement are concerned.

[90] There is no reason to think, like VAN BUITENEN (1975:645), that Atharvan is the same person as Aṅgiras. They are two different sages.

6.16.13 states that Atharvan rubbed the fire out of the lotus-flower.[91] In the late Veda Atharvan finds Agni hiding in a lotus-leaf, thus being the only sage credited with finding the hidden Agni in the later Veda. At times, Atharvan also seems to be a name of Agni himself.[92] Here Agni tries to appoint him in his stead in the office of carrying oblations (unlike in 3.207 where Aṅgiras replaces him without his prior knowledge), but it seems doubtful whether Atharvan actually ever does so. He seems more intent on finding the hidden Agni than on replacing him. In this, his behaviour follows the 'normal' pattern. In the same passage, when Agni dissolves in the earth, he flames up again (*jajvāla*) due to the combined *tapas* of Bhṛgu, Aṅgiras and other sages. In the transmission of the tapasic heat of the seers to the flaming of Agni, the common fiery nature of fire and sages is once again observed. This 'identical' nature is also revealed in a closely related mythical narrative, that of Skanda 's birth, which is told immediately after that of Agni's hiding in 3.213. There Agni falls in love with the seven *ṛṣis*' wives. Although Agni himself, at a superficial level, considers his lust to be adulterous (3.213.45), we know that this is not truly so, for if the seven *ṛṣis* are but manifestations of Agni himself, then it follows that their wives are his own too.

In the Anuśāsanaparvan, three different animals find Agni: the frog, the elephant and the parrot. From this point of view, this version of the myth is clearly indebted to the KS 25.7 and KapS 39.5.[93] In these two texts, Agni first hides in the ocean, whereupon a fish betrays him. Agni curses the fish to the effect that whosoever would come across a

---

91 As an aquatic plant, the lotus is a good combination of the waters and the plants as a hiding-place for Agni.

92 E.g. ṚV 8.9.7. See MACDONELL (1898:141). According to KUHN's interpretation (1859:7), following the Zend-Avesta, the name Atharvan means the "burning one" (der Feurige).

93 Another likely antecedent of this MBh version can be found in TB 1.1.3.9, where Agni, taking the form of a horse, hides in an *aśvattha*-tree.

fish should kill it. Then he takes refuge in a reed. A white horse finds him, touching the reed with his nose. Agni singes the horse's nose (which is why horses have a scorched nose).[94] Due to the pain, the horse neighs. That cry becomes the *suśloka* bird, a bird of good omen: whoever is looking for something will find it if he hears the cry of this bird. Hearing the bird's cry, the gods find Agni. In the Anuśāsanaparvan, the sequence of events has become more regularized, deprived of the beautiful metaphorical transformation of the voice into a flying bird: each one of the three animals (here the fish has become a frog, the horse an elephant and the *suśloka* a *śuka*, that is, a parrot) directly and voluntarily betray Agni to the gods, and each one is cursed in turn.

Now the question arises why the frog, the elephant and the parrot replace in the MBh the fish, the horse and the *suśloka* bird of the late Vedic version. Obviously, there isn't one single answer to this question, and a variety of factors might be at play. But one answer might be as follows: it seems to me that the frog, the elephant and the parrot[95] display certain 'Agni-like' qualities which are lacking in the other set of animals. Let me explain: all of them are animals which belong to two different realms. The frog, (and the etiologic myth means to explain this very fact), is an amphibian: it is both aquatic and terrestrial. The elephant, though basically terrestrial, loves to remain for a long time in the water. The parrot can fly but also move on the ground and on trees. Thus these animals share to some extent Agni's own aquatic, terrestrial and celestial births and hiding-places.[96] Even

---

94 This is probably meant to explain why some horses (especially white ones) have a pink nose, or a pinkish streak above the nose.

95 The *śuka* is quite straightforwardly a form of Agni. In different versions of the myth of Skanda's birth, Agni is sent to spy on Śiva and Pārvatī during their love-making and takes the form of a parrot. See DONIGER O'FLAHERTY (1973:277).

96 Unlike the fish, which is exclusively aquatic, the horse which is exclusively terrestrial and the *suśloka*, a mythical bird, which is a kind of embodied floating voice,

more than that: these animals show the Agni-like ambivalence of being wild and domesticated at the same time. All three of them would undoubtedly be classified among *āraṇyaka* (forest) animals, according to the Indian classification.[97] But both parrots and elephants, though basically wild, were and are commonly domesticated.[98] The frog, of course, cannot be called domesticated, but we know that it was used as a 'cooling-device' along with certain aquatic plants in the ceremony of the piling of the fire altar, when the fire's heat had to be reduced (TS 4.6.1.2; VS 17.6). (See OLDENBERG 1894:116 and KEITH 1925:156). And the frogs' chorus-like songs were assimilated to human speech and Vedic recitation. These factors to a certain extent also bring the frogs into the human realm, especially into the sacrificial realm, which is of paramount importance.

Agni's functions

The Ādiparvan is particularly relevant as far as three functions of Agni are concerned, namely those as witness, protector of the house and slayer of foes. Agni is called Jātavedas three times in the passage where the *rākṣasa* Puloman invokes him (1 5.17; 22; 25), just as in ṚV 10.51, where Varuṇa frequently addresses him by the name Jātavedas. Now, as FINDLY (1981:260-64) remarks, when Agni is called Jātavedas, he is especially connected with the family, the domestic life, the hearth or home-fire. Therefore it is appropriate that Puloman, speaking to the domestic fire in Bhṛgu's house, should call it Jātavedas. FINDLY (1981:349-50) further notes that there are several possible ways of translating this name: "who knows the creatures (lit. what has been born, the living beings)", or "who has innate wisdom",

---

and is therefore exclusively aerial. The case of the white horse is somewhat special, since the white horse is very commonly the theriomorphic form of Agni.

[97] Thus we read in BaudhŚS 24.5: "The seven jungle animals are [wild] cloven-hoofed animals, animals having feet like dogs, *birds*, crawling animals, *elephants*, monkeys, and *river animals* as the seventh." (Transl. by SMITH 1994:248). (My emphasis).

[98] The texts do not seem to make a special category for tameable wild animals.

or "in whose possession are the creatures", "in charge of the creatures", "in charge of the generations, who not only witnesses the passing of each successive family, but also regulates the generations of men and therefore directly participates in ensuring that the lineages of Vedic peoples will continue." (1981:353-54).

Now, one of the fire's most important functions, after the sacrificial one, is that of witness. If we take the name Jātavedas in the first two senses, those of "who knows the creatures" and "who has innate wisdom", we realize that the fact that Puloman insistently calls Agni "Jātavedas" in the Ādiparvan is one more way of emphasizing his status of knower of the truth and supreme witness. The fire is the witness *par excellence* (the ordeal by fire being an illustration of this), for the reason that it resides inside every human being (as the digestive fire, and also as the very life-principle or *ātman*) as the witness of their good and bad deeds, as Puloman himself tells Agni in 1.5.23. (See HOLTZMANN (1878:4-5)). It is in this sense that he "knows the creatures". Agni, being invoked by the *rakṣas* to bear witness, cannot but answer him truthfully, and the reasons he mentions for doing so are in perfect agreement with the precepts of the *smṛti*.[99] Moreover, in this case Agni is asked to testify about a marriage, and in Indian weddings up to the present day, the fire lighted for the ceremony has the function of witnessing the marriage. A few verses inserted after 1.5.26 and kept in the footnotes in the Crit. Ed. contain Agni's answer to the *rakṣas*' query, wherein Agni precisely mentions the fact that Bhṛgu married Pulomā as per the precepts of the *vidhi* and in front of himself, the fire, whereas Puloman had not done so.

---

[99] See e.g. Manusmṛti 8.79-130 on the duties of witnesses. Besides, as PIOVANO (1997-98:648) remarks, referring to the Dharmaśāstras of Gautama (13.6), Viṣṇu (8.37), and Yājñavalkya (2.79): "Some legislators agree that a witness who, questioned, refuses to answer the judge is as guilty as a witness who gives false evidence and should be punished in the same way."

If Agni cannot be blamed for answering truthfully Puloman's queries, he is however guilty of failing in two roles which are traditionally his in Vedic times, namely those of protecting the household[100] and slaying foes and *rākṣasas*.[101] It is true that since Vedic times, Agni always appears as the prototypical Brahmin or priest: this is due to the essential role he plays in the sacrificial performance, and he bears all the names of the various priests officiating in the ritual. Yet Agni has certain *kṣatriya*-like duties too in the Veda: he is often said to help Indra in the latter's heroic exploits, and his own martial deeds especially pertain to slaying demons, or *rākṣakas*. Agni's foe-slaying duties, as VARENNE (1977-78:376) shows, are directly related to his *purohita*-hood: "A *puróhita* is no ordinary priest; [...] his particular office is to slay in the most concrete sense of the word, the foes of the community. [...] the *puróhita* is a kind of military priest [...] a warrior using 'spiritual weapons' in [...] the battle." Agni's power to destroy the *rākṣasas* is probably also directly linked with the fire's natural manifestation, which is known to keep wild beasts at bay, and by extension also the 'night wandering' *rākṣasas*. But in these two respects (protecting the household and slaying *rākṣasas*), Agni in the Ādiparvan sadly fails in performing his duties: a *rākṣasa*, the very creature whom he is supposed to slay, abducts the lady of the household which he is supposed to protect, thus causing her to miscarry, or at least to give birth prematurely. It has generally been contended that the more war-like functions of the Fire-god are almost obliterated in the Epics, and that his priestly character is

[100] The third possible meaning of the term Jātavedas, which Findly prefers, that of "in whose possession are the creatures", "in charge of the generations", intimately connects Agni with his function of protecting the households.

[101] See OLDENBERG (1898:95) and KEITH (1925:158). That these are typical duties of Agni is also revealed in the 'orders' or prayers addressed to him: "kill /burn the foes/demons!" and "protect us!", "be patron of our household!" are usual addresses to Agni. See ELIZARENKOVA (1968:260; 265). Thus, as ELIZARENKOVA (1968:266) notes, Agni wavers between two Dumézilian functions, that of the priest and that of the warrior, and cannot be neatly classed in either of them.

dominant in these texts. (See HOLTZMANN 1878:1-2; 24-25). It is true that Agni's priestly function is of paramount importance in the myth of his hiding: we have had occasion to note that the distress caused by his disappearance chiefly pertains to the domain of sacrificial performances. Thus in this passage Agni's brahmanical functions of being *satya* (truthful) and bearing witness indeed outweigh his more *kṣatriya*-like functions. But we shall have occasion to qualify this statement below, in the section dedicated to the procreative fire.

These three functions of Agni: witness, protector of the household and slayer of demons, though they are important in the Ṛgveda as a whole, hardly play any role in the Ṛgvedic accounts of the myth of Agni's hiding. Thus it appears that in the Epic the myth of Agni's hiding has become a peg on which Agni's various functions were hanged. In the MBh, however, these functions are stressed only negatively: Agni is incapable of protecting the household and slaying the demon, and he is even punished for his truthfulness. Yet this applies only as far as the Ādiparvan is concerned, which is also the only account of the myth in the MBh where Bhṛgu's curse is described so circumstantially. Here Bhṛgu himself and his son Cyavana (who kills the *rākṣasa*) are the ones who take over all these functions which are traditionally associated with Agni. Thus it is noteworthy that the chief reason for which Agni is made to resume his sacrificial task is to make Bhṛgu's curse come true: thus Bhṛgu's truthfulness becomes more important than Agni's. This shift from Agni to the Bhārgavas concerning some of the Fire's main qualities and duties is not too surprising, since in the Ādiparvan this story is precisely told to the Bhārgava Śaunaka, in a context where the Bhārgavas' greatness would naturally be extolled. Yet it is noteworthy that the other versions of the same myth in the MBh, though some of them at least so to say pay 'lip service' to this version in mentioning Bhṛgu's curse, do not otherwise maintain the importance of Bhṛgu's role, and follow in this the more traditional pattern of the story, such as we have it since the

Ṛgveda, which emphasizes the importance of Agni's disappearance and the pains taken to find him.

The procreative fire

Most importantly, the myth of Agni's hiding is used to highlight another aspect of the fire, namely, that of the procreative fire. That the fire is potent to generate offspring is not surprising in itself, for the symbolism of fire, in India as in the West, is often that of love, of eroticism. (See KNIPE 1975:103). For FREUD (1932:6), the fire is a symbol of the libido. According to BACHELARD (1949:79-80) this sexualized conception of fire is due to the equivalence which is commonly established between the spark of fire and the seed: both being small causes which produce great effects. In the Vedic texts, the kindling of the fire is often likened to the sexual act in no vague terms (see KUHN (1859:70 ff.); PARPOLA (1994:239)), the lower *araṇi* (kindling stick) being the female (sometimes likened to Urvaśī) and the upper the male (sometimes likened to Purūravas). (KUHN 1859:78-79). The types of trees used to make the kindling sticks reveal the same sexual representations at work. The etiologic myth found in the Anuśāsanaparvan explains why the wood of the *śamī-garbha* (and presumably that of the *aśvattha* too, though the text does not explicitly say so) is used to make the kindling-sticks: it acquired the power of producing fire because Agni hid in it (13.84.42-43).[102] Now, the *śamī-garbha* is nothing but an *aśvattha*-tree, but one which, as its name shows, has grown parasitically on the trunk of a *śamī*. In fact, all these types of trees (*śamī, aśvattha* and *aśvattha śamīgarbha*) could be used to make the kindling sticks. The ritual texts differ on this point. ĀpŚS

[102] A glance at FRAZER's *Myths on the Origins of Fire* will show that in many cultures we find the mythical motif which consists in explaining why certain types of wood can be used as kindling sticks, by a story of how once upon a time Fire took its abode in them. The same holds for the reeds in which Agni hides in the KS. Reeds are also commonly used to produce fire by friction, and are even said to burst into flames spontaneously while rubbing against each other in the wind.

5.1.2; TB 1.1.9.1 and ĀśvŚS 2.1.16.16 recommend the *aśvattha śamīgarbha*. KŚS 4.7.22-23 and also Karmapradīpa 1.7.3 state that if a *śamīgarbha* is not available, one can also use another *aśvattha*-tree.[103] ŚB 11.5.1.14-17, in the context of the story of Purūravas and Urvaśī, relates how the Gandharvas gave Purūravas a fire and an *ukhā* (fire-pot). These two items vanished and became an *aśvattha* and a *śamī* tree respectively. Then they advised him to make a fire-drill out of the wood of these two trees: the upper stick (*uttarāraṇi*) out of the male *aśvattha*, and the lower stick (*adharāraṇi*) out of the female *śamī*. But this turned out to be an excessively *parokṣa* (hidden, indirect) procedure, owing perhaps to the fact that the two woods were one male, the other female. (Cf. HEESTERMAN 1983:93). Finally they advised him to make both *araṇi*s out of *aśvattha* wood, and this procedure was apparently successful. This text does not mention the *aśvattha śamīgarbha*, but it becomes apparent from this passage that this tree must have ultimately become the favourite because it combines the nature or essence of both *śamī* and *aśvattha*. HILLEBRANDT (1927-29/1980:374, note 27 to chap. III) emits the interesting hypothesis that this tree was holy because it grows neither on the earth nor in the sky. This intermediary position would thus make it an ideal receptacle for the fire, reflecting Agni's multiple origins. According to KUHN (1859:103), the use of the wood taken from an *aśvattha śamīgarbha* to make the kindling sticks symbolizes the sexual act: the 'male' tree which grows embracing a 'female' one is potent to produce fire. With such premises, when the production of fire itself is likened to the

---

[103] Perhaps this explains why the compensation made to the elephants is not as good as that of the parrots: because the *aśvattha* is a second-rate tree in this respect. The wood of the *aśvattha*-tree, whether *śamī-garbha* or not, seems to be highly inflammable, as HILLEBRANDT (1927-29/1980:96) notes, for it was prohibited in the construction of houses (Gobhilagṛhyasūtra 4.7).

sexual act,[104] it is not surprising that the Fire-god in turn came to be associated with procreation, and was considered to be especially potent to produce offspring. And Agni's offspring are indeed numerous in the MBh.

The Veda emphasizes Agni's predecessors: his (three) elder brothers. The MBh takes no notice of them, but on the contrary greatly stresses the theme of Agni's progeny. The long list of Agni's offspring through Aṅgiras in 3.208-211 is the most obvious case. Here Aṅgiras in all likelihood becomes the *dvitīya prājāpatyaka* fire, which Agni first proposed to become himself, in 3.207.15. We should probably interpret *prājāpatyaka* in the sense of 'generative' fire. Indeed, what follows the narration of the myth is the genealogy of all the descendants of Agni through Aṅgiras (3.208-211). These are all the various fires used for different sacrificial purposes.[105] Thus Agni in this version of the myth has the role of a demiurge, giving birth (though indirectly) to the whole lineage of fires. This generative activity may also explain why Agni was previously practising *tapas* in the forest. *Tapas* is a well-known generative technique. Thus Prajāpati, in ŚB 10.4.4.1-2, is said to do *tapas* for a thousand years before creating the world. (See KNIPE 1975:115-16).[106]

In the other MBh versions, the myth of Agni's hiding is told in connection with Cyavana's birth (Ādiparvan) or Skanda 's birth (second Āraṇyakaparvan version, Śalyaparvan and Anuśāsanaparvan). In the case of Cyavana, although Agni cannot of course be said to be his direct father, he is at least the indirect cause of his somewhat premature birth.

---

104 BACHELARD (1949:46-7) even claims that man learnt how to kindle the fire by rubbing two sticks in an imitation of the sexual act.

105 This long genealogy answers Yudhiṣṭhira's question in 3.207.3, who wants to know how various fires are seen in the rites, though Agni is one.

106 Though, arguably, Agni becomes weak due to his *tapas*, and does not seem to acquire by means of it the strength necessary for a procreative activity.

On the other hand, Agni is the direct father of Skanda.[107] Now we may note that both Skanda and Cyavana bear names whose semantic fields overlap to some extent and are inspired from a 'procreative' imagery: we have already had occasion to note that Cyavana means the "falling one" and in his case the term specifically refers to the falling of the foetus from the womb. The name Skanda comes from the root *skand-* which has the meanings of "to spurt out, to be spilt (also to drop down, to fall)" which is commonly used for the sperm. (See PARPOLA 1994:268). Apart from the similarity of their names, both new-born babies are also said to shine with a truly fire-like splendour. Thus the *rakṣas* Puloman is instantly reduced to ashes just by glancing at Cyavana. Skanda too in 13.84.68 and 70 is said to resemble Agni and the sun by his effulgence.[108] The birth of a third, equally shining but somewhat special offspring of Agni, is also narrated in the Anuśāsanaparvan along with the birth of Skanda. This offspring is gold. The frame-story of the Anuśāsanaparvan version is an etiologic myth explaining the origin of gold. Jamadagni asks what is the most purifying gift, and is told that it is gold. Then follows the story of Skanda's generation and birth, which is at the same time the story of the origin of gold. For gold was 'born' at the same time as the new god: everything became golden around the place where Skanda had

[107] Agni's paternity of Skanda is not a new trait. Already in the earliest reference to Skanda, in ŚB 6.1.3.18, he is called the ninth form of Agni and the son of Agni Gṛhapati. (See MUKHOPADHYAY 1985:314).

[108] However, this fire-like effulgence is not only characteristic of Cyavana and Skanda. For instance, Vyāsa's son Śuka, whose birth is described in MBh 12.311, is also said to "shine like a smoke-less fire" in 10-11. Śuka's manner of birth is very interesting: his father Vyāsa was churning the *araṇi* to light a fire when he saw the *apsaras* Ghṛtācī, who subsequently assumed the form of a parrot (*śuka*). Inflamed with passion, Vyāsa dropped his seed on the *araṇi*. Then he went on rubbing the *araṇi*, which, instead of fire, produced his son Śuka. Here the process of churning the fire literally becomes the generative act. Thus Śuka's birth has strong sacrificial connotations, which are made even more striking by the fact that the *apsaras* who kindles the sage's passion is Ghṛtācī, the one who "abounds in ghee" (ghee being one of the most common sacrificial oblations). For the story of Śuka's birth and its various implications, see HILTEBEITEL (2001:286-291).

been born (13.84.70). Thus Agni received the name of Hiraṇyaretas (who has golden seed) (13.84.74) and gold is considered to be Agni's progeny (*apatya*) (13.84.78).[109] From this point of view, this version of the myth is comparable to the second Āraṇyakaparvan version, where the origins of various metals and precious stones are explained, but in a different manner, by Agni's dissolution in the earth.

Agni is always involved in the paternity of Skanda, either principally, in the Āraṇyakaparvan and in the Anuśāsanaparvan, or secondarily, in combination with Śiva, in the Śalyaparvan.[110] In the Āraṇyakaparvan, Skanda's story is elaborately told in 3.213-221, immediately after the second narration of the myth of Agni's hiding. Here Svāhā takes the form of the *ṛṣis*' wives to seduce Agni, who is in love with them. Six times she keeps his seed in a golden vessel on a white mountain, and Kārttikeya is born from it. Śiva and Pārvatī are introduced only at the very end of the story, where it is revealed that Śiva is Skanda's real father, because he had impregnated Agni with his seed in the first place. In Śalyaparvan 9.43-45, the story is told shortly before the story of Agni's hiding, in connection with another *tīrtha* visited by Balarāma. In this version Agni's paternity is only secondary: Śiva's seed falls into the fire, who, unable to bear it, throws it into the Gaṅgā, who in turn unable to bear it throws it on a mountain, where the foetus finally grows and is fed by the Kṛttikās. In the Anuśāsanaparvan, the story of Skanda's birth is for the first time causally linked with that of Agni's hiding, and not just juxtaposed with it (told immediately before or after it), like in the other two versions. It is *because* Agni is absent at the time of Pārvatī's curse, and

109 In some versions of the myth (e.g. Brahmapurāṇa 128.3-46), Agni's 'gold-progeny' is explicitly personified as twins, a boy and a girl named Suvarṇa and Suvarṇā (= gold). (See DONIGER O'FLAHERTY 1973:96).

110 Skanda 's parentage is as a rule highly composite. His paternity is either attributed to Śiva, or Agni, or both. See DONIGER O'FLAHERTY (1973:261-277) for other versions of the myth of Skanda's birth.

therefore not affected by it, that he alone can produce a son capable of killing the Asura Tāraka. Certain text-critical problems are apparent in this passage,[111] and it is quite likely that the role of Śiva is superimposed on it, and that originally Agni had the sole paternity of Skanda in this version. Indeed, the story makes more sense if Śiva's contribution is omitted altogether: at the time when Pārvatī curses the gods, Agni is not there: *pāvakas tu na tatrāsīc chāpakāle* (13.83.51). The text does not mention where he is, but later, out of Brahmā's words, it transpires that "the eater of oblations did not get that curse, for he had vanished at that time": *sa tu nāvāpa taṃ śāpaṃ naṣṭaḥ sa hutabhuk tadā* (13.84.13). The terms *naṣṭa* and *pranaṣṭa* (= *adarśanaṃ gataḥ* according to Nīlakaṇṭha's commentary) are very commonly used from the ṚV onwards to express Agni's withdrawal from the world.[112] If Agni had disappeared at the time of Pārvatī's curse, how could Śiva's sperm later fall into him? This would mean that Agni reappeared and then disappeared again, since the gods subsequently have to go in search of him. Moreover, the last mention of Śiva's paternity is contained in Brahmā's speech (13.84.11), and afterwards Śiva is never mentioned again and Agni is considered as the sole father of Skanda throughout. Obviously, Śiva's role was added later to the story, in conformity with other versions of the myth. That there was some kind of 'rivalry' between Śiva and Agni in this respect is revealed by verses 13.84.15-17, wherein Brahmā recites a *stuti* of Agni, praising him as the master of the world, and concluding with these words: "he is even greater than Śiva": *jyeṣṭho rudrād api* (13.84.17).

---

[111] This is not unusually the case for Skanda's birth-stories, due to the wish of the redactors to accommodate as many parents as possible for the god, sometimes at the cost of logic and consistency.

[112] Here, since Agni is not affected by the curse, we must assume a complete withdrawal on his part, equivalent to a cessation of being.

As we can see from these different narrations of the myth of Skanda's birth, the tradition wavers between Agni and Śiva as the father of the new god, and accordingly, a much debated topic was to discover the 'original' father of Skanda.[113] The attribution of Skanda's paternity to Agni has sometimes been considered secondary (Śiva's parentage being original), and added in order to give a Vedic lineage to a new, perhaps even non-Aryan god.[114] However, the representations of Agni and Rudra-Śiva overlap to a certain extent, especially in Vedic literature,[115] and the question which arises in this connection is whether we should really make a choice between Agni and Śiva as far as Skanda's paternity is concerned. For just like Agni, who has many births and many origins, Skanda too displays an impressive array of 'parents': the fire, the water (Gaṅgā), the mountain, the clump of reeds, the Kṛttikās, Śiva, Pārvatī, Svāhā, and the list is probably far from exhaustive.[116] In MBh 3.213.25-30, Indra has a premonitory vision just before Skanda's birth: he sees at the hour of Rudra, on new-moon day, the sun rising on the mountain, the moon entering the sun, and the sacrificial fire entering the sun with the oblations; the dawn and the ocean are looking bloody. He then reflects that a son of Agni would be most powerful. But it is obvious that all the other elements described in this vision have their own role to play. In this way, the new god absorbs all the powers of the elements or gods whose son he is. Viewed from this perspective, it is perhaps futile to argue which god,

---

113 According to BEDEKAR (1975:168), it is Rudra-Śiva. According to HOLTZMANN (1878:20) and MUKHOPADHYAY (1985:316), it is Agni.

114 See BEDEKAR (1975:168).

115 As DANDEKAR (1953:98) remarks: "In one passage of the *Ṛgveda* (II 1.6), for instance, Rudra is included among the several deities identified with Agni. Rudra seems to be identified with Agni also in the *Atharvaveda* (VII 87.1), the *Taittirīya Saṃhitā* (V 4.3.1; V 5.7.4), and the *Śatapatha Brāhmaṇa* (VI 1.3.10). In the *Taittirīya Saṃhitā* (II 2.2.3), Rudra is called the terrific form (*ghorā tanuḥ*) of Agni."

116 It is perhaps due to the mystery of his origins that Skanda received the name of Guha, the 'secret one'. In this respect too, he is not unlike Agni, who in the ṚV is said to "move about in secret": *guhā catan*.

Śiva or Agni, is the original father of Skanda. The multiple origins of this god are probably from the start ingrained in the myth of his birth, just as they are ingrained in the myth of Agni's birth, whose son Skanda (at least partly) is.

It remains to be seen what can be the connection between Agni's hiding and his generating offspring (especially Skanda) in the MBh. There is evidently a direct relationship between these two stories, since the myth of Agni's hiding is told three times in connection with the story of Skanda's , and these three occurrences of the myth of Skanda's birth are the only ones in which this event is told in detail in the whole MBh. Agni's partial or temporary eclipse seems to be somehow necessary for the new god to be born. Does this mean that Skanda 'replaces' Agni in some of his functions? In Vedic times, Agni had certain war-like functions, like slaying foes and demons. For instance in ṚV 10.53.4, in the third hymn of the series, which we have not discussed because it moves away from the mythical events of Agni's hiding and is more like a usual sacrificial hymn, Agni declares, after being anointed *hotṛ*, that he will think of the means whereby the gods will be able to defeat the Asuras. Now Skanda is precisely born to become the general (*senāpati*) of the gods, and his first deed is to slay the Asura Tāraka.[117] Another offspring of Agni, whom we have not mentioned so far and who plays an important role in the central story of the MBh, is Dhṛṣṭadyumna. Dhṛṣṭadyumna is born of the sacrificial fire, and he becomes the *senāpati* of the Pāṇḍavas' army, leading the 'sacrifice of war', and slaying the Asuras incarnated in the Kaurava

[117] Another aspect of Agni which is in a way taken over by Skanda is that of Agni as the fire of illness. As GEIB (1976:208-9) shows, the Vedic Agni *kravyā́d* was a demon of illness, the death-bringing fire that rages in the body of a sick person. Skanda becomes associated with diseases, especially, in his case, the diseases afflicting small children (MBh 3.219). PARPOLA (1994:237) notes that Skanda is also mentioned in the Suśruta Saṃhitā (6.37) as one of the nine presiding deities of the diseases of infants. But according to MUKHOPADHYAY (1985:313-14), this trait is inherited from the Vedic Rudra. In any case, the topic of how Skanda inherits certain traits of the Vedic Agni would deserve further investigation.

camp; likewise, Skanda becomes the *senāpati* of the gods' army. Thus many of Agni's offspring exhibit marked warrior-like qualities, and therefore we should not underestimate Agni's relevance in the *kṣatriya*-function in the Epic.[118]

But over and above the idea of a 'replacement', or at least a 'taking over' of certain functions, which is present in the cases of both Cyavana and Skanda, but which can in any case at best be partial, I would like to propose the following hypothesis concerning the reason why the myth of Agni's hiding is narrated in connection with both Cyavana's and Skanda's births in the MBh: if my contention is correct that in the ṚV the myth of Agni's hiding is prominently a myth which tells us how Agni became a god, then it might not be too far-fetched to suppose that the Epic, retaining this essential significance of the mythological narrative, in turn used it as a kind of 'marker' whenever it narrated the birth of another new god – Skanda –, or of a quasi-divine *ṛṣi* like Cyavana.

Procreation and sacrifice

Notwithstanding the fact that, especially in the Anuśāsanaparvan, the task for which Agni is retrieved is no longer the sacrificial function, the new generative task he is appointed to after being retrieved by the gods and *ṛṣi*s came to be understood as sacrificial in its own way.[119] The terminology used in the Anuśāsanaparvan makes it clear that Agni's deed of fathering a son on the Gaṅgā is assimilated with a sacrificial duty. We have observed in the Ṛgveda that Agni is severally said to be

---

118 Besides, in the episode of the burning of the Khāṇḍava forest, though Agni's outward appearance is that of a Brahmin (which is indeed essential, for only as a Brahmin he can expect that the *kṣatriya*s Arjuna and Kṛṣṇa will give him the food he desires), the whole scenario of the forest-fire is a prefiguration of the war to come, or at least an initiation for the war (see HILTEBEITEL 1976/1982), and Agni moreover gifts weapons to his helpers.

119 This also applies for another one of Agni's functions, namely the consumption of food, which is considered to be offered into the digestive fire.

"yoked" (the verb *yuj-* is used) to the duties of a *hotṛ* (10.51.4: *mā yunájan*; 10.51.7: *yuktáḥ*). In the Anuśāsanaparvan, remarkably, the same verb (here with the prefix *ni-*, with the extended meaning of appointing to, assigning to) is used to designate the yoking of Agni to his duties of producing offspring. In 13.84.14, Brahmā tells the gods: *anviṣyatāṃ vai jvalanas tathā cādya niyujyatām* (you must look for the Fire and yoke him now in this manner). After finding Agni, the gods and *ṛṣis* tell him in 13.84.46: *tvāṃ niyokṣyāmahe kārye* (we shall yoke you to this task[120]), and Agni replies in 13.84.47: *bhavatāṃ hi niyojyo 'ham* (I must indeed be yoked by you).

This first impression concerning the ritual relevance of Agni's deed, which is based on purely linguistic evidence, is reinforced by the fact that in mythical thinking semen and *soma* often appear as multiforms of each other. (See DONIGER O'FLAHERTY 1973:277-79). OBERLIES (1999:42-44) further remarks that the relationship of *soma* with seed seems to date back to Indo-Iranian times when the *soma* developed a close connection with fertility. This connection is related to the representation that the *soma* comes down onto the earth along with the rain-water, which is conceived of as the seed of the heavenly bull.[121] Thus semen takes the place of *soma* in sacrificial-generative acts which lead to the procreation of offspring. We have seen one instance of this above, in the births of the seers Bhṛgu and Aṅgiras, who are born when seed is spilt into the sacrificial fire. Similarly, at the beginning of the Anuśāsanaparvan version, Śiva's seed falls into Agni,[122] who subsequently becomes mixed with the Gaṅgā and generates Skanda. In

120 Moreover, the term *kārya* can also mean "religious action".

121 OBERLIES (1999:31, note 145) further remarks that the ŚB often identifies *soma* with seed (3.3.2.1, 9.3.29).

122 In this connection SCHREINER (1999:130) remarks that "the role of Agni may actually even be the female role of receiving the semen." The female role of the fire is seen for instance in the Pravargya rite, where the jar pouring the milk is said to be the male organ, the milk the semen and the fire the womb. Cf. AB 1.22, quoted by DANGE (1979:60).

some other versions of the myth of Skanda's birth (see DONIGER O'FLAHERTY 1973:96), Agni is made to swallow Śiva's semen, just as he usually swallows the sacrificial oblations, being the 'mouth' of the gods. In R 1.36.11-14, Agni releases his own semen into the Gaṅgā. In this case, the sacrificial procedure is so to say inverted: the *soma* is not poured into the sacrificial fire, but the Fire himself pours the somic seed into the water. This similarity between *soma* and semen (in this case especially Agni's semen) is also revealed in the Āraṇyakaparvan version of the myth of Skanda's birth (3.213-221) where Skanda is begot by a different method: Svāhā is in love with Agni, but the latter is in love with the Kṛttikās, the seven *ṛṣis*' wives. Therefore Svāhā assumes in turn the form of each one of the *ṛṣis*' wives to seduce Agni, except that of the virtuous Arundhatī, Vasiṣṭha's wife. Then, hoping that this will prevent their recognition,[123] she flies away in the form of a Garuḍī bird, and keeps Agni's semen in a golden vessel on the top of a mountain. The Garuḍī or Suparṇī is of course a female Garuḍa, and Garuḍa is the mythical bird who steals the *soma* from heaven (in the Ṛgvedic versions the eagle steals it from the mountain) and brings it down onto the earth. Thus Svāhā's deed is an inversion of the *soma*-theft: she carries the somic seed from the earth onto the mountain, holding it in her hand (*pāṇinā*: 3.214.7), just as the eagle holds the

[123] However, the *ṛṣis* subsequently come to know of it, and, suspecting their wives' faithfulness, they repudiate them. PARPOLA (1994:206) notes that the motif of the Pleiades' (or Kṛttikās') separation from their husbands appears for the first time in ŚB 2.1.2.4-5, where it receives an astronomical interpretation: "originally the Pleiades were the wives of the Seven Sages, but are now precluded from intercourse with their husbands, as the Seven Sages (the stars of the Ursa Major) rise in the north, but the Pleiades in the east. Now the Pleiades have Agni as their mate, and it is with Agni that they have intercourse. [...] Only Arundhatī, the faithful wife of sage Vasiṣṭha, could not be seduced, and was allowed to remain as the star Alcor together with her husband, in the asterism of the Great Bear; the other wives were divorced." (See also pp. 241-2). He further remarks (1994:224): "[The] antiquity [of the myth of Skanda 's birth] is demonstrated above all by its connection with the Seven Sages and their wives: these mythological figures can be traced back to Harappan seals and fireplaces, and they are centrally connected with the nakṣatra calendar and its creation *c.*2300 BC." (See also 1994:225).

soma in his claw/foot (*padá*: ṚV 8.82.9; 10.144.5).[124] To make the analogy even more striking, the place where she keeps the semen, just like the *soma* in heaven, is said to be guarded by fierce snakes whose very look is poisonous (*dṛṣṭīviṣaiḥ*: 3.214.11; compare with *cakṣurviṣau* (1.29.6) in the episode of the *soma*-theft). Thus Agni's seed is indubitably kept on par with *soma* in the myth.

The resemblance between the fire itself and *soma* is revealed in the second Āraṇyakaparvan version of the myth of Agni's hiding. When Agni hides in the *mahārṇava*, Atharvan churns him out (*unmamātha*) of the ocean, a remarkable feat, if we reflect how difficult it is even to churn the fire by means of kindling sticks! The verb *math*, or here *un-math*, is commonly used both in the case of churning the *soma* (or rather the milky ocean out of which the *soma* is produced), and in the case of churning the fire from the *araṇis*.[125] Here Agni is churned out of the ocean just as the *soma* was churned out of it (see MBh 1.15-17). Thus there is a certain resemblance between this version of the myth of Agni's hiding, and the myth of the churning of the ocean to produce *soma*. In the myth of the churning of the ocean, the *soma* is produced out of herbs, resin of trees and gold, which, melted by the fire which burns the mountain used as a churning-stick, flow together into the ocean and conglomerate. In this version of the myth of his hiding, Agni subsequently dissolves into the earth, and out of various parts of his body are produced perfume, gold,[126] deodar pines, quartz, emeralds, mica and coral. The explanation of the origin of gold and

124 Anatomically speaking, the eagle's claws correspond of course to our feet. The fact that Svāhā (unlike the eagle) holds the seed in her hand probably hints at her (presumably) anthropomorphic original shape.

125 See KUHN (1859:12-16) for the similarity of the processes of churning milk and fire.

126 *Tejas* (13) may mean gold. This is how VAN BUITENEN translates it (1975:646). But perhaps we should rather read here *sugandhiteja(na)*, bdellium, a type of wood which was placed on the *uttara-vedī* during sacrifices. (Cf. TOKUNAGA 1997:273, note 93). This reading would correspond to BD 7.78 (MACDONELL); 7.59 (TOKUNAGA), which is perhaps inspired by this MBh passage.

precious stones as a combination of earth (in which they are found and whose heaviness they share) and fire (whose brilliance they share) seems quite logical, mythologically speaking.[127] Thus, the natures of *soma* and fire are to a certain extent coterminous. For if we combine the two cosmological myths, we see that fire, dissolving into the earth, becomes pines, gold and precious stones, which, in turn melting and dissolving under the influence of fire, produce the *soma*.

This equivalence of the fire or the fire's semen with *soma*, and the fact that the aim for which Agni is retrieved from his hiding-place is always represented as a sacrifice – whether he is really retrieved for actual sacrificial purposes or for purposes which are interpreted as sacrificial, like digesting food or generating offspring – make it likely that Agni's hiding in the myth should be interpreted at one level as a *dīkṣā* or initiation before the *soma*-sacrifice. As we know, the *dīkṣā* is a retreat from the world, a seclusion, an isolation, a death, or at least a regression to the embryonic stage, before the rebirth in the *soma*-sacrifice. All these elements play key-roles in the myth of Agni's hiding: Agni is *naṣṭa* and then 'reborn', he returns to the lap of his mothers, enveloped in an embryonic skin, he is isolated from, and opposed to all the others (be they gods, sages or animals) who look for him. The motifs of premature birth and premature death are also important for Agni himself as well as his offspring, especially Cyavana and Skanda.[128] At another level, Agni's hiding is a manner of proving his power negatively, that is, by withdrawing from the world in an unacceptable situation, not by fighting. In this, his behaviour reminds us of the Pāṇḍavas', who first retire to the forest and subsequently go

127 Not only mythologically, but also pre-scientifically and alchemically speaking. We find the same idea for instance in the Praśastapādabhāṣya 1.4.2, a treatise of the Vaiśeṣika philosophy. In the West too, the idea that metals and especially gold contain a high condensation of fire was prevalent till the 17th century. (See BACHELARD 1959:88;106;120).

128 Cyavana is born prematurely; Skanda, in many versions of the myth, is repeatedly aborted by various gods who are unable to carry him.

into hiding for one year, thereafter to reemerge more powerful than ever, like Agni. And as we know, the Pāṇḍavas' hiding can also be interpreted as their *dīkṣā* before the war-sacrifice.[129] The text itself never draws a parallel between both events, but the story of Agni's hiding – perhaps as a veiled allusion – is told in two different versions to the Pāṇḍavas, during their exile in the forest, in the Āraṇyakaparvan.[130]

Conclusions

In the ṚV, Agni, although he is said to be ancient, is at the same time frequently called a child. He is ever young, the youngest (*yaviṣṭh(y)a*), being kindled afresh every morning (MACDONELL 1898:91). Especially, he is the offspring or foetus of the waters, and when he hides in them he envelops himself in an embryonic skin. As such, he represents the life-principle or fiery germ of life lying in the primordial waters, his mothers.[131] But already in the ṚV, as VARENNE (1977-78:383-84) nctes, Agni is not only the son and embryo of the waters, but also their lover (ṚV 1.46.4), husband (2.35.13) and even father (1.96.2). In the epic myth of his hiding, Agni is no longer represented as a child or foetus. When he unites with the waters of the Gaṅgā in the Anuśāsanaparvan, it is no longer as a child hiding in the womb, but as a male uniting with a female, thereby producing a child in her. As

---

[129] The foetal symbolism is especially strong as far as the 13th year spent in hiding at Virāṭa's court is concerned. See GEHRTS (1975:217).

[130] We can also draw a comparison between Agni hiding in the water and Duryodhana who hides in the water of a lake at the end of the war (9.29). GEHRTS (1975:220) draws our attention to the foetal symbolism of Duryodhana's hiding. (We may add that the vanished Duryodhana is said to be *naṣṭa* (9.29.37), a term which is frequently applied to the hidden Agni.) Now, as GEHRTS notes, the lake in which Duryodhana hides bears the name of Dvaipāyana, which is also of course Vyāsa's name. Thus Duryodhana makes a "regressio in avum": he goes back to his grandfather's lap. But, as GEHRTS rightly remarks: "Nur aus dem Schoss des Weibes aber ist Wiedergeburt, und daher steigt Duryodhana zu seinem Tod aus dem See Dvaipāyana."

[131] See Stella KRAMRISCH. "The Triple Structure of Creation in the Ṛg Veda," in *History of Religions* II (1962-63:140-75; 256-85), p. 274, note 71. Quoted by KNIPE (1975:113).

BACHELARD (1949:85), paraphrasing an 18th century alchemist, notes: "le feu [...] est le principe mâle qui informe la matière femelle. Cette matière femelle, c'est l'eau." Even when such an explicit sexual encounter between the fiery male germ of life and the female waters does not take place, it is remarkable that some river always figures in the myth of Agni's hiding. In the Ādiparvan, we find the Vadhūsarā, and this river is moreover *produced* by the tears of Cyavana's own mother; and in the Śalyaparvan there is the Sarasvatī. We also find a list of rivers who are called the mothers of hearths or fire-altars in Āraṇyakaparvan 3.212.21-24.[132] Rivers in India are usually considered to be females and the mothers, not only of fire-altars, but also of people and the world in general, for they provide water and hence food. (See FELDHAUS 1995:82-85). Thus these rivers, whether the connection is explicitly made or not, always appear in the myth as Agni's watery and female counterpart, in union with which the generation of descendants can take place. Agni in the Epic is no longer the young god whose various origins and births are retold, but an 'old' god who produces new, typically epic, descendants. But the fundamental quality of the fire as the 'life-principle' has remained unchanged through the ages.

[132] It is interesting to note that the river Sindhu is explicitly excluded from this long list of rivers (*sindhuvarjam*: 3.212.21), because it is one of the rare rivers having a grammatically masculine name in Sanskrit and cannot therefore be called a 'mother'

3. Indra, the Lover of Ahalyā

Introduction

In the present chapter we shall deal with a subject which concerns the god Indra, namely, his seduction of Ahalyā, the wife of sage Gautama. This topic is first mentioned in a very laconic form in a few Brāhmaṇas, in the context of the Subrahmaṇyā litany, whereas the ṚV contains only a few motifs which go into the making of this story. But the most complete versions of this myth are certainly those which can be found in the Rāmāyaṇa. In an interesting reversal of the usual situation, the R presents two quite detailed and different versions of the story: 1.47.11-1.48 and 7.30.15-42, in the two *kāṇḍa*s which present numerous 'peripheral' narratives, whereas the MBh only contains a few allusions to it: 5.12.6; 12.329.14.i-ii; 13.41.21; 13.138.6. In this chapter, I shall first briefly narrate the two versions of the myth which appear in the R, in order to clarify the subject-matter. Then I shall attempt to disentangle the various Vedic threads out of which the epic narration is woven. A third step will be to present the Dumézilian interpretative framework as one of the means of explaining this mythical narrative, and see in the light of our findings from the history of the mythical motif whether Dumézil's theory concerning this particular myth is tenable or not. Finally, I shall try to answer the question why this theme was considered important enough by the redactors of the R to be introduced twice in this text (an unusual, if not unique occurrence),[1] whereas the MBh, usually so prolific as far as 'peripheral' narratives go, offers only a few allusions to it.

---

[1] See GOLDMAN (1984:367, note to 1.47.15): "The Uttarakāṇḍa version [...] marks the only repetition in the poem of a story peripheral to the epic narrative. The style and content of the two versions are quite distinct." As a matter of fact, the story of Indra slaying Vṛtra is also mentioned twice in the R, but it is true that only one version (in

The two Rāmāyaṇa versions

In the Balakāṇḍa (1.47.11-1.48), the story is told in the following circumstances: the young Rāma and his brother Lakṣmaṇa have been requisitioned by the sage Viśvāmitra to slay the *rākṣasas* who defile his sacrifices. This task accomplished, they proceed together to the town of Mithilā. On the outskirts of this town, Rāma sees an abandoned hermitage and questions Viśvāmitra about it. Then Viśvāmitra tells the two brothers about the events which took place there: in ancient times, the *muni* Gautama, one of the *saptarṣis* or seven great sages, lived in this hermitage with his wife Ahalyā, practising austerities. One day when Gautama was absent (as we learn later, he was only performing his ritual ablutions), Indra, who was infatuated with Ahalyā, took the sage's appearance and seduced her. Although she recognized Indra in spite of his disguise, she did not object, "swayed by her fascinated desire for the king of the gods":[2] *devarājakutūhalāt* (1.47.19). As Indra was leaving, quite pleased with himself, he met Gautama on the threshold of the hut. Realizing at once what had happened, the sage cursed him as follows:

> *mama rūpaṃ samāsthāya kṛtavān asi durmate /*
> *akartavyam idaṃ yasmād viphalas tvaṃ bhaviṣyasi* // 1.47.26 //
> Since you have done this deed which should not be done, having assumed my form, you fool, you will be deprived of testicles.

At once, Indra's testicles fell to the ground. Then Gautama cursed his wife to remain alone and invisible in their hermitage, doing *tapas,* till the day when Rāma's sight would free her. Then he vanished. In despair, Indra turned to the gods for help, claiming that he had done all this in order to lessen the sage's ascetic power, by provoking his anger.

7.75-77) is exhaustive, the other (in 1.23.17-23) is very brief, concerning not so much the deed itself, but the subsequent distribution of Indra's pollution.

[2] This translation is DONIGER O'FLAHERTY's (1975:94). It renders quite accurately the term *kutūhala,* which means both 'desire' and 'curiosity'.

The gods, with Agni at their head, offered a ram to the *pitṛdeva*s, requesting them to take this ram's testicles and to give them to Indra, promising them that henceforth their sacrificial share would be a castrated ram. The *pitṛdeva*s complied, and ever since, Indra has had the testicles of a ram. Then Viśvāmitra urges the two brothers to go into the hermitage and free Ahalyā from the curse. As they do so, she becomes visible once again, and, after offering them hospitality, she is reunited with her husband.

In 7.30, the story is told in entirely different circumstances, in the context of the description of the *rākṣasa*s' history and Rāvaṇa's exploits. The sage Agastya narrates to Rāma how Indra, defeated by Rāvaṇa's son Indrajit in the war between the *rākṣasa*s and the gods, was taken prisoner to Laṅkā. The gods contrived to negotiate his liberation, but he was still feeling dejected and gloomy due to the humiliation. Then Brahmā told him that he had only got what he deserved, and that his present condition was the retribution for a sin he had committed long ago. In ancient times, Brahmā says, he had created the living beings who all looked alike. Then, for the sake of variety, he created a woman of great beauty named Ahalyā (7.30.20).[3] Indra wanted to marry her, but Brahmā gave her to Gautama instead. Angry, Indra once went to their hermitage and raped Ahalyā.[4] He was seen by Gautama who

---

[3] After 20ab some manuscripts insert the following verse which contains an etymology of the name Ahalyā:

> *halaṃ nāmeha vairūpyaṃ halyaṃ tatprabhavaṃ bhavet /*
> *yasmān na vidyate halyaṃ tenāhalyeti viśrutā /*
> *Hala* here means ugliness, and *halya* is derived from that.
> Since (in her) ugliness is not found, therefore she is known as Ahalyā.

Ahalyā seems to be differentiated from the other creatures as much by the fact that she is a woman as by the fact that she is beautiful.

[4] In this version, apparently, Indra simply rapes Ahalyā and does not bother to disguise himself as Gautama. The only indication to this effect is found in a series of verses inserted by several manuscripts after 36 or 37 (presumably in conformity with the first version), where Ahalyā tries to disculpate herself by explaining to Gautama that she was deceived, for Indra had assumed his (Gautama's) form. In his reply, which is also in conformity with the first version, Gautama says that she will be purified by the sight of Rāma and subsequently reunited with him.

cursed him as follows: since he had raped Ahalyā, he would fall into the hands of the enemy during the war (7.30.29); besides, a similar state of affairs / emotion (*bhāva*) as the one Indra had inaugurated would exist among mankind, and half of the great *adharma* which would be produced thereby would fall to Indra's share (7.30.30-31); finally, the position of Indra would no longer be permanent, but would become a temporary post (7.30.32-33).[5] Then he orders Ahalyā to disappear from his hermitage, adding that since her beauty had been the cause of her downfall, all the creatures would henceforth be endowed with beauty too (7.30.34-37).[6] Then Brahmā advises Indra to take heart and perform the *vaiṣṇava-yajña* which would purify him.

The Vedic antecedents of the story of Indra and Ahalyā

At first sight, the story of Indra and Ahalyā seems to be new in the form in which it appears in the R. To my knowledge, it does not exist in the same detailed form in any earlier text. On the other hand, we can find scattered elements of it in many Vedic texts, which seem to have conglomerated in a subtle fashion in the R, perhaps for the first time.[7] Here I propose to disentangle the Vedic threads out of which the Epic narrative is woven. We can in fact distinguish no less than five originally distinct Vedic themes or motifs which go into the making of this particular story. These are:

1) Indra as the lover of Ahalyā.
2) Indra takes the appearance of Gautama.
3) Indra takes the appearance of a ram.

[5] Here Indra is not cursed to be deprived of testicles like in the first *kāṇḍa*. Only a few manuscripts, in conformity with the first version, present in 28cd the reading: *vikalo 'si kṛto deva tadā meṣavṛṣo bhavān*. "You have been mutilated, god, hence you have the testicles of a ram."

[6] No mention here of the fact that Ahalyā will be invisible.

[7] Obviously, we cannot be fully sure of the innovation of the R in this regard. Perhaps this text itself is based on earlier versions which are lost to us.

4) The importance of Indra's testicles.

5) Indra, who is overcome by the Nirṛti (Calamity, Perdition, Ruin) after metamorphosing into a woman, is freed by offering the sacrifice of a castrated domestic animal.

We shall examine each one of these themes separately, and if possible try to understand how they fused into a single narrative. The first three themes (Indra as Ahalyā's lover, as Gautama, and as a ram) appear together in the Subrahmaṇyā formula: a "chant which the Subrahmanyā priest sings while the soma is conveyed on the soma-cart to the sacrificial enclosure",[8] along with several other mythical motifs, most of them bearing on Indra's various metamorphoses.

Śatapathabrāhmaṇa 3.3.4.17-19, the Subrahmaṇyā litany:

> *átha subrahmaṇyā́m ā́hvayati / yáthā yébhyaḥ pakṣyánt syā́t tā́n brūyā́d ityahé vaḥ paktā́smī́ty evám evaìtád devébhyo yajñáṃ nívedayati subrahmaṇyóṃ subrahmaṇyóm*[9] *íti bráhma hí devā́n pracyāváyati triṣkṛ́tva āha trivṛ́d dhí yajñáḥ //17//*
> *índrā́gacchéti / índro vái yajñásya devátā tásmād āhéndrā́gacchéti háriva ā́gaccha médhātither meṣa vṛ́ṣaṇaśvasya mene / gaúrāva-skandinn áhalyāyai jāréti tád yā́ny evāsya cáraṇāni taír evaìnam etát prámumodayiṣati //18//*
> *kaúśika brāhmaṇa gaútamabruvāṇéti / śáśvad dhaitád ā́ruṇinā-dhunópajñātaṃ yád gaútama bruvāṇéti sá yádi kāmáyeta brūyā́d etád yády u kāmáyetā́pi nā́driyetetyahé sutyā́m íti yāvadahé sutyā́ bhávati //19//*[10]

17. Thereupon he recites the Subrahmaṇyā litany. Even as one would say to those for whom he intends to prepare a meal, 'On such and such a day I will prepare a meal for you;' so does he thereby

[8] This is the definition given by OERTEL (1895/1994:24-25).

[9] Although the litany says that the priest should say 'Subrahmaṇyom' three times, it is only repeated twice in the text. But in his translation (see below), EGGELING repeats it three times.

[10] Ed. ŚASTRI (1950:235).

> announce the sacrifice to the gods. 'Subrahmaṇyôm! Subrahmaṇyôm! Subrahmaṇyôm!' thus he calls, for the Brahman indeed moves the gods onward. Thrice he says it, because the sacrifice is threefold.
> 18. 'Come, O Indra!' Indra is the deity of the sacrifice: therefore he says, 'Come, O Indra!' 'Come, O lord of the bay steeds! Ram of Medhātithi! Wife of Vriṣaṇaśva! Bestriding buffalo! Lover of Ahalyā!' Thereby he wishes him joy in those affairs of his.
> 19. 'O Kauśika, Brāhman, thou who callest thee Gautama.' Just so has this (formula) been devised in these days by Āruni, to wit, 'thou who callest thee Gautama;' he may say it, if he choose, and if he does not choose, he need no attend to it. 'In so and so many days, to the Soma-feast,' (stating) in how many days from hence the pressing is to be.[11]

This formula is practically repeated verbatim in Taittirīyāraṇyaka 1.12.3:

> *subrahmaṇyoṃ subrahmaṇyoṃ subrahmaṇyom / indrā "gaccha hariva āgaccha medhātitheḥ/*[12] *meṣa vṛṣaṇaśvasya mene / gaurāvaskandinn ahalyāyai jāra kauśikabrāhmaṇa gautamabruvāṇa iti/*[13]

Indra, the lover of Ahalyā

Some Brāhmaṇas quote the Subrahmaṇyā with a commentary.[14] Presently we shall only quote the immediately relevant passage concerning the topic of Indra as the lover of Ahalyā, but it goes without saying that these texts also quote and discuss the rest of the litany. We shall deal with the other topics subsequently.

---

[11] Transl. by EGGELING (1885).

[12] The *daṇḍa* should probably be placed after *meṣa*. But this punctuation is present in all the editions of this text I have seen, which precludes the hypothesis of an editorial mistake.

[13] Ed. NATU (1967).

[14] The Subrahmaṇyā litany is also found in the DrāhŚS 1.3.3 and the LāṭŚS 1.3.1, which give several technical and practical recommendations on how, where and when to recite it.

Ṣaḍviṃśabrāhmaṇa 1.1.20-23:

1.1.20: *ahalyāyai jāreti* /
1.1.21: *ahalyāyā ha maitreyyā jāra āsa* /
1.1.22: *kauśika brāhmaṇeti* /
1.1.23: *kauśiko ha smaināṃ brāhmaṇa upanyeti* /
'Thou, Lover of Ahalyā!' he says.
He (scil. Indra) was the lover of Ahalyā, daughter of Mitrā.[15]
'Thou, brahman of the class of Kuśika!' he says.
He approaches her[16] as a brahman, Kauśika by name.[17]

Jaiminīyabrāhmaṇa 2.79 contains exactly the same statement as Ṣaḍviṃśa 1.1.20-21.

All that we learn from the above-quoted passages concerning this topic is that Indra was the lover (*jāra* designates an illegitimate lover, i.e., the lover of a married woman) of Ahalyā, the daughter of Mitrā. Sāyaṇa gives the following commentary on Ṣaḍviṃśabrāhmaṇa 1.1.23: *tasyāḥ jāraḥ san tadbhartṛsthāne tiṣṭhatīti kauśika brāhmaṇety upacārād āmantryate* // "Being her lover, he (scil. Indra) stands in the place of her husband, hence he is metaphorically called 'Kauśika, Brahman!'" If his interpretation is correct, then Ahalyā was probably the wife of the Brahmin Kauśika, (hence presumably a Brahmin herself), since Indra is called Kauśika precisely because he took her husband's place. In this case the germ of the idea that Indra takes the form of Ahalyā's husband to seduce her might be present here, but this passage is not entirely clear.

Indra as Gautama

In the Subrahmaṇyā litany in the Śatapathabrāhmaṇa and in the Taittirīyāraṇyaka, Indra receives the epithet of *gautamabruvāṇa*: 'thou

---

[15] Cf. Sāyaṇa: *maitreyī* = *mitrāyā duhitā* (daughter of Mitrā).
[16] But according to Sāyaṇa, *upanyeti* = *upayeme*: he married (her).
[17] Transl. by BOLLEE (1956).

who callest thee Gautama'. Ṣaḍviṃśabrāhmaṇa 1.1.24-25 further elaborates on this theme:

> 1.1.24: *gautamabruvāṇeti* /
> 1.1.25: *devāsurā hi saṃyattā āsaṃs tān antareṇa gautamaḥ śaśrāma / tam indra upetyovāceha no bhavānt spaśaś caratv iti / nāham utsaha iti / athāhaṃ bhavato rūpeṇa carāṇīti / sa yathā manyasa iti / sa yat tat gautamo vā bruvāṇaś cacāra gautama-rūpeṇa vā tad etad āha gautameti* //[18]
> 'Thou that callest Thyself Gotama (*sic*)!' he says.
> The Gods and Asuras contended with each other. Between them Gotama performed austerities. Indra went up to him and spoke: 'Do you act as a spy for us here!' 'I cannot do so' he answered. 'Then let me go in your shape' said Indra. 'As you think fit.' Because he then went about, calling himself Gotama or in the shape of Gotama, he therefore says: '(O Thou that callest Thyself) Gotama.'[19]

In Jaiminīyabrāhmaṇa 2.79, we find the following explanation of this expression:

> *kauśika brāhmaṇa kauśikabruvāṇeti* (*sic*)[20] / *yad dha vā asurair mahāsaṃgrāmaṃ samyete yad dha vedān nirācakāra / tān ha viśvāmitrād adhijage / tato haiva kauśika ūce / atha ha vā eke kauśika brāhmaṇa gautama bruvāṇety āhvayanti* //[21]
> 'O Kauśika, Brāhman, thou who callest thyself Kauśika!' he says. For when he (Indra) engaged in a great combat with the Asuras, and when he drove away the Vedas, he learnt them from Viśvāmitra. Then indeed he was called Kauśika. Then some call him 'O Kauśika, Brāhman, thou who callest thyself Gautama.'

18 Ed. SHARMA (1967).

19 Transl. by BOLLEE (1956).

20 This appears to be a misquote on the part of this Brāhmaṇa; the correct quote, i.e., *gautamabruvāṇa*, is given a few lines below.

21 Ed. VIRA and CHANDRA (1986).

Thus, from the Ṣaḍviṃśa we learn that Indra took the outward appearance of Gautama, just like in the R in the context of the story of Ahalyā's seduction. But the context of the Ṣaḍviṃśa seems to be entirely different (a war between Devas and Asuras) and Indra takes Gautama's form to act as a spy, not to seduce his wife. The Jaiminīya's explanation seems somewhat obscure: we can to a certain extent understand why Indra was called Kauśika after learning the Vedas from Viśvāmitra, for Kauśika is the patronymic of Viśvāmitra. But it is not quite clear why he should call himself Gautama for that matter.

Indra as a ram

Indra is called the "ram of Medhātithi" (*medhātither meṣa*) in the Subrahmaṇyā litany of the Śatapathabrāhmaṇa and Taittirīyāraṇyaka. This expression is elucidated in two different ways by the Jaiminīya and by the Ṣaḍviṃśabrāhmaṇa.

Jaiminīyabrāhmaṇa 2.79 makes the following comment:

> *medhātither meṣeti / medhātither ha meṣo bhūtvā rājānaṃ papau /*
> 'Thou ram of Medhātithi!' he says. Indeed, having become the ram of Medhātithi, (Indra) drank [his] *soma*.

The Jaiminīyabrāhmaṇa gives a more elaborate version of this story in 3.234: for the sake of obtaining cattle, Medhātithi, as the *yajamāna*, organizes a sacrifice. Indra, in the form of one of Medhātithi's rams, drinks the *soma*, and the performers drive him away, complaining. Finally, Indra reveals himself in his own form, and drinks the *soma*. From that time, he is summoned to the sacrifice with the words: 'O ram of Medhātithi!' (See DONIGER O'FLAHERTY 1985a:58).

On the other hand, Ṣaḍviṃśabrāhmaṇa 1.1.14-15 glosses this as follows:

> 1.1.14: *medhātither meṣeti /*
> 1.1.15: *medhātithiṃ ha kāṇvyāyanaṃ meṣo bhūtvā jahāra /*

> 'Thou ram of Medhātithi!' he says.
> Indra has carried him off to heaven,[22] the descendant of Kaṇva, Medhātithi by name, after having changed himself into a ram.[23]

Unlike the other mythological motifs we are dealing with here, that of Indra as a ram, more precisely as the ram of Medh(y)ātithi, is already found in the ṚV. In ṚV 1.51.1, 1.52.1, and 8.97.12, Indra is called *meṣa* (ram) in the context of hymns of prayers and invocations addressed to him. No further elucidation of the term *meṣa* is given there. Sāyaṇa glosses it as *śatrubhiḥ spardhamānam*: fighting (competing) with the enemies. Thus the epithet 'ram', according to Sāyaṇa, would mainly tend to emphasize Indra's war-like characteristics, perhaps even with an allusion to ram-fights.[24] ṚV 8.2.40 on the other hand contains a reference (the only one in this text) to the story of Medhyātithi:

> *itthā́ dhī́vantam adrivaḥ kāṇvám médhyātithim /*
> *meṣó bhūtò 'bhí yánn áyaḥ //*
> O lord of the pressing-stones, you (heard) Medhyātithi, the son of Kaṇva, whose mind was inclined that way, when you changed into a ram and carried him off (to heaven).[25]

The meaning of this verse depends on whether we follow the Padapāṭha: *abhí yánn áyaḥ*, or whether we read *abhí yán náyaḥ* with Sāyaṇa (= *agamayaḥ*), whom GELDNER follows in his translation. In the first

22 Sāyaṇa glosses *jahāra* "carried off" as *svargaṃ ninaya kila* "led him to heaven", quoting Ṛgveda 8.2.40.

23 Transl. by BOLLEE (1956).

24 Interestingly, DUMEZIL gives a similar interpretation. According to this author, the various animal forms that the great warriors assume in the literatures of many Indo-European cultures are meant to emphasize their physical strength and courage: "le guerrier éminent possède une véritable nature animale." (1985:207).

25 Translation according to GELDNER (1951): "Den Kanviden Medhyātithi, dessen Sinn darnach stand, hast du, Herr des Presssteines, (erhört), als du in einen Widder verwandelt (ihn in den Himmel) entführtest." GONDA (1963:222) thinks that GELDNER's translation of *itthā́ dhī́vantam* (dessen Sinn darnach stand) is wrong. According to this author, *dhī́vat* means 'inspired'.

case, it simply means that Indra came to Medhyātithi in the form of a ram, but in the second case it means that the god, in the form of a ram, carried off Medhyātithi. According to WEBER (1865:40), the gloss of Ṣaḍviṃśabrāhmaṇa 1.1.15 (viz. *medhātithiṃ [...] meṣo bhūtvā jahāra*) is based on a misreading of the Ṛgvedic verse: (*náyaḥ* instead of *áyaḥ*), and ṚV 8.2.40 simply means that Indra came to Medhyātithi in the form of a ram, i.e., with rich gifts. According to the same author, no allusion is meant to the legend of Medhyātithi in ṚV 1.51.1 and 1.52.1 (whereas Sāyaṇa does refer to it in his commentary): in these two verses, Indra is simply called 'ram' as he is more frequently called 'bull', as a metaphor of his bountifulness.[26]

Indra's testicles

In the ṚV, Indra often receives the epithet *sahasra-muṣka*: who has one thousand testicles.[27] This is obviously to emphasize his extraordinary virility and his fertilizing powers. Jaiminīyabrāhmaṇa 1.228 narrates the following story relating to Indra's testicles: Indra was tied down by the testicles by his own son Kutsa, who wished to test his power. Incidentally, this same Kutsa (imitating his father!)

---

[26] The story of Indra and Medhātithi is also found in the Bāṣkalamantra Upaniṣad, a short metrical Upaniṣad of 25 *triṣṭubhs*. This text was long known only through Anquetil du Perron's translation from Persian into Latin. (See WEBER 1865:§ 44, pp. 38-42). Sanskrit manuscripts were found in 1908 by F.O. Schrader in the Adyar Library. (This Upaniṣad is published for instance in LIMAYE and VADEKAR 1958). It gives an interesting version of the story of Medhātithi, on the one hand because it clearly shows Indra carrying Medhātithi to heaven (cf. stanza 1: *medhātithiṃ kāṇvam indro jahāra dyā meṣabhūyopagato* (= *meṣo bhūtvopagato*?) *vidānaḥ*: "changed into a ram, the wise Indra, approaching Medhātithi the son of Kaṇva, carried him to heaven"), and on the other hand because of the way in which Indra, while carrying off Medhātithi, eulogizes himself as the supreme god and *brahman*. (Cf. RENOU 1956). For a recent study of the Bāṣkalamantra Upaniṣad, see JEZIC (2002:46) who remarks that "the identification of Indra with the first principle takes the form of an almost monotheistic hymn, in which Indra reveals his divine nature with his own mouth. That hymn is comparable with Kṛṣṇa's self-revelation in the *Bhagavadgītā*....".

[27] Interestingly, in this text Indra is never called *sahasrākṣa*: "who has one thousand eyes". This epithet is reserved for other gods in the ṚV (See DONIGER O'FLAHERTY 1973:84 & 86), whereas it becomes a by-name of Indra in later texts. For instance, he is insistently called *sahasrākṣa* in the first R passage.

repeatedly seduced Indra's wife, using to his advantage the fact that he was Indra's exact look-alike. (JB 3.199-200).[28] Thus Indra's testicles were a well-known topic in Vedic literature, and a certain importance was attributed to them as a measure of the powers of this god. But whence comes the motif of Indra's substitute ram-testicles, which we have met nowhere so far? A tentative answer might be that it originates from the Subrahmaṇyā litany itself. For if we examine the Subrahmaṇyā attentively, we notice the juxtaposition of the two following expressions: *medhātither meṣa vṛṣaṇaśvasya mene*. If we suppress the gap between *meṣa* and *vṛṣaṇ(a)*, we obtain the term *meṣa-vṛṣaṇ(a)*: "who has the testicles of a ram".[29] Reinforcing this impression, the Taittirīyāraṇyaka, as we have already noted, moreover presents what appears to be a wrong punctuation,[30] i.e.: [...] *medhātitheḥ / meṣa vṛṣaṇaśvasya mene /*, thus grouping together the terms *meṣa* and *vṛṣaṇ(a)*. I am not trying to suggest that an actual misinterpretation or misreading occurred, but simply that the juxtaposition of the two terms *meṣa* and *vṛṣaṇ(a)* in the context of a well-known and probably often-heard sacrificial formula might have suggested the mythical motif of Indra's ram-testicles, supported by the fact that Indra does indeed take the shape of a ram in one myth, and by the fact that his testicles are an important element of his physical manifestation. Besides, as O'FLAHERTY (1985b:496) notes, the ram, with the bull and the stallion, belongs to the Indo-European 'macho trio' of animals which are considered to be extraordinarily virile. Hence Indra ultimately benefits from getting the testicles of a ram in that he

---

[28] Note that Indra's wife is not Kutsa's mother: Kutsa had been born from the thigh of his father, in the manner of an Indian Athene, hence his surname Aurava, "from the thigh". For these stories, see DONIGER O'FLAHERTY (1985a:74-76).

[29] After writing this passage, I noticed that the same observation was already made by SÖHNEN-THIEME (1996:48-49).

[30] However, we should perhaps not give too much importance to this point, for the punctuation in the manuscripts of the Brāhmaṇas is often inserted in a quite haphazard manner, when it is not lacking altogether.

receives the super-virility of this animal. (See DONIGER O'FLAHERTY 1973:85). What was initially meant as a punishment ultimately turns out to the god's advantage.

Indra's release from the curse

In the first version of the R, Indra is released from Gautama's curse, and his testicles are replaced with those of a ram, thanks to the gods', especially Agni's, intercession on his behalf with the *pitṛdevas*. The *pitṛdevas* are the gods who carry the oblations to the Manes, (the first of them being Agni Kavyavāhana, as opposed to Agni Havyavāhana, who carries the oblations to the gods).[31] The *pitṛdevas* tear out the testicles of a ram offered by the gods, and so to say graft them on Indra: *pitṛdevāḥ [...] utpāṭya meṣavṛṣaṇau sahasrākṣe nyavedayan* (1.48.8).[32] In exchange for this service they henceforth get sacrifices of gelded rams:

> *tadā prabhṛti kākutstha pitṛdevāḥ samāgatāḥ /*
> *aphalān bhuñjate meṣān phalais teṣām ayojayan* // 1.48.9 //
> Since then, Kākutstha, all the *pitṛdevas* enjoy castrated rams, for they provided (Indra) with the testicles of these (rams).

At one level, we can interpret this as an etiologic myth, which seeks to explain why the *pitṛdevas* get sacrifices of gelded rams. But at the same time, we can see here the transposition of an older myth, found in Kāṭhaka Saṃhitā 13.5 and in Maitrāyaṇī Samhitā 2.5.5. The Kāṭhaka Saṃhitā tells the following story:

> *indro vai vilisteṅgāṃ dānavīm akāmayata. so 'sureṣv acarat. stry eva strīṣv abhavat pumān puṃsu. sa nirṛtigṛhīta ivāmanyata. sa*

[31] See BIARDEAU (1999:1458, note XLIX, 2).

[32] The editor of the Critical Edition remarks here rather comically: "Note the art of grafting glands wonderfully developed in modern times by Scientific Researches." (Vol. 1, Critical Notes, p. 454).

> *etam aindrānairṛtaṃ vipuṃsakam apaśyad. yena rūpeṇācarat tam ālabhata.*[33]
>
> "Indra desired the Dānavī Vilisteṅgā. He went to the Asuras and became a woman among women and a man among men. He thought he was seized by Nirṛti (the goddess of Calamity or Misfortune). He saw (as a sacrificial offering) this castrated animal consecrated to Indra and to Nirṛti. In that form in which he went about (i.e. castrated), such an animal he offered in sacrifice."[34]

The Maitrāyaṇī Saṃhitā relates nearly the same thing, but in connection with Indra as the wife of Vṛṣaṇaśva, a mythical motif which occurs in the Subrahmaṇyā litany:

> *yátra vā́ adá índro vṛ́ṣaṇaśvasya ménā́sīt tád enaṃ nírṛtiḥ pāpmā́gṛhṇāt / sá yáṃ pāpmā́nam apā́hata sá nápuṃsako 'bhavat / yáḥ pāpmánā támasā gṛhītó mányeta sá etáṃ aindrám nápuṃsakam ā́labheta /*[35]
>
> "When Indra became Vṛṣaṇaśva's Menā (or wife) he was seized by Nirṛti, Calamity. When he chased it away, that Calamity became a castrated animal. Whoever thinks he is seized by Calamity, Darkness, he should sacrifice this castrated animal to Indra."[36]

Both in the R and in these two texts of the Black Yajur Veda, Indra is in trouble because he is deprived of his virility, but in different ways. In the Yajur Veda, this happens because he changes into a woman, and in the R, as we know, because he loses his testicles as the result of a curse punishing his excess of virility. But the end-result is the same.[37]

---

33 Ed. VON SCHROEDER (1970-72).

34 Transl. acc. to DEPPERT (1977:363).

35 Ed. VON SCHROEDER (1970-72).

36 Transl. acc. to DEPPERT (1977:363). See also ŚB 12.7.1.10-12; 5.2.3.8: "Indra lost his virility. The gods used the ram, the male goat, and the bull as recompense. And therefore the bull is sacred to Indra." (Transl. by DONIGER O'FLAHERTY 1973:134).

37 As O'FLAHERTY (1985b:491) remarks: "Or it may simply be that to be changed into a woman is to be castrated; here, as so often in Indian mythology, change of sex, androgyny, castration, and the eunuch are closely related."

The R thus presents a variation of this Vedic motif. The *pitṛdeva*s here get the castrated animal as a sacrificial offering, instead of Indra (as in the Maitrāyaṇī Saṃhitā) or instead of Indra and the Nirṛti (as in the Kāṭhaka Saṃhitā). What is clear is that in the R the *pitṛdeva*s fulfill the same function as the Nirṛti (a goddess who has hardly any importance in the Epics), since Indra has to be bought off from them. Besides, already in the AV, the Nirṛti and the *pitṛ*s are shown to be roughly equivalent, since two hymns which deal with the soul's destination after death say that "the deceased should come out of the lap of perdition" (*nírṛter upásthāt*) (3.11.2) and "should not go to the Pitṛs" (8.1.7).[38] The *pitṛdeva*s, who precisely carry the oblations to the *pitṛ*s, are probably here the representatives of the world of the dead, into whose realm the emasculated Indra would have fallen if he had remained maimed, unwhole, whereas of course he rightly belongs to the world of the *deva*s. We know of the strong opposition between the *pitṛyāna* or way of the Manes, and the *devayāna* or way of the gods, which are two different destinations of the souls of the dead. Why the sacrificial animal has to be a castrated one is readily explainable by the fact that the sacrificial victim is always considered to be a substitute for the sacrificer's own self: since Indra is unmanned in each occasion, though by different means, it naturally follows that the victim he offers is castrated too.

To sum up, the R tale has carefully interwoven the various motifs listed above to produce its own version of the tale of Indra's seduction of Ahalyā. How this process of conglomeration took place is hard to tell with any certainty, but it is likely that the Subrahmaṇyā litany, listing as it does many of the mythical motifs which appear in the R, must have played a crystallizing role in this process. Most of these mythical motifs appear to be very poorly attested in Vedic literature, and are at best allusive and fragmentary. But we must probably suppose that

[38] See BODEWITZ (1999a:112).

already at that time there existed fully developed myths around these topics (otherwise the allusions would have made no sense to anybody), which have simply not come down to us. It is interesting to note that the two versions of the R use the myth to explain two very different things: the first version uses it to explain why the *pitṛdeva*s get sacrifices of gelded rams. This sacrificial connotation, which first appears somewhat surprising, if not unusual, in the context of the R, becomes more readily understandable if we reflect that the myth is a conglomeration of several motifs which appear in a sacrificial litany. The second R version uses the myth to explain in a rather typical manner (why could such a thing happen? because once upon a time such and such a wrong deed was committed, for which the present event is the retribution) why Indra could be defeated in a war between the gods and the *rākṣasa*s. A similar background of a war between Devas and Asuras during which Indra takes the shape of Gautama, or calls himself Gautama, already appears in the Ṣaḍviṃśabrāhmaṇa (1.1.24-25) and in the Jaiminīyabrāhmaṇa (2.79), and it is therefore possible that this new setting is not an innovation of the second R version, but that it is precisely inspired from these Vedic passages.[39]

The Dumézilian theoretical framework

The mythological motif of Indra's seduction of Ahalyā is central to Georges DUMEZIL's theory concerning the Indo-European cycle of the 'three sins of the warrior' (les trois péchés du guerrier).[40] These sins of the warrior are sins committed against what Dumézil calls the 'three functions', which, according to this author, divided and organized the Indo-European society. Although Dumézil's three functions are well-known, I will briefly summarize them here.

---

[39] However, in an interesting reversal, Indra does *not* take the form of Gautama in the second version of the R.

[40] See his *Heur et Malheur du Guerrier* (1985).

1) The function pertaining to the government, and to the religious and juridical domain. In India, on the social level, the Brahmins are the representatives of this function.

2) The function pertaining to the domain of war, brute strength and violence. The Kṣatriyas are the representatives of this function.

3) The function pertaining to the 'mass' of the people, agriculture, reproduction, fertility, sexuality and beauty. This function is represented by the Vaiśyas.[41]

In the Indian context, the main perpetrator of these 'sins of the warrior' is the god Indra, the warrior-god *par excellence*. His sins are, most notably:

1) Against the first function: the murder of the Brahmin Triśiras.

2) Against the second function: the murder of Vṛtra, committed in a treacherous fashion, against the warriors' code of honour, and not by dint of strength and courage, as would befit a warrior.

3) Against the third function: his seduction of Ahalyā, a married woman and a Brahmin.[42]

In each case, Indra is punished in a fashion which is commensurate to his crime:

[41] For DUMEZIL's application of this framework to the MBh, see his *Mythe et Épopée* (1968).

[42] Indra has a solid reputation as a womanizer, but Ahalyā's seduction is certainly paradigmatic of this type of transgression. SÖHNEN-THIEME (1996:39) argues that in fact his seduction of Ahalyā is the only instance on record. It is true that it is the only clear and unambiguous instance of a successful seduction on the part of Indra, but there are quite a few other cases which are, it is true, less clearly stated: thus the cases of Menā and Vilistengā, which we have discussed above, and also the case of Ruci, which we will discuss below. BROCKINGTON (2001:78) adduces a few other examples. In any case, the intention to do wrong often matters just as much as the deed itself.

1) He loses his *tejas*: splendour, renown, spiritual power.
2) He loses his *bala*: physical strength.
3) He loses his beauty, etc. (See DUMEZIL 1985:89-90).

According to Dumézil, this theme of the 'sins of the warrior' goes back to the remotest Indo-European antiquity, since it appears in the literatures of most Indo-European languages, ranging over a vast geographical area from India to Ireland. Thus, he notes, it seems even more strange that the theme of Indra's sins in general, and of his seduction of Ahalyā in particular, are not found in the oldest Indian literary testimony, the ṚV. Dumézil explains this state of affairs in the following way: since the ṚV consists practically exclusively of hymns of prayers and praise addressed to various divinities, begging from them favours like riches, cows, sons, long life, and so on, it is logical that the poets do not heavily insist on the misdeeds of the gods, but on the contrary emphasize their glorious and beneficent actions, as a *captatio benevolentiae*.[43] This does not mean, then, that Indra's sins were unknown, but simply that the Ṛgvedic poets, for the above-listed reasons, did not mention them.[44] This state of affairs, according to DUMEZIL (1985:83-84), changes at the time of the Brāhmaṇas, where we start to find allusions to Indra's sins. This is due to the fact that those texts mainly emphasize the overarching importance of the sacrificial ritual, in which the personal favours of the gods, and the belief in their omnipotence, have greatly lost their importance. Finally, the theme of Indra's sins reemerges in its full vigour in the Epics, where Indra has lost most of his power and importance, and is defeated in numerous instances. The great gods are now Viṣṇu and Śiva, and in

[43] To substantiate his theory, DUMEZIL even claims that Indra's one misdeed which is mentioned in the ṚV but finds few echoes in the later literature, namely, slaying his father, results from a faulty transmission of the text (1985:81-82).
[44] See DUMEZIL (1985:82-83).

many cases the epic poets do not hesitate to depict Indra as a mere buffoon. Thus we can see at work here one of Dumézil's theoretical leïtmotivs, namely, that many ancient Indo-European mythological themes went so to say underground in early Vedic times and reemerged in full force at the time of the Epics.

Reassessing Dumézil's Theory

How can we reassess Dumézil's theory in view of what we have seen above, in the R and in the Vedic texts, concerning the myth of Indra's seduction of Ahalyā? I propose to examine the problem from two different points of view: first, the question of the punishment meted out to the sinners in the R: to what extent is in commensurate with the crime, and to what extent does it correspond to Dumézil's trifunctional theory; then the question of whether there really is a direct continuity from Indo-European times to epic times as far as the representation of Indra's 'sins' (more precisely Ahalyā's seduction) is concerned, as Dumézil claims, or whether, on the contrary, there was a change of attitude concerning Indra which accounts for the greater emphasis given by the Epics to Indra's misdeeds.

Let us first consider the question of the punishment. In the first R version, Indra is indeed punished in a fashion which is commensurate to the sin he has committed. His sexual transgression or adultery is punished by castration. This is not only in accordance with Dumézil's trifunctional theory, but also with what we read in the Smṛtis on the one hand, and in other mythological narratives on the other. In the Manusmṛti for instance we read that if a man had intercourse with his *guru*'s wife, one of the options available to him to expiate his deed was to cut off his own sexual organs and walk toward the southwest region of Nirṛti till he dropped dead.[45] Of course, Ahalyā is not the wife of Indra's *guru*, but she is a Brahmin (whereas Indra is admittedly the prototypical *kṣatriya*), and the wife of a great *ṛṣi*. The *saptarṣi*s or seven great sages, to whose group Gautama belongs, certainly function as the supreme *guru*s, if not fathers, of the world. Thus, as GOLDMAN (1978:360-61) notes, Indra's adventure with Ahalyā has very clear incestuous undertones.[46] Besides, Ahalyā literally means "who should not be ploughed",[47] and we know of the usual imagery which likens the sexual act to the ploughing of a field (i.e., the womb). Thus her name itself shows that Ahalyā, who is both a Brahmin and a mother-figure, is definitely off limits for Indra. Not only in treatises of law, but on the mythological plane too, we find instances where the punishment affects the organ whereby one has sinned; this motif is also prominent in the myth of Agni's hiding, as we have seen in the preceding chapter.

In some other versions of the myth (e.g. MBh 13.41.21; Padmapurāṇa 1.56.15-53; Kārttikeya Māhātmya 4.32; Kampaṉ's Irāmāvatāram, canto 1[48]), Indra is punished by getting a thousand vulva-marks on his body. These are subsequently transformed into eyes either by divine intercession, or because Gautama relents. As DONIGER O'FLAHERTY (1973:85-86) remarks, the effects of both castration and branding with *yoni*-marks is the same: it unmans Indra, depriving him

---

[45] This is stated in MSmṛ 11.105:

> *svayaṃ vā śiśnavṛṣaṇāv utkṛtyādhāya cāñjalau /*
> *nairṛtīṃ diśam ātiṣṭhed ānipātād ajihmagaḥ //*
>
> "Or he himself [the man who has violated his *guru*'s marriage-bed] may cut off his penis and testicles, hold them in his two cupped hands, and set out toward the southwest region of Ruin, walking straight ahead until he dies." (Transl. by DONIGER and SMITH 1991).

[46] GOLDMAN (1978:327) rightly notes that "scholars have tended to overlook the very marked tendency in some types of Oedipal story toward the substitution of various males figures, notably the guru or aged brahman sage, and to a much lesser extent the elder brother, for the father and female figures such as the guru's wife, the sister-in-law, and often a cow, for the mother." And he further remarks (1978:341): "so many [...] legends regularly equate brahmans with fathers and *kṣatriyas* with sons".

[47] See BIARDEAU (1997:105).

[48] See RAMANUJAN (1991).

of his virility.[49] But ultimately both punishments turn to Indra's advantage, since the ram's testicles confer added virility on him and the thousand *yoni*s become 'erotic' eyes (to use DONIGER O'FLAHERTY's words).[50] Apparently, the R does not refer to this other punishment of Indra, but throughout the passage Indra is insistently called *sahasrākṣa*, undoubtedly as an allusion to it. Ahalyā's curse to become invisible is also certainly meant as a reaction against Indra's *sahasrākṣatva*, so that her beauty will no longer be able to attract Indra's one thousand erotic eyes.

On the other hand, the punishment Indra gets in the second R version (he will be defeated in the war and his post will become temporary), mainly pertains to the realm of kingship and war, i.e., the first and second function. Thus it is out of keeping with his sexual offense. Perhaps Dumézil would have called the redactor of this passage of the R a bad myth-maker! Yet the motif of the loss of beauty, which, according to Dumézil's theory, would be the proper punishment for an offense against the third function, is not absent in R 7.30, but it pertains to Ahalyā, the co-sinner, rather than to Indra. Strictly speaking, there is no actual loss of beauty: Ahalyā simply loses the prerogative of being the only beautiful creature, since beauty is henceforth distributed among the other creatures as well. But in effect, it does mean that Ahalyā will no longer stand out as the only beautiful woman in the world, and will henceforth be much less likely to attract the attention of the likes of Indra. Thus both curses,

49 Interestingly, branding with the mark of the *yoni* is also a possible punishment for a man who has had intercourse with his *guru*'s wife. See MSmṛ 9.237.

50 There is another story which explains the origin of Indra's thousand eyes: once, as the newly-created *apsarus* Tilottamā was doing a *pradakṣiṇā* around the gods, Indra was so smitten by her beauty that he grew one thousand eyes all over his body so as not to lose sight of her. (MBh 1.203). Thus on both occasions Indra's lechery is the cause of his thousand eyes. We can contrast this with the thousand eyes of the kingly Varuṇa in the ṚV, in whom they denote the power to oversee everything.

invisibility and the distribution of her beauty, ultimately have the same effect.

Concerning the second question asked above (were Indra's sins suppressed in the ṚV, or do the Epics reflect a change of attitude towards Indra, which explains why they talk more about the 'sins' of this god), we can make the following observations. First, as far as we can tell from the scanty evidence at hand, we observe that the Vedic passages do not seem to attach any sort of blame to Indra, and he is not punished for being Ahalyā's lover. The fact that he is her lover is not mentioned in connection with his so-called 'sins'[51] (this in itself would be astonishing, since the expression *ahalyāyai jāra* appears in the context of a formula recited during a sacrifice to call Indra to the sacrifice), but rather in connection with Indra's versatility and his various metamorphoses: the other metamorphoses which are mentioned in the Subrahmaṇyā are that he became Gautama and a ram (which we have discussed above) and also that he became Menā or the wife of Vṛṣaṇaśva (seed-bearing stallion? bull-stallion?),[52] and a *gaura* (Bos gaurus, a species of wild bovine).

According to DUMEZIL (1985:85-6), if the Vedic literature does not insist much on Indra's sexual transgressions it is partly because the Brahmins, as a new class which had to assert itself, did not wish to create an unwelcome precedent by depicting the king of gods appropriating one of their own women. In other words, the warrior class, which as a class had but too many propensities for sexual *débordements*, should not be encouraged to trespass into Brahmin territory. This statement is probably true to a certain extent. But if this were the reason for the Veda's truly scanty references to Indra's seduction of Ahalyā, they would at least mention this topic negatively, attaching blame to Indra,

[51] Whereas these texts do contain lists of Indra's sins, i.e. deeds which are mentioned negatively and shown to be condemned by the other gods themselves. See DUMEZIL (1985:83-4).

[52] For this particular mythical motif, see O'FLAHERTY (1985b).

whereas this is not so. In the Epics, on the other hand, Indra is blamed and punished. On one occasion, in MBh 12.329, a passage which belongs to the Nārāyaṇīyaparvan, Indra's seduction of Ahalyā is even mentioned in the context of Indra's sins (killing Triśiras, Vṛtra, etc.) and his various defeats at the hands of Brahmins. MBh 12.329.14.i-ii laconically states the following:

> *ahalyādharṣanimittaṃ hi gautamād dhariśmaśrutām indraḥ prāptaḥ* / 1 / *kauśikanimittaṃ cendro muṣkaviyogaṃ meṣavṛṣaṇatvaṃ cāvāpa* / 2 /[53]
>
> Because he raped Ahalyā, Indra got a reddish[54] beard from Gautama. And because of Kauśika[55], Indra was deprived of his testicles and obtained those of a ram.

Similarly, in 13.138.6, the god Vāyu tells king Arjuna Kārtavīrya how Gautama cursed Indra because the latter was lusting after Ahalyā,[56] in the context of a general praise of Brahmins, which he undertakes because the king was intoxicated with pride and thought that nobody was his equal. Thus Vāyu, to dampen his arrogance, enumerates numerous

---

53 Perhaps this series of sentences which rather tersely enumerate Indra's various (mis)deeds is a deliberate imitation of the Subrahmaṇyā litany, but in a more negative vein.

54 The term is *hari*. DONIGER O'FLAHERTY (1973:85) translates it as green. But *hari* is a color which is very frequently used to describe Indra, especially in the ṚV, where it means 'reddish' or 'golden': his hair, his beard are *hari*, his horses are *hari*, etc. Perhaps it should rather be taken in the same sense here in the MBh. This is the only occurrence of this type of punishment I have come across in connection with the story of Indra and Ahalyā. I do not quite understand why and how this is in fact a punishment. The same point already puzzled SÖHNEN-THIEME (1996:46), who further proposes the following explanation: "Perhaps the ideal of beauty had somehow changed after the immigration of the ancient Aryans, who were presumably fair-haired, and in later periods blond hair and beard were regarded as abnormal." (1996:49). However, this interpretation involves too many imponderables.

55 We have already met with Kauśika in the context of the Subrahmaṇyā litany. Here the MBh seems to make a confusion between Kauśika, a name which usually designates Viśmāmitra, and Gautama. The same already happens in the Jaiminīyabrāmaṇa (2.79). It is also possible that Kauśika plays Gautama's role in some versions of the myth which have not come down to us in a better attested form.

56 The content of the curse is not mentioned, and the verse adds that Gautama did not harm Indra, for the sake of *dharma*: *dharmārthaṃ na ca hiṃsitaḥ*.

instances where the Brahmins proved to be more powerful than anybody else.

Therefore a change of attitude seems to have taken place, a hardening of morals and of class distinctions between Vedic and epic times, and if anything, the hierarchy of the *varṇa*s seems to have become more rigidly fixed at the time of the Epics than previously, and the Brahmins asserted their domination more vigorously. Indeed, if we look at the R passages, and also at MBh 13.40-41 (Vipulopākhyāna), we observe that it is mainly the Brahmins who blame Indra for his deed. Gautama is enraged for obvious reasons and curses Indra. R 1.47-48 offers a very finely drawn description of Indra's moral and physical turpitude as opposed to Gautama's absolute purity (one of the preconditions for the efficacy of his curse). As Indra is hurriedly leaving Ahalyā's hut, afraid of meeting Gautama, he meets the sage on the threshold. Gautama is here described as follows:

> *devadānavadurdharṣaṃ tapobalasamanvitam /*
> *tīrthodakapariklinnaṃ dīpyamānam ivānalam /*
> *gṛhītasamidhaṃ tatra sakuśaṃ munipuṃgavam* // 1.47.23 //
> The bull-like *muni*, unassailable by gods and demons, invested with the power of his penance, wet with the water of the sacred bathing-place, shining like the fire, holding fuel and *kuśa*-grass.

The *muni*'s absolute power and purity is opposed to Indra's troubled state of mind (he is afraid)[57] and his state of physical pollution (he has just had adulterous sexual intercourse, that too not at the proper time, i.e., not during Ahalyā's fertile period,[58] and has presumably not washed himself yet). Gautama, on the other hand, invincible and full of tapasic strength, is just coming back from his ritual ablutions (he is

[57] This fear itself is a sign of decadence on the part of Indra, the king of the gods and the prototypical *kṣatriya*.

[58] See 1.47.18, where Indra himself declares: *ṛtukālaṁ pratīkṣante nārthinaḥ* (lustful people do not wait for the fertile period.)

even still wet), he shines like a fire, the purifier par excellence, and he holds fuel and pure *kuśa* grass, indicating that he is about to perform a sacrifice. All these elements combined together contribute to form the picture of Gautama's perfect purity.[59]

And the depiction of Indra's character does not improve when he tells the gods, adding lies to debauchery, that he has seduced Ahalyā with the sole aim of provoking a great outburst of anger in Gautama, thus diminishing his ascetic power (1.48.2). From what comes before, we know that he has simply acted out of lust and wished to avoid a confrontation with Gautama by all means.[60] Besides, great dharmic sages like Gautama are not usually hampered in their *tapas* by the gods, unlike ordinary humans or demons who thereby try to gain harmful power. On the whole, this passage gives a psychologically very insightful depiction of Indra's character: cowardly, boastful, lying and cheating!

Another passage with a reference to Indra's seduction of Ahalyā, which also glorifies brahmanic power as opposed to the cowardice and debauchery of Indra, and contains a strong condemnation of Indra's behaviour on the part of a Brahmin, is found in MBh 13.40-41, the Vipulopākhyāna. This story is quite similar to that of Indra and Ahalyā (perhaps even a double of that story), but with a happy ending, at least for Indra's prospective victim, if not for Indra himself. This narrative serves as an illustration for the topic discussed in the two previous chapters (13.38-39) entitled *Strībhāvakathana,* the "description of the nature of women", whose gist is that 'women are the root of all

---

59 I cannot quite agree with GOLDMAN's translation of the second part of the verse (1984:216): "That bull among sages was still damp with he water of the bathing place, *but* carrying kindling and *kuśa* grass, he shone like fire." (My emphasis). In my opinion, there is no opposition here between water and fire: both represent Gautama's perfect purity.

60 According to DONIGER O'FLAHERTY (1975:94), this version of the myth "satirizes the widespread mythological belief that the gods must dispel the dangerous powers of an ascetic by stirring him to lust or anger."

evil'.[61] Bhīṣma tells Yudhiṣṭhira that once there was a *ṛṣi* called Devaśarman who had a very beautiful wife named Ruci. Indra was infatuated with her. Knowing the weakness of women and Indra's nature, the sage did everything in his power to protect her. But one day he had to leave his hermitage to attend a sacrifice, and requested his *śiṣya* Vipula, a Bhārgava (see 13.40.21), to see to it that no harm came to her, especially warning him against Indra, who could take any form at will. After some reflection, Vipula decided that the only way to protect her efficiently was to 'possess' her by means of his yogic powers.[62] When Indra arrived to seduce her, Vipula first spoke to him harshly through her mouth, and then, revealing himself, thoroughly rebuked the king of gods for his vile behaviour, asking him, among other things:

> *kiṃ nu tad vismṛtaṃ śakra na tan manasi te sthitam /*
> *gautamenāsi yan mukto bhagāṅkaparicihnitaḥ* // 13.41.21 //
> Have you really forgotten this, Śakra, has this not remained in your mind, how you were released by Gautama, branded with vulva-marks?

As we can observe from these two passages, there was certainly no lesser fear in epic times of this sort of '*kṣatriya* incursion on Brahmin

[61] Probably for the sake of additional credibility, these words and the whole description of the fundamentally evil nature of women are placed in the mouth of a woman, the *apsaras* Pañcacūḍā, whom Nārada is interrogating on this topic.

[62] Interestingly, the passage even describes by what means Vipula 'possesses' her, or enters into her, which is very similar to the way in which Vidura enters into Yudhiṣṭhira at the moment of his death (see MBh 15.33.24-27):

> *netrābhyāṃ netrayor asyā raśmīn saṃyujya raśmibhiḥ /*
> *viveśa vipulaḥ kāyam ākāśaṃ pavano yathā* //13.40.56//
> Having joined the rays of her eyes with the rays from his own eyes, Vipula entered her body like the wind enters the atmosphere.

However "yogic", it turns out that this possession is in fact equivalent with the sin of sleeping with his *guru*'s wife, especially because Vipula never tells Devaśarman the exact manner in which he protected his wife. As a consequence of this action, as he subsequently comes to know, he is condemned to the worst tortures in hell. But after he confesses everything to his master, the latter gives him full forgiveness and promises him heaven. (See MBh 13.42-43.)

territory' than in earlier times. Besides, the fact that the story could still be used as a precedent to justify certain types of reprehensible behaviour is shown in the MBh by the case of Nahuṣa (a human king who replaces Indra on the throne when the latter is overcome by *brahmahatyā* after killing Triśiras), who precisely quotes the story of Indra's seduction of Ahalyā as a precedent for his own evil intentions of appropriating, not a Brahmin's wife it is true, but Indra's own wife Śacī, an idea which the gods and *ṛṣi*s alike strongly disapprove of:

> *ahalyā dharṣitā pūrvam ṛṣipatnī yaśasvinī /*
> *jīvato bhartur indreṇa sa vaḥ kiṃ na nivāritaḥ* // 5.12.6 //
> Once upon a time, the glorious Ahalyā, the *ṛṣi*'s wife, was raped by Indra, whereas her husband was still alive. Why did you not try to prevent him?

On the whole, the MBh only alludes to the story of Indra and Ahalyā in contexts which describe the superiority of Brahmins over *kṣatriya*s, and it serves as an illustration for the fact that *kṣatriya*s can afford to insult Brahmins (and their wives) only at their own risk and peril. If the Brahmins at least strongly seem to disapprove of Indra's behaviour with Ahalyā and other Brahmin women, the situation is not so clear as far as the gods are concerned. In R 1.48, when Indra calls to them for help, not a single word of reproach escapes their lips. They at once get down to the task of restoring Indra's testicles. Agni plays a special role here, acting as the gods' spokesman, but perhaps we should not make too much of this, since it is his usual behaviour, especially in times of crisis.[63] Why are the gods so ready to help the truant Indra,

---

[63] Besides, the text is not entirely consistent here. According to 1.48.5, all the gods speak to the *pitṛdeva*s, but according to 1.48.8, only Agni speaks. DONIGER O'FLAHERTY (1973:134) remarks that "Agni then replaced Indra's testicles with those of a ram, the animal sacred to Agni himself", probably implying that here Agni, as in some other myths (e.g. JB 2.134), is the first to provide a means to save Indra. But here not only is it nowhere clearly stated that only Agni gave the ram, besides, it is rather the goat which is Agni's animal, and not the ram. (See SMITH 1994:258-260).

without ever blaming him?[64] Another variant of the same myth, found in Padmapurāṇa 4.101.174-9 (quoted in DONIGER O'FLAHERTY 1973:246) suggests that in this affair the other gods were equally guilty, if not in deed then at least in thought:

> "Formerly the gods lusted for Gautama's wife and raped her, for their wits were destroyed by lust. Then they were terrified and went to the sage Durvāsas (an incarnation of Śiva), who said, 'I will remove all your defilements with the Śatarudrīya Mantra (an ancient Śaiva prayer).' Then he gave them ashes which they smeared upon their bodies, and their sins were shaken off."

Moreover, we know from other myths that Agni had also been guilty of lusting not only for Ahalyā but for all the seven wives of the seven great sages! Thus, even if in the R the misdeed is Indra's alone, we can understand that this version is just a variant of other versions of the myth where all the gods are equally guilty. This certainly explains their cooperating behaviour here.

But another, far more weighty reason might also account for the gods' behaviour. Indra, especially in the Epics, is not only a war-god, but also a rain-god, who fertilizes the earth by sending rain. His sexual *débordements* at a human level are only the extension of his fertilizing activities at the cosmic level. Hence no moral judgment should be passed on them.[65] Now, an Indra deprived of testicles, (and the word mostly used here for testicles is *vṛṣaṇa*, from the root *vṛṣ-* 'to rain, to fertilize'), is an Indra who cannot rain. And we know the catastrophic consequences of a drought at the human and at the cosmic level. This

[64] We have already noted that the excuse Indra himself offers (viz. that he was trying to destroy Gautama's *tapas*) is rather weak.

[65] As BHATTACHARJI (1970:273) rightly remarks. But according to her, Indra's adulterous behaviour is due to the fact that he is a solar god. See also HILTEBEITEL (1976:47): "when Indra commits his assorted crimes, these are pure deeds. They invite no moral investigation. The gods act out of their own essential natures, and that is that." The gods themselves seem to understand this very well in the R, but not the Brahmins!

undoubtedly explains why the gods are in such a hurry to redress the situation. One of Dumézil's shortcomings, in my opinion, is that he exclusively insists on Indra's warrior-nature to explain his sexual excesses (a trait which, according to him, is typical of all great warriors who refuse to be tied by established social conventions), but he does not correlate them to this god's raining and fertilizing function. Now, it is true that in the Veda (especially the Ṛgveda), Indra is prominently the warrior-god, and that the god Parjanya is more closely connected with the raining function. But at the time of the Epics, Indra's quality as the rain-god has gained much more prominence,[66] and this is perhaps the reason why the Epics mention his sexual excesses more frequently, precisely because they are but an aspect of his cosmic fertilizing activities.

Thus on the whole, it seems much more likely that the importance of Indra's sexual adventures in the Epics,[67] and the negative judgment pronounced on them, cannot so much be attributed to the sudden resurgence of a mythical motif which had remained suppressed in early Vedic times, but are rather due to a change of attitude towards this god. His loss of importance on the one hand, due to which, at a perhaps more superficial level, he can safely be made the object of ridicule. And, on the other hand, the shift of his functions from warrior-god to rain-god: in this connection, at a higher level, his propensities to sexual adventures are but an extension of his raining functions, and cannot therefore come under any moral judgment. Yet the tension between these two levels is all too evident, especially in the first R version. It appears that the Brahmins especially were hostile towards Indra, and resented his behaviour towards Ahalyā as if it were a human

[66] See BHATTACHARJI (1970:256; 269). BROCKINGTON (2001:81), according to his stages-of-composition theory, maintains that the shift from war-god to rain-god can be observed within the Epics themselves.

[67] And, subsequently, even more prominently, in the Purāṇas. See SÖHNEN-THIEME (1996).

king's misbehaviour towards a Brahmin woman. Certainly, it appears that they cited the story as an example of what *kṣatriya*s should not do.

Conclusions

It now remains to be seen why the R attaches so much importance to the story of Indra and Ahalyā as to relate it twice extensively, whereas the MBh contains only four brief allusions to it. Arguments *ex nihilo* are usually rather hazardous, it is therefore difficult to ascertain why the MBh, which narrates so many other tales, does not contain a complete version of the story of Indra and Ahalyā. Moreover, in the MBh, the allusions are always so to say 'twice- (if not thrice-) removed', i.e., always in a context where somebody tells someone else how once upon a time in the distant past somebody mentioned to someone else Indra's seduction of Ahalyā, as an event which itself had taken place in an even more distant past![68] This procedure cannot fail to produce the impression of a certain distance, if not of a certain lack of relevance for the central events of the Epic.

In the R, on the other hand, (although it is true that the story of Indra and Ahalyā is also in both cases narrated to Rāma by Viśvāmitra and Agastya), it is directly attached to the main events of the story. In the second version, it is narrated in connection with the history of the *rākṣasa*s, especially that of Rāvaṇa and his son Indrajit, who have just been slain in the war by Rāma and his brother. And in the first version, Rāma himself intervenes in the *dénouement* of the story by delivering Ahalyā from the curse, as he delivers so many people from curses in his

[68] Thus (not even taking into account the fact that the whole MBh is retold by the *sūta* to the *ṛṣi*s of the Naimiṣa forest as he heard it from Vaiśaṃpāyana): in 5.12.6, Vaiśaṃpāyana tells king Janamejaya how king Śalya told Yudhiṣṭhira how Nahuṣa reminded the gods of Indra's seduction of Ahalyā; in 12.329.14, Vaiśaṃpāyana tells Janamejaya how Kṛṣṇa, speaking to Arjuna, alluded to the story of Indra's adventure with Ahalyā; in 13.41, Vaiśaṃpāyana relates to Janamejaya how Bhīṣma told Yudhiṣṭhira the story of how Vipula mentioned to Indra his own adventure with Ahalyā; in 13.138.6, Vaiśaṃpāyana explains to Janamejaya how Bhīṣma told Yudhiṣṭhira how Vāyu told Arjuna Kārtavīrya how Indra was cursed by Gautama.

career. Thus he acts as the perfect king who protects the Brahmins, unlike Indra the king of the gods who 'violates' the Brahmin Ahalyā, thereby threatening the social world-order.[69] Moreover, both versions of this mythical motif are placed at crucial junctures of the plot: in the first book, just before Rāma's marriage to Sītā, and in the seventh book, just before he repudiates her. Thus the story of Indra and Ahalyā serves as a sort of multiform or echo of one of the most striking events of the R, namely Sītā's repudiation, a function which it cannot serve in the MBh.

[69] Yet at the same time, if we follow DUBUISSON (1986), Rāma would be the inheritor of Indra's sins in the R. His murder of the *brahmarākṣasa* Rāvaṇa reduplicates Indra's murder of the Brahmin Triśiras. The treacherous fashion in which he slays Vālin, Sugrīva's brother, reduplicates Indra's murder of Vṛtra. And finally, his own repudiation of Sītā is a variant of Indra's sin against the third function, as indeed it reduplicates Gautama's repudiation of Ahalyā. However, this theory is not without flaws. As Alf Hiltebeitel (personal communication) points out: the order of Rāma's sins does not follow the usual order: 1st function, 2nd function, 3rd function. Even more importantly, Rāma is nowhere blamed for killing Rāvaṇa and does not appear to be overcome by *brahmahatyā* for that matter. Nor is it ever stated that his *aśvamedha* is performed to expiate this 'sin'.

4. The Theft of the Soma

Introduction

In this chapter, my aim is to deal with the myth of the theft[2] of the *soma*, under which denomination I refer to the Vedic allusions to the theft of the *soma* by the eagle,[3] and to the theft of the *amṛta* by Garuḍa in the MBh and elsewhere.[4] This particular mythical motif has attracted the attention of scholars since the inception of indological studies. Writing a century ago, BLOOMFIELD (1894-96:3), referring, it is true, more particularly to the studies of the Ṛgvedic allusions to this myth, makes the following remark: "My own treatment of the myth [is] undertaken somewhat shamefacedly after so many painstaking efforts on the part of my predecessors". Writing a century after him, with all the additional baggage of scholarly research devoted to this myth since then, how shall we justify our present endeavour? A general answer might be that we no longer share some of the prejudices evidenced by early Indologists, and also that looking at a myth from a

---

[1] This chapter is a revised version of FELLER JATAVALLABHULA 1999b.

[2] 'Theft' is not actually the accurate word to use, for the eagle's act is not a sneaky robbery committed in the dark, but a heroic deed. The word 'rape', which is sometimes used in connection with this myth, which corresponds to French 'rapt' and German 'Raub' would be more appropriate, but has become obsolete in the sense of 'carrying away forcefully'; but interestingly a similar connotation has survived in the technical usage of 'raptor' for 'bird of prey'. I thank Mrs Mary Brockington for this observation.

[3] We shall use the word 'eagle' throughout, more for the sake of convenience than to refer to a specific zoological species. In the ṚV, the bird who brings the *soma* is sometimes called *śyena*, which designates a bird of prey (hawk, falcon or eagle). Some authors have tried to determine more precisely the zoological species to which the *śyena* belongs: according to SCHNEIDER (1971:32-37), who reaches this conclusion on the basis of the behaviour of the bird as it is described in the ṚV, it is a falcon; according to STAAL (1983:vol.1, 88-90), who bases himself on the outlines of the *śyena*-shaped fire-altar, it is a species of vulture, probably Gyps himalayensis. Garuḍa, in the later literature, is an entirely supernatural bird.

[4] The myth of the theft of the nectar of immortality by an eagle is also wide-spread in other Indo-European cultures. See DUMEZIL (1924); KNIPE (1966-67) and OBERLIES (1998:244, note 471), with references to further literature.

particular perspective amounts to a new reading of this myth. More particularly, we shall here deal with the myth with a special concentration on its epic occurrences (and again with more emphasis on the MBh) and compare them with the earlier occurrences in the ṚV and later Vedic literature, with the aim of understanding the relation that the chosen narrative from the Epics has with the earlier Vedic versions of this particular myth.

In the first part of this chapter, I will pass in chronological review all the accounts of this myth as they appear in the ṚV, later Vedic literature, Suparṇākhyāna, R and MBh, in order to get a clear picture of the different versions of the myth. Whenever it is possible, I will try to see what function the narration of this particular myth serves in the immediate as well as in the larger context of a given text. The second part, entitled 'Power-relations', will deal with the theme of power-struggle, which is, in my view, particularly prominent in all versions of this myth. This struggle for supremacy appears:

1) at the historical-religious level, reflecting the changing fortunes of various divinities: here the power seems to be mainly related to the possession or non-possession of the *soma-amṛta*, but ultimately transcends it;
2) at the social level, reflecting the domination of the Brahmins;
3) at the symbolical level. This last point will be dealt with in the third part of this chapter, called 'The protagonists of the story'. There we shall examine the symbolism attached to the main protagonists of the myth, the *soma*, the snakes and the eagle, hoping that this will throw some light on the nature of this particular mythological narrative.

By giving the myth this particular interpretation, within these paradigms, I do not pretend (far from it!) to exhaust all that can be said about it, but I do think that it will enhance our understanding of the relationship between the MBh narrative and the other earlier versions of the myth, as well as of its function in the MBh.

The history of the mythical motif

The Ṛgveda

We find the first occurrence of the myth of the theft of the *soma* by the eagle in the ṚV. This myth appears mainly in hymns 4.26-27, which form a whole, according to the tradition. They belong to a series of Indra-hymns (4.16-32) which are attributed to the seer Vāmadeva. We also find a number of other allusions to this mythical exploit scattered in other books of the ṚV: 1.80.2; 1.93.6; 3.43.7; 4.18.13; 6.20.6; 8.82.9; 8.100.8; 9.48.3-4; 9.68.6; 9.77.2; 9.89.2; 10.11.4; 10.144.3-5. On the basis of the unambiguous elements of these allusions, we can summarize the Ṛgvedic account as follows: the bird (*ví, śakuná*) or eagle (*suparṇá, śyená*) steals the *soma* from afar, from the mountain or from heaven.[5] On whose instigation he acts is not mentioned. ṚV 3.43.7, which is addressed to Indra, simply states that the eagle brought the *soma* for "you who desired it": *te [...] uśaté*. He brings back the *soma*, holding it in his claw (literally "foot"): *padā́* (8.82.9; 10.144.5). On the way, an archer named Kṛśānu (4.27.3; 9.77.2), usually interpreted (according to the later testimonies) as a *gandharva*,

[5] From the mountain: *pári [...] ádreḥ* (1.93.6); from there (i.e. the other world): *átaḥ* (4.26.5; 9.48.3); from afar: *parāvátaḥ* (4.26.6; 9.68.6; 10.144.4), a term which can also denote the underworld (see KUIPER (1971:93-94)), or more precisely the realm of the dead, which is distinct from heaven (see BODEWITZ 2000); from the highest heaven: *divó amúṣmād úttarād* (4.26.6); from the vast surface of the sky: *bṛható ádhi ṣṇóḥ* (4.27.4); from the sky or heaven: *dívam* (8.100.8), *diváḥ* (9.48.3). As KNIPE (1966-67:357) notes, mountain and heaven do not have to stand in contradiction to each other: "growth on a mountain by no means precludes celestial identification with poetic mountains. 'The oldest heaven is the mountain-top.'" On the other hand, the term *parāvátaḥ* seems to stand in contradiction to heaven. As BODEWITZ (2000:106) remarks: "Agni and Soma are fetched from heaven and sometimes nether world and highest heaven alternate, a problem which is difficult to solve."

the guardian of the *soma*,[6] shoots an arrow at him. One of the eagle's feathers, shot off by the arrow, falls in mid-air (4.27.4). The eagle gives the *soma* to Indra (3.43.7; 4.18.13; 6.20.6; 8.82.9; 8.100.8, 10.144.5). Thanks to the possession of the *soma*, Indra gets a standing among the gods (4.18.13),[7] and, in the intoxication of the *soma*, he is able to perform several of his well-known exploits, notably slaying Vṛtra.[8] Alternatively, the eagle is said to give the *soma* to Manu or mankind, so that men can perform sacrifices with it (1.93.6; 4.26.4; 4.26.7; 9.48.4; 10.11.4).[9] But in this case too, its ultimate recipients include Indra (as well as other gods, of course), the receiver of the oblations and the *soma*-drinker *par excellence*.[10] One more theme which is implied in this mythical account, is that the *soma* was originally in the possession of Indra's enemies, since it is protected by an archer, and either the eagle or the *soma* are kept guarded in a hundred metal forts to prevent the theft: *śatáṃ mā púra ā́yasīr arakṣan*: "a hundred metal forts guarded me" (4.27.1);[11] perhaps these

---

[6] Sāyaṇa, *ad* 4.27.3, glosses the name Kṛśānu as *etannāmakaḥ somapālakaḥ*, quoting Aitareyabrāhmaṇa 3.26.

[7] This interpretation holds only if we accept that Indra is speaking here. According to Sāyaṇa, it is the author of the hymn who is speaking.

[8] Apart from the slaying of Vṛtra (1.80.2), the other exploits of Indra which are mentioned in direct connection with the eagle bringing him the *soma* are: shattering the 99 forts of Śambara (4.26.3), uncovering the cow-pens (3.43.7) and shaking / dispersing the tribes of men (3.43.7).

[9] SCHNEIDER's (1971) main thesis is that the falcon not only gave the *soma* to Manu, but that the entire scenario of the theft was organized by Manu himself. But this hypothesis lacks all textual support.

[10] Also, in the intoxication of the *soma*, the seers are able to compose hymns in praise of the gods: again the gods ultimately benefit from it.

[11] In 8.100.8, there is only one metal fort: *ā́yasīm [...] púram*. Who exactly is guarded or imprisoned is far from clear. To quote a few interpretations: according to Sāyaṇa, in his commentary *ad* 4.21.1, it is the *ṛṣi* Vāmadeva, the composer of the hymn; acc. to BLOOMFIELD (1894-96:13-18), it is Agni as the lightning; acc. to PISCHEL (1889:215) and SIEG (1902/1991a:181; 1926/1991b:350), it is Indra; acc. to GELDNER (1951:I,455), CHARPENTIER (1920:139), DONIGER O'FLAHERTY (1981:129), it is the eagle; acc. to HILLEBRANDT (1927-1929/1980:192-3), SCHNEIDER (1971:2), GONDA (1975:120), MYLIUS (2002/1978:16) it is the *soma*; DONIGER O'FLAHERTY also gives the *soma* as an alternative interpretation (1981:130, note 11). In the Epics it is without possible doubt

enemies are the older gods or Asuras, who are afraid that Indra, once in the possession of the *soma*, will usurp their position of supremacy, which is indeed what seems to happen (OBERLIES 1998:246-7).

However, as KNIPE (1966-67:332) already remarked, hymns 4.26-27 present considerable difficulties of interpretation, so that many controversies arose around them. These difficulties are mainly due to:
– the extreme allusiveness of the narration;
– the dialogical form of these hymns: hence, already Sāyaṇa sometimes offers variant interpretations concerning the identity of the speakers;[12]
– (due to the previous point) the use of personal pronouns (he, I, it, etc.) without certainty as to who or what is meant;
– the identity of certain characters remains obscure: we find twice, in 4.26.7 and 4.27.2, the expression: *púraṃdhir ajahād árātīr*: "Puraṃdhi left the Arātis behind", or, "the bountiful one left the non-liberal ones behind". Who exactly is meant by these terms is not known, and this point has given rise to long debates.[13] Here, my purpose is not to deal with all these controversial matters extensively, but I hope that the points established above will suffice to go about the examination of this myth in the later literature.

the *soma* which is guarded in a place made out of metal: *ayojālāni* (metal net-works) in R 3.33.34 and *cakraṃ [...] ayasmayam* (metal wheel) in MBh 1.29.2.
Note that the term *ayas*- translated as "iron, metal" in MW, probably did not designate iron in the ṚV, but another type of metal. As WITZEL (1989:247) notes: "[The AV and YV] are the first (texts) which mention iron at all: AV 11.3.7, 9.5.4 first speaks of the "black metal"."

[12] For instance, about the speaker of 4.26.1-3, he presents an alternative between Indra and Vāmadeva: *vāmadeva indro vā*.

[13] On this point, see BLOOMFIELD (1894-96:19-20), PISCHEL (1889:202-216), SIEG (1926/1991b:351), CHARPENTIER (1920:146), GELDNER (1951:455), SCHNEIDER (1971:7-10; 37-60).

The later Veda

We find the myth of the *soma*-theft in the following texts of the later Veda, mostly in texts belonging to the black and white Yajur Veda:[14] TS 3.5.7; 6.1.6; MS 3.7.3; 4.1.1; KS 23.10; 34.3; ŚB 1.7.1.1; 3.2.4.1-7; 11.7.2.8; AB 3.25-26; TMB 8.4.1; TB 1.1.3.10; 3.2.1.1-2. These different versions present certain variations. Some of these passages briefly state that the *soma* is in the third heaven. The Gāyatrī-meter (sometimes assuming the form of a *śyena* or bird) fetches it. On the way back, one of the *soma*'s leaves (*parṇa*) is cut off, and it becomes a *parṇa*-tree. That is why, if a person makes the oblation-spoon (*juhū*) out of *parṇa*-wood, then his oblations become similar to *soma* (TS 3.5.7); or, if his *saṃbhāra* consists of *parṇa*-wood, then he obtains a draught of *soma* (TB 1.1.3.10); or, whoever drives the calves away with a *parṇa*-branch obtains *soma* (MS 4.1.1); alternatively, if the sacrificial post (*yūpa*) is made out of *palāśa*- (= *parṇa*) wood, a *paśubandha* sacrifice performed without *soma* becomes equivalent with one performed with *soma* (ŚB 11.7.2.8).

Other versions (TS 6.1.6; MS 3.7.3; KS 23.10; ŚB 3.2.4.1-7; AB 3.25-26; TMB 8.4.1) present a more developed and complete form of the story, which can be summarized as follows: Kadrū (the Earth) and Suparṇī (Speech; sometimes the Sky) hold a bet, whose object is either unknown or very unclear, which Suparṇī loses. Kadrū tells her to get for her the *soma*, which is kept in the third heaven, to pay for her freedom. Suparṇī sends one after the other her three children, the meters Jagatī, Triṣṭubh and Gāyatrī. (Alternatively, the gods and *ṛṣis* request the meters to get the *soma* which is in heaven: ŚB 3.2.4.1-7; AB 3.25-26; TMB 8.4.1). Only the Gāyatrī, although she is the smallest meter, manages to bring back the *soma*, holding two pressings in her 'feet' and one in her beak. Some of these versions have one common point

[14] For a detailed treatment of the myth in the late Veda, see CHARPENTIER (1920:chapt. III).

with the Ṛgvedic account, namely that a *soma*-guardian (a *gandharva* named Viśvāvasu or Kṛśānu) cuts off either a *soma*-leaf, or a feather (or claw) of the Gāyatrī, as she flies away with the *soma*.[15] This leaf / feather / claw undergoes certain transformations when it falls down. Alternatively, in an interesting reversal, the *soma* is stolen from the Gāyatrī by a *gandharva* who is not the *soma*'s legitimate guardian. The gods, knowing that *gandharva*s are fond of women, send Vāc (Speech), who is a woman, in exchange for the *soma*. The *gandharva*s agree to this exchange, but Vāc does not want to remain with them. The gods and *gandharva*s vie with each other for her: exchanging their respective roles, the *gandharva*s chant the Vedas and the gods sing (sometimes also dance and play the *vīṇā*) to charm her. Vāc is pleased with the gods' singing and goes back to them: that is why women are fond of men who sing and dance. (Cf. TS 6.1.6; MS 3.7.3; ŚB 3.2.4.1-7).

The late Vedic accounts of the myth differ in several ways from the Ṛgvedic accounts:

1) the personages of Kadrū, Suparṇī and Suparṇī's children, the meters, appear for the first time in the story.

2) the eagle is actually the meter Gāyatrī, a trait which does not appear in the ṚV, though Sāyaṇa, obviously inspired by the late Vedic versions of the myth, sometimes interprets *śyena* as *chandorūpaḥ suparṇaḥ* (in his commentary *ad* ṚV 3.44.7), or *pakṣyākārā gāyatrī* (*ad* 1.93.6; also 1.80.2) or *pakṣirūpadhāraṇī gāyatrī* (*ad* 8.82.9).

3) the transformations of the fallen *soma*-leaf, or Gāyatrī's feather or claw. This leaf, feather or claw, as it falls onto the earth, changes into various plants used as *soma*-substitutes in sacrifices: the *palāśa*- or *parṇa*-tree (Butea frondosa) (TS 3.5.7; MS 4.1.1; TB 1.1.3.10; 3.2.1.1-2; ŚB 1.7.1.1; 11.7.2.8); or the *pūtīka* plant (Basella cordifolia) (KS 34.3). According to TMB 8.4.1, the filaments of the

[15] One version (ŚB 1.7.1.1) offers an alternative between the bird's *parṇa* and the *soma*'s *parṇa* (with pun on *parṇa* as leaf or feather).

soma became the *pūtīka*s, its flowers the *arjuna*s, and what 'shook' or 'puffed out' (*prāprothat*) became the *praprotha*s, which are also *soma*-substitutes. According to AB 3.26, the Gāyatrī's claw became the porcupine, and out of the arrow discharged by Kṛśānu came varieties of snakes. On the whole, these texts provide etiologic explanations for the use of *soma*-substitutes: either because by performing the sacrifice with certain implements made out of *parṇa*-wood, one obtains *soma*, and a sacrifice peformed without *soma* is made equivalent to a sacrifice performed with *soma*. Or, as KS 34.3 states more straightforwardly, if one does not have *soma* to offer as an oblation, one can use the *pūtīka* (which grew out of the Gāyatrī's claw), and if that is not available, one can also take *ārjuna*s. This might indicate that *soma* was no longer available easily, and that some mythical validation for the use of surrogates had to be provided.

We see that the late Veda is mainly concerned with ritual interpretations. The *soma* is no longer merely obtained by a heroic deed, it is through the power of the word (*vāc*) and of the meters that it is brought down onto the earth. This is in keeping with the ideology of the Brāhmaṇas which stress the power of the *mantra*s in the sacrificial ritual. OBERLIES (1998:445) holds that, especially in the ŚB, Kadrū and Suparṇī's betting contest is comparable to a *brahmodya*, a verbal contest in which visionary insight plays a great role. Following the lead of Heesterman's writings, he concludes that this way of winning the *soma*, involving a verbal contest, is a "ritualized, and thus non-dangerous form of the violent *soma*-theft" (1998:447). Why a meter should assume the role of the *soma*-bringing eagle is at first puzzling. But we can note that already in the ṚV we find associations between the bird on the one hand and speech, meters and poetic inspiration on the other. In ṚV 10.177, the 'Hymn to the Bird' (called, it is true, *pataṅgá*, and not *śyená*, *ví*, or *suparṇá*, like the *soma*-bringing eagle), the 'bird' symbolizes poetic inspiration or 'visionary insight' (see GONDA 1963:31-32; 1975:66). What is more, in ṚV 5.44.11 we find the expression *śyená āsām áditiḥ*. According to GELDNER (1951:II, 49), *āsām* refers to the hymns or verses, and he makes the following remark: "Aditi ist die Göttermutter und Urmutter der Welt. Der Falke hat zuerst den Soma auf die Erde gebracht, der Soma regt die Lieder an. So kann der Falke die Aditi der Lieder heissen." As a further step, one might consider that through the hymns recited at sacrificial performances, one obtains a long life of a 'hundred autumns', a favour frequently requested from the gods, if not a type of immortality (also bestowed by *soma*), as a consequence of which the *soma*-bringing eagle was conceptualized as a personified meter.

The Gāyatrī is here given special prominence: she alone, though she is the shortest meter, is capable of bringing the *soma*, that is, the goods for the sacrifice. As BLOOMFIELD (1894-96) was the first to show, the *gāyatrī* meter is closely associated with the divinity Agni[16] (the *jagatī* being connected with the Ṛbhus and the *triṣṭubh* with Indra).[17] BLOOMFIELD contends that the *śyena* in the Ṛgvedic myth is the lightning (i.e. the atmospheric form of Agni) which brings down the *soma* from the clouds, which, according to him, explains why the Gāyatrī, "the mystic sacerdotal name of Agni",[18] takes the form of an eagle in the late Vedic versions of the myth. Though I cannot wholeheartedly accept this very one-sided interpretation, for the eagle also has other connotations than that of the lightning or fire,[19] it remains indisputable that the eagle is closely associated with the fire, being compared, if not assimilated with it in his deeds and

[16] See also VON SIMSON (1989-90:357) and SMITH (1994:296).

[17] BLOOMFIELD (1894-96:5).

[18] BLOOMFIELD (1894-96:3).

[19] Besides, as KNIPE (1966-67:334) rightly remarks: "And it occurs to us [...] that 'lightning' presents a further problem undisclosed by Bloomfield, that of 'one way' versus the 'round trip': lightning does not go up. In this poetic form Ṛgveda IV.26 and 27 *imply* that the eagle flies up to steal, although admittedly all of the verbs describe *śyená* as descending, bearing *from* the heavens."

functions.[20] If we accept this close association of the eagle with the fire, and the connection between the fire and the Gāyatrī meter, it becomes easier to understand why, in the late Vedic versions of this myth, the eagle is replaced by the Gāyatrī.

The Suparṇākhyāna

We find the same mythical theme once again in the Suparṇākhyāna,[21] a poem of 165 stanzas composed in the so-called 'pseudo-vedic' style,[22] whose date is quite uncertain.[23] Unfortunately, the text is in a bad state of preservation, and were it not for the more complete account of the MBh, it would even be incomprehensible at places. Moreover, certain late additions to it seem to derive from the MBh itself, so that it is at times difficult to ascertain which text borrowed from which.[24] In the Suparṇākhyāna, the story has undergone further changes and closely resembles the account of the MBh. The snakes, as the sons of Kadrū, appear for the first time in connection with this story as the ones who want the *soma*. But Viṣṇu does not play any role in it, which seems to indicate the poem's relative priority. Charpentier considers the Sup to be the main source for the MBh as well as R accounts of the *soma*-theft.

The Rāmāyaṇa

In R 3.33.27-35, the story of the theft of the *soma* is told in the following circumstances: Rāvaṇa flies from Laṅkā to the mainland to find Mārīca who is practising *tapas* in the Daṇḍakāraṇya. When he

[20] See below, the section entitled 'The snakes and the eagle'.

[21] For a detailed study of this poem, see CHARPENTIER (1920). The Suparṇākhyāna is the text on which OLDENBERG (1883) mainly based his *ākhyāna*-theory.

[22] RENOU (1945:124, under Suparnādhyāya) and GONDA (1975:47).

[23] According to CHARPENTIER (1920:199 & 395-396) it dates back to the Brāhmaṇas and early Upaniṣads, an idea which GONDA (1975:47) does not share: according to him, the poem is probably later.

[24] MEHTA (1971:58).

reaches the mainland, he sees on the shore of the ocean the huge banyan-tree whose branch Garuḍa broke. Then there follows a very short evocation of some points of Garuḍa's *soma*-stealing exploit, which roughly correspond to those in the MBh though the order of the episodes is changed (it corresponds more closely to the order in the Sup): Garuḍa breaks the branch, flies away with it, eats the tortoise and elephant while flying, kills the Niṣādas with the branch and finally releases the ascetics who are still on the branch. Then he flies up to heaven and steals the *soma*. The whole account is rather disconnected and even disjointed:[25] eating an elephant and tortoise while flying and carrying a huge branch is no mean feat, even for Garuḍa, and killing the Niṣādas with the branch when the ascetics, for whose welfare Garuḍa is so concerned, are still clinging to it, seems downright absurd.[26] The real object of this description is the banyan-tree (which is even given a personal name here: Subhadra (3.33.35)), and in connection with it the exploit of Garuḍa (especially the episodes which are directly related to the tree) is mentioned in passing. Garuḍa's motivations (why he steals the *soma* and for whom) are passed over in silence. The snakes are not mentioned, and the only explanation which is given for Garuḍa's deed is that he felt so elated because he released the ascetics that he decided to get the *soma* (3.33.33-34). Of course, we can assume that the story

25 "[A]n obviously inserted passage of the second stage", according to BROCKINGTON (1998:445).

26 At least, this sequence of events seems to be implied in verses 3.33.31-32:

teṣāṃ dayārthaṃ garuḍas tāṃ śākhāṃ śatayojanām /
jagāmādāya vegena tau cobhau gajakacchapau //
ekapādena dharmātmā bhakṣayitvā tadāmiṣam /
niṣādaviṣayaṃ hatvā śākhayā patagottamaḥ /
praharṣam atulaṃ lebhe mokṣayitvā mahāmunīn //

Out of pity for these [ascetics], Garuḍa quickly flew away, taking along that branch which was a thousand *yojana*s long, and these two, the elephant and the tortoise. Then the dharmic one, that best of birds, after eating the flesh [of the elephant and tortoise] with one claw, and after smiting the country of the Niṣādas with the branch, obtained an incomparable joy, after releasing the great *muni*s.

was well-known and that therefore the poet did not feel obliged to tell it in full detail.

On the whole, it is at first sight difficult to discern in what way this account of the myth is relevant in the immediate as well as larger context of the R.[27] Why should the description of the banyan-tree whose branch was broken by Garuḍa occur in this passage, which describes Rāvaṇa's journey from Laṅkā to the mainland? The story of the *soma*-theft as it is told in the Kathāsaritsāgara (2.12.135-144) may throw some light on this point. This passage narrates the origin of Laṅkā: a character of the story, named Lohajaṅgha, is unwittingly carried by a Garuḍa bird to the other side of the ocean, in the vicinity of Laṅkā, and received hospitably by king Vibhīṣaṇa.[28] Lohajaṅgha notices that the earth of Laṅkā is made of wood: *kāṣṭhamayī* (2.12.136), and asks Vibhīṣaṇa the reason for this phenomenon. Vibhīṣaṇa explains it as follows: Garuḍa released the broken branch (here it is the branch of a *kalpavṛkṣa*, a wishing-tree) in a deserted place, and subsequently Laṅkā was built on the top of this branch. This is why the earth of Laṅkā is made of wood. The Kathāsaritsāgara, though much younger than the R, is based on the older Bṛhatkathā, and

27 We may note here that Garuḍa plays a rather negligible role in the R. He appears as Viṣṇu's vehicle, and once, in his quality of arch-enemy of snakes and master of the antidote for venom, saves Rāma and Lakṣmaṇa from Indrajit's serpent-arrows (6.40.33-59). In a general way, one might conjecture that his role is to some extent usurped by Hanumān in the R. Hanumān is not only explicitly likened to Garuḍa (4.65.4; 6.61.62), but he sometimes carries Rāma (Viṣṇu's *avatāra*) during the war, like Garuḍa carries Viṣṇu. His well-known childhood exploit (told in 7.35) when he jumps up to the sun in an attempt to eat it, presents many structural similarities to Garuḍa's flying up to the sky to steal *soma* (their hunger is common, so too is Indra hitting them with his *vajra*). Even more similar is Hanumān's exploit during the war: he brings back the mountain on which grows the reviving herb (6.61), which is of course in many ways comparable to *amṛta*: the mountain is said to stand near the place where the churning of the ocean took place. Moreover, the verbs used to describe the act of tearing out the mountain: *unmamātha* (6.61.61) and *samutpāṭya* (6.61.62) are commonly used to designate the plucking of the *soma*.

28 It is interesting to note that the Kathāsaritsāgara, which is a much later text than the R (composed around 1070 C.E.), also places this story in later mythical-historical times. Thus here the king of Laṅkā is no longer Rāvaṇa (who is killed by Rāma in the R), but his virtuous younger brother Vibhīṣaṇa, who was anointed king by Rāma himself, after Rāvaṇa's death.

we cannot rule out that a form of the story existed even at the time of the R, in which the broken branch was somehow connected with the island of Laṅkā.[29] At least, this might explain why the first thing Rāvaṇa sees on the shore of the mainland is the tree: for Rāvaṇa here is so to say taking the same trip as Garuḍa in the Kathāsaritsāgara, but in the reverse direction.

The Mahābhārata

Let us now turn to the MBh's version of the *soma*-theft. We find it in the Ādiparvan (1.14-30), in the Āstīka-sub-parvan.[30] This *parvan* contains an enormous amount of material concerning snakes,[31] including the mythical account which concerns us here. In 1.11, the *sūta* mentions Janamejaya's snake-sacrifice to Śaunaka, who requests him to tell the whole story in detail. Accordingly, the *sūta* starts his narration: Vinatā and Kadrū are two sisters, the daughters of the Prajāpati Dakṣa and the wives of Kaśyapa. Kaśyapa offers a boon to each one of his wives, and Kadrū chooses to become the mother of one thousand *nāgas* (snakes) and Vinatā the mother of two sons who will surpass in might those of Kadrū. In time, both sisters lay eggs, but Kadrū's eggs hatch first, and Vinatā becomes envious and impatient. She breaks one of her own eggs. Thus her elder son, Aruṇa, is born, but only half-formed. Angry, he curses his mother to become the slave of her rival Kadrū, but also foretells that she will be delivered from the curse by her second son, if she patiently waits for his birth and does not maim him too. Then he flies up to the sky where he is now seen as

[29] MEHTA (1971:61-62) also thinks that the R used partly different sources than the MBh as far as this account is concerned.

[30] In the Southern recension, the story of the *soma*-theft also appears in the Anuśāsanaparvan, after *adhyāya* 8. It can be found in appendix IA of the Critical Edition. The story is narrated by Bhīṣma to Yudhiṣṭhira, in a fairly elaborate form (461 lines), which roughly corresponds to the version found in the Ādiparvan. For the differences between the two versions, see MEHTA (1971:62-64).

[31] As MINKOWSKI (1989:416) says: "the Mahābhārata becomes the most complete compendium of Indian snake-lore that we have in Sanskrit literature."

the red dawn.[32] Some time later, Kadrū and Vinatā see the divine steed Uccaiḥśravas, who was born out of the churning of the ocean, just like the *amṛta*. (This furnishes a pretext to tell the story of the churning of the ocean, in 1.15-17). Then Vinatā becomes the slave of Kadrū, due to a bet concerning the colour of Uccaiḥśravas' tail, which Kadrū wins through cheating: Kadrū claims that his tail is black, whereas Vinatā rightly maintains that it is white. In order to win the bet, Kadrū forces her sons to become black hairs and hang on to the horse's tail. When they first refuse to comply with her wish, she curses them to be burnt at Janamejaya's snake-sacrifice.

When he is born, Garuḍa learns of this state of affairs and asks the snakes what he can do to release his mother and himself from slavery. They tell him to get for them the *amṛta* which is kept in the heavens. Garuḍa agrees to this, but before flying up, he stills his hunger by eating the Niṣādas, a tribe of fishermen, and a giant elephant and tortoise. To eat these two, he tries to land on the branch of a huge tree. But the branch breaks under his weight. Seeing some tiny ascetics, the Vālakhilyas, clinging to the branch, Garuḍa, afraid of killing them, flies around with it, till his father helps him to release them. Then, after getting rid of the branch and eating the two huge creatures, Garuḍa flies up to heaven. Ominous portents announce his arrival to the gods, who get ready for battle. But Garuḍa easily defeats them, takes the *amṛta* from the rotating wheel where it is guarded by two poisonous snakes, and flies back with it. On the way, he meets Viṣṇu, who is pleased with Garuḍa's selflessness (he did not even taste the *amṛta*!) and grants him immortality and the right to be on his banner. When Garuḍa in turn offers him a boon, Viṣṇu requests the bird to be his

---

[32] The motif that Aruṇa subsequently becomes the charioteer of the sun-god is only found in a few manuscripts of the MBh, in verses inserted after 1.14.21, and in the Sup (1.5).

vehicle.[33] Meanwhile Indra arrives on the scene, and hurls his *vajra* at Garuḍa, who is not in the least hurt, but sheds a single token feather to acknowledge Indra's deed. Then the two strike up a friendship and Garuḍa describes to the awed Indra his supernatural strength. Indra gives Garuḍa the boon to have the snakes for his food, and then requests him not to give the *amṛta* to the snakes, who would make a bad use of it. Garuḍa explains to him why he has to do it, but adds that Indra can come and pick up the *amṛta* wherever he, Garuḍa, would put it down. So the bird flies back to the snakes, shows them the *amṛta* and makes them formally declare his and his mother's freedom. Then he advises them to go and take a bath before partaking of the divine drink, in order to purify themselves. The snakes eagerly follow this piece of advice, and in the meantime Indra takes the *amṛta* back to the heavens, before the snakes even get a chance of tasting it.

In the MBh, the myth of the *soma*-theft is a kind of sub-plot of the story of Janamejaya's *sarpa-sattra*. Very generally speaking, it is told to give moral justification to the sacrifice of the snakes, attributed to their mother's curse: because they first refused to become black hairs on the tail of Uccaiḥśravas, to allow her to win her bet with Vinatā, she cursed them to be burnt at Janamejaya's sacrifice (1.18.7-8).[34] On the whole, we may notice that the MBh version of the myth shows a clear effort at bringing together and compiling the previous accounts. The only point left out in the MBh is the identification of the eagle with the meters, which originated in the late Veda and is still kept alive in

[33] Yet RAVEN (1994: I, 21) notes that "[a]part from this tale on how Garuḍa's service to Viṣṇu came about, there are hardly any epic references to him actually carrying that deity, and none in which he appears on his banner. It is especially in the *Purāṇas* that Garuḍa operates in those functions." I have noted at least one instance where Garuḍa carries, not Viṣṇu, but Kṛṣṇa, namely in 13.14.26. In this passage, Garuḍa carries Kṛṣṇa to the Himālaya, where Kṛṣṇa wants to perform *tapas* in order to get sons. (See more about this episode in the next chapter.) And in 2.22.22, Garuḍa comes and sits on the flag mast of Kṛṣṇa's chariot, and then, rather curiously, seems to merge into the flag itself (2.22.23-24).

[34] That the link between the two plots is artificially done and shows signs of 'piecing together' was already noticed by OLDENBERG (1883:83-84).

the Suparṇākhyāna (see 1.1.2; 6.12.4-5; 7.14.4; 14.27.3). The MBh's narration is also very systematic: for the first time, we find the myth told in a detailed, exhaustive and logical way, and the motivations of the characters are made explicit, which is far from being the case in the Suparṇākhyāna (inasmuch as we can judge from the text we have). The MBh adds several episodes to the narrative: the content of Aruṇa's curse to his mother (1.14.16-18),[35] maybe Indra's insult to the Vālakhilyas and their revenge (1.27),[36] the previous history of the giant elephant and tortoise (1.25.10-25), and mainly the churning of the ocean to obtain the *amṛta* (1.15-17). These episodes are added ostensibly with the aim of explaining, legitimizing and even morally justifying certain happenings (as we have already noticed in the case of the linking of this myth to the story of the *sarpa-sattra*): Vinatā deserves her slavery because she crippled her elder son, breaking his egg-shell before he was fully grown; it is possible for Garuḍa to steal the *amṛta* from Indra because of the curse the latter got from the Vālakhilyas, due to his disrespectful behaviour towards them; Garuḍa is justified in eating the elephant and tortoise because they were quarrelsome brothers who fought over their inheritance and cursed each other, etc.

Let us now attempt to understand the purpose for which this particular mythical motif is narrated towards the beginning of the MBh. We may first note that many episodes of the myth prefigure or

[35] In the Suparṇākhyāna, Aruṇa curses his mother, but the content of the curse is not mentioned (1.3.4). According to CHARPENTIER (1920:212) this verse itself might be a later addition.

[36] Kaśyapa offered up a sacrifice in order to obtain a son. All the gods and other divine beings helped him. Kaśyapa requested them to fetch firewood. Indra carried a big load without effort. But the tiny Vālakhilyas barely managed to carry one single leaf, and fell into a cow's hoof-print filled with water. Seeing this, Indra burst out laughing and, puffed up with pride, stepped over them. Enraged, the Vālakhilyas undertook a great sacrifice to produce another Indra, but Kaśyapa soothed them and convinced them to produce an Indra of birds instead. They agreed, adding that this Indra of birds would be Kaśyapa's son (Garuḍa).
This episode appears very briefly at the very beginning of the Suparṇākhyāna (1.2.3-5), but might be a late addition according to CHARPENTIER (1920:210).

announce episodes belonging to the central epic story of the MBh. Thus Vinatā prematurely breaking Aruṇa's egg out of impatience and envy towards her co-wife Kadrū, whose eggs have already hatched, prefigures Gāndhārī aborting her foetus which is taking too long to be born, when she comes to know that Kuntī has already given birth to Yudhiṣṭhira (1.107).[37] More importantly, the rivalry of the mothers is transmitted to their respective sons. The theme of the enmity between brothers (not 'real' brothers, but half-brothers or cousins) appears both between the snakes and Garuḍa on the one hand, and the Kauravas and the Pāṇḍavas on the other. In both instances we have one set of numerous and wicked brothers,[38] and one set of virtuous brothers, who are limited in number.[39] The hundred Kauravas are a 'brood' just like

---

[37] In this case there is an inversion: Gāndhārī is the mother of the Kauravas, who correspond to the *nāga*s. Moreover, as KUIPER (1983:32) rightly remarks: "It is further a striking feature of Kadrū (Aditi), that in the Suparṇākhyāna she is said to be one-eyed (*kāṇā*). [...] A parallel in the epic is that not only the father of the hundred Kauravas (who bears the name of a snake-god, Dhṛtarāṣṭra) is blind but also the mother Gāndhārī symbolically blinds herself at her marriage by bandaging her eyes. This deed, hardly motivated at all in the epic (cf. *MhBh.* I. 103. 12f) can only be understood if Gāndhārī is considered equivalent to Kadrū."

[38] Of course, in Indian literature and beliefs in general, the *nāga*s do not always appear as wicked, their nature being at best ambivalent. But in the episode of the *soma*-theft, it is clear that the sympathy of the narrator lies with Garuḍa, unlike for instance in the episode of Mātali and his *nāga* son-in-law (see below) or in the Nāgānanda, a play by Harṣa, where Garuḍa practically plays the role of the villain. In the myth which concerns us here, Brahmā himself does nothing to prevent Kadrū's curse and the destruction of the snakes, because, he says, the *nāga*s are very strong, extremely numerous, poisonous, mordacious and vicious (1.18.9-11 and 1.34.9-10).

[39] For an explanation concerning the way in which the five Pāṇḍavas correspond to the two sons of Vinatā, see KUIPER (1983:34). The same theme of the enmity or at least opposition between two sets of brothers also appears in the story of Sagara's sons (MBh 3.104-106; R 1.37-40): Sagara has 60'000 sons by one wife and one son (Asamañja) by another, who perpetuates the dynasty. In the MBh, these 60'000 sons are described as wicked and torturing the worlds with warfare, for which reason the gods decide to do away with them, stealing Sagara's sacrificial horse for that purpose. The R does not mention why Indra steals the horse, but the Sāgaras, in spite of their efforts, fail to get it back, whereas Aṃśumān (Asamañja's son) manages to do so. The 60'000 sons are reduced to ashes (just like the snakes in the *sattra*) by Kapila Vāsudeva due to their improper behaviour (they have been digging up the whole earth and killing the creatures in their search for the horse.) The Sāgaras' resemblance with snakes is further emphasized by the fact that they mainly roam about underground, digging up the earth: in this they resemble snakes, who are said to live in holes, and are specially connected with the earth.

the snakes, and their manner of birth accounts for, or symbolically represents, their 'reptilian' evil and vicious nature. Even more strikingly, we see that in the end the 'good' brothers eliminate the 'bad' ones: Garuḍa eats the snakes, the Pāṇḍavas kill the Kauravas.[40] Also, the wicked ones are killed in a sacrifice: the *nāga*-race is nearly exterminated at Janamejaya's *sarpa-sattra*, and the Kauravas are killed in the 'sacrifice of war' (*raṇa-yajña*). Furthermore, the enmity between the snakes and Garuḍa is a variation on the theme of the eternal and ever-recurring enmity between another set of half-brothers, namely the Devas and Asuras,[41] who are of course partly incarnated as the Pāṇḍavas and Kauravas. Thus the attempt of the snakes to get supremacy through the possession of the *soma* announces the whole fight, which is central to the Epics, between the powers of 'good' and those of 'evil', or, to use more accurate terminology, those of *dharma* and *adharma*, and the attempt of the Asuras to win supremacy over the gods. On the whole, the Suparṇādhyāya of the MBh directly links the *sarpa-sattra* of Janamejaya (an event which happened within the direct experience of the story teller) with events which took place at the beginning of the world, in the Devayuga (= Kṛtayuga) (1.14.5).[42]

In the R Garuḍa, who is the maternal uncle of the 60'000 Sāgaras, appears to Aṃśumān and instructs him how his fathers' *jalakriyā* should be performed: the water of the Gaṅgā should be brought to wash their ashes and allow them to go to heaven (an operation subsequently performed by Aṃśumān's grand-son, Bhagīratha, in the Gaṅgāvataraṇa story): here Garuḍa appears as the one who presides over death and, more specifically, over the death-rites.

[40] OOSTEN (1985:64 & 71) notes that in many Indo-European myths pertaining to the acquisition of the mead, paternal relatives initially cooperate to obtain it, but then make war, while the mead is subsequently shared among maternal relatives.

[41] As DUMEZIL (1924:48) notes, the Bhāgavatapurāṇa (8.6-11), in its description of the churning of the ocean, explicitly compares the Asuras to snakes, for Viṣṇu reflects that giving the *amṛta* to the Asuras, these naturally cruel beings, would be as foolish as giving it to snakes.

[42] And the *sarpa-sattra* itself is also a Vedic rite, described in the Pañcaviṃśabrāhmaṇa, TMB, and in the *śrautasūtras*. (VOGEL 1926:14; WINTERNITZ 1904/1991b:374; MINKOWSKI 1989:413-416; 1991:386-391). But, as MINKOWSKI (1991:386-387) writes: "this is not a rite that draws snakes into the fire. Rather, it is made up of the ordinary ritual components of *sattras*, i.e. Soma sacrifices."

Those events (Kadrū's curse) even serve as a direct justification for the sacrifice, without there being any sense of oddity or discrepancy evidenced in the telling.

Power-relations

We shall now turn to a theme which appears prominently in the myth of the *soma*-theft, namely the various power-relations, that is, struggles for the power and also shifts in the distribution of the power evidenced in the different versions of this myth. OBERLIES (1998:432-447; 489-493) shows that in Ṛgvedic times the legitimatization of power and kingship (not only in the case of gods, but also in the case of human kings) was vastly derived from the possession of the *soma*. Thus first and foremost, it appears that the possession of the *soma-amṛta* amounts to the possession of power, and inversely, that the lack of *soma* amounts to a lack of power.

In the Ṛgvedic account, the *soma* is stolen *for* Indra, who thereby obtains a position of supremacy among the gods. One of the most striking traits of the epic and Sup versions of this myth, as compared to the Ṛgvedic one, is of course that it is *from* Indra that Garuḍa steals the *soma*. It is no doubt true that even in the MBh and Sup Indra ultimately gets back the *amṛta*, and that Garuḍa sides with the gods; but the structural inversion of Garuḍa's deed is too striking to be explained away easily and has, as is to be expected, provoked a number of different, sometimes radically opposed, interpretations. Some hold, for various reasons, that the Vedic and epic versions do not have much in common, and that the Epic tells a new story, with different protagonists.[43] Others have tried to reconcile both Vedic and epic

[43] See for instance SIEG (1926/1991b:357); DANGE (1969:XXXIX; 151-3); SCHNEIDER (1971:32). KUIPER (1971:88) seems to thinks that the Sup and MBh misinterpreted the myth: "Not until the Suparṇākhyāna and the Mahābhārata was the fundamental character of this myth so much forgotten that the Soma could be said to have been stolen from Indra."

versions and contend that already in the Veda the *soma* is stolen from Indra. This is notably CHARPENTIER's view (1920:141), who further propounds the hypothesis that the eagle later returns the *soma* to Indra. But he himself has to admit that the latter episode is never explicitly mentioned in the ṚV (1920:150).[44] According to MEHTA (1971:42), the ṚV knows two versions of the myth: according to one, the eagle steals the *soma* for Indra, and according to the other, he steals it from him. The crux of the last type of interpretation seems to lie in one single word, namely *índrāvataḥ*, found in ṚV 4.27.4, in the sentence: *īm* (scil. *somam*) *índrāvato [...] śyenó jabhāra*. PISCHEL (PISCHEL & GELDNER 1889:211-212) renders *índrāvataḥ* as "from Indra's heaven", in the sense of an ablative singular. (See also BLOOMFIELD's discussion in 1894-96:21-23). But GELDNER (1951:I,455) translates it as "zu den Indraanhängern" (to the followers of Indra), taking it as an accusative plural, thus obtaining an exactly opposite meaning. The precise signification of this word is in any case quite obscure, as a result of which many emendations have been, not quite successfully, proposed. The meaning "from Indra's heaven" stands of course in stark contradiction with the many other passages which state quite unequivocally that the eagle gives the *soma* to Indra. But it is not ruled out that this interpretation of *índrāvataḥ* might have given rise to the inverted version of the myth in the later epic literature, where the eagle steals the *soma* from Indra's heaven. At least part of the later tradition did interpret *índrāvataḥ* as meaning "from Indra's heaven". Sāyaṇa renders it quite unequivocally as *indro rakṣako yasya tasmāt*, but it is likely that Sāyaṇa knew the MBh version of the myth, and his gloss might be influenced by it.

44 Moreover, he tries to prove that Viṣṇu, in the shape of the *soma*-bringing eagle, already figures in the Ṛgvedic myth (1920: passim), for according to him, the eagle is Viṣṇu himself, a view which GONDA (1954:102) disputes.

VON SIMSON, following his 'mythology of nature' type of interpretation,[45] views the episodes of Indra first receiving and then being robbed of the *soma* as cyclical events, in which Indra, as the alternately waxing and waning moon, alternately attains a position of superiority or inferiority.[46] Whether or not one follows this type of 'astronomical' interpretation, one fact remains indisputable, namely, that Indra's position underwent a sea change between Vedic and epic times. Therefore, in my opinion, this inversion of situation is simply due to the fact that the same mythical motif is used in the Epic, but applied to the new conditions of mythical history and time. In Vedic mythology, Indra was originally an outcast and had no status (see ṚV 4.18.13): obtaining the *soma* allowed him to achieve a position of supremacy among the gods. In the epic mythological situation, on the other hand, Indra's status as the king of the gods and the possessor of the *soma* is well-established. Yet at the same time, his importance has waned and he is no longer considered to be the greatest god. This in turn enables some non-gods, the snakes, to try and get the *soma* from him in order to escape the sacrificial death which awaits them, and probably too, in order to get divine power and attain the status of immortals.[47] At one level, this may be a way of stating, in mythical language, that the snake-worship was getting powerful and threatening the worship of the higher gods. In any case, we see that the essential value of the *amṛta-soma* is that it bestows superior power on its possessor.[48]

---

[45] VON SIMSON (1984) develops a tightly-knit 'astronomical' interpretative paradigm, in the light of which he explains the major characters of the MBh, as well as their deeds. The interpretation of one element makes sense only on the general background of his theory.

[46] VON SIMSON (1989-90:354).

[47] We must admit, however, that the snakes' motivations in asking Garuḍa to get the *soma* for them are nowhere clearly spelt out. It is also not ruled out that, along the lines of the 'labours of Hercules', they are just setting the young bird a task assumed to be impossible. in the hope of keeping him and his mother forever in slavery.

[48] As DUMEZIL says: "le *sôma* est l'arme essentielle des *Dêva*." (1924:34).

In the Ṛgvedic account, the *soma* is the bestower of strength, or brute force to conquer one's enemies and gain the lordship over them: Indra defeats Vṛtra after drinking the *soma*. The epic *amṛta* bestows immortality, which was also understood as a form of power. But in the MBh, the power of devotion (*bhakti*), as a bestower of immortality, is made equivalent, if not superior to that of the *amṛta*, and on the whole, we can notice that the epic *amṛta* does not enjoy as much prestige as the Vedic *soma*. In fact, we see that in the myth which concerns us here, nobody drinks it in the end: the snakes fail to obtain it and Garuḍa specifically refuses to get immortality through the 'lunar' *amṛta* (perhaps as a way of showing his superiority over the other gods, who obtained it through it). He gets it from the 'solar' god Viṣṇu:[49] "May I be free of old age and immortal, even without *amṛta*!": *ajaraś cāmaraś ca syāṃ amṛtena vināpy aham* (1.29.14). If we combine the two boons Garuḍa gets: immortality from Viṣṇu and the right to have snakes for his food from Indra, the end result is that Garuḍa gets immortality through eating snakes, that is, through the very opposite of the life-giving drink, namely, through the deadly poison of snakes.[50] The implication is that for a superior being like Garuḍa, eating poison or *amṛta* is one and the same thing.[51] Likewise, in the R's version of the churning of the ocean (Crit. Ed. 1 App. 8.15; Gorakhpur Ed. 1.45.26), Śiva drinks the Halāhala poison which is then described as *amṛtopama* (similar to *amṛta*).[52]

[49] What I mean by lunar and solar is explained below in the section on 'The Snakes and the Eagle'.

[50] In one variant reading of the churning of the ocean in the R, the Halāhala poison, which emerges out of the ocean before the *amṛta*, is drunk precisely by the snakes (explaining the origin of their venom), and not by Śiva. (See DUMEZIL 1924:49).

[51] This is a very old trait. DANGE (1969:93) quotes AV 5.4.6.3 which states that poison turned into food for Garutmān. Garuḍa is after all the master of the antidote for poison, the *gāruḍī-vidyā* or *sarpa-vidyā* (DANGE 1969:20ff.).

[52] In some versions of the myth, Śiva is offered the poison by Viṣṇu as if it were the choicest produce of the churning. This seems to correspond to the usual procedure in sacrifices. LONG (1976/1982:197-8) notes that Śiva gets the remainder (*ucchiṣṭa*) of the

As far as Indra is concerned, and although he is now the *soma*'s legitimate possessor, he can no longer boast of absolute supremacy. In the Epics, unlike in the Veda, Indra-hood has become a 'post' and is not permanent. This is clearly shown in our story, in the episode where the Vālakhilyas perform a sacrifice to produce another Indra. In the Epics, the king of gods is regularly defeated by other powers.[53] Here Indra is defeated by Garuḍa, the new "Indra of birds": *patatrīṇām indro* (1.27.20), who manages to steal the *soma* from him, against whom his *vajra* is useless, and who, we may add, speaks very condescendingly to him (1.29.18-20; 1.30.12). Moreover, Indra is divested of his ancient serpent-killing prowess, since this becomes Garuḍa's characteristic *par excellence*. Indeed, Indra graciously hands it over to him, by giving Garuḍa the boon of having snakes for his food (1.30.12-13). This does not mean that Indra loses his quality of 'Vṛtrahan', but Vṛtra in the Epics appears in an anthropomorphic form: as an Asura, and also as a Brahmin, giving rise to the problem of *brahmahatyā* for Indra.[54] In the MBh, Garuḍa is in turn defeated (or at least tricked) by a power which figures for the first time in the story of the *soma*-theft, namely Viṣṇu, who appears here as the supreme god. Viṣṇu grants the bird a first boon, and Garuḍa asks to "stand above Viṣṇu": *tava tiṣṭheyam upari* (1.29.13), obviously meaning, to be superior to him. But the god tricks him by making him 'above him' in the sense that Garuḍa will be on his banner. When Garuḍa in turn gives him a boon (which in itself

sacrificial offering, which is "praised as the choicest and most favorable portion (*bhāga*) of the oblations and as that portion which brings immortality (*amṛta*)."

53 He is overcome by *brahmahatyā* after killing Vṛtra and Triśiras; the sage Gautama punishes him for seducing his wife Ahalyā; the sage Agastya easily stays him when he tries to prevent him from giving *soma* to the Aśvins; the 'five Indras' are overcome by Śiva, etc. See also BROCKINGTON (2001:77-78). Often Indra is thus punished for his sins. His offense against the Vālakhilyas (due to which Garuḍa is able to defeat him) would be a sin against the first function (to use Dumézilian terms), that is, against the brahmanical power.

54 BENVENISTE et RENOU (1934:167, note 1). For the list of passages, see Introduction, footnote 13.

reveals that the bird considers himself Viṣṇu's equal),[55] Viṣṇu chooses him as his *vāhana* (1.29.16), a very direct way of making him subordinate to him.[56] In this episode, Viṣṇu, who makes Garuḍa immortal, reveals himself as the real master of immortality, which he can grant at will. Thus the *bhakti* element in turn appears in the myth: immortality is no longer dependent on a particular drink, but can be given by the supreme god to his *bhakta*.

In the Udyogaparvan (5.95-104) we find a tale which presents certain structural similarities to this episode, and which reveals the same hierarchy of the powers of the three protagonists, Viṣṇu, Garuḍa and Indra. The story is as follows: Mātali, Indra's charioteer, is looking for a suitable husband for his daughter. He selects a young *nāga* called Sumukha, but the latter tells him that Garuḍa has designated him as his next victim. In doubt, Mātali takes him along to Indra and Viṣṇu. Viṣṇu suggests to Indra that the solution would be to feed him some

[55] DANGE (1969:126-7).

[56] Here I am dealing with the *vāhana*-hood of Garuḍa only from the point of view of the power-relations it implies. But I do not at all disagree with GONDA's (1965:83) more general contention that "an animal which was, in the Vedic period, closely associated with a definite deity served him, in later times, as a vāhana", and "that these animals which are more or less intimately or regularly connected with gods are, in the Vedic as well as the Hindu period, theriomorphic manifestations of an aspect of the god's essence or nature." (About Garuḍa becoming the vehicle of Viṣṇu, see GONDA 1965:86). It is interesting to note that Viṣṇu also appropriates Śeṣa, the eldest *nāga*, as his resting-place: he notably sleeps on him as Nārāyaṇa between two *kalpas*. Thus these two *vāhanas* of the supreme god symbolize his dominion over the two opposite parts of the cosmos. (See below the section entitled 'The snakes and the eagle'.) On this aspect of Viṣṇu's nature, KUIPER (1983:48) remarks: "So we are driven to the conclusion that at an early date Viṣṇu occupied a more *central* position than either Indra or Varuṇa, who are the protagonists of the opposed groups of Devas and Asuras and thus stand each for one of the moieties only. In contrast with them, Viṣṇu must consequently represent the unity of the two antagonistic parties, upper world and nether world. He stands for, and *is*, each of the two worlds (just as later he is, in a way, the heavenly bird Garuḍa and the serpent of the subterranean waters Śeṣa), but under the aspect of their unity".
We may note that Viṣṇu does not appear in the Anuśāsanaparvan version of the *soma*-theft (appendix IA). There Garuḍa himself is said to be one with Viṣṇu-Kṛṣṇa. Thus, before telling the story to Yudhiṣṭhira, Bhīṣma requests Kṛṣṇa's permission to do so, since, he says, Kṛṣṇa himself is Garuḍa (ll. 11-12). And, at the end of the story (ll. 456-57), Indra is pleased with Garuḍa and predicts that he will be born as Kṛṣṇa, "having divided himself for the protection of *dharma*": *svayaṃ dharmasya rakṣārthaṃ vibhajya*, a formulation which is reminiscent of BhG 4.8.

amṛta. Indra hesitates, remembering the superior power of Garuḍa: *saṃcintya vainateyaparākramam* (5.102.25). Finally, he grants him long age instead, and the *nāga* marries Mātali's daughter. Then the incensed Garuḍa arrives on the scene, having learned what happened. He berates Indra: how dare he take away his appointed food, condemning him to starvation? Then he boasts of his own greatness, enumerating his exploits, notably that he is capable of carrying all the worlds: *aham apy utsahe lokān samastān voḍhum añjasā* (5.103.10), and Indra himself, on the tip of one wing, without any fatigue: *so 'haṃ pakṣaikadeśena vahāmi tvāṃ gataklamaḥ* (5.103.17). (Compare with Garuḍa's description of his own strength in 1.30.4-5). At this point Viṣṇu intervenes: if he is able to carry just one of his arms, he tells the bird, then his boasting is justified. He rests his arm on Garuḍa's shoulder, who collapses and swoons under the weight of this arm, which is as heavy as the whole earth with its mountains: *yāvān hi bhāraḥ kṛtsnāyāḥ pṛthivyāḥ parvataiḥ saha* (5.103.23). Then, duly repentant, he asks Viṣṇu's forgiveness. As we see, in this episode, just as in the *soma*-theft, Garuḍa shows himself superior to Indra, whom he scolds without restraint, but infinitely inferior to Viṣṇu, the Supreme God.[57]

Another power which turns out to be stronger than either Indra or Garuḍa is that of the Brahmins. This is a trait which is typical of the Epics, in which the Brahmin power is regularly shown to be superior to the *kṣatra*-power, and hence to Indra's, the *kṣatriya*-god *par excellence*. But this trait concerning the superiority of the spiritual brahmanical power is not an innovation of the MBh in this particular mythical narrative, but already appears in the late Vedic versions of the myth, where only the Gāyatrī, though she is the shortest meter (i.e.

---

[57] This story is told by Kaṇva in the great *sabhā* of Hastināpura, during Kṛṣṇa's embassy to the Kauravas, with the aim of praising the greatness of Viṣṇu (that is of course of Kṛṣṇa himself) and warn Duryodhana against the evils of boasting.

lacks physical strength), manages to bring back the *soma*. As we know, the Gāyatrī is the meter reserved for Brahmins (the Jagatī being that of *vaiśyas* and the Triṣṭubh of *kṣatriyas*).[58] It seems indeed that the *soma* became the prerogative of Brahmins at an early date,[59] which probably (partly) accounts for the fact that the Brahmin-meter is the only one capable of getting it from the heavens. In the MBh, this superiority of the brahmanical power is also shown in various other episodes of the myth: in connection with the Vālakhilya episode (1.27), Indra, with all his physical strength and stamina, is defeated and humiliated by the superior power of their penance and sacrifice. Garuḍa is allowed to eat the Niṣādas, a tribe of outcasts,[60] but his mother warns him not to eat the Brahmins, who are said to be "the ones who eat first among (all) beings": *bhūtānām agrabhuk* (1.24.3-4).[61] Similarly, when he whishes to drop the giant branch, he requests his father to show him a place "devoid of Brahmins": *varjitaṃ brāhmaṇair deśam*, lest any harm should befall them (1.26.16). He pays respect to Indra's *vajra* by shedding one feather, not so much to acknowledge Indra's power, but to show reverence to the sage Dadhīca's bones, out of which the *vajra* was made (1.29.19).[62] Thus we see that some of the various shifts the telling of the myth undergoes in the MBh are due to the ideological and religious changes reflected in this text: emergence of *bhakti* and

58 GONDA (1975:177) and SMITH (1989:99-100).

59 HILLEBRANDT (1927-1929/1980:159;174).

60 In the MBh, the Niṣādas, as tribal hunters or fishermen, are treated with general hostility and contempt. See GOLDMAN (1996:7-10).

61 Or perhaps more accurately: "who are the top-eaters of all beings". The idea is comparable to that of a biological food-chain, in which the Brahmins are the top-eaters and can 'eat' all the others, but cannot be eaten themselves. Even the king cannot 'feed' on them, because they have Soma as their king. See SMITH (1991:541) and (1994:210). AV 5.18.4 states that one who regards the Brahmins as food consumes poison.

62 The Brahmins' superiority over Garuḍa is similarly shown in an episode narrated in MBh 5.111.1-18, where Garuḍa loses his wings and "becomes similar to a ball of flesh endowed with a beak and feet": *māṃsapiṇḍopamo 'bhūt sa mukhapādānvitaḥ khagaḥ* (5.111.4c-5a), due to the curse of a Brahmin ascetic woman named Śāṇḍilī, whom he had (mentally) scorned.

superiority of Viṣṇu; decline of Indra's prestige; glorification of the Brahmin- over the *kṣatriya*-power.

The protagonists of the story

The soma

Let us now examine more closely the nature of the *soma*, around whose possession the myth centers. While reading the Vedic and epic accounts of the myth, we cannot fail to notice that the *soma* and the *amṛta* referred to in these two different layers of literature are not quite the same thing.[63] This is the thesis which is central to DUMEZIL's book, *Le festin d'immortalité* (1924). According to Dumézil, the *amṛta*, as well as the myth of the churning of the ocean to obtain it, have an Indo-European origin (he quotes many parallel myths from other ancient Indo-European cultures), whereas the *soma* is typical of Indo-Iranian times, having replaced the more ancient *amṛta* in popularity. Like many other mythical motifs, the myth of the churning of the ocean lived so to say 'underground' during Vedic times,[64] (though some of the characteristics of the old *amṛta* were transferred to the *soma*), and later resurfaced in a full-fledged form in the Epics.[65] In the ṚV, the *soma*, however disputed its actual identity might be,[66] is clearly a plant: a 'real' plant, which grows on the mountains,[67] has

[63] Though certain Brāhmaṇas strive to establish the identity in nature of *soma* and *amṛta*. BLOOMFIELD (1894-96:11, note*).

[64] CHARPENTIER (1920:389) tries to find traces of it in ṚV 10.72.6-7, which describes the gods dancing in the sea while holding each others' hands, but his thesis seems somewhat far-fetched. This is also the opinion of KUIPER (1983:99).

[65] His theory is disputed by KEITH (1925:623-624, Appendix D), but quoted with approbation by GONDA (1965:67).

[66] For the 'history' of the theories concerning the identity of the *soma*-plant, see DONIGER O'FLAHERTY (Part Two of WASSON:1968). For a more recent reinterpretation of the problem, see FALK (1989).

[67] However, OBERLIES (1999:15) makes us attentive to the fact that the mountains are polyvalent: they do not only belong to the earth, but also to the heavens. They function as a link between heaven and earth, and are conceived of as a piece of heaven placed

certain well-defined characteristics, and is used as a sacrificial oblation. In the myth of the *soma*-theft, it is referred to both in its natural state as a stem: *aṃśú* (4.26.6; 6.20.6), as well as in its pressed state, ready for sacrifice, as a juice or drop: *índu* (8.4.4), *drapsá* (9.89.2; 10.11.4), etc.

In the MBh episode of the *soma*-theft, the drink of immortality is interchangeably called *amṛta* or *soma*[68] (the latter term being perhaps used to mark the continuity between the Vedic myth and that of the MBh), whereas the term *amṛta* is rare in the Veda.[69] The identity of the *amṛta* in the MBh is somewhat obscure, for its real nature is never clearly described. But since the churning of the ocean, during which the *amṛta* was obtained, is elaborately described in connection with the myth of the theft, we may assume that the *amṛta* Garuḍa steals is the same as the one which was churned out of the ocean, and that the story of the churning is told with the intention of clarifying the nature and origins of the divine drink.[70] The *amṛta* is said to result from the mixing of the sap of trees, the juice of herbs and of gold, all present in

on the earth. He further notes (1999:16): "In dem Bild des auf dem Berge wachsenden Soma verschmelzen somit geographische und botanische Realität, (uralte) religiöse Vorstellungen und klassifikatorische Konzeptionen, und man sollte in ihm nicht allzu eindimensional einen blossen Hinweis zum Wachstumsort einer Pflanze sehen."

[68] But in the story of the churning of the ocean, the drink of immortality is called *amṛta*, whereas *soma* designates the moon, which is also born out of the churning.

[69] See GONDA (1965:61-63) and DUMEZIL (1924:3). Moreover, in the ṚV, *soma* and *amṛta* did not necessarily mean the same thing. The term *amṛta* can designate the *soma*, but more often it means 'immortal' or 'immortality'. See GRASSMANN (1996), under *amṛta*.

[70] The description of the horse Uccaiḥśravas, who was born out of the churning just like the *amṛta*, prompts Śaunaka to ask the *sūta* to describe the churning of the ocean (1.15.4.). The role of Uccaiḥśravas in the episode of the *soma*-theft is limited (he is the object of the bet between Kadrū and Vinatā), but revealing: he too, just like the *amṛta*, becomes an (innocent) object of dispute and strife.
Here one might object that the story of the churning is a late addition to the MBh text, and that therefore this episode cannot be said to reflect the exact nature of the *amṛta* as it was originally conceptualized. DUMEZIL (1923:4) accepts the lateness of this passage: "Dans sa rédaction actuelle, cet épisode n'est certes pas une des parties les plus anciennes du poème", but, he adds: "Mais l'ancienneté du fond n'est pas contestable" and "[le texte] du MBh offre un état de la légende incontestablement plus ancien." In brief, however late this passage might be, it deals with a very ancient myth.

the mountain used as a churning-stick. Due to the fire which burns the mountain, they flow into the sea, and, conglomerating, produce the *amṛta* (1.16.15-17). This *amṛta* is then brought out of the ocean by Dhanvantari, kept in a *kamaṇḍalu*, a small water-jar (1.16.37). Thus we see not only that it is probably a liquid, but also that it is a unique concoction, artificially produced, something like a chemical, not a freely growing plant. But memories of the *soma* as a plant still remain in the MBh. Thus Garuḍa is said to "tear out" (*samutpāṭya*) (1.29.10) the *amṛta* from its guarded place, like one would tear out a plant.[71] Also, as DANGE (1969:71, note 177) remarks, Garuḍa carries the broken branch of the tree in his beak and the two monsters in his claws, which might be a reminiscence of TS 6.1.6.4; AB 3.25-26; TMB 8.4.1, where the Gāyatrī carries back three pressings of the *soma*, one in her beak and two in her claws. Thus the branch of the tree is equated with a *soma*-pressing.[72] In MBh 1.15.31 (and also in Sup 8.15.4), this tree is said to be a *rohiṇa* or *rauhiṇa*; the identity of this particular tree is somewhat doubtful: it might be a sandalwood tree or a species of fig-tree.[73] The fig-tree (though usually the *aśvattha*) is said to be "*soma*-bestowing" and probably worked as a *soma*-substitute.[74] In the R the tree is a *nyagrodha*, that is, a banyan tree. According to the AB 7.5.30, this tree grew out of spilt *soma*-drops. The juice of its fruits was used as a *soma*-surrogate for *kṣatriya*s, the banyan-tree being

[71] Inversely, we might see a prefiguration of the churning of the *amṛta* in ṚV 6.20.6, where the eagle is said to 'churn out': *mathāyán*, the *soma*.

[72] This statement begs of course the question whether the giant elephant and tortoise also represent *soma*-pressings. The answer might be yes, for, as DANGE (1969:44) shows, the two creatures are called *nāgau*: two elephants or two *snakes*, in some versions of the myth, and, as we have seen above, the poisonous snakes Garuḍa gets for his food are as good as *amṛta* for him.

[73] CHARPENTIER (1920:369).

[74] HILLEBRANDT (1927-1929/1980:158).

the tree of *kṣatriyas*, for it represents the *kṣatra*-power.[75] Thus the *nyagrodha* explicitly stands as a *soma*-substitute, and this might well be its significance in the R episode.[76]

The most important difference between the Vedic *soma* and the epic *amṛta*, apart from their difference in nature, which we have discussed above, resides in the fact that the Vedic *soma* was used in the ritual, but not the epic *amṛta*. The reason for this is of course obvious: as we have seen, the *soma* was a real, freely available plant, whereas the *amṛta* is a purely mythical drink. This ritual relevance (or lack of it) probably accounts for the fact that the *soma* is omnipresent in the Veda, which deals extensively with sacrifice, whereas the *amṛta*, except in the myths of the theft and of the churning, hardly plays any role in the later literature. The *amṛta*, once the gods have drunk it (and drinking it once was enough to ensure ever-lasting immortality, as the story of Rāhu (MBh 1.17.4-8) shows), becomes practically redundant. The Vedic *soma* is the sacrificial oblation *par excellence*: the eagle brings it not only for Indra, but also for man and for the sake of sacrifice, thus instituting the receiving and giving cyclical exchange between men and gods. This sacrificial dimension of the *amṛta* is totally lacking in the Epics. In the MBh, the only connection the *amṛta* retains with sacrifice is that the snakes want it, not in order to sacrifice with it, but in order not to be sacrificed themselves. If we may risk a comparison between the Vedic *soma* and the *amṛta* of the MBh, we could say that the *soma*, due to its importance in the sacrifice, is like a freely circulating currency, with a buying and selling power, with an exchange-value. The *amṛta* on the other hand is like a highly

---

[75] HILLEBRANDT (1927-1929/1980:158-159); SMITH (1989:98) and (1994:221-3). For instance, Rāma and Lakṣmaṇa, before going into exile in the forest, smear their hair with the milk of this tree, in order to make it matted, as befits ascetics (R 2.46.55-56).

[76] In any case, the tree is certainly comparable to the famous cosmic tree, attested in so many cultures. See KNIPE (1966-67:353).

precious treasure kept in a safe at the bank: it is useless for all practical purposes and its worth is felt only when it is stolen.

The *amṛta,* it is well-known, is the drink which bestows immortality; but death, so to say the 'other side of the coin' of immortality, seems to be inseparable from it. In keeping with its 'treasure-like' nature, strife and slaughter inevitably arise for its possession: the gods and Asuras, who were previously in agreement, if only temporarily, start fighting for the *amṛta* as soon as it appears out of the ocean (MBh 1.17). Moreover, the churning of the ocean does not only produce the *amṛta*, but also its opposite, the deadly Kālakūṭa or Halāhala poison, which threatens to destroy the worlds.[77] The ambiguous nature of the *amṛta* is also reflected in the etiologic myths relating to the transformations of the fallen *soma*-leaf, or the feather (or claw) of the *soma*-bringer: in the late Veda, as we have seen, it changes on the one hand into snakes (death-giving elements) and on the other hand into various *soma*-substitutes (life-giving elements). In the Suparṇākhyāna too, the feather changes into a variety of poisonous snakes, and also into animals which are the natural enemies of snakes, the mongooses and peacocks (14.28.1). In the MBh, Garuḍa's feather is not transformed into anything,[78] it merely accounts for Garuḍa's name, Suparṇa, which literally means, according to the etymology given in MBh 1.29.21, "who has a beautiful feather". But in the MBh, it is the *soma* itself, when it is kept on the ground by Garuḍa, which gives rise to the etiologic myths. But here we have so to say attenuated etiologic interpretations: the *soma* does not become the origin of any new things

---

[77] The episode of the Kālakūṭa or Halāhala poison is not preserved in the critical editions of the MBh (1.15-17) and R (1.44), although, as DUMEZIL (1924:49) points out: "Il semble bien qu'il y ait là un élément ancien du cycle hindou". Subsequently, he demonstrates the existence of the poison-episode in the Indo-Iranian version of the myth of the churning of the ocean.

[78] Only one manuscript inserts a verse, which is rejected by the Critical Edition, after 1.29.20, which states that out of the feather came the peacock, the mongoose and the two-headed snake. In the Anuśāsanaparvan version (appendix IA, ll. 412-13), the peacocks take hold of Garuḍa's feather.

or creatures, it merely accounts for certain transformations, which again concern a *soma*-substitute on the one hand and the snakes on the other: the *darbha*-grass on which the *soma* is kept becomes holy due to being in contact with it;[79] and the snakes' tongues become forked when they lick the sharp *darbha*-grass in the hope that some *soma* might have been spilt there, and cut their tongues on it (1.30.20). As we have seen above, ŚB 1.7.1.1 presents an alternative between the eagle's feather and the *soma*'s leaf to account for the origin of *soma*-substitutes. The MBh has actualized the alternative and made two separate incidents out of a single one.[80] Thus on the whole, we see that the immortality-bestowing drink (as well as its substitutes) is regularly accompanied by its opposite: death in the form of war, deadly poison, snakes, etc.

The snakes and the eagle

After this discussion on the nature of the *soma-amṛta*, let us now turn to the other main protagonists of the story, the snakes and the eagle, and see what is their function in this myth. The eagle is an old acquaintance: he already figures in the Ṛgvedic account of the myth. But the snakes are relatively speaking new-comers, since they appear for the first time in the Sup in connection with the myth of the *soma*-theft.[81] Here the myth of the *soma*-theft is combined with another wide-spread motif, namely that of the enmity between the snakes and

[79] The *darbha*-grass (or *kuśa*-grass) is also a *soma*-substitute, the least desirable one, according to ŚB 4.5.10.2-6.

[80] We find an interesting continuation of the same mythical motif in two later texts, but which both very probably draw the story from the older Bṛhatkathā, namely in Harṣa's Nāgānanda (7th c. C.E.) and in the Kathāsaritsāgara, in the context of the story of Jimūtavāvana. There, the repentant Garuḍa himself revives all the dead snakes he has devoured, by fetching the *amṛta* from heaven and sprinkling it on their bones. (Nāgānanda, end of 5th act; Kathāsaritsāgara 4.22.248-249). Thus, though the story and its purport is changed, we still find the motif of the drops of *amrta* producing snakes. The Nāgānanda (verse 35b) moreover preserves the episode of the snakes (who have just been resurrected) "licking the earth with the tip of their forked tongues, greedy for a taste of *amṛta*-juice": *jihvākoṭidvayena kṣitim amṛtarasāsvādalobhāl likhantaḥ*.

[81] However, in certain late Vedic versions, the *soma* guardian Kṛśānu is said to be 'footless', which might denote a snake.

the eagle.[82] It should be made clear from the start that these snakes (*nāgas*) are by no means ordinary snakes. They are of course conceived on the model of the cobra, but are usually described as altogether supernatural, semi-divine beings: of huge size, able to change their form at will (*kāma-rūpa*) and able to roam about at will (*kāma-gama*).[83] They are also the objects of worship since times immemorial.[84] As for the eagle, he is apparently 'just' an eagle in the ṚV, though we cannot conjecture much about his nature, since this text simply does not say much about him, except that he brought the *soma*. In the Sup, MBh and R, Garuḍa is an altogether supernatural bird: he is the king of birds, of huge size (which he can increase or reduce at will) and great effulgence.[85] He is even praised as the Supreme Being in some passages of the Sup (see e.g. 15.30.2) and in some verses attached by certain manuscripts after MBh 1.20, discarded to the critical apparatus.

Here the following question arises: what is it that attracts specifically the snakes and the eagle around the *soma*, and why are these two animals, and not some others, chosen (in the Sup and MBh) to exemplify the struggle for the drink of immortality? We may first note that the *soma*, since Ṛgvedic times, seems to have certain

82 ELIADE (1978:205). This mythical motif is of course partly based on reality. See for instance CHARPENTIER's discussion on the various species of snake-eating eagles which are worshipped as Garuḍa in India (1920:344-349).

83 For general information on the nature and deeds of the *nāgas* in Indian literature, see VOGEL (1926).

84 WINTERNITZ (1888/1991a:46-47).

85 In the secondary literature on Garuḍa and the *nāgas*, these are often described as having semi-human, semi-animal forms. This is certainly due to the influence of their representations in art, where Garuḍa is often depicted or sculpted as a bird with a human face, and the *nāgas* as human beings with several cobra-hoods growing from their neck and rising above their head, or else with a human torso and a snake-tail. These iconographic devices are necessary in artistic representations in order to make them immediately recognizable as Garuḍa or *nāgas*, and not just as an ordinary bird or snakes. But in the MBh, Garuḍa is described only as a bird, albeit of a supernatural kind, and the *nāgas* either appear as snakes or as human beings, never as a mixture of both. However, the manner in which they are represented in art in turn influenced certain later texts. See RAVEN (1994:19).

affinities with both snake and eagle. ṚV 9.86.44 states that "*soma*, like a snake, slips out of its old skin": *áhir ná jūrṇā́m áti sarpati tvácam*; here the *soma*-juice flowing out of its squashed stem evokes for the poet the image of the serpent sloughing off its old skin. On the other hand, the *soma* is sometimes also called a bird in the ṚV: *divyáḥ suparṇó* (ṚV 9.71.9; 97.33; 85.11).[86] The bird-like nature of the *soma* is also revealed in R 3.33.34, where the *soma* in the heavens is said to be kept in "metal net-works": *ayojālāni*, an expression which is reminiscent of a bird-cage.[87] In other words, the *soma* partakes of the nature of both snakes and eagle. The opposite is also true: snakes and eagle partake of the nature of *soma*; they are both connected with immortality and also with death, its reverse side.

In this section we shall try to read the myth of the *soma*-theft once more as a struggle for power, but this time a struggle which takes place at the cosmic level, in which the elemental forces themselves (incarnated, so to say, as snakes and eagle) confront each other in order to obtain the highest form of power, namely immortality. As ELIADE (1958:277) remarks:

> "The fight between the eagle and the snake, like the struggle between Garuḍa and the reptile, is a cosmological symbol of the struggle between light and darkness, of the opposition between two principles, that of the sun and that of the underworld."

Or, as KNIPE (1966-67:328) poetically puts it:

> "And, often enough in the worlds of prehistory, the mythopoeic mind could effortlessly project this single struggle [between the eagle and the snake] onto a definitive plane, where the great free-flying bird is truly the boundless sky and the slithering serpent or

[86] See HILLEBRANDT (1927-1929/1980:208), who uses the comparison between the *soma* and a bird to support his theory of the identification of *soma* with the moon.

[87] In the Anuśāsanaparvan version (appendix IA) of the MBh, the *amṛta* is also kept in big metal net-works: *jālena mahatā [...] ayasmayena* (ll. 224-5).

> dragon becomes the chthonic power par excellence. Sky and earth, light and darkness; the beneficent and lofty against the shadowy and chaotic; the all-seeing, all-knowing heavens and the hidden depths of the primordial womb-earth."

According to certain archetypal symbolic values, which, as we shall see, apply particularly well in the present case, serpent and eagle have exactly opposite symbolism on all planes: the serpent is connected with the earth, the water and the moon, whereas the eagle is associated with the air, the fire and the sun.[88] The myth of the *soma*-theft reflects the thirst for transcendence: the quest for immortality and escape from death. The elements are the imperishable matter out of which all things perishable are constituted. Their union means life, and their dissolution, death. A common Sanskrit expression, *pañcatvaṃ gam-*: to go to the five elements, means 'to die'. Thus we might venture the hypothesis that the even distribution, or separation, of the elements among the two sets of inimical protagonists jeopardizes the achievement of immortality (i.e. the coming down onto the earth of the *amṛta*), which might have been accomplished by their union.

Our main reference for this section is Mircea ELIADE, especially his *Traité d'histoire des religions*, translated as *Patterns in Comparative Religions*. In this respect, we may mention that most of the symbolic values that the snakes and eagle display in the texts concerning us here are present in many other cultures as well, and might thus be called 'universal'. On the other hand, the idea of 'multivalence' can also be seen at work here. This is particularly noticeable in the case of the eagle or Garuḍa: in the ṚV, the *soma*, the sun and the fire are at times called *suparṇa*. In turn, in a process of reverse assimilation, the eagle himself came to be compared, associated, assimilated with the *soma*, the sun and the fire. Therefore the symbolism that we make use of does not

[88] On the other hand, their common father is "Kaśyapa (tortoise), a typical representative of the totality" (KUIPER 1983:32).

necessarily have to imply a 'Jungian' or an 'Eliadean' type of collective unconscious or archetypal theoretical presuppositions, but can as well be simply the encyclopaedic information that was available to the culture, which made possible the redistribution of various epithets, powers, etc. among the protagonists of a myth. The ubiquity of symbolisms and the proliferation of associations have been made evident by the literature which deals with them. The selections that we make for our investigation are necessarily restricted to those objects whose symbolic value makes possible a particular reading of the myth. This does not mean that what we do not make use of in this particular reading has no symbolic value, or that the other elements involved in the myth, if studied, do not lead to a significant reading of the myth. We shall now examine in the texts how the various symbolism attached to the snakes and eagle are worked out.

That the snakes are connected with the earth, since they crawl on the surface of the earth and live in holes,[89] is made explicit in the myth by the fact that their mother is Kadrū. This name, which means the "tawny one", designates the earth, and she is also sometimes called *surasā* (she of the good smell), a designation typical of the earth (see e.g. MBh 5.101.4 or R 5.1.130). The identity of Kadrū as the earth is explicitly stated in the late Vedic versions of the myth: *iyaṃ* (scil. *pṛthivī*) *vai kadrūr*, and in the Sup 1.2.1. In the AB 5.23, the earth is also called *sarparājñī,* the queen of snakes.[90] In the Sup, Suparṇī addresses her as Aditi, another denomination of the earth (3.6.4). Indeed, both in the Sup as well as MBh accounts of the *soma*-theft, the *nāga*s appear singularly earth-bound. As we have noted above, the *nāga*s are often described as able to roam about at will and change their shape at will, but none of these traits is manifested here: Garuḍa has to carry them to the Ramaṇīyaka-island; they are apparently unable to get the *amṛta*

[89] ELIADE (1949:§ 52) and WINTERNITZ (1888/1991a:6-7).
[90] WINTERNITZ (1904/1991b:377, note 7).

themselves; they helplessly lick the *darbha*-grass when Indra carries away the *soma*, without attempting to pursue him. This contrasts sharply, for instance, with the way in which Takṣaka flies away through the atmosphere after biting king Parikṣit (MBh 1.40.2-3).

Just as the snakes reveal their intimate relationship with the chthonic element by being the sons of the earth, in the very same manner the eagle is related to the sky by being the son of the sky: this is made explicit in the late Veda, where the eagle's mother, Suparṇī, is identified with the sky (KS 23.10: *dyaus suparṇī*). In the MBh her name itself, Vinatā, "the bent one", probably designates the cupola of the sky. (See WINTERNITZ 1904/1991b:377, note 7). In the Sup she appears in the form of an eagle, whereas Kadrū has the shape of a snake: these are the theriomorphic forms of sky and earth respectively. In the MBh, both Kadrū and Vinatā are apparently represented as women: the two sisters address each other by means of epithets such as *bhadre* (fortunate one), *śubhe* (fair one), *śucismite* (brightly smiling one), *bhāmini* (beautiful woman) (1.18.2-4) which would hardly suit an eagle or a snake. The only reminiscence of Vinatā's eagle-shape lies in the fact that she carries Kadrū to the island of the snakes (1.21.5): this makes sense only if we visualize her as an eagle carrying the snake, whereas if we imagine her as a woman carrying another woman, it looks somewhat incongruous,[91] especially when Garuḍa is at hand to carry them all. This motif of the myth is obviously a 'left-over' of the account of the Sup which was not worked over to fit Vinatā's human shape.

In Indian mythology, snakes are closely connected with water: they are thought to live in the ocean, in ponds and in rivers.[92] This

[91] This happens for instance in the cartoon version of the Amar Chitra Katha series (*Garuda*. Ed. Anant Pai. vol. 547. Bombay: India Book House, 1993). Kadrū and Vinatā are represented as women, and Vinatā (who seems to be wading across the ocean) carries Kadrū on her shoulders (pp. 10-11).

[92] VOGEL (1926:4) and ELIADE (1949:§71).

association with the watery element clearly appears in the story which concerns us here: the Ramaṇīyaka-island, to which Garuḍa carries the snakes, is said to be an island of the snakes and is situated in the middle of the ocean (1.21.4). We also find a long description of the ocean in the context of Kadrū and Vinatā's bet (1.19). In the Sup, Kadrū even takes the ocean as a witness for their betting contest: according to CHARPENTIER (1920:220), this is because no one else is at hand. But Varuṇa, who appears in epic mythology as the king of the ocean, which is the abode of the snakes, and even, from the AV onwards, as the king of snakes,[93] is the ideal witness to invoke for Kadrū, the mother of snakes and a snake herself. The snakes are not only connected with the water of the ocean, but with that of the sky as well.[94] Thus they can become rain-clouds. For instance, while discussing how to escape the *sarpa-sattra*, one of the *nāga*s proposes that they should become clouds and rain on the sacrificial fire to extinguish it:

> *apare tv abruvan nāgāḥ samiddhaṃ jātavedasam /*
> *varṣair nirvāpayiṣyāmo meghā bhūtvā savidyutaḥ* // 1.33.21 //
> Other Snakes again said, 'Let us become clouds with lightning and all, and put out the kindled fire of Sacrifice with rain showers!' (Transl. VAN BUITENEN 1973).

Likewise, in another narrative found in the Ādiparvan, Uttaṅka, whose ear-rings were stolen by the *nāga* Takṣaka, sings a hymn in praise of the snakes when he enters the *nāga-loka*, in which he describes them as follows. *Varṣanti iva jīmūtāḥ savidyutpavaneritāḥ*: "they rain like clouds which are driven by the wind accompanied by lightning" (1.3.139).[95] Perhaps in connection with their affinity to

93 ELIADE (1978:202-3).

94 ELIADE (1949:§53).

95 For this passage, see the next chapter.

clouds, lightning and rain-water, the snakes receive favours from Indra, in his status of rain and storm-god: thus Indra rains on them to protect them from certain death when Garuḍa carries them on his back towards the sun which scorches them (MBh 1.22). And we may note that elsewhere too in the MBh this affinity between Indra and the snakes is apparent, especially in his friendship with Takṣaka:[96] he tries to save him from Janamejaya's *sattra* (1.51); he is said to have repeatedly prevented Agni from burning the Khāṇḍava forest, since Takṣaka had his abode there (1.215.6-9); Mātali, his charioteer, marries his daughter to a *nāga* (5.95-104). This general affinity of snakes with water makes them the guardians of springs, especially of the springs of life and immortality. In this status we find them in the Sup (12.23.3-6) and MBh (1.29.5-6) guarding the *amṛta* in the heavens.[97] In this connection, we must note that in the ṚV the snake Vṛtra also guards (in the more negative sense of obstruction) the waters and hence prevents life and creation. In certain accounts, he is also said to have *soma* in his belly.[98] Not only are the snakes the traditional guardians of the source of immortality, they are also said to be immortal themselves: the periodical sloughing of their skin is interpreted as a rejuvenation.[99]

If the snakes have a close affinity with water, the eagle is on the contrary connected with fire. As BLOOMFIELD (1894-96:11) notes,

---

[96] About Indra's friendship with Takṣaka, BIARDEAU (1978:140, note 1) remarks: "Takṣaka, 'le Façonneur', s'oppose comme Nāga à Ananta ou Śeṣa, le serpent qui connote au contraire l'informe, le chaos. Tandis que ce dernier représente le côté négatif du chaos, résidu d'une destruction, Takṣaka en est plutôt le côté fécond, créateur. C'est pourquoi il est l'ami d'Indra qui le protège."

[97] While reading the story in the MBh, we might of course wonder who are these two snakes who guard the *soma*, who resemble the *nāga*s like brothers, and yet are obviously not connected with them. Their presence in the heavens is all the more surprising in that the *nāga*s are apparently the first snakes, the original representatives of the race. The answer to this puzzle is very simple: the two *soma*-guardians are present here in their traditional role of guardians of treasures and of the sources of life, a role in which they figure in so many Indian tales (VOGEL 1926:20-23).

[98] KUIPER (1971:87).

[99] VOGEL (1926:14), WINTERNITZ (1888/1991a:8), ELIADE (1949:§ 51).

Agni is frequently spoken of as a bird from the ṚV onwards. The fire-altar (*agni-cayana*) itself was sometimes built in the shape of a *śyena*.[100] In the MBh, Garuḍa fire-like nature is emphasized from the start: as soon as he is born he grows to a huge size, and his effulgence is such that the gods take him for Agni (1.20.6-7).[101] He is also praised as the fire in 1.20.10 & 13; 1.26.8. His name itself, Garuḍa, which might mean the "devourer"[102] probably refers to the all-devouring aspect of fire. Garuḍa's hunger indeed plays a great role in the MBh. Unless his hunger is satisfied, he cannot perform his *soma*-stealing exploit. We may notice that the creatures Garuḍa gets for his food are all related to water, therefore antithetical by nature to fire: the Niṣādas, a fisher-folk who live "in the belly of the ocean": *samudrakukṣau* (1.24.2), and eat various fish: *bahuvidhamatsya-bhakṣiṇaḥ* (1.24.14); the giant elephant and tortoise, both animals related to the water, who inhabit a lake (1.25.20);[103] and finally the snakes, who become his food *par excellence* and are eminently connected with the water, as we have seen. His devouring snakes makes Garuḍa's function similar to that of the fire, for Agni too in the MBh is

---

[100] VON SIMSON (1989-90:356); for drawings of one, see RENOU & FILLIOZAT (1985:351) and especially STAAL (1983:vol.I), which also contains photographs of (modern) *śyena*-shaped fire-altars . (See esp. plate 16).

[101] And his affinity with Agni is also revealed by the fact that Agni seems to be the only one who knows Garuḍa's identity (cf. 1.20.8).

[102] This is the etymology given by Uṇādi-sūtra 4.155, which derives the name *garuḍa* from the root 2. *gṝ:* "to devour" (see MW under *garuḍa*). Another possible etymology would be to connect *garuḍa* with *garut-mat*, another, older, name of the eagle, which simply means 'winged'. For further etymologies of this word, see DANGE (1969:99-108). The Anuśāsanaparvan version (appendix IA, ll. 323-24) offers the following etymology of the name Garuḍa, explaining it, it seems, as a combination of *gurubhāra* and *krīḍan*. Seeing Garuḍa effortlessly carrying the huge branch and the two animals, the *munis* exclaim:

> *asau gacchati dharmātmā gurubhārasamanvitaḥ /*
> *ayam krīḍann ivākāśe tasmād garuḍa eva saḥ /*
> That dharmic one goes, carrying a heavy burden,
> as if playing in the sky. Therefore he is Garuḍa.

[103] One may wonder if these preliminary deeds of Garuḍa, before his great exploit of seizing the *soma*, do not have a certain initiatory value. As ELIADE (1949:§ 63) says: "l'obtention de 'l'eau vive' implique une série de consécrations et d' 'épreuves'".

bent upon devouring the snakes and is generally speaking their enemy. He burns them at Janamejaya's *sattra* (1.47-48); he is said to have repeatedly tried to burn the Khāṇḍava forest, Takṣaka's abode, and finally manages to do so, and, though he fails to get Takṣaka himself, he burns some of his family (1.214-225); in the shape of a horse,[104] he helps Uttaṅka in his endeavour to get his ear-rings back from Takṣaka, by filling the *nāga-loka* with smoke (1.3.157-158; 14.57). His similarity to the destructive aspect of the fire makes Garuḍa a symbol of the fire of destruction at the end of the world, and therefore of death itself. This is how the gods praise him as soon as he is born (MBh 1.20.13.c-d):

> *bhayaṃkaraḥ pralaya ivāgnir utthito*
> *vināśayan yugaparivartanāntakṛt* //
> "And terrible at the Dissolution dost thou rise firelike,
> Destroying and ending the revolution of the Eon."
> (Transl. VAN BUITENEN 1973).

(See also 1.24.10; 26.9). And the *pralaya* imagery evoked by Garuḍa's appearance in the heavens previous to his stealing the *soma*, with all the bad omens preceding it (1.26.27-34) and the dust he whirls up with his wings, which seems to be the sign of the confusion which reigns at the end of the world (1.28.5-6),[105] is especially prominent. This ominous side of Garuḍa's character, connecting him with death, is also found in the later Garuḍapurāṇa, which probably accounts for the inauspicious connotation of this text.[106]

---

[104] In the ṚV we also find the snake-killing horse of Pedu. The horse is a theriomorphic shape of Agni.

[105] Whirling up dust seems to be one of Garuḍa's favourite tactics of war: he also whirls up dust to blind the Niṣādas (1.24.11) and the two snakes who guard the *soma* (1.29.8).

[106] For instance, VASU (in BASU 1911:I) remarks: "It was used all over India at funeral ceremonies, but some are afraid to read it on other occasions, thinking it inauspicious."

Let us now turn to the last set of opposed symbolisms of the snakes and eagle, namely those connected with the moon and the sun.[107] The snakes are believed to be immortal due to the periodic sloughing of their skin. This is what links the snakes especially to the moon (with which *soma* is moreover identified at an early date):[108] just as the moon decays and grows again, so do the snakes by sloughing their old skin. The *soma* plant itself also shares in the same cyclical process: as a plant, the *soma* naturally undergoes growth, decay and death. And during the pressing, the 'dead' and dried-out *soma* plant is swelled with water and reborn in the form of the juice.[109] (See OBERLIES (1999:52-54)). This is not an absolute and permanent immortality, but one which undergoes decay and rebirth.[110] This is also what the near-destruction of the *nāga* race through the *sarpa-*

The Garuḍapurāṇa also reflects the ambiguous nature of Garuḍa: besides numerous other matters, it contains on the one hand treatises on medicine, the life-prolonging and life-giving science (1.146-204) and *mantras* against poisons in general and snake poison in particular (1.20 & 27). On the other hand, it contains a long disquisition on the after-life (the various worlds, esp. hells) and on the *śrāddha* or death ceremonies (Kāṇḍa 2, the so-called Dharma or Preta Kāṇḍa). Reference is given to *The Garuḍa Purāṇa*, ed. SHASTRI (1978).

107 In Indian thought, the sun and the moon are conceived as sub-forms of fire and water. This is not only the case in mythical thinking, but can also be found in astronomical texts. Thus in Āryabhaṭīya 4.37 (ed. SHUKLA 1976), we read: *candro jalam arko 'gniḥ*.

108 Though not yet, apparently, in Ṛgvedic times. HILLEBRANDT's thesis (1891-1899-1902), that already in the Ṛgveda the *soma* was the moon, and that therefore the moon was the greatest deity of Vedic times, was opposed already by OLDENBERG (1894:599-612) according to whom the identification was firmly established only at the time of the Brāhmaṇas, and later by KEITH (1925:171) and GONDA (1965:50-51). ŚB 11.1.4.4, for instance, expresses the idea that "[t]he moon is the vessel of the beverage of life, from which the gods drink their *amṛta* [...] and which is periodically refilled." KUIPER (1983:127). MYLIUS (1978/2002:43), on the other hand, sees the emergence of this idea already in ṚV 10.85.2

109 It is perhaps due to this very similarity in nature of the snakes and *soma* that the *sarpa-sattra*, which, as we have noted above (footnote 42), is a Vedic rite consisting of *soma*-offerings, could be called *sarpa-sattra*, or "snake-sacrifice". In Janamejaya's sacrifice, these *soma*-offerings become real snake-offerings. The metaphor is actualized.

110 ELIADE (1949:§ 47 and §§ 54-55).

sattra, in which most of the snakes are killed, and the subsequent revival of the race, might imply.[111]

The eagle, on the other hand, is by essence a solar bird.[112] The sun itself is sometimes compared to a bird, for it flies through the sky (see e.g. ṚV 1.191.9).[113] And in ṚV 1.164.46 & 52, the expressions *divyáḥ sá suparṇó garútmān*: "he is the divine bird Garutmat", and *divyáṃ suparṇám* probably designate the sun. The solar nature of this bird may also account for the fact that in the late Vedic versions of the myth, it is the Gāyatrī meter in eagle shape who brings back the *soma*. The Sāvitrī-*mantra* too, which is composed in the Gāyatrī meter and which, according to GONDA (1975:52), was ritually recited since ancient times, is connected with the sun: not only is it addressed to that luminary, it also has to be recited at sun-rise, noon and sun-set and literally makes the sun rise and set. As soon as he is born, Garuḍa is praised by the gods as the sun (MBh 1.20.12-13), and his quality of younger brother of Aruṇa also identifies him with the sun: Aruṇa, dawn, appears before the sun, just as the character Aruṇa was born before Garuḍa. As GONDA, who agrees with the theory which sees the sun-bird in Garuḍa, remarks: "His [Garuḍa's] brother, moreover, is Aruṇa, the charioteer of the Sun (Sūrya), or the foregoer of this god, the 'personification' of dawn, and, in a striking and apposite manner, distinguished from his well-made younger brother by being not full-grown." (1954:102). The sun-god has another characteristic which makes Garuḍa's function similar to his, namely that of a 'food-giver',

---

111 And the same holds perhaps also for the 'lunar dynasty', to which the Pāṇḍavas and Kauravas belong, which is nearly exterminated in the *raṇa-yajña*, the sacrifice of war. As already noted by HOPKINS (1915/1974:24), VOGEL (1926:4-5) and MINKOWSKI (1991:396), we find many *nāga*s and Kurus bearing identical names, such as Kauravya, Dhṛtarāṣṭra, Dhanaṃjaya, Janamejaya, etc. (See the lists of *nāga*-names in MBh 1.31 and 5.101.) This parallelism of the names is probably no coincidence. It reflects the parallelism observable in the fates of both 'dynasties' or 'races'.

112 ELIADE (1949:§38).

113 Also CHARPENTIER (1920:127;141).

since plants grow under the beneficent influence of that luminary. Thus in the Āraṇyakaparvan (3.4), it is Sūrya who undertakes to feed the Pāṇḍavas and their numerous following of Brahmins during their sojourn in the forest. This is one more sense in which the eagle who brings the *soma-amṛta*, which is after all the food *par excellence*,[114] can be compared with the sun.

Garuḍa's affinity with the sun is also clearly shown in the episode when he carries the snakes on his back towards the sun. He is not affected by the sun's heat, whereas the snakes, whose nature is antithetical to that of the sun, are badly burnt and swoon (Sup 4.8.3-5; 5.9.1-2; MBh 1.21.6). In this episode, we can discern another trait which is typical of the sun, namely his character of a psychopomp who carries the souls of the dead to the underworld: for the journey of the sun round the earth during the night can be interpreted as his journey through the realm of the dead. But the sun itself, unlike the moon, is not believed to die. Thus his is a permanent type of immortality.[115] The snakes are often linked with the cult of the dead and even represent the souls of the dead, for they live underground.[116] Garuḍa carrying the snakes can therefore be compared to the sun carrying the souls to the nether world. The same motif might again be seen in the episode where Garuḍa carries the tiny Vālakhilyas hanging on the branch of the *rauhiṇa* tree (MBh 1.26). The Vālakhilyas are said to be of the size of a thumb (MBh 1.27.8), and the R adds that they drink the sunshine: *marīcipāḥ* (3.33.30). In the account of the R, some other ascetics, the Vaikhānasas, designated as *māṣa*s, that is to say beans, also live on the tree (3.33.30). This thumb- or bean-size, as CHARPENTIER already remarked (1920:333), makes them similar to the *ātman*, which is often said to be of that size. Thus these tiny ascetics too might represent the

---

114 DUMEZIL (1924:228).

115 ELIADE (1949:§§ 42 &45).

116 ELIADE (1949:§52); WINTERNITZ (1888/1991a:11).

souls of the dead (according to CHARPENTIER (1920:334) they are originally soul-beings living on the sun) carried by the sun-bird Garuḍa.[117]

Thus we see that, though basically antithetical in their natures, the snakes and the eagle share two common points: first, their destructiveness which identifies them with death; for the *nāga*s are of course highly poisonous and their poison is often likened to a fire,[118] and Garuḍa, through his devouring activity, can bring death like the fire of destruction at the end of the world. On the other hand they are both intimately connected with the ambrosia: the snakes as its guardians and the eagle as the bringer of the drink of immortality. Moreover, as we have seen, the snakes are thought to be immortal, for they rejuvenate themselves by sloughing their skin, and the eagle, as a solar symbol, is immortal too, though in a different way.[119] Thus the life-death ambivalence lies within them, just as it resides in the *soma-amṛta* itself.

Conclusions

Among all the opposite elements which are at work in this myth, it seems to me that the polarity sky-earth plays a great role. For basically, the following problem is actualized in the myth of the theft: should the *soma* belong to the sky or to the earth? Or, should it belong to the

[117] See also VON SIMSON (1989-90:358) and DANGE (1969:133).

[118] Thus when Takṣaka bites the banyan tree in MBh 1.39, it is reduced to ashes. When he bites king Parikṣit in 1.40, the whole palace bursts into flames. See also WINTERNITZ (1888/1991a:9) and VOGEL (1926:15).

[119] In some cultures, the eagle is also thought to rejuvenate himself by shedding his feathers, but I have not been able to find traces of this in Indian literature. FRAZER (1918:78) mentions this belief among the Hebrews. KNIPE (1966-67:353, note 102) quotes Psalm 103:5: "Your youth is renewed like the eagle's." We also find the motif of the eagle's rejuvenation in the Physiologus, a Medieval Latin text attributed to Theobaldus. And there is of course the well-known legend of the Phoenix who is reborn out of its own ashes. But perhaps, as KNIPE (1966-67:358-59) claims, it is precisely the feather that the eagle, the Gāyatrī, or Garuḍa shed, which is shot off by an archer or by Indra's *vajra*, which is the price they have to pay for their immortality. Yet this would not be a cyclical event, unlike the serpent's sloughing.

inhabitants of the sky or to those of the earth? The *soma* is first in the sky. An eagle, acting as the go-between, brings it down onto the earth. The choice of the eagle as the messenger is of course dictated first by the realistic trait that this bird flies particularly well and high, but also by the fact that the eagle, as a sun-symbol, is immortal in his own right, and would therefore not feel tempted to use the *soma* for his own purpose.[120] In the ṚV, the *soma* really comes down onto the earth and is then used for the sacrifice. This might reflect the historical reality of those times: the *soma* was indeed a plant commonly used by the people in the sacrificial ceremonies.

In the late Veda, the earth and the sky are personified as Kadrū and Suparṇī. Again, the earth wants the *soma* and orders the sky to get it for her. The eagle brings it down. As we see, Kadrū and Suparṇī, though they appear personified for the first time, are not merely some alien figures from another legend which conglomerated with the myth of the theft, as most scholars hold. It is true that the characters of Kadrū, Suparṇī and their children are indeed 'new', in the sense that they do not figure in the Ṛgvedic occurrences of the myth in this form. But it was possible for them to be incorporated in the myth only because they stand for something (earth and sky) which was already present in the myth before. The sky-earth competition for the *soma* was already prominent in the Ṛgvedic versions. But in the late Veda, the fate of the *soma*, once it is brought down, is mostly not further dealt with. What is emphasized, on the other hand, are the various *soma*-substitutes which grow out of the fallen leaf or feather. Again, this

[120] The only text in which Garuḍa is said to taste the *amṛta* is Sup 14.3. In the MBh, Garuḍa does not partake of the *amṛta*. In the ṚV too (see esp. hymns 4.26 & 27), emphasis is laid on the fact that the eagle flies straight, with great speed and unwaveringly, as he brings back the *soma*. SCHNEIDER, basing himself on the behaviour of hunting falcons who drink the blood of their victims, suggests that the Ṛgvedic *śyena* first nibbles at the *soma*-stalk, thereby gaining *tvákṣas* and *vīryà*, an act which, as he himself admits, is nowhere mentioned in this text. (See SCHNEIDER 1971: 8; 15; 35; 67). But in view of what we have just said, his conjecture seems quite untenable.

probably reflects the concrete fate of the *soma* in late Vedic times: though it was still known and used, it was increasingly difficult to come by, and therefore its substitutes and the need to validate them became more important.

In the Sup, Kadrū and Suparṇī become a snake and an eagle. According to CHARPENTIER (1920:305-312) we have here a typical animal fable of the weaker animal who manages to defeat the stronger one by a trick:[121] Kadrū the snake (and a one-eyed snake at that!)[122] defeats by cheating the eagle (with her famous eagle-eye: *sauparṇaṃ cakṣur* (3.5.5)) in a competition which involves the ability to see at a great distance. This animal-fable trait may indeed be present in the Sup, but here again, we should not forget that the snake and eagle are nothing but the theriomorphic forms of earth and sky, an identification which is moreover explicitly made in this text, and that therefore what is represented here is once again their age-old conflict for the possession of the *soma*. In the Sup the *nāga*s, as a class of beings, appear for the first time as the representatives (literally, as the sons) of the earth. In this text, and also in the MBh, we see that the *soma-amṛta* cannot remain on the earth even for an instant. In the MBh Indra immediately snatches it back to the heavens. Again, this reflects the concrete historical situation: the epic *amṛta* is an entirely mythical drink, which has no place in the ordinary life of earthly creatures. Therefore it is brought back to the imaginary realm of the heavens, where it properly belongs.

But the *nāga*s do not just symbolize the earth in this particular myth. They also stand for the Evil, or the powers of *adharma*, into

---

[121] And according to DANGE (1969:140) the story of the competition between Kadrū and Suparṇī is a typical folk-tale of rivaling co-wives. But being the wives of one and the same sage implies also the togetherness of sky and earth, which are frequently mentioned together in the ṚV in the compound form *dyāvapṛthivī*. This fact exemplifies our general contention that the Ṛgvedic material can reappear according to various criteria in the later literature.

[122] According to Sup 1.2.2, Kadrū lost one eye in a sacrificial performance.

whose possession the *soma* should not fall. This is the Vṛtra-quality of the *nāgas*.[123] The basically antithetical and inimical nature of snakes and eagle makes the attempt of the snakes to get the *soma* through him go wrong: they fail to get the *soma*. On the contrary, the *soma*-theft becomes a means of destroying the snakes: in the ṚV, Indra kills Vṛtra, the "first-born of snakes": *prathamajā́m áhīnām* (1.32.3-4),[124] after winning the *soma*, and in the intoxication of the *soma*. Thanks to his theft of the *soma*, Garuḍa gets as a boon from Indra to have the snakes for his food: he thus in turn becomes the arch-destroyer of snakes.

---

123 Obviously the *nāgas* are not to be equated with Vṛtra, though Vṛtra himself may have been conceptualized as a cobra in the ṚV (SCHMIDT:1963). As BROCKINGTON (1981:28) remarks: "Of course, even in the Ṛg-Veda Vṛtra is represented as a snake or serpent, but the use of a new term and the attitudes involved in the post-Vedic period indicate quite a different source. [...] It is clear that the nāgas were a very ancient object of worship, a type of chthonic deity obviously significant for good or ill to the peasants." But in this particular myth, the negative side of their character is specially emphasized.

124 BENVENISTE et RENOU (1934:105).

5. Upamanyu's Salvation by the Aśvins

Introductory

In the present chapter, we shall mainly deal with the story of Upamanyu's salvation by the Aśvins as it is told in MBh 1.3.19-82 (in the Pauṣya-sub-parvan), along with the stories of Upamanyu's co-students, and with that of Uttaṅka, which is narrated immediately afterwards (1.3.83-176), and presents striking structural similarities with that of Upamanyu. After giving a summary of the story of Upamanyu, we shall first examine its various Vedic antecedents. Then we shall deal with the patterns of initiation-ceremonies which underlie the narrative, and finally we shall examine the other versions of these stories which figure in MBh 13.14 and 14.52-57.

The twin-gods named Aśvins have a very limited role in the Epics. They hardly figure at all in the R, and in the MBh they are connected to the main epic events only because they are the fathers of the two youngest Pāṇḍavas, Nakula and Sahadeva,[1] and they appear in 'peripheral' narratives only in the tale of their rejuvenation of Cyavana, and in that of Upamanyu's adventures, with which we are dealing in this chapter. On the other hand, in Ṛgvedic times, they were very prominent gods: "The Aśvins are, next to Indra, Agni, and Soma, the gods most frequently mentioned in the Rigveda, where they claim more than fifty hymns and are mentioned over 400 times." (KEITH 1925:113). Here we shall not try to investigate in general terms the Aśvins' decline in the Epics, but try to find out more specifically what motivations lie behind their exceptional appearance in the story of Upamanyu as it is told in the MBh. In this story, the Aśvins rescue Upamanyu who has become blind and has consequently fallen into a

[1] And we must note that unlike their three elder brothers, the twins never meet their divine fathers (resp. brother in the case of Bhīma) in the MBh.

well. Their function of saviours, let us note first of all, is entirely consistent with their Vedic role.

Summary of MBh 1.3.19-82.

Presently we shall give a summary of the passage which concerns us here. MBh 1.3.19-82 abruptly introduces the story of the 'tests' of the three students of the teacher Āyoda Dhaumya, with no immediate connection with what comes before.[2] Here we are more specifically concerned with the adventures of the second student, named Upamanyu, but the tests of the other two may shed some light on particular details of Upamanyu's own. The story is as follows: there was a teacher (*upādhyāya*),[3] Āyoda Dhaumya by name, who had three students (*śiṣyas*): Āruṇi Pāñcālya, Upamanyu and Veda. The first pupil, Āruṇi, was once sent by his teacher to fill a hole in a dike. Unable to do so,[4] he finally lay down in the hole himself, thus effectively stopping it. After some time, the teacher asked his other two *śiṣyas* what had happened to Āruṇi. They reminded him that he had sent him to fill the hole, and then all three went in search of him. When his teacher called out his name, telling him to come, Āruṇi got up from the hole, (thereby letting the water flow out of the field

---

[2] MBh 1.3.1-17 relates the somewhat mysterious story of Saramā's son (i.e., a dog) who is unjustly beaten during Janamejaya's horse-sacrifice. Then Saramā curses Janamejaya to be overcome by an invisible fear, but we never hear of the curse again. (See however HILTEBEITEL's very interesting discussion on this topic in (2001:170-171)). Janamejaya is reintroduced at the end of the Pauṣyaparvan, when Uttaṅka urges him to take revenge on Takṣaka. Thus Uttaṅka's story has a direct link with what follows. This is one of the reasons why WILHELM (1965:24-27) thinks that the Pauṣyaparvan originally consisted of the story of Uttaṅka, and that the stories of Dhaumya's students were subsequently attached to it.

[3] As WILHELM notes (1965:12, note ad 95), in the Pauṣyaparvan, the teacher is mostly called *upādhyāya*, seldom *guru*, and never *ācārya*. Usually, the *ācārya* is the real teacher of the Vedas, and the *upādhyāya* is a lower sort of teacher. But, as WILHELM, in my opinion, rightly remarks: "Es ist zu bezweifeln, ob im Buche Pauṣya diese Bedeutungsdifferenz gemacht wird".

[4] According to Nīlakaṇṭha (commentary ad 1.3.23 = Crit. Ed. 1.3.21), because his teacher, by his yogic powers, prevented the hole from being filled.

again),[5] presented himself in front of Dhaumya and explained to him what means he had resorted to in order to fill the hole. His teacher praised him for his obedience, adding that since he had got up, tearing out the hole in the dike, he would be known as Uddālaka (here this etymology derives the word from the root *ud-dal-*, to tear out). Then, pleased with him, Dhaumya granted him *śreyas* and knowledge of all the Vedas and Dharmaśāstras, and sent him away, his time as a student being over. (MBh 1.3.19-31).

Then Dhaumya sent his second pupil, Upamanyu, to guard cows. At the end of the day, after guarding the cows, Upamanyu came to his teacher and saluted him. Observing that Upamanyu was very fat: *pīvān [...] dṛḍham* (31), Dhaumya asked him by what means he obtained food. By begging, replied Upamanyu. Then Dhaumya told him not to eat what he got by begging without first giving it to himself.[6] Agreeing to this, Upamanyu again went to guard the cows, and then again presented himself before his teacher. Observing that he was still fat, Dhaumya asked him what he had been eating now, since he was taking from him all that he got from begging.[7] Upamanyu replied that he was going on a second begging-round after giving the produce of the first to his teacher. Dhaumya told him that it was not proper for him to do so, since thereby he was depriving others of their food. Agreeing

[5] The way Āruṇi describes it, the water was flowing out of the field: *niḥsaramāṇam udakam* (28). Perhaps we should imagine a rice-field, which must initially be kept under water. But according to Nīlakaṇṭha (commentary ad 1.3.22 = Crit. Ed. 1.3.21), a *kedāra* (i.e., a sort of earthen mound raised around a field) prevents the surplus water from flowing into the field and destroying the seeds: *bahujalapraveśena bījanāśo mā bhūd iti bhāvaḥ*, an opinion shared by MW (*vide sub kedāra-khaṇḍa*).

[6] As WILHELM (1965:6, note ad 37) remarks, the Dharmaśāstras prescribe that the students must first offer their teacher the food they obtain by begging, quoting Gautamadharmaśāstra 2.39, Āpastambadharmasūtra 1.1.3.31-32 and Manusmṛti 2.51.

[7] Presumably for the sake of clarity, MS N (except Ko. 3 Ñ1) inserts the following after 37: *sa tathety uktvā bhaikṣam caritvopādhyāyāya nyavedayat / sa tasmād upādhyāyaḥ sarvam eva bhaikṣam agṛhṇāt /* "Having consented, and after going on a begging-round, he gave it all to his teacher. The teacher took from him absolutely everything that he had begged." We must assume that in each case at least a few days elapse between each visit of Upamanyu to his teacher, but this is never clearly mentioned. In spite of the many repetitions in this narration, the style is also quite terse.

not to do so again, Upamanyu went to guard the cows and came back to his teacher. Dhaumya still found him fat, and after being questioned, Upamanyu revealed that he was now drinking the milk of the cows. His teacher told him that it was not proper for him to drink the cows' milk without first asking for permission. Promising not to do it again, Upamanyu went off to guard the cows, and when he came back, he was still fat. This time he confessed that he was drinking the milky froth which the calves were spitting out after drinking from their mothers' udders. As is to be expected, Dhaumya reprimanded him again: he was not to drink the froth, thus depriving the calves of their food.[8] These virtuous calves: *guṇavanto vatsāḥ* (49) were surely spitting out more froth than usual, out of pity for him! Promising not to drink the milk-froth again, Upamanyu went back to guard the cows. This time he did not eat anything. One day, tortured by hunger, he ate *arka*-leaves,[9] which made him blind. Wandering about blind, he fell into a pit or well: *kūpe* (1.3.32-52).

Noticing his absence, his teacher told his *śiṣyas*[10] that surely Upamanyu, prohibited from eating, was angry with him, which is why he was not coming back. They went in search of him. The teacher called out to him. Upamanyu replied from the bottom of the well, revealing his presence there, and explained how he had come to this plight. Dhaumya then advised him to praise the Aśvins who, being the heavenly physicians: *devabhiṣajau* (58), would restore his eye-sight.

[8] Yet, as WILHELM (1965:7, note ad 48) remarks, the *muni* Śamīka, on whose shoulders king Parikṣit places a dead snake, is also said to live on milk-froth dripping from calves' mouths (MBh 1.36.15). Thus it seems that (unlike eating food without first offering it to one's *guru*), drinking milk-froth was not reprehensible from the point of view of *dharma*, and was even a common ascetic practice.

[9] "*arka* (Calotropis Gigantea) is a bush widely spread in northern India; it has some medicinal properties: that it may cause blindness is further unknown." (VAN BUITENEN 1973:440, note 50). For a more precise description of the plant, see WILHELM (1965:7, note ad 51).

[10] *śiṣyān avocat* (1.3.53). The text is not quite consistent here: as a matter of fact, since Āruṇi has already left, Dhaumya now has only one other *śiṣya* apart from Upamanyu, namely Veda.

Accordingly, Upamanyu started praising the Aśvins in *ṛc*es or metrical *mantras*: *vāgbhir ṛgbhir* (59). (1.3.53-59).

1.3.60-70 contains the hymn Upamanyu sings in praise of the Aśvins. Pleased, the two gods appeared to him. They offered him an *apūpa*,[11] telling him to eat it. But Upamanyu refused to comply, explaining that he could not possibly eat it without first offering it to his teacher. The Aśvins insisted, telling him that once upon a time they had similarly offered an *apūpa* to Dhaumya, who had eaten it without offering it first to his own teacher. But Upamanyu adamantly refused to eat the *apūpa*, and then the Aśvins declared themselves pleased with his behaviour towards his teacher. They told him that his teacher had iron teeth: *kārṣṇāyasā dantāḥ* (75), but he, Upamanyu, would have golden ones: *hiraṇmayā*. Besides, his eyesight would be restored, and *śreyas* would accrue to him. Thus cured, Upamanyu went back to Dhaumya and told him all that had happened. Dhaumya was very pleased with him, and dismissed him after granting him knowledge of all the Vedas. Thus was Upamanyu's test: *parīkṣā* (78). (1.3.71-78).

As for the last student, Veda, he stayed for a long time in his teacher's house, enduring all kinds of hardship "like a bullock": *gaur iva* (81),[12] till finally Dhaumya declared himself pleased with him and dismissed him after granting him *śreyas* and omniscience. Thus was Veda's test. (1.3.79-82).

---

[11] *apūpa*: rice-cake or honey-comb. The term appears a few times in the ṚV, where the *apūpa* is offered in sacrifices to Indra (3.52.1 & 7; 8.91.2) and Agni (10.45.9). Sāyaṇa says it is a rice-cake. According to Nīlakaṇṭha (commentary ad 1.3.69 = Crit. Ed. 1.3.71), the *apūpa* is a type of food containing lots of holes and cooked in oil: *bahucchidraṃ snehapakvaṃ bhakṣyam*, thus looking like a honey-comb.

[12] According to Nīlakaṇṭha, *gauḥ* = *balīvardaḥ*.

The Vedic antecedents

This story presents a number of immediately perceptible Vedic antecedents. In the ṚV, the Aśvins are well-known saviours and physicians: *bhiṣajau*, and, though no Upamanyu appears there in the long list of their protégés, they have to their credit the cure of many blind(ed) people, as well as the salvation of personages who have been buried, kept in holes, pits, wells, and such like.[13] All these references appear in hymns addressed to the Aśvins: 1.112.4-6 & 8; 1.116.11 & 14 & 16 & 24; 1.117.5 & 12 & 17-18; 1.118.6-7; 1.119.6-7; 8.5.23; 8.8.20; 10.39.3 & 8-9.[14] ṚV 1.112.8 and 10.39.3 mention in general terms the Aśvins' power to heal the blind, without mentioning any particular names: *prā́ndhaṃ [...] cákṣasa [...] kṛtháḥ*: "you made the blind to see"[15] (1.112.8); *andhásya [...] yuvā́m [...] āhur bhiṣájā*: "they called you the physicians of the blind" (10.39.3). Among specific blind people whose eyesight was restored by the Aśvins figure Trimantu (1.112.4), whom the Aśvins made "far-sighted": *vicakṣaṇá*,[16] and Kavi (or perhaps simply a 'seer') (1.116.14), whom they made to see: *kavím [...] yuvám [...] akṛṇutaṃ vicákṣe*. Slightly more detailed are the references to the healing of Ṛjrāśva and Kaṇva. Ṛjrāśva had been blinded by his wicked father, literally "led to darkness": *támaḥ práṇītam* (1.117.17), because he offered 100 rams to a she-wolf. As ZELLER (1990:59) notes, the wolf represents the wilderness, what is outside, alien, inimical. Thus by offering a sacrifice to a wolf, Ṛjrāśva transgressed the ritual order, hence his punishment.[17] The Aśvins gave

[13] For general information on the Aśvins in the ṚV, see especially ZELLER 1990.

[14] OBERLIES (1993:183, note 53) makes us attentive to the fact that these saving acts of the Aśvins are never mentioned in the Aśvin hymns of books 2 to 4.

[15] However, according to Sāyaṇa, the blind is here the *ṛṣi* Ṛjrāśva.

[16] Perhaps, this should be taken in a metaphorical sense. This is at least implied by Sāyaṇa, according to whom *vicakṣaṇa* means "omniscient": *sarvārthānāṃ jñātā*.

[17] But according to Sāyaṇa's commentary on 1.117.17, this she-wolf is nothing but the Aśvins' donkey in disguise: *vṛkye* = *vṛkīrūpeṇa avasthitāya aśvinor vāhanāya rasabhāya*.

him eyes to see (1.116.16; 1.117.17-18; Khila 1.12.7). As for Kaṇva, who was "smeared over": *ápiriptāya*, the Aśvins gave him back his eye-sight (1.118.7; 8.5.23).[18] Sāyaṇa here refers to a story told in Jaiminīyabrāhmaṇa 3.72-73, which goes as follows: Kaṇva is married to the daughter of the Asura Akhaga. Angry, she goes to stay with her relatives. In order to get her back, Kaṇva has to prove to the Asuras that he is a real Brahmin and a seer. The Asuras, "smearing (his eyes) with a salve": *avalepenāvalimpanta[ḥ]*, make him blind and tell him that he must announce the coming of dawn. The Aśvins, who have come to know of this, tell him that at dawn they will fly over him, sounding their *vīṇā* to warn him. During the night, the Asuras repeatedly give false alarm, but of course Kaṇva is not cheated and correctly announces the coming of dawn after hearing the Aśvins.

Antaka, Vandana and Rebha were rescued out of pits by the Aśvins. Thus, they revived Antaka who was exhausted or starving in a hole: *ántakaṃ jásamānam ā́raṇe [...] jijinváthuḥ* (1.112.6). The rescue of Rebha is mentioned a few times: *úd rebháṃ [airatam]*: you made Rebha come out (1.118.6). And in 10.39.9 we read: *yuváṃ ha rebhám vṛṣaṇā gúhā hitám úd airayataṃ mamṛvā́ṃsam aśvinā*: "O Bulls, you dug out the hidden Rebha who was dying, O Aśvins." According to Sāyaṇa, 1.117.12 also refers to Rebha,[19] though no name is mentioned: *híraṇyasyeva kaláśaṃ níkhātam úd ūpathur daśamé āśvinā́han*: "you dug up, on the tenth day, the one who was buried like a pitcher of gold, O Aśvins." Sāyaṇa here comments that Rebha was buried in a well by the Asuras for ten nights and nine days. In these passages, Rebha seems to be buried in a dry place, but in 1.116.24, we read that Rebha was kept in the water by his enemy for ten nights and nine days, and was all but dissolved, when the Aśvins "spooned him

[18] ṚV 1.112.5 and 8.8.20 also mention that the Aśvins protected Kaṇva, but without mentioning his blindness.

[19] However, according to BAUNACK (1896:266) this verse alludes to Vandana.

out" like *soma*.[20] Most frequently mentioned is Vandana's salvation (1.112.5; 1.116.11; 1.117.5; 1.118.6; 1.119.6-7; 10.39.8). They brought out (the verbs most frequently used are *úd ūpathuḥ* and *úd airayatam*) the buried Vandana from a field: *kṣétrād* (1.119.7) or a pit for catching antelopes: *ṛśyadā́d* (10.39.8). He was decayed due to old age: *nírṛtaṃ jaraṇyáyā*, and they put him together again, like wonderfully skilled artisans a chariot: *rátham ná dasrā karaṇā́ sám invathaḥ* (1.119.7). He was like a hidden treasure: *nidhím ivā́pagūḷham* (1.116.11). Verse 1.117.5 contains the most telling set of comparisons: he was as if sleeping in the lap of Perdition: *suṣupvā́ṃsaṃ ná nírṛter*[21] *upásthe*. He was like the sun residing in darkness: *sū́ryaṃ ná [...] támasi kṣiyántam*. He was like a buried golden ornament, fair to see: *rukmáṃ ná darśatáṃ níkhātam*. Vandana was brought out "so that he could see the sun": *svar dṛśé* (1.112.5). The Ṛgvedic hymns themselves never mention the reason why Vandana was thus buried, but Sāyaṇa (cf. 1.116.11) adduces a similar story as for Rebha, namely that he was kept in a pit by Asuras, and, unable to get out, invoked the Aśvins who came to his rescue.

The people listed above who were saved by the Aśvins are either blind or have fallen into holes. None of them is both. The MBh story has united both events in the case of Upamanyu, and even causally linked them: it is because Upamanyu was blind that he fell into a pit. Besides, in the case of the Ṛgvedic personages, we can notice that in many cases they find themselves in their unfortunate circumstances due to some actively malignant intervention: Ṛjrāśva was blinded by his wicked father, and Kaṇva was "smeared over", presumably by Asuras. Likewise, for Rebha and Vandana, Sāyaṇa adduces stories where they are said to be buried by enemies or Asuras. On the other hand, Upamanyu brings about his plight by his own behaviour. Of course,

[20] Also 1.112.5 mentions that Rebha is tied up and kept in the water.

[21] According to Sāyaṇa, Nirṛti means the earth here.

one might say that his teacher had more than a hand in it. This is certainly true, but it is far from certain that Dhaumya had evil intentions in doing so: as we shall see, the opposite is almost certainly the case.

Thus, by its very subject-matter, this MBh tale affiliates itself directly with the Vedic tradition. This Vedic affiliation is strengthened by the Vedic hymn which Upamanyu sings in praise of the Aśvins. This hymn is composed in Triṣṭubhs, like many Ṛgvedic hymns addressed to the Aśvins.[22] Now, though the text says that Upamanyu sings in "metrical *mantra*s": *vāgbhir ṛgbhir*, it is well-known that this is in fact no genuine hymn from the Ṛgveda,[23] not even from a lost recension, but rather an imitation in what Renou has styled 'hybrid Vedic Sanskrit'.[24] HOPKINS (1915:168) calls this hymn a "ridiculous laudation", but in fact this comment is far from correct. For, as RENOU (1939/1997:763) shows, although the grammar of this hymn is modern, "le vocabulaire est foncièrement mantrique", and this poem adduces several truly Vedic motifs. Thus many epithets given to the Aśvins figure in the Ṛgveda, likewise certain deeds for which they are praised here, like saving the quail which was half-swallowed by a wolf (1.3.62). Also, the type of 'enigma poetry' which is manifest throughout the hymn is typical of many Ṛgvedic hymns (1.164 being the most typical example) and at least of one hymn addressed to the Aśvins, namely ṚV 10.106.[25] On the other hand, what is curiously lacking in this hymn, and, (or so it seems), would be particularly apposite, is any mention of the various people saved by the Aśvins

22 The meter is at times irregular, with lacking or extra syllables, due to the faulty transmission of the text.

23 See RENOU (1939/1997:763).

24 To this category belong the Suparṇākhyāna, the Bāṣkalamantra Upaniṣad, *et al.* See RENOU (1956b:3).

25 The reader is referred to RENOU (1939/1997) for a detailed analysis of Upamanyu's hymn, the exact Vedic references it contains, and its textual reconstruction which at times slightly differs from the text proposed by the Crit. Ed.

from distressing situations, such as we listed above. It is of course hazardous to venture an explanation for this omission. But one answer might be that although the Aśvins prominently figure as saviours in the ṚV, none of the people mentioned as their *protégés* in that text had any noteworthy posterity in post-Ṛgvedic texts. Even in the ṚV, most of the references to them are at best allusive, if not downright obscure (at least for the modern reader), for this text does not tell us anything about the people saved by the Aśvins, apart precisely from the fact that they were saved by them. Thus any mention of names (like Vandana, Ṛjrāśva, etc.) might have been lost on the Epic's audience. Perhaps in epic times the salvation of the quail, which is mentioned here, had remained as the paradigmatic saving act attributed to the twin gods. The hymn also mentions that the Aśvins freed the cows after cleaving the mountain (66), a deed which is usually attributed to Indra. And Upamanyu quite appositely mentions the Aśvins' power to bring light (61, 68) and dispel darkness (61), since he hopes of course to regain his own eye-sight.[26]

Thus, the immediate and explicitly mentioned reference for the hymn to the Aśvins are the *ṛc*es. And Upamanyu's blindness, his fall into a well and subsequent salvation and cure by the Aśvins, have an immediate Ṛgvedic resonance. But on the whole, the story of Dhaumya's *śiṣya*s also evokes another literary genre. I am referring here to two stories which appear in the fourth Prapāṭhaka of the Chāndogya Upaniṣad.[27]

ChU 4.4-9 narrates the story of Satyakāma Jābāla who becomes the *śiṣya* of one Hāridrumata Gautama. The latter gives him four hundred emaciated cows to guard, and Satyakāma swears not to return before they have multiplied to one thousand. He guards them for many years,

[26] See VAN BUITENEN (1973:440, note 60).

[27] SENART (1930:XIX) sees things the other way round. For him, the stories of the ChU are reminiscent of the stories of Dhaumya's students: "deux histoires d'étudiants brahmaniques [...], du genre de celles que conte le début en prose du *Mahābhārata*."

till they have reached the required number. Then, in turn, a bull of his herd, the fire, a *haṃsa* and a *madgu* bird tell him one quarter of the *brahman*. When he returns to his *guru*, the latter tells him what remains to be known.

ChU 4.10-14 tells the story of Upakosala Kāmalāyana, who is the *śiṣya* of Satyakāma Jābāla. For twelve years, the latter does not instruct him in the true knowledge (in spite of his wife's warnings) and the poor Upakosala feels fully dejected and stops taking any food. Then the three sacrificial fires take pity on him and decide to instruct him themselves. Accordingly, they reveal to him their own true nature and the nature of the *ātman*. Then Upakosala's *guru* completes the fires' teaching.

In these two stories, the motifs which remind us of the story of Dhaumya's students are first of all the trials which the *śiṣya*s are subjected to before being taught. None of them is directly taught by his teacher: at best, the teacher only completes his *śiṣya*'s instruction. Satyakāma Jābāla is first sent to guard the cows, just like Upamanyu. And like Upamanyu too, Upakosala Kāmalāyana has to fast before he receives the revelation. Thus it appears that these two ingredients (or at least one of them) are necessary preliminaries before receiving the true knowledge. Also, all these students receive a similar supernatural revelation. Upamanyu sees the Aśvins, Upakosala is taught by the sacrificial fires, and Satyakāma by various animals and by the Fire. Obviously, the names of the *śiṣya*s in both texts do not tally. But we may note that the ChU mentions one Prācīnaśāla Aupamanyava (i.e. son of Upamanyu) in 5.11, and Uddālaka Āruṇi (the name is the same as that of Dhaumya's first *śiṣya*), is mentioned in 5.11.2 as one who studies the *ātman*. In 6, he is the father of Śvetaketu Āruṇeya whom he instructs in the knowledge of the *ātman*. (The Upaniṣad makes no mention of Uddālaka's own apprenticeship under Dhaumya, nor of how he came to have his name.)

The stories in both texts are similar not only content-wise, but also style-wise: for, quite unusually for the MBh, practically the whole Pauṣya-sub-parvan (like the ChU), is narrated in prose,[28] except for the hymns[29] and the very last verses of the *parvan* (1.3.178-195). Moreover the manner of telling the tale in the MBh is quite unlike the usual epic flow, but very similar to the style of Buddhist *sūtra*s, or, precisely, that of certain Upaniṣads. The story of Upamanyu unfolds slowly, with many repetitions, especially in the dialogues, where the same words and even whole sentences are repeated over and over again, and what has been said or has happened before is again passed in review.[30] Likewise, in the story of Satyakāma in the ChU, the same stock phrases are used four times in the passage describing the teaching he receives from the fire and the three animals.

The question which might arise here is that of chronology: which came first, the ChU or the Pauṣyaparvan of the Mahābhārata? The sub-*parvan*s at the beginning of the MBh are usually considered to be late. (See e.g. HOPKINS 1915:169). On the other hand, the ChU is considered to be one of the oldest Upaniṣads. As OLIVELLE (1998:12) writes:

> "The scholarly consensus, well founded I think, is that the Bṛhadāraṇyaka and the Chāndogya are the two earliest Upaniṣads.

[28] WINTERNITZ (1927:I, 321, note 1) remarks that prose is also used in the Mārkaṇḍeya section of the Āraṇyakaparvan and in the Nārāyaṇīya of the Śāntiparvan. He considers that the use of prose is a sign that these pieces are late insertions. On the contrary, VOGEL (1926:61) remarks that "the *Paushya-parvan* [...] is composed in very archaic prose", and GOPAL (1982:236) claims, without justifying his opinion, that: "It goes without saying that these prose portions intermixed with sporadic verses constitute the earliest stratum of the Epic."

[29] Apart from Upamanyu's hymn to the Aśvins, there is also subsequently Uttaṅka's hymn to the snakes in 1.3.139-146, and 1.3.150-153, where he describes the visions which appear to him in the *nāga-loka*. Perhaps the use of prose throughout the *parvan* is precisely a means to give special emphasis to the hymns, which are naturally in verse.

[30] This should still be visible enough in the summary of the story given above, although I have tried to avoid a few repetitions, especially in the dialogues, for fear of boring the reader.

> [...] The two texts as we have them are, in all likelihood, pre-Buddhist; placing them in the seventh to sixth centuries BCE may be reasonable, give or take a century or so."

Thus, *prima facie*, it is likely that the ChU antedates the Pauṣya-subparvan of the Mahābhārata by at least a few centuries. However, nothing can be affirmed too categorically in this regard. In any case, we are not trying to prove here that the MBh 'borrowed' from the ChU: as we have noted above, the affiliation to the *ṛc*es is explicitly stated in this passage, but we find no such clear reference to an Upaniṣadic source.[31] It is more likely that stories such as those of Uddālaka Āruṇi and other *śiṣya*s were a common stock in certain Brahmanical circles, and were put to different uses by different texts.

Patterns of initiation

Now that we have examined the Vedic antecedents of this particular narrative, it remains to be seen what is its meaning. At first reading, the stories of Dhaumya's students are rather apt to make us smile. Thus Āruṇi, who rather dull-wittedly finds no better means to fill the hole in the dike than lying down in it (so that the water immediately starts flowing out again as soon as he gets up), and the greedy Upamanyu who is never at a loss to find new sources of food, till harm befalls him. And what about Dhaumya, we may ask, who seemingly tortures[32] his students till they are driven to rash acts?

---

31 However, generally speaking, the MBh does refer to the Upaniṣads. As HOPKINS (1920:27) notes: "[the Bṛhadāraṇyakopaniṣad] is the only one of the oldest Upanishads certainly cited, though the Chāndogya, Aitareya and Kauṣitaki have many parallels with the epic". Similarly BIARDEAU (1997:171): "the Upaniṣads were used as much as the ritual texts".

32 This impression is not just the modern reader's. According to Nīlakaṇṭha (commentary ad 1.3.21 = Crit. Ed. 1.3.19), Dhaumya's iron teeth elliptically designate his cruel words: *upādhyāyasya te kārṣṇāyasā dantā itivākyaśeṣāt krūravacā ity arthaḥ*. In his commentary ad 1.3.73 (= Crit. Ed. 1.3.75), he writes that they represent Dhaumya's lack of compassion (*nirdayatvam*) towards his *śiṣyas*.

But once we go beyond the superficially humorous nature of this narrative, we start perceiving in it certain motifs which immediately remind us of patterns of initiation ceremonies. According to Eliade,[33] the basic pattern of all initiation ceremonies is that of death and rebirth, including a promise of immortality, out of which the initiate emerges as a entirely different person: he is literally reborn.[34] These death and rebirth are not literal of course, but symbolic. More precisely, the motifs which are reminiscent of initiation ceremonies in the story of Upamanyu, and Āruṇi, and also in that of Uttaṅka, which is subsequently narrated, are the following: fasting; isolated sojourn in a secluded place; blindness; burial; tests and temptations; visions and revelations; rebirth and immortality. This initiatory pattern is very well

[33] For the topic of initiations, ELIADE's basic book is *Initiation, rites, sociétés secrètes. Naissances mystiques.* (1959); (the second edition, also by Gallimard, is simply entitled *Naissances mystiques*). It describes and analyses initiation ceremonies in various types of societies. But many of Eliade's works deal with this topic. See the bibliography given in SNOEK (1987:99, note 13).

[34] Eliade's general representation of various societies and his interpretation of initiation rites in particular has been criticized by certain modern anthropologists. Thus for instance LA FONTAINE (1985:22-23): "Mircea Eliade, the distinguished religious philosopher, published in 1958 a book called *Rites and Symbols of Initiation* which reads curiously like the work of nineteenth-century anthropologists. He retains all the assumptions of that time; in particular he assumes that western Europe represents the greatest development of civilization, and Christianity the highest form of religion. He places other societies on a historical ladder according to their modes of making a living. [...] He assumes that their initiation rituals, which he sees as coterminous with their religion, must reveal the crude forms of ideas which receive their highest development in Christianity. Thus, what he is doing is to take the idea of life after death, of spiritual rebirth, which he sees as central to Christianity, and seek counterparts to it in the other rituals he studies. What purports to be a study of development from most primitive to most civilized is, in fact, an interpretation of other religions in the light of the assumption that Christianity is the end-product towards which those religions will ultimately develop. Hence, while his discussion provides us with interesting insights into religious symbolism it is prejudiced from the beginning." This is not the place to discuss whether Eliade really draws the model for his death/rebirth/immortality initiatory pattern from Christianity. It is true that this initiation-pattern is strikingly present in certain Biblical narratives, but Eliade is also perfectly acquainted with the Indian material. Whatever the case may be, it seems to me that this model applies particularly well too in the case of the Indian myths we are dealing with here. Another initiatory schema, (but one which, in my opinion, does not apply so well in the present case), is the tripartite one proposed by VAN GENNEP (1909/1981:14): "le schéma complet des rites de passage comporte en théorie des rites *préliminaires* (séparation), *liminaires* (marge) et *postliminaires* (agrégation)".

attested elsewhere in the Indian context, on the one hand in the *dīkṣā* ceremony (a term which is usually precisely translated as 'initiation'), which the *yajamāna* has to undergo before offering a *soma*-sacrifice, and mainly involves fasting, keeping oaths of silence, isolated residence in a secluded hut, which the texts themselves[35] clearly describe as a return to the embryonic stage, followed by a rebirth in the sacrifice; and also, on the other hand, in the *upanayana* ceremony, which young boys of the three upper *varṇa*s have to undergo before becoming *brahmacārin*s, which is literally a rebirth into the knowledge of the Vedas, and allows them to become *dvija*s, or "twice-born". (See ELIADE 1959:118-123). The motifs of fasting, keeping silence, covering the eyes and residing in an isolated place also appear in Gobhilagṛhyasūtra 3.2.32-33, which describes what the Vedic student should do before his teacher initiates him in the knowledge of the three *stotriya* verses of the Mahānāmnīs:[36]

> *pariṇaddho vāgyato na bhuñjīta trirātram ahorātrau vā* // 3.2.32 //
> *api vā 'raṇye tiṣṭhed ā 'stam ayāt* // 3.2.33 //
> "With veiled eyes, keeping silence, he should abstain from food through a period of three nights, or through one day and one night. Or he should stand in the forest till sunset (and spend the night in the village)."[37]

As far as mythology in general, and the MBh in particular, are concerned, we can note that another myth narrated in MBh 1.71-72, that of Kaca, was analyzed in terms of an initiation-rite by DEFOURNY (1986:269-282). This myth lends itself particularly well to such an

---

35 E.g. ŚB 3.3.3.12. See SEN (1978:74) under *dīkṣā*.

36 "Name of a group of 3 *tṛca*s (9 verses) of the Sāma Veda. Beginning with the words *vidā maghavan*; also called *śakvarī* verses; chanted on various occasions (*ahīna*). Lāṭyāyana Śrautasūtra VII.5.9." (SEN 1978:97).

37 Transl. by OLDENBERG (1892/1964). In the translation, the numbers are 3.2.37 & 38.

analysis, and the Eliadean components of initiations (death, rebirth and immortality) are strikingly present in it.

Before analyzing in detail the various initiatory motifs which appear in the story of Upamanyu, we must first of all mention that already the Ṛgvedic stories of salvations by the Aśvins have strong initiatory undercurrents, reminding us of *rites de passage*. This was first remarked upon by BAUNACK (1897), and further developed by ZELLER (1991:76): "Viele der beschriebenen Einzelheiten erinnern [...] an Initiationsriten, etwa der versteckte, unzugängliche Aufenthalt, die grundsätzliche Einsamkeit und ein todesähnlicher Zustand, dann die Rettung als Geburt und Erneuerung." Why the Aśvins have this sort of tutelary function, presiding over these *rites de passage,* was most convincingly elucidated by OBERLIES (1993; 1998). According to this author, the Aśvins are principally the gods of "intermediary realms" (die Götter der Zwischenbereiche). Due to their twin-birth, from different origins (one from a human, the other from a divine father), the Aśvins belong neither fully to the earth, nor to heaven (OBERLIES 1993:171), and therefore they must keep moving from one to the other, hence their well-known *vartis* (circuit). The precise moment in time usually attributed to them is dawn, that is, between night and day. Likewise, they are often described in connection with Uṣas, Dawn, or Sūryā, the daughter of the sun, who is the young morning sun according to OBERLIES (1993:175). The number three is characteristic for them. As OBERLIES (1993:176-177) says: "Die Drei scheint – dies formuliere ich bewusst als eine Vermutung! – die Zahl mit *einem* characteristischen 'Dazwischen', mit einer 'Mitte' zu sein. Sie hat die Struktur 1-1-1, die die Dreizahl zugleich zu einer Zahl der Ganzheit macht." Their birth is somewhere mid-way between the Devas and the Asuras, who were previously in power. They share the latters' *māyā*, or magic power, which comes to the fore in their miraculous saving acts (OBERLIES 1993:177). Finally, and most importantly for our present investigation, they typically bring their help to people (or animals) who find themselves in 'intermediary states': between non-being and being, life and death,[38] darkness and light, old age and rejuvenation, celibacy and marriage, etc. This applies to all the Ṛgvedic personages we have listed above, who are usually hovering between life and death, who are fallen into wells, i.e., are neither quite fully buried nor in the open air, who have been blinded, and are made to see again. "Immer wenn Belange eines prägnanten 'Dazwischen' betroffen sind, werden die Aśvin angerufen; dann werden sie *zwischen* diversen Bereichen tätig". (OBERLIES 1993:182). And: "Die Handlungssequenz des 'Ausscheidens aus und des anschliessenden Wiedereintritts in die Gemeinschaft' deutet daraufhin, dass die Berichte der Heilungen durch die Aśvin mythische Thematisierungen von Initiations- und Übergangs-Riten sind." (OBERLIES 1993:184).

OBERLIES' expression: "mythische Thematisierungen von Initiations- und Übergangs-Riten" is very accurate. Likewise, the stories of the *śiṣya*s in the MBh indeed deal with initiations, but not with initiation-rites. We are here dealing with mythical, prototypical initiations, which are much more drastic and 'real' than initiation-rites. What is described is not a 'dramatic' *mise en scène*, but the 'real thing', if we may say so. Thus, the initiate is not simply kept in a hut representing the darkness of the tomb or womb, but he really falls into a well or even goes to the underworld (as in Uttaṅka's case). Upamanyu really goes blind, his eyes are not just covered. The gods appear in person to these *śiṣya*s, they are not just dealing with people masquerading as gods, as is the case in certain initiation ceremonies, and they receive truly supernatural visions and revelations, which are (sometimes) subsequently explained by their *guru*.

We shall presently deal with the different aspects of these myths which are reminiscent of initiation-rites. Let us make it clear from the

[38] Some of them, like Rebha, are apparently even quite dead, since the Aśvins dig him out only on the tenth day. Death in this case is more than just symbolic.

start that we are not trying to fit the different initiatory motifs which appear in these *śiṣyas*' stories into well-defined initiatory models, such as: puberty rites, shamanic initiations, or initiations into secret societies, etc.[39] Many motifs are in any case common to all these different types of initiation-rites, and we shall try to examine them in the stories which concern us here.

Fasting

In the Indian context, any *tapas* (penance) necessarily involves gradually decreasing the intake of food. Usually, the order is: eating roots and fruit, then only dry leaves, then water, and finally only wind (*vāyubhakṣa*), i.e., nothing at all. In Upamanyu's diet we see the same gradual (though involuntary) lessening of food intake: first he lives on what he gets from begging, then on what he gets from a second begging-round (presumably less than during the first), then on milk, then on milk-froth, and finally on nothing at all, except for the fatal *arka*-leaves which cause his blindness. Thus Upamanyu is systematically starved by his teacher, who forbids him, one after the other, all the means of nourishment he devises. This may first appear as sheer cruelty on the part of Dhaumya, but the import is clear: Upamanyu has to refrain from eating before he can have access to any kind of revelation. As GERLITZ (1965:272) says:

> "Auch von der Nahrung gehen bestimmte Kraftwirkungen aus, die leibliche oder seelische Schäden verursachen können. Das Fasten nun vermag neben anderen asketischen Übungen Unreines fernzuhalten, die eigenen Kräfte zu vergrössern und sogar in die Ekstase zu führen."

---

39 And neither can the initiations of Dhaumya's students be compared to *upanayanas*, since they are already *śiṣyas* living in their *guru*'s house.

Fasting is well-known in most initiation-rites (see ELIADE 1959:47-48) and it is the necessary precondition for entering into a kind of *état second*, which facilitates 'hallucinations' or 'visions' of divine revelations. As such, it is used by many societies and in the context of various religions, especially in the context of initiation-rites. As GERLITZ (1965:273) says: "Tatsächlich wird hier die Verbindung von *Initiation* und *Vision* so stark, dass man geradezu von einem 'Erfasten' der Gnade sprechen muss". This author speaks in some detail about this type of fasting which he calls *jejunium ecstaticum* or *jejunium propheticum*: the visionary fast. He notes that it is a preparatory factor of the highest importance before any religious initiation. Through fasting, the initiate becomes detached from mundane problems and realities and is filled with an intense, meditative concentration. Visited by visions and dreams, he imagines that he is filled with supernatural powers. "Der durch die Entsagung geschwächte Organismus mag dabei eine gewisse psychische Reizbarkeit zeigen und so 'zur Phantasietätigkeit beitragen', wie allgemein angenommen wird." (1965:279).

In the light of the above, we realize that Dhaumya, far from acting out of any gratuitous malice towards Upamanyu, is consciously leading his *śiṣya* along the proper path which will enable him to receive the divine vision of the Aśvins, and also to become a real 'seer', in the true Vedic sense of the term, namely one who 'sees' or composes hymns.[40]

[40] We may contrast and compare this passage with ChU 6.7.2, where the motif of fasting similarly appears in the context of an 'initiation' or 'revelation', but with a very different purport. Uddālaka Āruṇi is instructing his son Śvetaketu in the true knowledge. He orders his son to stop eating for a fortnight: "Śvetaketu did not eat for fifteen days. Then he came back to his father and said: 'What shall I recite, sir?' 'The Ṛg verses, the Yajus formulas, and the Sāman chants.' 'Sir, I just can't remember them,' he replied." (Transl. by OLIVELLE 1998:251). His father wishes to make Śvetaketu understand that breath is composed of water (hence by drinking, though without eating, he keeps alive). And mind is composed of food: hence without eating he cannot remember the Vedas he has learnt by heart. We may contrast this with Upamanyu who is starving and blind but recites hymns. But the vast difference is that Śvetaketu cannot remember the texts he has learnt by heart, whereas Upamanyu becomes inspired to 'see' new *ṛc*es. Fasting may dull memory, but stimulates visionary and poetic powers.

And indeed, Upamanyu learns the lesson very well (albeit the hard way and slowly), for when the Aśvins offer him the *apūpa*, he refuses to eat it, in spite of his truly desperate situation. And the reward is not slow to come: he gets golden teeth, unlike his teacher who got iron ones, because in his time he did eat the *apūpa* without offering it first to his own teacher.[41] We understand by this episode that Dhaumya had probably gone through the same trials as his pupil (although this is not clearly spelt out), and that all his teachings and admonitions so far had the aim of preparing Upamanyu to affront the trial better than himself in his time, and reap the reward. And this reward is not unnaturally related to the instruments used for eating, namely, the teeth. Thus we realize that from the start Dhaumya had only good intentions towards his *śiṣya*, and this is confirmed by the fact that, far from being jealous or angry, Dhaumya is delighted when Upamanyu tells him the outcome of all his adventures.

The secluded place

As we have seen above in the quotation from GobhGS 3.2.33, one of the options for a *śiṣya*, before being taught certain verses, was to sojourn in the forest (*araṇye*) for a day. It is a common pattern in initiation-ceremonies that they have to take place in an isolated, uninhabited spot:

> "Le lieu du rite est séparé de l'espace domestique. Il instaure une rupture dans l'espace, alors que le rite consacre la rupture avec la vie antérieure. [...] Endroit éloigné, il est 'perdu', dans la brousse, dans la montagne, dans la jungle, des espaces intermédiaires qui

---

[41] Dhaumya's iron teeth have given rise to different interpretations: we have already noted that according to Nīlakaṇṭha they represent Dhaumya's cruel words and lack of compassion. According to VAN BUITENEN (1973:440, note 75), it means that he is a miserly man. But VAN BUITENEN does not say how he reaches this conclusion. WILHELM (1965:8, note *ad* 75) says: "Nach den Rechtsbüchern sind schwarze Zähne von Übel und erfordern besondere Sühne". He gives no reference to his sources.

> symbolisent le chaos, les modalités latentes, toutes les potentialités." (SIMON 1986:113).

Now, it is striking that both Upamanyu and Satyakāma Jābāla in the ChU receive their initiatory visions or teachings while they are guarding cows.[42] Guarding cows may of course really have been one of the tasks for which *śiṣyas* were commonly employed. Perhaps the cows confer additional auspiciousness and purity to this preparatory stage before receiving the revelation. In the present case, we immediately perceive what is the import of this occupation: the person who guards cows is alone, and in the jungle, i.e., in a territory which is outside the area inhabited by humans and therefore particularly suitable for the reception of initiations and visions.

Blindness

Another element which seems to be an essential step towards receiving the true vision or revelation, is Upamanyu's temporary blindness. Here his blindness, like his subsequent fall into the well, represents a 'death' before rebirth. As ELIADE (1959:50) notes: "Les ténèbres sont un symbole de l'*Autre Monde*, aussi bien de la mort que de l'état foetal." At the same time, it is not before he has become blind that Upamanyu truly 'sees'. As DONIGER (1999:109) puts it: "the myths tell us that we often see better without our eyes." Upamanyu's visions are recorded in the hymn he sings to the Aśvins. In many societies, blind people are credited with 'far-sightedness'. They see beyond what mere mortal eyes can see, with a visionary, even prophetic foresight. By becoming blind to the real world, Upamanyu gets access to a higher plane of reality.

This blindness, in Upamanyu's case, is caused by the *arka* leaves he eats when his hunger becomes unbearable. Why do these leaves cause blindness? At a first level of explanation, we must note that Upamanyu

42 The same applies to Kaca (MBh 1.71-72), who is twice killed by the Asuras (and subsequently revived), the first time while he is guarding his *guru*'s cows (1.71.26).

was not supposed to eat anything, since his teacher had practically forbidden him to eat without first offering the food to himself, or asking his permission. Upamanyu did none of these, and nevertheless ate the leaves. Hence, at this level, the resultant blindness is certainly in a way a punishment for this transgression. But as we have seen in footnote 9, *arka*-leaves do not seem to have the noxious power of causing blindness. Hence the explanation of this blindness must probably be sought at a symbolic level. What do these *arka*-leaves stand for? First, we may here quote TS 5.1.5.5 which contains the following curious statement: "One gathers things with a donkey, and therefore the donkey grows fat beyond all other domestic animals even on bad grazing, for people gather food and the *arka* plant with him." (Transl. by O'FLAHERTY 1985b:495).[43] It appears from this statement that the *arka* plant causes fatness, though the connection between the two is not immediately clear. And we remember that Upamanyu was at first "very fat": *pīvān dṛḍham*, a condition which, in his case, should clearly be avoided. Therefore, eating *arka*-leaves may have been more than a desperate expedient in his hunger, equal, in other words, to eating just about anything which was handy in the forest, but on the contrary a deliberate and well-aimed attempt at regaining his lost fatness, against his teacher's wishes. This still does not explain why the leaves provoke blindness. Here we should look at the meaning of the word *arka*. *Arka* does not primarily designate a plant. Its first meaning is that of 'sun' and then 'fire'. And Upamanyu is said to be "hit in the eye": *cakṣuṣy upahato*, after eating the leaves which are moreover described as "acrid, pungent, hot, and ripening": *kṣārakaṭūṣṇavipākibhiḥ* (1.3.52). Now we can understand how an excess of solar and fiery food causes Upamanyu's blindness, as if he had been 'hit in the eye' by the rays of the sun or of the fire. Besides,

[43] But here KEITH (1914) translates *arka* as "light". However, this does not seem to make any immediate sense.

the sun, which makes the plants grow, is considered as the nourisher *par excellence*,[44] which explains at the same time why these sun-leaves have the power to make one fat.

Burial

Due to his blindness, Upamanyu falls into a well or a hole. This fall into a well represents the fourth motif listed above, which we can broadly describe as burial (with different variants), and which is very well attested in most initiation ceremonies. (See ELIADE 1959:50). The meaning of the various sorts of burials is that of death before the rebirth which follows when the novice is initiated. In the Indian context of the *dīkṣā* ceremony, this burial has taken the milder form of a secluded sojourn in a hut. On the whole, the symbolism of burial is closely connected with that of blindness. While being 'buried', the novice returns to an embryonic stage, which is a necessary passage to his rebirth. The sojourn in a hole is not only Upamanyu's prerogative: Dhaumya's first *śiṣya* Āruṇi undergoes the same test. He keeps himself in the hole in the dike to prevent the water from flowing out. This motif is also shown in the story of Uttaṅka, which follows that of Dhaumya's students (1.3.83-115). Since Uttaṅka's story also contains

[44] Thus in MBh 3.2-4, when the Pāṇḍavas are exiled in the forest, a group of people, especially Brahmins, follow them, and refuse to leave them even when Yudhiṣṭhira explains that it would be difficult for him to feed them all. Then Dhaumya, his *purohita*, advises him to propitiate Sūrya, the sun-god. Yudhiṣṭhira does so, and Sūrya grants him an inexhaustible supply of food for the whole duration of his exile. We do not know whether the two Dhaumyas are the same person. To my knowledge, the Pāṇḍavas' *purohita* is never called Āyoda. Besides, the chronology does not quite tally: Dhaumya Āyoda, according to the context, lives roughly at the same time as king Janamejaya, the great-grand-son of the Pāṇḍavas. Of course, this argument is not entirely conclusive, since in the Epics people are often said to live for thousands of years. However, for reasons which will be explained below, it is unlikely that Dhaumya is such an immortal personage. Yet strikingly, both Dhaumyas guide their *protégés*, and direct them to the proper (Vedic) god to invoke in their particular trouble; besides, both exhibit the same mastery over food: negative, in the case of Dhaumya Āyoda, who deprives Upamanyu of food, and positive in the case of the Pāṇḍavas' *purohita*, who provides them with the means of obtaining food.

the motifs of the test, visions and rebirth, we shall briefly summarize it here.

The story of Uttaṅka

Veda, (who, we remember, was the last student of Dhaumya and was kept for a long time in the latter's house, enduring hardship), after "returning from living in his teacher's house": *pravṛttas tasmād gurukulavāsād*, became a householder in turn: *gṛhāśramaṃ pratyapadyata* (83). He too had three students. But he never used to tell them to do anything at all, because, "knowing full well the misfortune of living in a teacher's house, he had no wish to inflict any hardship on his students": *duḥkhābhijño hi gurukulavāsasya śiṣyān parikleśena yojayituṃ neyeṣa* (84). But once Veda was requested by two *kṣatriya*s, Janamejaya and Pauṣya, to perform a sacrifice for them, and had to leave the hermitage, which he kept in the care of one of his students, Uttaṅka. One day, the women came to tell Uttaṅka that his *upādhyāyinī* (teacher's wife) was in her fertile period, which should not be allowed to pass in vain, and that he should take his teacher's place. But Uttaṅka refused to comply. When he returned, Veda was pleased with his *śiṣya*'s behaviour, and told him that his time as a student was now over. But Uttaṅka did not want to go before offering his *gurudakṣiṇā*. Veda tarried, and did not name his fee, but on Uttaṅka's insistence he finally told him to go and ask his wife. The *upādhyāyinī* told Uttaṅka to get for her a pair of earrings which belonged to Pauṣya's wife. Uttaṅka set off to obtain the earrings. On his way, he met a huge man, riding an enormous bull. The man enjoined him to eat some of the bull's dung and urine. Uttaṅka first refused, but finally complied when the man told him that his *guru* had eaten the same before him. Then Uttaṅka reached Pauṣya's place, and, after certain incidents which are not particularly relevant for our present inquiry, he obtained the earrings from his wife. The latter told him that these jewels were hotly sought after by Takṣaka, the *nāga*-king, and that he should look after them well. On his way back, Uttaṅka observed a naked ascetic coming towards him. Then Uttaṅka kept the earrings on the ground and went for water.[45] Meanwhile, the presumed ascetic pounced on the earrings and ran away with them, Uttaṅka in hot pursuit. But at the very moment when he was catching hold of the ascetic, the latter changed back into his own form, that of Takṣaka of course, and vanished into a big hole in the earth. Uttaṅka followed him there, into the *nāga-loka*. He sang a hymn to the snakes, in order to propitiate them, but Takṣaka did not reappear. Then Uttaṅka saw visions: two women weaving black and white threads on a loom, a wheel turned by six young boys, and a handsome man (147-8). He praised them all in *mantravādaślokaiḥ*: "verses containing a sacred text" (see MW), (1.3.149).[46] Then the man declared himself pleased with him, and Uttaṅka explained his problem to him. The man told him to blow into the anus of a certain horse. When Uttaṅka did so, flames and smoke issued from all the apertures of the horse's body, filling the *nāga-loka*. Takṣaka, scared, returned the earrings to Uttaṅka, who managed (riding the same horse) to bring them to his teacher's wife just in time for the particular ceremony during which she wished to wear them, and in time to escape her curse. Subsequently, being questioned by Uttaṅka, his *guru* Veda explained to him the meaning of the various personages he had met on the way: the huge man on the bull was Indra, and the bull was Indra's elephant Airāvata. The dung and urine he gave him to taste was *amṛta*, thanks to eating which he could go to the underworld and come back unharmed. The two women

[45] Probably in order to purify himself after the polluting sight of this *śramaṇa*, as VAN BUITENEN (1973:440, note 135) suggests.

[46] WILHELM (1965:18, note ad 149) opines that these verses need not have been composed ad hoc, but notes that they are not found elsewhere.

were Dhātā and Vidhātā,[47] and the white and black threads were the days and nights. The wheel was the year, and the six youths the six seasons. The man was Parjanya,[48] and the horse was Agni.[49]

Uttaṅka, unlike Āruṇi and Upamanyu, does not merely enter/fall into a hole, but he goes down to the nether world, more specifically, to the *nāga-loka*. Here Takṣaka plays, perhaps involuntarily, the role of a psychopomp, leading Uttaṅka to the underworld.[50]

Tests and temptations

Another important element of these stories, and one which is also tightly linked with the initiation pattern, is that of the test and temptation which the students have to undergo before receiving their various visions and revelations. The stories of Upamanyu and Veda are described by the MBh itself as *parīkṣās*, or "tests".[51] What is tested is not only the physical courage of the *śiṣyas*, but also their resourcefulness and their moral fiber. Dhaumya deliberately puts his students to the test, knowing that only in this way they will obtain the

---

47 About these two names, VAN BUITENEN (1973:441, note 170) makes the following remark: "Dhātā and Vidhātā, creator and dispenser, [are] masculines in *-tar*, which here surprisingly seem to be taken for feminine *ā*-stems."

48 Here Parjanya is probably synonymous with Indra (who in post-Vedic times has taken over many of Parjanya's functions), for in his hymn Uttaṅka unmistakably praises him as Indra.

49 For Agni as a horse, see SMITH (1994:266-7).

50 After his adventure, Uttaṅka keeps a great resentment against Takṣaka and decides to take revenge. He goes to King Janamejaya, and tells him that Takṣaka had killed his (Janamejaya's) father Parikṣit, (something which Janamejaya had apparently never known), and convinces him to undertake the *sarpa-sattra* to get rid of Takṣaka.
We never learn why Takṣaka wants these earrings so badly. In the other version of Uttaṅka's story (14.54), it is said that not only the *nāgas*, but *devas* and *yakṣas*/*rākṣasas* as well are after the same earrings, which are described as magical earrings endowed with wonderful powers, which protect the wearer against all sorts of dangers. Perhaps, (but this is never explicitly said), Takṣaka wants them in order to escape from the impending *sarpa-sattra*. (Whereas he actually precipitates the event by this theft, since, as we have noted, it is precisely due to his anger at having been robbed by Takṣaka that Uttaṅka encourages Janamejaya to undertake the snake-sacrifice.) Or perhaps, it is simply in his quality of *nāga*, i.e., guardian of treasures and of gems, that Takṣaka wants to own these earrings.

51 That of Uddālaka is only indirectly called a test. See WILHELM (1965:35).

true revelation. Veda, on the other hand, who perhaps does not understand the ultimate aim of such tests, does not set any tasks to his own students. But the unavoidable nature of the ordeal is shown by the way in which Uttaṅka is put to the test anyway, even without his teacher's wish. What do these tests consist of? The thing which is preeminently put to the test seems to be the students' obedience to their master. And, as WILHELM (1965:33-36) notes, obeying the teacher provokes in each case a dilemma. Dhaumya shows himself pleased with Āruṇi for no better reason, it appears, than because the latter fulfilled his orders to the letter: entering into the hole of the dike when he found that no other method would do (and remaining there for some time), and coming out again at his teacher's call, even if doing so involved breaking the dike again.[52] Certainly, or so it seems to us, his actions do not display a penetrating intelligence, but the obedience with which they are executed is all that matters here.

As far as Upamanyu is concerned, he finally understands that the purport of all his teacher's prohibitions is that he should abstain from food, and he too passes the obedience test with flying colours when he refuses the *apūpa* proffered by the Aśvins. In this case, we are no longer dealing with a simple test, but with a temptation. The motif of the Aśvins as tempters seems to be an innovation of the Epic. In all the above-listed Ṛgvedic passages where they appear as saviours, the Aśvins are content with saving the blind and buried persons from the deplorable situation in which they find themselves without further putting them to the test.[53] In the story of Cyavana's rejuvenation

---

[52] As WILHELM (1965:5, note ad 20) remarks: "Dem Ruf des Lehrers Folge zu leisten, ist eine wichtige Vorschrift der Dharmaśāstras". He cites Gautamadharmaśāstra 2.25 and Āpastambadharmasūtra 1.2.6.5.

[53] Unless the she-wolf to whom Ṛjrāśva offers 100 sheep is really the Aśvins' donkey in disguise, as Sāyaṇa claims. In this case, the test might have been to recognize the she-wolf's real self, for which the Aśvins would naturally reward the seer. However, although the ṚV does mention the Aśvins' donkey (*rāsabha*) who draws their chariot (for instance in 1.34.9 and 1.116.2), it never explicitly states that the wolf is the Aśvins' donkeyă, and I do not know whence Sāyaṇa has the story.

(MBh 3.121-125; 13.141), the Aśvins also tempt Sukanyā, Cyavana's wife. Since Sukanyā, who has an old and decrepit husband, is presumably sexually starved, they tempt her with their own beautiful bodies (the Aśvins being the most handsome gods). Whereas Upamanyu is starving (with hunger), and the Aśvins accordingly tempt him with food,[54] and that too with a very powerful argument: "Do as your own master did before you!" In Upamanyu's case, the dilemma is whether he should obey his teacher or the Aśvins, all of them being in equal degree figures of authority.

In Uttaṅka's case, the test or temptation is first sexual, and emanates from his *guru*'s wife, who requests him to take her husband's place, since it is her fertile period which should not be allowed to pass in vain. Here again, Uttaṅka is in a dilemma. On the one hand, his teacher has told him before leaving to see to it that nothing is left undone, and it is a notorious sin to let a woman's fertile period go by in vain. But on the other hand, having intercourse with one's *guru*'s wife is one of the worst possible crimes, equivalent to incest, and Uttaṅka refuses. But he refuses, he says, "because I have not been told by my teacher to do even that which should not be done": *na hy aham upādhyāyena saṃdiṣṭaḥ / akāryam api tvayā kāryam iti //90//* Does this mean that he would unhesitatingly have done it if Veda had enjoined him to do so, against all the precepts of the *smṛti*? If yes, then again it is primarily the obedience towards one's *guru* which is at stake, above everything else. It is probable (though not explicitly stated in the text) that the *upādhyāyinī* keeps a grudge against Uttaṅka for having refused her favours, which is why she sends him on the difficult and dangerous quest for the earrings. (Her desire for revenge is also

[54] We have already discussed above the meaning of *apūpa*: rice-cake or honey-comb. If a honey-comb is meant here (which cannot entirely be ruled out, since honey (*madhu*) is the prerogative of the Aśvins), the transgression involved in eating it would be double, for a *brahmacārin* was strictly prohibited from eating honey. See for instance MSmṛ 2.177 & 11.159; GobhGS 3.1.23.

clearly evidenced by the alacrity with which she prepares to curse him, thinking that he will not return in time.)

On his way, Uttaṅka undergoes yet another test: Indra offers him *amṛta*, but in the shape of the *purīṣa* and *mūtra* (dung and urine) of the bull he is riding. It is only by consuming this disguised *amṛta* that Uttaṅka will be able to go to the *nāga-loka*, (as his teacher subsequently reveals), but he is initially unaware of this. In a way, this test is the reverse of Upamanyu's: the starving Upamanyu is offered something delicious which he must not eat, whereas Uttaṅka is given something disgusting[55] which he must eat. To complicate matters further, the Aśvins and Indra try to convince them both to eat with the same argument, namely, that their teacher had eaten the same before them. However difficult the choice, both *śiṣyas* make the right one: in Upamanyu's case, the right choice is not to imitate his teacher, whereas in Uttaṅka's case, the right choice is to imitate him.[56] Later, in the *nāga-loka*, Uttaṅka is again asked to do something disgusting: the man tells him to blow into the anus of the horse. Since this horse is Agni, blowing into it is of course the logical way to kindle his flames, but Uttaṅka is not initially aware of this. Again, by overcoming his disgust,[57] he manages to save the situation.

Visions and revelations

As in Upamanyu's case, the underground (world) is the place where Uttaṅka's visions occur. It is precisely for the sake of these visions that

---

[55] Though perhaps we should slightly qualify this statement. Eating cow-dung and urine may not seem as disgusting in the Indian context as it is to our eyes, for eating the *pañcagavya* or the "five products of the cow", i.e., milk, curds, ghee, dung, and urine, is considered to be a very meritorious and purifying act. A story told in MBh 13.81 explains in a rather amusing way how the cows' dung came to be full of *śrī* (auspiciousness).

[56] Of course, as WILHELM (1965:37) notes, Uttaṅka's teacher has not forbidden him to eat.

[57] In the second version of Uttaṅka's story, the horse specifically tells him: *mā jugupsāṃ kṛthāḥ*: "Don't be disgusted!" (14.57.40).

all the preceding ordeals had to be borne. What do these visions consist of? First of all, both *śiṣyas* see gods: Upamanyu sees the Aśvins (although in his case it is not sure whether he really sees them with his physical eyes, for he is blind at that time). Uttaṅka, on his way, first sees Indra mounted on Airāvata, whom he does not then recognize, and subsequently, in the underworld, he again sees Indra, and Agni in the form of a horse. These gods guide and direct Uttaṅka on his way, functioning as teachers.[58] Then, most importantly, both have visions of hymns, and thus become real 'seers' in the true Vedic sense of that word. Now we understand how important it is that Upamanyu should praise the Aśvins in *ṛc*es of his own composition, not just by quoting verses he has learnt by heart.[59] As for Uttaṅka, he first praises the *nāga*s (1.3.139-146), and then recites verses describing the visions of Time he has seen in the underworld and praising Indra and Agni (1.3.150-153). In this hymn, Uttaṅka seems to have perfectly recognized the identity of the handsome man and the horse, although he later requests Veda to explain the meaning of these visions to him. For in 1.3.152-153, he praises Indra in no equivocal terms, mentioning many of his exploits which were well-known since Vedic times: "killer of Vṛtra and Namuci": *vṛtrasya hantā namucer nihantā* (1.3.152), and pays homage to the "lord of the three worlds": *lokatrayeśāya*, and the "breaker of forts": *puraṃdarāya* (1.3.153). Likewise, he calls the horse "the ancient foetus of the waters": *garbham apāṃ purāṇaṃ*, and

---

[58] Interestingly, as WILHELM (1965:41) notes, Śatapathabrāhmaṇa 11.5.4.2 contains a formula which has to be recited by the teacher at the time of the *upanayana*, in which both Agni and Indra are mentioned as the new student's future teachers, along with his actual teacher. KUIPER (1983:182) calls Agni the "*guru par excellence*".

[59] On this subject, GOPAL (1982:236) makes the following remark: "So far as I know, this phenomenon of praying to gods in self-composed Ṛcās is extremely rare in later Sanskrit and the only other example of a similar nature is met with in the fourth act of Kālidāsa's Abhijñāna-Śākuntalam [4,7] where the sage Kāśyapa blesses Śakuntalā with a verse composed in a Ṛgvedic meter at the time of her departure." On the contrary, WILHELM (1965:34) supposes that Upamanyu has learnt the hymn from his teacher.

"belonging to all men": *vaiśvānaram* (1.3.153), which are well-known names of Agni, especially in Vedic literature.

Most interesting are the visions of Time, shared by both Upamanyu and Uttaṅka. These are mainly related to the cyclical nature of time: the "wheel of time" (*kāla-cakra*).[60] Thus 1.3.64, where the 720 spokes are the days and nights of the year. According to VAN BUITENEN (1973:440, note 60), the wheel of the year is said to be rimless, because it is not a real wheel.

> *ekāṃ nābhiṃ saptaśatā arāḥ śritāḥ*
> *pradhiṣv anyā viṃśatir arpitā arāḥ /*
> *anemi cakraṃ parivartate 'jaraṃ*
> *māyāśvinau samanakti carṣaṇī //*
> "Seven hundred spokes do rest on one nave
> To the wheel rims are stuck another twenty:
> But rimless runs this Wheel forever –
> Popular Aśvins, magic adorns ye!"[61]

Or 1.3.65, which describes the year with its twelve months and six seasons:

> *ekaṃ cakraṃ vartate dvādaśāraṃ pradhi-*
> *ṣaṇṇābhim*[62] *ekākṣam amṛtasya dhāraṇam* / [...]
> "One is the Wheel, with its twelve spokes,[63]
> Six naves, one axle, that bears the Elixir [...]."

---

[60] Vipula, the *śiṣya* of the sage Devaśarman, (see above the chapter entitled "Indra the lover of Ahalyā") has similar visions of the cyclical nature of time, although not in the context of an initiation, which are subsequently explained by his master. See MBh 13.42-43.

[61] The translations of these verses are VAN BUITENEN's (1973).

[62] RENOU (1939/1997:769) notes: "*ṣaṇṇābhim*: substitué par modernité à *trinābhi-* [ṚV] I 164 2 Khil. I 2 8." In the early ṚV, the year was divided into three seasons. The division into six is found from the Yajur Veda onwards. See FELLER (1995:7-9).

[63] Here van Buitenen translates "rims", probably a translation of *pradhi* (felly of a wheel). "Spokes" is the translation of *ara*. Here, as the faulty meter shows, we should probably choose between *ara* and *pradhi* while establishing the text, as RENOU (1939/1997:764) suggests, and unlike what the Crit. Ed. does.

We can compare this with Uttaṅka's verse in 1.3.150, where the three hundred and sixty spokes are the days of the year:

> *trīṇy arpitāny atra śatāni madhye*
> *ṣaṣṭiś ca nityaṃ carati dhruve 'smin /*
> *cakre caturviṃśatiparvayoge*
> *ṣaḍ yat kumārāḥ parivartayanti //*
> "Three hundred and sixty spokes are fixed to the nave in this abiding wheel, forever moving in a cycle of twenty-four fortnights, which the six boys keep turning."

The cyclical nature of time is also revealed by means of a different metaphor, that of the old year giving birth to the new:

> *ṣaṣṭiś ca gāvas triśatāś ca dhenava*
> *ekaṃ vatsaṃ suvate taṃ duhanti /*
> *nānāgoṣṭhā vihitā ekadohadās* [...] // 1.3.63//
> "Those three hundred sixty milking cows
> Give birth to one calf, and yield milk for it.
> Many sheds divide them, but they suckle one [...]."[64]

Here the three hundred and sixty cows are the days of the old year, which in a way 'give birth' to the new year, their calf. The 'many sheds' are the fortnights, months and seasons.[65] A similar image, but with a different metaphor, is used in 1.3.70:

> *mukhena garbhaṃ labhatāṃ yuvānau*
> *gatāsur etat prapadena sūte /*
> *sadyo jāto mātaram atti garbhas* [...] //

---

[64] Incidentally, this verse also betrays Upamanyu's fondness for milk.
[65] See VAN BUITENEN (1973:440, note 60).

"Let, youths, it conceive the child through the mouth:
This dead man bears it along the path:
No sooner than born the child eats the mother –"[66]

Here VAN BUITENEN comments as follows: "the notion is that the next year is conceived at the mouth, i.e., head or beginning, of the present year, and is borne for a period of a year, as the old year goes along [...]. Simultaneously the Year expires in a year ('this dead man'), so that it can be said that the new year kills the old, which produced it." (1973:440, note 70).

Yet another image, that of the 'weaving' of time appears in both Upamanyu and Uttaṅka's laudatory hymns:

śukraṃ vayantau tarasā suvemāv
abhi vyayantāv asitaṃ vivasvat // 1.3.61 //
"Who on fine looms swiftly weave the light in,
And swiftly weave out that darker sun."

tantraṃ cedaṃ viśvarūpaṃ yuvatyau
vayatas tantūn satataṃ vartayantyau /
kṛṣṇān sitāṃś caiva vivartayantyau
bhūtāny ajasraṃ bhuvanāni caiva // 1.3.151 //
"Two young women are weaving this colorful loom, forever turning back and forth their threads, turning them from black ones to white ones, which are for always the past creatures and the present."[67]

On the one hand, these visions of the cyclical nature of time, of the ever recurring rebirth of the new year from the old, aptly illustrate the process of death and rebirth after being 'initiated', which the two *śiṣya*s

---

[66] This last line contains what is usually a description of Agni, who eats his 'mothers', the kindling-sticks, as soon as he is born. But taking it in this sense here does not seem to be very meaningful.

[67] *Bhūtāni* and *bhuvanāni* could also be translated as "creatures" and "worlds". But according to Veda's subsequent explanation, these black and white threads are days and nights.

are undergoing at the very moment of their visions. Moreover, according to VASSILKOV (1999:17), we find in these two hymns of Upamanyu and Uttaṅka traces of the ancient doctrine of *kālavāda*, or the "Doctrine of [cyclical] Time". In this doctrine, which finds expression from the Atharvaveda onwards, Time (*kāla*) is described as the 'Highest Lord', creating the worlds and beings and destroying them in turn. (See VASSILKOV 1999:17-18). Although it was greatly superseded in the Epics by didactic passages of a different purport, or by the worship of Viṣṇu and Śiva as the highest gods, and by the doctrine of *karman*, nevertheless, according to Vassilkov, this doctrine is central to the epic world-view. In the light of this, Upamanyu and Uttaṅka's revelations, their visions of the cyclical nature of *kāla*, turn out to be far from banal: they are revelations of the highest religious and philosophical order, unveiling the truth about the supreme Being (Kāla) and the origin and end of the world.[68]

Rebirth and immortality

While reading these stories, we have already become aware of the fact that what is at stake here for the initiates is not just mere survival in the face of the various ordeals they are made to undergo. It is not even just receiving a 'vision' or 'revelation', however important this factor is. In short, what is at stake here is the acquisition of immortality.

[68] Revelations concerning time also seem to play a certain role in initiation ceremonies elsewhere. For instance, BRANDON (1965) draws our attention to initiatory rituals in Orphism. One of the lines engraved on a gold leaf found in an Orphic grave says: "I have flown out of the sorrowful weary Wheel". According to Brandon, "The 'sorrowful weary Wheel' [...] mentioned here, is, without doubt, the endless cycle of metempsychosis, to which the Orphics believed every unenlightened soul was condemned. This process, like the Indian concept of saṃsāra, was equated with the cyclic process of Time in which all existence in the phenomenal world was involved. [...] In some way, therefore, initiation into the Orphic mysteries was believed to lead to ultimate deliverance from Time as manifest in the 'sorrowful weary Wheel' of the unceasing transmigration of the soul." (BRANDON 1965:45-6).
It would be a moot question whether the *kālavāda* doctrine was also linked with the belief in transmigration from the oldest texts onwards. In a few passages of the MBh, the Wheel of Time is sometimes interpreted as the wheel of *saṃsāra*. (See VASSILKOV 1999:20).

This immortality is proffered under various, more or less disguised forms. Uttaṅka obtains immortality by consuming *amṛta*, which Indra offers him in the form of his bull's dung and urine. As for Upamanyu, he receives golden teeth from the Aśvins. What do these stand for? This gift of golden teeth makes HOPKINS (1915:168) say that the Aśvins appear as dentists in this passage. But this is probably not the point here. As far as we know, Upamanyu's teeth were in no way defective. The golden teeth represent something else. Now, as ELIADE (1959:124) notes:

> "L'or est, dans l'Inde comme ailleurs, un symbole de l'immortalité et de la perfection. Se transformant dans un 'embryon d'or',[69] le récipiendaire s'approprie en quelque sorte l'indestructibilité du métal et participe à l'immortalité. L'or est solaire; d'autre part, il existe tout un complexe mythico-iconographique qui présente la descente du Soleil dans les ténèbres tout comme le novice pénètre, en tant qu'embryon, dans les ténèbres utérines de la hutte initiatique."[70]

We have already met with the comparisons with buried gold and the hidden sun in the case of the Vedic seers rescued by the Aśvins. In ṚV 1.117.12, the buried Rebha is compared to a pitcher of gold.[71] Vandana is like a hidden treasure (1.116.11); like the sun residing in darkness; like a buried golden ornament, fair to see (1.117.5).

Thus the golden teeth are the tokens of the immortality which Upamanyu gains by successfully undergoing his 'épreuve initiatique'. Now we can compare the case of Upamanyu with that of Dhaumya,

---

[69] Here Eliade is more specifically referring to the rite called *hiraṇyagarbha*, but this remark is certainly also valid for the type of initiation which Upamanyu is undergoing.

[70] Instead of sojourning in a "hutte initiatique", Upamanyu, more dramatically, falls into a well. But as we have noted above, the meaning is the same.

[71] In ṚV 1.116.24, as we have noted above, the dissolved Rebha is spooned out by the Aśvins *like soma*. Here the comparison is not with gold, but with the *soma*, ambrosia, which conveys much more straightforwardly the notion of the immortality achieved by Rebha.

who has iron teeth. Nīlakaṇṭha (commentary *ad* 1.3.21 (= Crit. Ed. 19)) interprets the name Āyoda as deriving from *ayodaṃtaḥ*: who has iron teeth. Instead of Āyoda, quite a few manuscripts have the reading Āpoda. This is interpreted by Nīlakaṇṭha as coming from *apo 'tti*: he eats water. I do not propose here to discuss whether these etymological interpretations are well-founded or not: as a matter of fact, they seem to be somewhat fanciful, but they are nevertheless very revealing. For now indeed we see that the golden-toothed and milk-drinking Upamanyu has fared incomparably better than his teacher, the iron-toothed, water-drinking Āy/poda. Thus Dhaumya, by succumbing to the temptation of eating the *apūpa*, undoubtedly missed his chance of gaining immortality, and his perishable (or at least rusting!) iron teeth are the visible token of his mortality.[72]

MBh 13.14 and 14.52-57

Interestingly, the stories of both Upamanyu and Uttaṅka are retold in the Anuśāsanaparvan and in the Āśvamedhikaparvan of the MBh, but in very different contexts. The story of Upamanyu is narrated in the Anuśāsanaparvan (13.14), in the following circumstances: Yudhiṣṭhira requests Bhīṣma to tell him the thousand names of Śiva. Bhīṣma asks Kṛṣṇa (whom he calls Viṣṇu in 2) to do it in his stead, since nobody is as qualified to do so as he. Kṛṣṇa accordingly starts relating under what

[72] We can also draw an interesting parallel with the story of Śyāvāśva, as it is told in BD 5.50-81 (ed. MACDONELL 1904). Śyāvāśva, the descendent of a long lineage of seers, wishes to marry the daughter of king Rathavīti Dārbhya. But the girl's mother objects, on the ground that Śyāvāśva himself is not a seer: he has not received the vision of *ṛcs*. As he is dejectedly reflecting on his misfortune in the forest: *araṇye* (5.67), the host of the Maruts, who have gold on their breasts, appears in front of him. After an initial hesitation concerning their identity, Śyāvāśva recognizes them and praises them with the stanzas *yá īṃ váhante* (ṚV 5.61.11). Pleased with his praise, the Maruts take off the gold from their breasts and give it to Śyāvāśva. Subsequently, having now become a seer of *ṛcs*, Śyāvāśva obtains the king's daughter. We recognize the common motifs of the sojourn in the forest, the unfortunate situation, the apparition of helpful deities, the importance of recognizing them and praising them with new *ṛcs*, and finally the gift of gold.

circumstances he himself heard Śiva's names. Once, he (Kṛṣṇa), desiring progeny, went to the Himālaya. There, in a beautiful hermitage, he met the sage Upamanyu who advised him to do *tapas* in order to propitiate Śiva, who would grant him offspring. Then Upamanyu told Kṛṣṇa how he himself had obtained boons through propitiating Śiva (72 ff.). He was born in the Kṛtayuga, as the son of the *ṛṣi* Vyāghrapāda and the brother of Dhaumya. Once, as young boys, both Upamanyu and Dhaumya went to another hermitage and saw a cow being milked. Upamanyu felt very tempted by the "milk which [...] was like *amṛta*": *kṣīraṃ [...] amṛtopamam* (13.14.77). As a milk-surrogate, their mother made them drink some flour, or a cake: *piṣṭam* (78) dissolved in water, but Upamanyu, who had once before tasted milk, was not cheated. He requested his mother to give him a rice-pudding cooked in milk: *kṣīrodana*. His mother felt very sad for him. Whence could hermits like themselves, living in the forest on roots and fruit, and not possessing a cow, obtain milk? She advised him to propitiate Śiva, who would grant him his wish. Accordingly, Upamanyu started a terrible *tapas*, which lasted for thousands of years. Standing on his toes, he first ate only fruit, then dry leaves, then subsisted on water, and finally only on air (13.14.86-87). Then Śiva was satisfied with him, and appeared to him, but in the guise of Indra. He asked him what boons he desired, but Upamanyu, rather indignantly, refused any boons from him, adding that he would accept them only from Śiva, and then he praised Śiva's greatness. Pleased, Śiva revealed his true form, and, after receiving a long *stuti* from Upamanyu, granted him the boons of immortality, and eternal youth (191-2), and also promised him that an ocean of milk-pudding: *kṣīrodaḥ sāgaraḥ*, would appear whenever he wished (192). Besides, that milky rice-pudding would be "full of *amṛta*": *kṣīrodanaṃ [...] amṛtena samanvitam* (193).[73]

[73] Subsequently, Kṛṣṇa in turn propitiates Śiva and obtains the boon of numerous

At first sight, this version of Upamanyu's story does not seem to have much in common with the Ādiparvan version, were it not for the names, which remain the same. Dhaumya here is Upamanyu's brother, and not his teacher. Besides, he hardly plays any role in the story. The motif which remains constant in both versions of the story is Upamanyu's fondness for milk, which is here explicitly likened to *amṛta*. He gets as a reward an ocean of milky rice-pudding, which immediately evokes the milky ocean out of which the ambrosia was churned. In both versions, he refuses to eat/drink the surrogate milk or *amṛta* (i.e., the *apūpa*, in the first story, and the dissolved flour or cake, in the second). Thus this second version spells out much more clearly the motif of the achievement of immortality than the first version, where it was revealed only allusively by means of the golden teeth.[74] Here Upamanyu's hunger, or his thirst for milk, is explicitly made equivalent with the desire for *amṛta* or immortality, which the devotee can obtain only by the benevolent intercession of the supreme god. Thus in this second version, the whole ideological framework has changed, and is wholly subordinate to *bhakti* (devotion) towards Śiva. Even Kṛṣṇa himself is here shown as a devotee of Śiva. The initiatory pattern has been entirely replaced by the more classical *tapas* which Upamanyu undertakes, and by the grace given by the supreme god to his devotee. The devotional tone of the whole passage, which mainly consists of long eulogies of Śiva,[75] is quite striking, the role of the Aśvins has been entirely suppressed, and Indra (or rather the supposed Indra) is told politely but firmly by Upamanyu that he has no use for

offspring from him and Umā. Then Upamanyu tells him the 1000 names of Śiva.

[74] The text quite clearly reveals that Upamanyu is as good as immortal, for he says himself that he was born in the Kṛtayuga, whereas his meeting with Kṛṣṇa necessarily takes place towards the end of the Dvāparayuga (i.e., myriads of years later), since the Mahābhārata-war is said to take place at the junction between the Dvāpara- and the Kaliyuga.

[75] This is even more striking in the Vulgate, where Upamanyu's mother also recites a long praise of Śiva. The whole passage is quite abridged in the Crit. Ed.

him whatever. The motif of the test is also present here; but the aim of the test is not to recognize the true nature of the god under his disguise (this will be the case for Uttaṅka, as we shall see below), but to proclaim allegiance to Śiva and denigrate the ancient Vedic affiliations.[76]

The story of Uttaṅka is retold in the Āśvamedhikaparvan (14.52-57), in a passage which shows clear vaiṣṇavite tendencies. The circumstances are as follows: Kṛṣṇa is returning to Dvārakā after the great war. On the way, he meets the sage Uttaṅka. Hearing from Kṛṣṇa that nearly everyone has been killed in the war, Uttaṅka threatens to curse Kṛṣṇa, whom he holds responsible for the massacre. But he desists after hearing the revelation of Kṛṣṇa's real nature as the supreme god, and his reasons for having brought about the war. Then Kṛṣṇa shows him his true cosmic form, and, on Uttaṅka's bidding, he gives him the boon of obtaining water whenever he thinks of him. (Here Uttaṅka is said to live in a desert.) Sometime later, Uttaṅka feels very thirsty and remembers the boon. He thinks of Kṛṣṇa. Then a frightful, dirty and naked Mātaṅga (an untouchable or tribesman), carrying weapons and surrounded by a pack of dogs, approaches him. Uttaṅka sees a lot of water beneath him (flowing) from his urethra: *tasyādhaḥ srotaso 'paśyat vāri bhūri* [...][77] (14.54.16), and the Mātaṅga offers him this 'water' to drink. But Uttaṅka obstinately refuses to accept the 'water' in this polluting form and from this polluting personage, however much the latter insists. Then the Mātaṅga vanishes and Viṣṇu appears in his stead. Uttaṅka bitterly reproaches him for sending such an impure person to offer him water, but Viṣṇu explains to him the

---

76 As LAINE (1989:237) notes: "In Indian literature, the appearance of gods in māyic forms in order to test heroes and sages is common and it plays upon two themes; (1) the test of the purity of human intentions and (2) the inability of humans to apprehend divinity when it appears in a form which does not conform to human expectation."

77 In Suśruta, *srotas* designates the spout of a jar or an aperture in the human body. Here probably the urethra. Like in the Pauṣya-sub-parvan, Uttaṅka is offered urine to drink.

reasons why this happened: he went to Indra, he says, to request him to give *amṛta* to Uttaṅka, but Indra first refused. Finally, he accepted to do so on one condition: he (Indra) would go to Uttaṅka in the guise of a Mātaṅga and offer him the *amṛta* in this form.[78] Uttaṅka would obtain immortality only if he accepted it from him in this polluting form. Then Kṛṣṇa consoles Uttaṅka and assures him that 'Uttaṅka-clouds', roaming over the desert, would rain for him whenever he would feel thirsty. (14.52-54).[79]

Then Janamejaya wants to know who was this Uttaṅka, who was so powerful that he was not even afraid of cursing Kṛṣṇa himself. Vaiśampāyana accordingly tells him the previous history of Uttaṅka, in very similar terms as it is told in the first book of the MBh, and with but slight divergences: Uttaṅka, who is here said to be a descendent of Bhṛgu,[80] was the *śiṣya* of Gautama and grew old in his *guru*'s house. The latter was so pleased with his student that he never dismissed him from his house.[81] One day, due to old age, Uttaṅka was unable to carry a load of fuel, threw it on the ground, (at the same time tearing out his silvery *jaṭā* which had got caught in the wood), and started crying. His tears were so scalding that not even the earth could bear them, which shows the great *tapas* Uttaṅka had accumulated by his service to his *guru*. Gautama, when he heard the cause of his misery, declared himself pleased with him, and gave him back his youth, and his own daughter in marriage, and dismissed him. But like in the first version,

[78] LAINE (1989:162, note 2) notes that WASSON (1968:29-34) "claims that the Uttaṅka story is a reflection of the old Soma cult, in which the initiates drink the urine of priests who have ingested it."

[79] For a structural analysis (including a diagram) of this passage, see LAINE (1989:169-171).

[80] This is perhaps meant to explain his irascibility, Bhārgava sages being notably prone to anger.

[81] Here it seems that Uttaṅka also assumes the role of his *guru* Veda in the first version, who had to remain for a long time in his teacher's house, serving him. Compare also with the story of Upakosala in ChU 4.10-14, who is neglected for a long time by his teacher.

Uttaṅka refused to go without offering his *gurudakṣiṇā*, and his *guru*'s wife (here Ahalyā) sent him to get the earrings. The rest of the story is roughly similar to the first version, except that the earrings belong to Madayantī, the wife of king Saudāsa (and not Pauṣya) who is moreover said to be a man-eater;[82] Uttaṅka does not meet Indra and Airāvata on the way, but instead Indra helps him with his *vajra* to open the small hole leading from an ant-hill to the *nāga-loka*, through which "a snake of Airāvata's family"[83] has vanished with the earrings; inside, he does not see Indra and the visions of time-cycles, but only meets Agni in the shape of a horse who helps him like in the first version of the story. (14.55-57).

In the case of Uttaṅka's story, two versions are juxtaposed:[84] one is very similar to that of the Pauṣyaparvan, the other presents striking structural similarities with it, but the personage of Kṛṣṇa/Viṣṇu plays the major role in it, and it exemplifies *bhakti* towards the supreme god rather than the worship of Vedic gods. Like in the story of Upamanyu in Book 13, the visions of time-cycles, which might represent the *kālavāda* world-view, do not figure here. Indra does not appear as the bestower of *amṛta* in the story of Uttaṅka's quest for the earrings, but

---

[82] This is the same king as Mitrasaha, also called Kalmāṣapāda, a king of Ikṣvāku's dynasty, who was cursed to become a man-eater. His story is told in numerous different versions. Besides in many Purāṇas, it appears for instance in R 7.57, where he is cursed to become a man-eater by Vasiṣṭha, after offering him by mistake human flesh to eat. In MBh 1.166, he is cursed to become a *rākṣasa* by Śakti, Vasiṣṭha's son, because he has whipped the latter who was refusing to go out of his way. Śakti's curse is subsequently reinforced by the curse of another Brahmin, to whom Kalmāṣapāda, (who is by now possessed by a *rākṣasa*), deliberately offers human flesh to eat. In the Pauṣyaparvan version of Uttaṅka's story, though the king is said to be Pauṣya (not Kalmāṣapāda) and is nowhere said to be a *rākṣasa*, Uttaṅka also has a dispute with him over some impure food which Pauṣya has given him to eat, and they curse each other.

[83] Even in the Pauṣyaparvan, where the earrings are stolen by Takṣaka, Uttaṅka mentions Airāvata not less than four times in his hymn to the snakes. As WILHELM (1965:17, note ad 139) remarks, there is a certain amount of overlapping in the representations of Airāvata the elephant, and Airāvata the snake king, and a general confusion about the term *nāga*, which means both elephant and snake.

[84] According to a text-historical analysis, this might be a clue that this narrative is later than that of the first book.

he appears instead in 14.54, where his gift of '*amṛta*' is rejected. Thus Indra retains his role as the master of *amṛta*,[85] but he is shown as a grudging dispenser of the divine drink. Here, unlike in the Pauṣyaparvan, Uttaṅka does not make the right choice. He refuses to drink the *amṛta* in the form of the Mātaṅga's urine, (as Indra had cunningly reckoned he would), which shows that a bull's urine may still be quite acceptable, but an untouchable's urine is definitely off limits. However, the bull and the Mātaṅga ultimately turn out to be one and the same thing: in the first version of the story, the bull is said to be Airāvata, Indra's elephant, and the first meaning of the term *mātaṅga* is also that of 'elephant'. By refusing the 'water' from the Mātaṅga, Uttaṅka fails in his test and forfeits his chance of obtaining immortality. Another inversion as compared to the story of Upamanyu as it is told in book 13 is also apparent here: Upamanyu is rewarded because he does not recognize Śiva in Indra's shape and refuses to accept boons from him, whereas Uttaṅka is punished for not recognizing Indra in the Mātaṅga's shape and refusing to accept water from him.[86] On the whole, the purport of the whole passage is rather unclear. If its aim is to glorify Viṣṇu, as the context would have us believe, then it is not quite fulfilled, since Viṣṇu here, although he is shown as the supreme god, still depends on Indra to offer immortality to his devotee,[87] and since Indra is obviously far from eager to enter into his designs. But it is also possible that Uttaṅka, unlike Upamanyu, simply lacks *bhakti*.

[85] He also appears as such in the episode of the *soma*-theft in the Ādiparvan.

[86] We had already noted a similar inversion in the Pauṣyaparvan, where Upamanyu is rewarded for not accepting the *apūpa*, whereas his own master had done so before him, and Uttaṅka is rewarded for accepting the bull's dung and urine, like his master had done before.

[87] Like in the story of Sumukha (see above, in the chapter on the theft of the *soma*), but unlike in the episode of the *soma*-theft, where Viṣṇu grants immortality to Garuḍa without making it depend on *amṛta*. Unless the water subsequently shed by the Uttaṅka-clouds is a form of *amṛta*. But this is nowhere explicitly stated. Judging from Kṛṣṇa's apologetic way of speaking, the rain-water rather seems to be a consolation prize.

Conclusions

As we have seen throughout this chapter, similar stories are told in different (con)texts: in the Chāndogya Upaniṣad, in the Ādiparvan of the MBh and in the last books of the Epic. But they are told with very different aims in each case: the Chāndogya Upaniṣad makes use of them to teach the new doctrine about the nature of *ātman* and *brahman*. The Pauṣyaparvan on the other hand, continuing the line of the old Vedic tradition, uses them to (re)assert orthodox Vedic values: obedience to one's teacher, veneration of the ancient Vedic gods, knowledge of the Vedas (all the *śiṣya*s receive as a reward the knowledge of all the Vedas,[88] and Upamanyu even becomes a true Vedic *ṛṣi*, 'seeing' new *ṛce*s[89]), and perhaps the doctrine of *kālavāda*.[90] This is in agreement with BRONKHORST's more general

---

[88] Dhaumya does not teach the Vedas to his students, and they do not learn them by heart (which is usually what *gurus* and *śiṣya*s do). Instead, Dhaumya grants all his students the immediate, 'magical' revelation of the *śruti* at the end of their time as students. This type of instantaneous revelation of the Vedas is usually no easy thing to come by, as a story told in MBh 3.135 shows: Yavakrī, the son of Bharadvāja, performed a terrible *tapas* in order to get the revelation of all the Vedas. After trying to dissuade him by all sorts of arguments, Indra finally had recourse to the following subtle stratagem: disguised as a Brahmin and lugging around great buckets of sand, he started building a bridge of sand across the river near which Yavakrī was doing *tapas*. Yavakrī pointed out to him that all his efforts were in vain, since the sand was immediately washed away by the river. Smiling, Indra replied that all his efforts to get a revelation of the Vedas by means of *tapas* were equally pointless. Yet in the end he nevertheless granted him his wish.

[89] We can contrast Upamanyu's case with that of Vālmīki. Whereas Upamanyu 'sees' *ṛce*s, Vālmīki, in a comparable moment of emotional upheaval, 'sees' a new verse, the *śloka*, in which he composes the R (1.2). Upamanyu is obviously not the author of the MBh, and the MBh is of course also composed in *śloka*s, just like the R. Yet the two passages are similarly situated toward the beginning of the texts, and might thus be considered to hold a paradigmatic value, emphasizing the MBh's look 'backward', to the Vedas, and the R's look 'forward', to the *kāvya* tradition.

[90] WILHELM (1965:40), on the contrary, supposes (though admittedly without proof) upaniṣadic representations behind these narratives of the Pauṣyaparvan: "Möglicherweise verbergen sich in diesem nachvedischen Text [...] vermutlich schon Konzeptionen der Upaniṣadenmystik: das Aufgehen der Einzelseele in die Weltseele, die mystische Einheit von Ātman und Brahman."
Nīlakaṇṭha too gives a Vedāntic interpretation of the story of Upamanyu in the first book of the MBh. Thus in his commentary ad 1.3.73 (= Crit. Ed. 1.3.75), he says that the teeth are the actions, because of the enjoyment/eating of happiness and unhappiness: *dantāḥ sukhaduḥkhabhojakatvāt karmāṇi*. His overall interpretation of Dhaumya's iron

contention that the Upaniṣads had a marginal position outside the Vedic main-stream, and became popular and orthodox only at the time of the Vedānta system of philosophy (1993:61-3). In the last books of the MBh, similar stories are again used, this time to teach the doctrine of *bhakti*. Upamanyu and Uttaṅka are shown to be devotees of the supreme gods Śiva and Viṣṇu (and both meet Kṛṣṇa), in passages which have a strong devotional flavour. In this regard, we may quote VASSILKOV (1999:28), who makes the following remark:

> "It is known from European history that a Christian temple would often be built in place of an older heathen shrine. Likewise, the brahman 'editors' of the MBh would place, next to a piece of heroic-didactic preaching of an earlier time,[91] a new layer, now in the spirit of a new, Hinduist world-view. True, there is a fundamental difference: a heathen shrine in Europe would be destroyed while in the MBh, in keeping with certain basic principles of traditional Indian culture, some earlier texts were left intact although their contents seem to agree poorly with the preaching of the Hindu *dharma* placed next to them."

This type of stories illustrating the revelations of certain truths and the initiations undergone by students are an ideal vehicle for the propagation of either new doctrines, or the reassertion of old ones. The audience of such tales (listener or reader) is made to identify with the one who is being initiated, suffering the same trials as him, though

teeth versus Upamanyu's golden ones is that by being devoted to his teacher, even if the latter does not know the *ātman*, the devotee obtains the knowledge of the *ātman*: *anātmajñasyāpi guror ārādhanād ātmajñānaṃ bhaktasya bhavati.* In any case, his Vedāntic interpretation is noticeable in the whole of the MBh. As BIARDEAU (1997:88) notes: "Nīlakaṇṭha [...] vedānticised the Mahābhārata."

91 It is Vassilkov's contention that the *kālavāda* doctrine precisely belongs to this layer of 'heroic didactics'. A view which is very commonly held is that the MBh is basically composed of two subsequent layers: an (older) 'epic-heroic-*kṣatriya*' layer and a (later) 'brahmanic-Smṛti' layer. In his article, VASSILKOV (1999:27) proposes yet another layer, that of 'heroic didactics', representative of the epic-heroic world-view, which antedates the brahmanic-Smṛti layer. Against this view of a 'layered' composition of the Epic, see for instance HILTEBEITEL (1999).

vicariously, and receiving in the end the same revelation. Thus the immortality passed on to these initiates, which takes various forms, is in the final instance nothing but the immortality which they (and the audience) gain through the revelation, knowledge or belief which is imparted to them. Thus most of these passages consciously reuse the age-old initiation pattern, involving death (to the old beliefs) and rebirth (to the new), including the promise of immortality tendered by the new belief. Perhaps we might even go so far as to claim that the MBh, by narrating, as its first (but one) story, that of Dhaumya's *śiṣya*s and their initiation, is thus reinforcing its *śruti*-like status and claiming that the 'revelation' is the MBh itself, and the reward for hearing or reciting the text is nothing less than immortality.

6. *Raṇa-yajña*: the Mahābhārata War as a Sacrifice[1]

Introductory

This chapter takes up two central themes from the ancient brahmanical tradition and from the Mahābhārata respectively, namely, sacrifice and the Mahābhārata war. As the title shows, my aim is to explain the significance of repeated references to the war as a sacrifice in the text of the Mahābhārata: *raṇa-sattra*: 3.242.14; *raṇa-yajña*: 5.57.12 and 5.154.4; and *śastra-yajña*: 5.139.29.[2] This chapter differs from the preceding ones, in that its main subject is not myth, but sacrifice. The inclusion of this topic here can be justified on several grounds. First, the subjects of myth and sacrifice are often closely linked. We have seen in the preceding chapters how frequently myths refer to, or concern, sacrifice. Furthermore, we shall examine here the way in which sacrifice is so to say 'mythified' in the MBh. If sacrifice, or *yajña*, is the heart of the Veda, the war is the heart of the Mahābhārata Epic. This fact itself justifies one's effort to understand this predication.

What kind of sacrifice might be a 'war-sacrifice'? How to analyze the terms *raṇa-sattra, raṇa-yajña* and *śastra-yajña*?[3] Should we attribute a metaphorical meaning to them or should we take them literally? Is any war considered as a sacrifice? Or, is this particular war which takes place in the Epic conceived as a special sort of sacrifice,

---

1 This chapter is a revised version of FELLER JATAVALLABHULA (1999 a).

2 Other, non-critical editions give more references to *raṇa-yajña*: see the list given by BIARDEAU (1976a:132, note 4).

3 Obviously, we cannot analyze them in the same way as for instance *aśvamedha, sarpa-sattra* or *soma-yajña* (horse-, snakes- and *soma*-sacrifice), in the sense that a horse, snakes or *soma* are offered as the oblations of a sacrifice. This would make no sense for war, an abstract concept.

designed for its own special purpose, like for instance Janamejaya's snake-sacrifice?[4] Before attempting to answer these questions, let us first of all examine the role of *yajña*s in the Mahābhārata both from historical and textual points of view.

The society represented by the Mahābhārata is one in which sacrifice plays a major role. The text itself as we have it was recited at Śaunaka's twelve-year sacrificial session by the bard Ugraśravas. He himself heard the story at the snake-sacrifice of king Janamejaya (whose significance we shall see later), where it was recited by Vaiśampāyana, a direct disciple of the composer, Vyāsa or Kṛṣṇa Dvaipāyana. Apart from these, (and without even mentioning the numerous sacrifices described in 'peripheral' tales), two sacrifices play a pivotal role in the plot of the central epic story, namely Yudhiṣṭhira's *rājasūya* (royal consecration) and his *aśvamedha* (horse-sacrifice).

As we can see, the society depicted in the Mahābhārata still fully follows the ritualistic ideology of the Vedic brahmanical tradition. But the text of the Mahābhārata was composed at a later time, and we do perceive in it the influences of the age of the composition. As THAPAR (1993:147) says, it is "a later age reflecting on an earlier one", and we sometimes feel a sense of rupture between the two ages thus represented in the text, a rupture which manifests itself at various levels: social, ideological and mythical-historical. As far as the social level is concerned, we can again quote THAPAR's words:

> "Any of the seeming contradictions in the stances and configurations characterizing the epics can perhaps be explained by these texts (and particularly the Mahābhārata), reflecting something of a transitional condition between two rather different structures, the societies of the lineage-based system and that of the monarchical state." (1993:148).

---

4 See MBh 1.47: the *sarpa-sattra* was specially conceived by the gods to allow Kadrū's curse to be fulfilled.

In lineage-based (or tribal) societies, kings sought the validation of their kingship in their ancient *kṣatriya* lineage, whose mythical origins were drawn from Manu and his two children, Ikṣvāku and Iḷā (solar and lunar dynasties). The pastoral-agricultural society of the lineage progressively gave way to the mainly monarchical state system with its agrarian society, urban centers and emerging private ownership of the land, in which the person of the king as well as his immediate family were all-important, and where the legitimatization of the power was no longer drawn from the lineage (indeed at that time many kings were not necessarily *kṣatriya*s, but might be Brahmins, *śūdra*s, tribals, etc.). Whereas the Mahābhārata as a whole clearly represents a society of the lineage type, certain didactic sections, in the Śāntiparvan for example, propound the monarchical state as the ideal type of society. Incidentally, the Mahābhārata war itself can be said to be a mythical explanation for the decay of the lineage-based system, since it is said to have virtually wiped out all the *kṣatriya* lineages (at least of the lunar dynasty). (See THAPAR 1993 & 1975).[5]

At the level concerning the sacrificial ideology, we can also discern two contradictory trends. On the one hand, many sacrifices are performed (and their performance strongly recommended) in the story of the Mahābhārata: Yudhiṣṭhira's *rājasūya* and *aśvamedha*, as well as the *raṇa-yajña* itself. On the other hand, some passages express the general idea that sacrifice started declining during the Dvāparayuga (the third world-age or eon, at the end of which the war is supposed to have taken place) and that only remnants of it are left in the Kaliyuga (that is, the present age). (See BIARDEAU 1976a:80-81). More precisely, according to the theory of the *yugadharma*s, the "duties according to the *yugas*), sacrifice is said to be the *dharma* of the Dvāparayuga,

---

[5] But THAPAR seems to take the war as a historical reality, an opinion which I do not share. See also HILTEBEITEL (2001:chapter 5) concerning this motif of the "Passing of the old order".

whereas the *dharma* of the Kaliyuga is *dāna* (giving). (See KOSKIKALLIO 1994:254). In other passages, the violence of bloody sacrifices in particular is condemned. Thus many passages concerning the social *dharma* proclaim the ideology of *ahiṃsā paramo dharmaḥ*: "non-killing is the highest *dharma*" (e.g. 13.114-117). In the Śāntiparvan (12.248-267),[6] especially in 260-262, we find long disquisitions to the effect that non-harming is higher than sacrificial violence. (See HOUBEN 1999:134-5).[7] Likewise, Vaiśaṃpāyana, after narrating to Janamejaya how Yudhiṣṭhira's *aśvamedha* was performed, warns the king that in the present age violent sacrifices should not be performed any longer (14.94-95).

Finally, at what we might call the mythical-historical level, the Mahābhārata is the depiction of a by-gone era made in the present age. For the battle marks the end of a *yuga* (eon). The war is said to take place at the very tail-end of the Dvāparayuga, and its completion marks the beginning of the last and worst of all *yuga*s, the Kaliyuga, in which moral and religious values reach further levels of degradation. The catastrophe of the war is thus to be taken as a minor sort of *pralaya*, a feeble foretaste of the great destruction which will take place at the end of a *kalpa* (a period of one thousand *yuga*s or 4.320.000.000 years, measuring the duration of the world).[8]

Thus the war happens at a sort of *saṃdhyā* or twilight-time, a period of transition in many ways, and therefore one of increased

---

6 For a detailed analysis of this passage, see SCHREINER (1979).

7 See also HILTEBEITEL (2001:202-214) for a discussion on *ahiṁsā* and *ānṛśaṁsya* (noncruelty) in the MBh.

8 This is especially BIARDEAU's view (see her "Etudes de mythologie hindoue"), according to whom the MBh is the transposition of the eschatological myth of the cosmic dissolution. On the other hand, GONZALEZ-REIMANN (2002:203) rightly cautions that "the meanings of yuga, yugānta, *kali*, *kṛta*, and even Kali Yuga and Kṛta Yuga, cannot be taken for granted", for, as they are used in the MBh, these terms rarely refer to the theory of world-ages, but can have a range of different meanings. According to this author, only "late" passages of the MBh unequivocally state that the war takes place at the turn of two eons (for a list of the passages, see chapter 3), and this view gained a wide notoriety only subsequently.

danger and insecurity. In this connection we must remember that many sacrifices too have to be performed at similar periods of transition, such as dawn and dusk, new- and full-moon days, in-between seasons, etc. In this sense, sacrifice functions as a 'bridge' between two different times.[9] Just as *yajña*s are meant to help in tiding over such critical moments, in the same way, one of the functions of the war-sacrifice is to mark the transition from one *yuga* to another.

Raṇa-yajña

Having highlighted the above mentioned points of rupture and transition, let us now examine the possible analogies between a war and a sacrifice. First we shall see what analogies between them are explicitly stated by the text.

Two such comparisons between the ritual of battle and the sacrificial performance are drawn in the text, one by Duryodhana addressing his father (5.57.12-14) and the second, more at length, by Karṇa for the benefit of Kṛṣṇa (5.139.29-51).[10] Both establish correspondences between the implements and acts of the war and those of the sacrifice. Thus, Duryodhana says that the chariot will be the sacrificial ground (*vedī*), the mace will be the oblation-spoon (*sruk*), the arrows will be the *darbha*-grass, etc. (13). Similarly, Karṇa says that the soldiers' heroism is the ghee poured into the fire (30), the sounds of the conches and of the drums, as well as the shouts of the warriors, are the *subrahmaṇyā*-recitation (35), the staffs supporting the banners of the chariots are the sacrificial posts (37), some weapons are the bricks of the sacrificial altar (39), the (chopped off) heads and the blood are the various oblations (39-40), and so on and so forth. This description

[9] ELIADE (1964:483) makes the following remark: "numerous rites are conceived of as symbolically 'building a bridge' or a 'ladder', and as accomplishing this by the sheer power of the rite itself. This idea is documented for example in the symbolism of the Brāhmanic sacrifice (Cf. Taittirīya Saṃhitā VI, 5,3,3; VI, 5,4,2; VII, 5,8,5; etc.)."

[10] It is rather curious that these sacrificial descriptions of the war to come are placed in the mouths of those who will lose the war.

presents an inversion of the situation we find in certain Vedic texts, where the sacrificial implements are called the 'weapons' of the sacrifice: *yajñāyudhāni*. (See HEESTERMAN 1993:53). In the MBh, the real weapons and implements of the war become sacrificial implements. We can certainly discern here traces of the identificatory mode of thought, typical of brahmanical ritual texts, which is greatly indebted to the ancient Vedic 'pensée à énigmes'.[11]

We also find a list of comparisons concerning the protagonists of the war. Thus Duryodhana proclaims in 5.57.12:

> *ahaṃ ca tāta karṇaś ca raṇayajñaṃ vitatya vai /*
> *yudhiṣṭhiraṃ paśuṃ kṛtvā dīkṣitau bharatarṣabha //*
> I myself, father, as well as Karṇa, have taken religious initiation, after organizing the war-sacrifice and after making Yudhiṣṭhira our sacrificial victim, o bull of the Bharatas.

As we see, Duryodhana considers that this war is his own, as well as Karṇa's sacrifice, in the sense that it is performed on their instigation, and they are both *dīkṣitau* (initiated) for it. On the other hand, Yudhiṣṭhira will be their *paśu* (sacrificial victim), a piece of wishful thinking which of course will not come true: for Duryodhana on the contrary ends up as one of the *paśu*s at his own sacrifice. Karṇa too expresses the opinion that this will be Duryodhana's war-sacrifice (*dhārtarāṣṭrasya [...] śastrayajño bhaviṣyati*) (5.139.29), and that he is initiated for it (42). But Karṇa, less misguided than Duryodhana in this respect, (and indeed, as it seems, gifted with second sight, since he foresees in this passage the whole course of the war), far from considering the Pāṇḍavas and other great warriors of their army as the *paśu*s of the sacrifice, sees them on the contrary as various priests officiating in the ritual.[12]

---

[11] See HEESTERMAN (2001).

[12] Thus Kṛṣṇa will be the *vettṛ* (knower) of the sacrifice, as well as the *adhvaryu* (the priest who is in charge of all the practical duties of the sacrificial performance) (29),

In order to explain the fact that both Duryodhana and Karṇa consider that the war-sacrifice is organized by Duryodhana, we should perhaps briefly examine the events which lead to the war. In the MBh, the whole feud between the two closely related branches of the family arose due to practically unsolvable succession problems. As they grew up, the Pāṇḍavas should probably have inherited the kingdom which was their father's previously, since Dhṛtarāṣṭra, though the eldest, was disqualified by his blindness.[13] But instead of getting the kingdom, the Pāṇḍavas were more or less openly banished from Hastināpura, and Duryodhana attempted to take their life by roasting them alive in a lac-house. The second, partly successful means he resorted to later, was to banish the Pāṇḍavas to the forest after defeating them at the dice-game. But, their time of exile being over, they again claimed their share of the kingdom. Now nothing else was left to Duryodhana but an open war, in which he hoped to 'sacrifice' once for all his rival to the throne, and continue to enjoy the kingdom. Now we can understand why Duryodhana says that the war is called on his instigation. Obviously, he is indeed the one who brings about the war, since he adamantly refuses to strike any compromise with the Pāṇḍavas, whereas the latter would have been satisfied with a share of the kingdom.

On the whole, one cannot but feel that Duryodhana made a grave mistake by sending the Pāṇḍavas in exile to the forest, and that their

and Arjuna the *hotṛ*, one of the most important priests, the one who recites the formulæ. This is explained in verse 31, where his various *astras* (magic weapons) which are precisely invoked by means of *mantras* (magical formulæ) are said to be the *mantras* of the sacrifice. Bhīma will be the *udgātṛ* (the priest who sings certain parts) apparently because of his loud shouts (33). As for Yudhiṣṭhira, because he is *dharmātmā*, being the son of Dharma, he will be the *brahman* priest, the general supervisor of the sacrifice (34). These four types of priests are, respectively, the priests of the Yajur-, Ṛg-, Sāma- and Atharvaveda. Other Pāṇḍavas and their allies too are said to be certain types of priests, excepting Dhṛṣṭadyumna, who is said to be the *dakṣiṇā* (fee) of the sacrifice.

[13] However, king Pāṇḍu, the Pāṇḍavas' father, had abdicated due to a curse, and retired to the forest, leaving the kingdom in Dhṛtarāṣṭra's care. As VAN BUITENEN (1973:xvi) rightly notes: "The succession rights of the male descendants are a genealogist's nightmare, and, to me at least, there is little doubt that the story was in part *designed* as a riddle."

sojourn there was one of the reasons for Duryodhana's failure to sacrifice them as the *paśus* of his sacrifice. To explain this, we should turn to the notion of *dīkṣā* (the initiation which the sacrificer has to undergo before the *soma*-sacrifice), which Duryodhana precisely claims to have undergone. Now the *dīkṣā* is actually a sort of *tapas*: the sacrificer is made to sit alone in a hut, without talking and fasting till exhaustion. The Brāhmaṇas see in the *dīkṣā* a means of access to the sacred, and it is also interpreted as a rite of rebirth following a corporeal purification achieved by the removal from the common life. In a way, it is a death followed by a rebirth in the sacrifice. (See RENOU & FILLIOZAT (1985:§708); ELIADE (1979:221); COOMARASWAMY (1977:108)). Thus we see that it is Yudhiṣṭhira, through the life of hardship and penance he lead in the forest,[14] and not Duryodhana, who was meanwhile enjoying his kingdom, who has truly undergone the *dīkṣā* for the war-sacrifice, though the latter, as we have seen above, claims to be *dīkṣita*. And indeed, before the war, the elders repeatedly warn Duryodhana against Yudhiṣṭhira, telling him that the latter has gained great powers by his penance in the forest.

Another important equivalence between this war and sacrifice is found in the notion of 'share' (*bhāga* or *aṃśa*). About these terms, HILTEBEITEL (1976/1991:318) remarks that "they are used with the combined meaning, pertinent to both the sacrifice and the battlefield, of 'victim'."[15] Thus in 5.161, Dhṛṣṭadyumna, the general of the Pāṇḍava-army, who is himself born of a portion of the sacrificial fire and thus

---

[14] According to BIARDEAU (1976b:153-154) and (1978:187, note 3), it is more specifically the 13th year the Pāṇḍavas spend in hiding (i.e., in an embryonic state), which represents their *dīkṣā* for the sacrifice of war. As HILTEBEITEL (2001:137, note 21) remarks, it is very interesting to note that Bhaṭṭa Nārāyaṇa in his Veṇisaṃhāra (1.25) says that king Yudhiṣṭhira is *dīkṣita* for the sacrifice of war, and that the Kauravas are the *paśus* of the sacrifice, expressing in so many words what the MBh only hints at.

[15] Interestingly, the terms *bhāga* and *aṃśa* are also used interchangeably in the MBh to denote the partial incarnations of deities (see SULLIVAN 1990:69). Besides, Bhaga and Aṃśa are Vedic gods.

ideally suited to lead the war-sacrifice, appoints a victim or share to each one of the Pāṇḍavas and their allies, finally appointing Droṇa as his own *aṃśa* (10). Similarly in 5.56.12-25, Saṃjaya enumerates a list of the future victims of the Pāṇḍavas and of other members of their army, repeatedly using the terms *bhāga* or *aṃśa*.

The term *paśu* (sacrificial victim) is frequently applied to the slain warriors. We have already seen one instance above, in Duryodhana's speech, applying to Yudhiṣṭhira. The expression *paśumāram amārayat* (he made him die the death of a sacrificial animal) appears all through the war description.[16] Similarly, after killing Duḥśāsana, Bhīma proclaims in 8.61.16:

> *adyaiva dāsyāmy aparaṃ dvitīyaṃ*
> *duryodhanaṃ yajñapaśuṃ viśasya /*
> Even today, after slaughtering him, I shall offer Duryodhana as another, second, victim of the sacrifice.

Violence and human sacrifice

It has become clear from the above that the sacrificial victims (*paśu*, *bhāga* or *aṃśa*) of the war-sacrifice are the warriors slain in the battle. This does not come as a great surprise to us, for one of the premises on which the idea of the war-sacrifice is based, and which makes the term immediately comprehensible, is that both sacrifice and war involve violence. It is of course true that not all sacrifices involve the killing of *paśu*s, but many of the major ones do.[17] Moreover, as far as violence

---

[16] See also BIARDEAU (1976a:234, note 2). My attention was drawn to this expression by Prof. Minoru HARA in his lecture delivered at the Xth World Sanskrit Conference (Bangalore, January 1997) entitled "A Note on the Epic Phrase *jīvan-mukta*". In his lecture, Prof. HARA noted that the expression *paśumāram amārayat* is peculiar to the Mahābhārata, and is never found in the Rāmāyaṇa. This concords with the concluding part of this chapter.

[17] In any case, HEESTERMAN (1993:9), referring to TS 6.6.9.2 and ŚB 2.2.2.1-2; 4.3.4.1-2; 11.1.2.1, makes us attentive to the fact that even offerings of *soma* or other vegetal matters were conceptualized as killings: "The pressing of the soma stalks, the killing and cutting up of the animal victim, and the grinding of the grain are all equally killings, and, to drive the point home, the text uses the verb *hanti*, 'to slay, kill', here."

is concerned, the resemblance between war and sacrifice is not just restricted to the killing itself. According to HEESTERMAN, the sacrificial performance itself is, at its very core, and from its origins, a conflict: conflict between rival sacrificers, between the host and guest parties and also between the sacrificer and his officiants, the priests, who are given very precise instructions in the ritual texts on how to harm their patron, should they wish to do so. As HEESTERMAN (1993:40) remarks: "sacrifice is not just concerned with conflict. It *is* conflict writ large," and, "The place of sacrifice, then, must be viewed as the battleground on which the parties engage in the contest of life and death." (1993:43). If one accepts such an interpretation: sacrifice = conflict, the inverse equation: war = sacrifice, which concerns us here, becomes even more pregnant with meaning and readily understandable.

Thus the war is represented as a human sacrifice. The topic of human sacrifice in Ancient India is highly debated. KEITH (1925:282) holds that though it was probably never very common, it was yet far from unknown in Ancient India. And HOUBEN (1999:123) says: "the human sacrifice was not just a theoretical construct of ritualists, but a 'real option' which, in one form or the other, may very well have been occasionally put to practice." Indeed, the Brāhmaṇas often express the view that man is the first and best sacrificial victim, and that other creatures are mere substitutes for him.[18] During the *agni-cayana*, or the building of the great sacrificial fire-altar, it seems to have been customary to sacrifice five victims, one of them a man, whose heads were then built into the altar.[19] DONIGER O'FLAHERTY (1988:83) notes that there is "archaeological evidence of human skulls and other human bones at the site of such fire-altars". Later Brāhmaṇas tell us of

However, as far as the ritual slaughter of animals is concerned, we must note that the texts also frequently use euphemisms, such as *sáṃjñapayanti*: "they make [the animal] consent [to its fate]". See e.g. ŚB 4.5.2.1.

[18] See KEITH (1925:273-4).

[19] See KEITH (1925:281-2); RENOU & FILLIOZAT (1985:§701).

a *puruṣa-medha*, a "man-sacrifice", which closely followed the model of the *aśvamedha*, but on a grander scale.[20] The Śatapathabrāhmaṇa (13.6.2.13) mentions the offering of 166 men at the *puruṣa-medha*, but this is described as a symbolic offering, and the men are released and not put to death.[21] The story of Śunaḥśepa, which is customarily told during the *rājasūya*, has been interpreted as the reminiscence of actual human sacrifices performed on such occasions,[22] and it is also quite possible to interpret in this light the slaying of Śiśupāla by Kṛṣṇa at Yudhiṣṭhira's *rājasūya*. Human sacrifices are moreover explicitly mentioned in the Mahābhārata. For instance, king Jarāsaṃdha is killed in a duel by Bhīma, on Kṛṣṇa's instigation, because he was planning to offer in sacrifice numerous kings whom he had taken prisoners.[23] And after the war, Vyāsa suggests various types of sacrifices which Yudhiṣṭhira might perform as expiatory ceremonies, one of them being a *nara-medha*, a man-sacrifice (14.3.8). Thus we see that the offering of human sacrifices is in no way an impossibility in the society represented by the Epic.

Rules and expiations

Another point of convergence between war and sacrifice might be found in the rules to be followed in both of them. It is a well-known fact that sacrificial ceremonies have to be performed strictly according to the

20 See KEITH (1925:282 & 347); RENOU & FILLIOZAT (1985:§727).

21 See KEITH (1925:347).

22 See KEITH (1925:282 and 341, note 2); RENOU & FILLIOZAT (1985:§701). On the other hand, SMITH (1994:251) doubts the reality of human sacrifice: "Whether humans were in practice sacrificed is uncertain, however; and even theoretically (i.e. categorically) man does not always appear in the lists of the proper victims. We recall here Śunaḥśepha's horror when he is seized as a sacrificial victim in the famous myth: 'They will slaughter me as if I were not a man' (AitB. 7.16)."

23 This might make us think that human sacrifices were frowned upon in Mahābhārata times, since Jarāsaṃdha is thus punished for his intended action. But it is not necessarily the human sacrifice as such which is rejected here. For as we shall see below, it is an essential prerequisite in sacrifices that the victim, whatever its species, should be consenting, which is obviously not the case here since these kings are kept imprisoned.

regulations, with minutely planned ritual acts and *mantra*s and that the slightest omission, mistake or accident would render them invalid. While things are obviously not carried so far in a war, it is nevertheless true that wars too have to follow a set code of rules. Thus, before getting down to the business of battle, the two armies of the Kauravas and of the Pāṇḍavas agree on a series of rules to be respected (6.1.26-32). These rules can be summarized as follows:

a) Only warriors belonging to similar army-divisions should fight against each other: infantrymen against infantrymen, chariots against chariots, elephants against elephants, etc.
b) A list of persons who should not be killed is given: those who are fleeing, or distressed in some way or wounded, who are unarmed or fighting with someone else, etc. Moreover, people who are involved in the battle but not in the quality of warriors, such as charioteers, drummers, conch-blowers, etc., as well as horses, should not be killed either.

Reading the battle-descriptions, we find that the first set of rules is usually respected, though with a few occasional exceptions which do not seem to incur any sort of blame.[24] But the second set of rules is broken more often, especially the injunction not to kill charioteers and horses, which is ignored without any compunction. Indeed, reading the *parvans* of the war, we find that it is nearly a ritual in fights between *rathas*, to dispatch first the horses, then the charioteer,[25] and finally, if

[24] But indeed, most of the fights described in the MBh are those between *rathas*, the chariot being considered as the most noble vehicle, and hence used by the majority of great warriors. As BASHAM (1954:136) remarks: "it is clear that at most times great emphasis was placed on single combat between picked warriors. Though the mass fighting of the rank and file must often have played a decisive part in the encounter, it is given little notice in the literary sources".

[25] Thus HILTEBEITEL (1982:92) remarks: "In the roughly nine hundred and sixty-six combat scenes at the battle of Kurukṣetra, there is individual reference to the killing of one hundred and fifty-five *sūtas*, or a 16% ratio of charioteers killed per duel."

possible, the warrior himself, if he has not already taken refuge on someone else's chariot. These occurrences, in spite of the explicit rules against them, seem to be considered as perfectly normal, and no reproaches are voiced against them.

On the other hand, it is clear that serious *adharma* results from killing opponents who are in some sort of disadvantageous position, and it is a well-known and often remarked fact that most of these offenses happen on the Pāṇḍavas' side, and frequently on Kṛṣṇa's instigation. (Duryodhana enumerates them in 9.60). But the Kaurava camp of course also commits its share of infractions.[26] At this point, we can again note a similarity between sacrifices and wars: in the same way as the lapses occurring in a sacrifice could, and indeed had to, be expiated by a special ceremony called *prāyaścitta*, the same was also valid for social offenses, or crimes against *dharma*. This type of expiations, varying according to the gravity of the crime, were also called *prāyaścitta*.[27] And indeed, at the end of the war, we see that Yudhiṣṭhira, tormented by his somewhat oversensitive conscience, performs expiatory ceremonies. Mainly by organizing an *aśvamedha*, which was considered to be the *prāyaścitta* par excellence, and also by

[26] Thus, on the Pāṇḍavas' side, Droṇa's death, and the events leading to it: he was demoralized by being told, falsely, that his son was dead and Dhṛṣṭadyumna cut off his head and threw it at the enemy, though Droṇa was already dead (7.164-165). Karṇa's death, whom Arjuna killed though he was begging for mercy (8.66). Bhūriśravas' death, whom Arjuna hit though he was fighting against someone else (7.117). Duryodhana's death, whom Bhīma hit below the belt in the mace-fight (9.57-58), etc. On the Kauravas' side, most notably, Abhimanyu's death, killed while he was fighting alone against many (7.48) and, probably the worst deed of all, Aśvatthāman's slaughter of the sleeping army of the Pāṇḍavas (Sauptikaparvan).
In this connection, it is interesting to note that some of the above-mentioned deeds, which are utterly condemned in the MBh, are on the contrary coldly recommended by the Arthaśāstra: for instance, spreading false information among the enemies to create a panic (cf. 10.6.48-50) or making night-raids on the sleeping enemy camp (cf. 10.3.20).

[27] Cf. RENOU & FILLIOZAT (1985:§1243-9).

giving donations to those left orphaned and widowed by the war. Such gifts were also considered as a form of *prāyaścitta*.[28]

The aims of the raṇa-yajña

Let us now briefly contrast and compare the purposes of sacrifices in general and of the *raṇa-yajña* in particular. The primary aim of a sacrifice (prominently reflected in the Ṛgveda), and based on the *do ut des* principle, is to obtain from the gods something concrete in exchange for the sacrifice, such as wealth, cattle, sons, a long life, etc.[29] At a higher level, sacrifices also eminently purport to maintain the world-order (variously, and at different times, called *ṛta* or *dharma*). This conception already figures in the Ṛgvedic Puruṣasūkta (ṚV 10.90) where the whole world is created out of the sacrifice of a primordial giant. And in a sense, any sacrifice is said to repeat this act of creation. This idea gained a great predominance in the literature of the Brāhmaṇas where sacrifices were conceived of as bringing about this effect by a formidable power of their own, achieved by the magic potency of their *mantras*.[30]

If these are the two most important aims of sacrifices, what are the aims of the war-sacrifice? The primary, concrete, purpose of the war is the lordship over the earth, which Duryodhana wants to retain and

---

[28] In this connection, we must remember that according to Karṇa's words, Yudhiṣṭhira is the *brahman* priest of the war-sacrifice, that is, the one whose duty is to *supervise* the performance, notice whatever faults might occur and *redress* them.

[29] Cf. KEITH (1925:259); also BhG 3.12.

[30] Cf. KEITH (1925:260) and ELIADE (1979:229). Also BhG 3.14-15 (probably from MSmṛ 3.76):

annād bhavanti bhūtāni parjanyād annasaṃbhavaḥ /
yajñād bhavati parjanyo yajñaḥ karmasamudbhavaḥ //
karma brahmodbhavaṃ viddhi brahmākṣarasamudbhavam /
tasmāt sarvagataṃ brahma nityaṃ yajñe pratiṣṭhitam //

From food creatures come forth; the production of food is from rain; rain comes forth from sacrifice; sacrifice is born of action; know thou that action comes from Brahman, and that Brahman comes from the Imperishable. Therefore, the all-pervading Brahman ever rests in sacrifice. (Transl. by SASTRY 1979).

Yudhiṣṭhira wants to obtain. This idea is expressed very frequently. Thus in 6.5, at the beginning of the war, Dhṛtarāṣṭra reflects that the earth must be marvellous indeed if so many warriors are ready to die for her possession, and he requests Saṃjaya to describe the earth to him, which the latter accordingly does, at some length.[31]

As for the second aim of sacrifices, that of maintaining the world-order, how can it possibly be fulfilled by a battle which apparently has the absolutely opposite effect of causing general doom and destruction? The very idea seems basically absurd. And yet, if we follow ELIADE (1979:190), we might discern here the heritage of a very ancient Indo-European ritual, which is attested in ancient India, in Rome, and in the Celtic tradition:

> "They [i.e. the Indo-Europeans] possessed concepts and rituals that enabled them to consecrate space and to 'cosmicize' the territories in which they settled [...] *and this also enabled them periodically to renew the world* (*by ritual combat between two groups of celebrants*,[32] a rite of which vestiges still remain in India and Iran.)"

Thus the aim of such ritual battles was the 'renewal of the world'. This conception plays a role of primordial importance in the Mahābhārata too. For we must remember that the Mahābhārata is not just a "tale of petty jealousy, intrigue and strife", (as SUKTHANKAR (1975:62) rightly notes), but it describes a war of cosmic dimensions between Good and Evil (or *dharma* and *adharma*) and most of the protagonists are incarnations of gods or demons, who have taken human form to fight

[31] Less optimistically, Arjuna says in BhG 1.35:
etān na hantum icchāmi ghnato 'pi madhusūdhana /
api trailokyarājyasya hetoḥ kiṃ nu mahīkṛte //
These, O slayer of Madhu, I do not wish to kill, though they kill me, even for the sake of dominion over the three worlds; how much less, for the sake of the earth! (Transl. by SASTRY 1979).

[32] My italics.

out their age-old and ever-recurring battle. As SULLIVAN (1990:90) writes: "The war between the gods and demons is a frequent topic of Vedic literature; indeed, from the *Vedas* on, it has been the central myth of Indian civilization", and "[it] is certainly the central myth of the MBh." (1998:91). Thus the primary aim of this war is to re-establish the *dharma*, the world-order, social order, and also moral law (see SUKTHANKAR 1975:69), which threatens to be overcome at a critical moment.[33] This explains why the battlefield is called a *dharma-kṣetra* and the battle itself a *dharma-yuddha*.

As we can see from the above, the aims of this battle are basically twofold: at a concrete level it is obtaining the earth, and at a higher level it is maintaining the cosmic world-order. In these two respects, the aims of the *raṇa-yajña* are essentially the same as those of sacrifices.

The deities of the raṇa-yajña

Three divine beings are propitiated through the war-sacrifice, namely the Earth,[34] Kṛṣṇa and Śiva. These three divinities are closely related to the war and to the sacrifice performed by it. We shall therefore examine their respective roles in the Mahābhārata as the gods of the sacrifice.

The Earth

The fact that the Earth is one of the recipients of the sacrifice is made clear by various events and implications of the war-sacrifice:

---

[33] My thanks to GONZALEZ-REIMANN (2002:116, note 71) for correcting my imprecise quotation.

[34] Here I propose to argue that the goddess Earth plays an important role in the Epic, especially during the war. SMITH (1989:182) on the contrary claims that "Goddesses are relatively unimportant in the *Mahābhārata* and *Rāmāyaṇa*, but they play a major role in many vernacular epics." Judging from the importance of Draupadī (who, as any queen, is a representative of the earth) in the South Indian versions of the MBh, HILTEBEITEL (1988:135) on the contrary concludes that the goddess already plays an important role in the MBh.

– the promise she receives from Viṣṇu before the war.
– the way in which the dead warriors are left lying on the ground as oblations for her.
– the way in which she is described as enjoying the gift of these oblations.
– the active role she plays in the war, evidenced through the various biases she displays.

We shall presently take up these points in the above sequence. In Mahābhārata 1.58 and 11.8, we find a typically Purāṇic story which is the prelude to most of Viṣṇu's incarnations: the Earth is overburdened by the weight of too many creatures and complains about it to the gods. The two passages slightly diverge: in the first, the Earth is specially oppressed by the numerous Asuras and Daityas who have incarnated themselves. The gods promise her that they will incarnate themselves too in order to defeat them. The second version does not specify who oppresses her particularly, but Viṣṇu tells her that her wish would be fulfilled when Duryodhana, Dhṛtarāṣṭra's eldest son, would rule over her, and provoke a great war in which the kings would kill each other, thus lessening her burden (11.8.24-26). Thus we see that at one level, the Earth causes the war.

Another legend, which also purports to take place before the war, reveals that the earth of the Kurukṣetra will be the sacrificial ground of the sacrifice. In 9.52, the *rājarṣi* Kuru, the legendary founder of the Kaurava-dynasty, is observed ploughing the Kurukṣetra (field of Kuru), and as a reward for this action he gets as a boon from Indra that those dying in a battle in this particular field would go to heaven (to this point we shall return later). Now, ploughing is a well-attested sacrificial act: the ground is always ploughed before the erection of a fire-altar (KEITH 1925:308). This act thus prefigures the future *raṇa-yajña*.

The fact that the goddess Earth is one of the recipients of the war-sacrifice explains one point which would otherwise seem quite incomprehensible, namely, why the corpses of the dead warriors are left lying on the ground till the end of the war (the sight is graphically described in the Strīparvan (11.16, ff.). This is understandable in the case of the common soldiers who often come from distant lands and who have no one to take care of their mortal remains, but quite surprising for the great war-lords, close allies or relatives of the Kauravas and Pāṇḍavas, who are left exactly to the same fate after their death. It is of course true that there is probably no time to perform funeral ceremonies in the midst of the battle, but one feels that a certain religious sentiment, if not simple human affection and emotions, should prompt the living to keep their dead in a safe place till the end of the war.[35] The sad fate of the slain warriors is pathetically described in 7.48.46:

> *praviddhavarmābharaṇā varāyudhā*
> *vipannahastyaśvarathānugā narāḥ* /
> *mahārhaśayyāstaraṇocitāḥ sadā*
> *kṣitāv anāthā iva śerate hatāḥ* //
>
> [These] men, provided with the best of weapons, with their fallen armours and ornaments, following their destroyed elephants, horses and chariots, who were always used to precious beds and couches, [now] they lie on the ground, slain, as if they had no protector.

---

[35] Indeed we find that as certain emphasis was laid on the fact that the bodies of the dead should be preserved whole (R̥V 10.16.6) and if a part should prove missing it had to be replaced symbolically (ŚB 11.6.3.11; 14.6.9.28). This was probably dictated by the belief that the dead would be reunited with their bodies in the after-life (R̥V 10.14.8 and 10.16.5). (See KEITH 1925:405-6). On the other hand, it is also true that bodies were often merely dumped on burial grounds (*śmaśāna*), (see KEITH 1925:417 & 424), but this was in all probability due to economic factors (wood is scarce and dear in many parts of India). (See BASHAM 1954:177). But that this is not ultimately intended here is shown by the fact that all the slain warriors are duly cremated after the war (MBh 11.26).

This state of affairs appears all the more surprising to one familiar with Homer's Iliad, where great fights are fought around the bodies of dead warriors, to prevent them from falling into enemy-hands, as for instance the fight around the body of Patroclus in Canto 17. It is true that, with a few notorious exceptions, no offenses are usually done to corpses in the Mahābhārata war (this would entail great *adharma*), quite unlike the situation in the Iliad (one may think especially of the shameful treatment inflicted to Hector's corpse by Achilles in Canto 22).

But if the dead have nothing to fear from men, they undergo nevertheless great depredations due to man-eating demons such as *piśāca*s and *rākṣasa*s, and various carrion-eating beasts such as vultures and jackals, who invade the deserted battlefield at night-time to feast on the corpses (see e.g. 7.48.47-48; 7.72.13-15; 8.21.42; 8:36.33-35, etc.). These descriptions often evoke the purest *bībhatsa-rasa*, or "sentiment of disgust". Thus for instance verse 7.48.48:

> *tvaco vinirbhidya piban vasām asṛk*
> *tathaiva majjāṃ piśitāni cāśnuvan /*
> *vapāṃ vilumpanti hasanti gānti ca*
> *prakarṣamāṇāḥ kuṇapāny anekaśaḥ //*
>
> Having pierced the skin (of the corpses), drinking the fat and the blood and eating the marrow and the flesh, they (i.e. the *rākṣasa*s and *piśāca*s) tear out the omentum,[36] laugh and sing, dragging around corpses in great numbers.

---

36 The omentum, as LINCOLN (1986:55) remarks, is "the fattiest piece of visceral tissue, which burned brightest". During the sacrifice, the omentum is the first part of the sacrificial victim to be taken out, and it is brought to the altar called *uttara-vedī* where it is cooked. The *uttara-vedī* is a notoriously dangerous place, apt to change itself into a fierce lioness should anything go wrong during the ritual. The *vapā* is thus probably offered in/to it first, as a placatory measure (See JAMISON 1991:88 ff.). Similarly, the *rākṣasa*s and *piśāca*s are also wild and dangerous creatures, and the fact that they appropriate the *vapā* makes the sacrificial analogy of their act even more striking.

We can understand why the corpses are left lying on the battlefield to undergo the above-described treatment only if we consider them to be the oblations to the Earth and to her creatures who are thus partaking in the sacrifice.[37] This is corroborated by Karṇa's words (5.139.39-40), who says that the heads and blood are the oblations of the war-sacrifice. As a matter of fact, the *paśu*s of a sacrifice are always eaten after the sacrificial ceremony. As LINCOLN (1986:84) aptly and succinctly puts it: "every sacrifice is followed by a meal". Since in the present case the victims are human beings, they can only be eaten by *rākṣasa*s, etc. Moreover, it seems to have been a common ritual in ordinary sacrifices to offer aside, to the snakes and to the *rākṣasa*s, certain parts of the victim which were considered impure, such as the blood, the entrails, etc. Maybe to propitiate the powers of evil, but maybe also as serious offerings to them as the embodied chthonic powers of the earth.[38] At a more concrete level, the act of leaving the bodies on the battlefield can also be interpreted as a ritual of fertilizing the earth.[39] This concept can be explained by a very ancient Indo-European mythological theme,

[37] This also explains why Bhīṣma, mortally wounded by Arjuna's arrows, chooses to remain till his death supported and lifted up on his bed of arrows: for only the dead lie on the ground, and of course, Bhīṣma is not destined to die as yet. (For different interpretations of Bhīṣma's bed of arrows, see GEHRTS (1975:237-39), BIARDEAU (1978:201) and VON SIMSON (1984:195)). Not only do the dead lie on the ground: it also seems to be true that whoever lies on the ground is as good as dead. This is especially noticeable in the case of Duryodhana, who, though suffering only from broken thighs, is left lying on the ground and considered as good as dead. No one attempts to rescue him from his fate. Indeed, to my knowledge, there is never a description in the entire Mahābhārata war (unlike the situation in the Rāmāyaṇa) of the wounded soldiers being rescued from the field, or given medical care.

[38] See KEITH (1925:273, 281, 326, 382). In the light of the above, Bhīma's deed of drinking Duḥśāsana's blood (8.61) gains a new dimension. Seeing Bhīma's deed, the horror-struck spectators exclaim: *nāyaṃ manuṣyaḥ* (he is not human!) (8.61.10). Bhīma is of course behaving here in a 'rākṣasic' way (other instances of this trait of his character are not lacking). (See GITOMER 1991:299). But Bhīma is not only behaving in an inhuman way in the common sense that his deed is horrible, but also in the sense that he places himself at the level of a divinity who receives the sacrificial oblation.

[39] See ELIADE (1960:187), who notes that when human sacrifices were performed by certain Indian tribes, parts of the body were cut into pieces and buried in various villages, and the rest was burnt and the ashes strewn over the land, in order to fertilize the earth.

namely, that the earth was formed out of the flesh of the primordial sacrificial man. Though this trait is not preserved in the Ṛgvedic Puruṣasūkta (10.90), it appears for instance in MBh 12.175.17, and also very commonly in other texts belonging to Indo-European cultures.[40] Thus earth and flesh are 'alloforms of each other (to use Lincoln's terminology), and this explains how the devastated earth is very literally replenished by the offerings of human flesh left lying on her surface.

The fact that the Earth enjoys the offering of these oblations explains why we often come across poetic descriptions of the beauty of the earth of the battlefield in the midst of battle-descriptions. These descriptions are often made by Saṃjaya for the benefit of Dhṛtarāṣṭra (6.85.31-34; 6.92.54-75; 7.48.22-30 & 44; 8.36.8-9; 9.8.13-23) or by Kṛṣṇa for Arjuna (7.123.30-41; 8.14.26-59). The striking point of these descriptions is that the horrible sight of the earth strewn with corpses, severed limbs, fallen weapons and ornaments, dead or dying elephants and horses, and covered with flowing rivers of blood, is described as a picture of beauty when it should only inspire revulsion. Thus, the earth, covered with all the above-listed relics of the war, is said to "shine, as if she was covered with flowers in spring": *saṃcchannā vasudhā bhāti vasante kusumair iva* (6.85.34), or, to "look as if she was wrapped in colourful clothes": *vasudhāṃ [...] citrapaṭṭair ivāvṛtām* (7.123.38). In 8.36.8, Saṃjaya describes her as follows:

> *rudhireṇa samāstīrṇā bhāti bhārata medinī /*
> *śakragopagaṇākīrṇā prāvṛṣīva yathā dharā //*
> O descendent of Bharata, the earth, covered with blood, shines like the earth during the monsoon when she is covered with multitudes of *śakragopa*[41] insects.

---

40 See LINCOLN (1986: chapter 1).

41 The (red) cochineal insect.

We may notice that two of the above (partly) quoted verses mention certain seasons: spring and the monsoon. (Verse 6.85.34 contains another allusion to spring.) Now, these two seasons are those which are most directly connected with the fertility of the earth and of its vegetation. Spring because it produces young shoots and blossoms on all the trees, and the rains because they drench the earth which was parched during the long summer-months, and thus provoke a general revival of the vegetation. Therefore, it may not be too daring to say that the blood and flesh of the dead warriors soak and revitalize the earth, like the sap of spring and the rain of the monsoon.

In these passages, the earth is sometimes personified, mainly by means of comparisons (*upamā*s). Thus, in verse 8.36.9, reddened by the flesh and blood with which she is covered, and shining due to the warriors' fallen jewellery, she is likened to a beautiful dark-complexioned woman wearing colourful clothes and dazzling golden ornaments. (See also 6.92.65; 8.68.34).[42] Some verses even have erotic undertones, which probably aim at intensifying the sense of the enjoyment that the earth experiences through the offerings of the sacrificial oblations. Thus, verse 9.8.13 likens the imprints of horse-hooves on the surface of the earth, to the nail-marks left by her lover on a woman:

> *teṣāṃ tu vājināṃ bhūmiḥ khuraiś citrā viśāṃ pate |*
> *aśobhata yathā nārī karajakṣatavikṣatā ||*
> And the earth, speckled by the hooves of these horses, o King, shone like a woman wounded by the marks [left] by [her lover's] nails.

But there is one description of the earth of the battlefield which fails to stress her beauty, namely that made by Śalya to Duryodhana in

---

42 HILTEBEITEL (1980) more specifically analyzes such passages in terms of reclothing the earth, which had been stripped in the person of Draupadī (the queen, hence the representative of the earth) in the great *sabhā* of Hastināpura.

8.68.14-31, after Karṇa's death. Here on the contrary, Śalya likens the Earth to a ghastly-looking Vaitaraṇī, a river of hell carrying blood and corpses:

> *tathāpaviddhair gajavājiyodhair*
> *mandāsubhiś caiva gatāsubhiś ca /*
> *narāśvanāgaiś ca rathaiś ca marditair*
> *mahī mahāvaitaraṇīva durdṛśā* // 8.68.18 //
>
> With the pierced elephants, horses and soldiers who have little life left or none at all, with the smashed men, horses, elephants and chariots, the earth is horrible to look at, like a great Vaitaraṇī.[43]

Further, in 8.68.22, Śalya remarks that the earth, strewn with various corpses in the path of Arjuna, is inaccessible and unattainable: *agamyā vasudhātidurgā*. These terms, which can also have the meaning of sexually unapproachable, are in stark contrast with the term used in verse 8.68.34, where Saṃjaya himself is speaking again, and where the earth is on the contrary likened to a young woman clad in bright attire, who is said to be *sarvagamyā*: accessible to all. Of course, Śalya is one of the future *paśu*s of the war-sacrifice, and thus he is struck only by the horror of the picture. As HILTEBEITEL (1980:107) remarks, referring to a comment made by Duryodhana in 9.28.16 before his duel with Bhīma, where he compares the Earth to a widow: "To the vanquished the Earth appears stark." Kṛṣṇa on the other hand, being the 'knower' of the sacrifice, besides being the Supreme God, knows that the Earth is enjoying the offerings given to her in the war-sacrifice. Saṃjaya too 'knows', having been gifted with second sight. In a sense,

---

[43] Descriptions of flowing rivers of blood carrying corpses and compared to the Vaitaraṇī are frequent in the battle books (6.55.125; 6.99.38; 7.48.50; 7.146.48; 8.55.42). But only in one other instance is the earth of the battlefield (*raṇabhūmi*) itself compared to the Vaitaraṇī (8.58.7).

these passages, which are mostly very poetic, could be considered as the hymns of the sacrifice.[44]

In some instances, the Earth actively interferes in the course of events during the battle, showing favour to some, and disfavour to others. For instance, at the decisive moment before the great fight between Arjuna and Karṇa, all the gods and other divine or semi-divine beings take sides: some with Arjuna, and others with Karṇa (8.63). Here significantly the Earth sides with Arjuna, "like a mother with her son": *mātā putrasya* (8.63.32).[45] In this connection we can quote AV 12.1.37, from the well-known hymn to the Earth, which states clearly that in the fight between the powers of good and those of evil, the earth is ever on the side of the gods, here represented by Indra (Arjuna's father), against the powers of evil, here exemplified by the serpent of chaos Vṛtra: "She that delivers (to destruction) the blasphemous Dasyus, she that takes the side of Indra, not of V*ri*tra, (that earth) adheres to *S*akra (mighty Indra), the lusty bull." (BLOOMFIELD (1992 [1897]:203)). Again, during the fight with Karṇa, the Earth helps Kṛṣṇa and Arjuna by allowing their chariot to sink down into her: *avagāḍhe rathe bhumau* (8.66.11), so that Karṇa's arrow, which was aimed at Arjuna's throat, merely strikes his coronet. Inversely, the Earth is the cause of Karṇa's downfall since the wheel of his chariot gets stuck in a rut at a critical moment (8.66.59): *agrasan mahī cakraṃ rādheyasya* (the Earth swallowed up Karṇa's chariot-wheel), an ominous image of

44 Indeed, we must not forget that hymns are one of the most important aspects of the sacrificial performance, if not the most important. See POTDAR (1953:18), and GONDA (1975:83). Similarly, all through the war, Kṛṣṇa gets his share of hymns in praise of his deeds and of his divine nature, and Śiva gets his share specially in 10.7, in the long *stuti* Aśvatthāman addresses to him.

45 The Earth is of course not literally Arjuna's mother, but, since very ancient times, the Earth is considered as the primeval Mother of the world and of the gods. Arjuna's 'real' mother is Kuntī / Pṛthā, who is said to be the incarnation of another, rather insignificant goddess, Siddhi. But the name Pṛthā might also suggest Pṛthivī (Earth). This is hinted at by KARVE (1974:38) and BIARDEAU (1997:98). According to BIARDEAU (1976b:225), Kuntī, as the principal queen of king Pāṇḍu, represents the kingdom and hence the earth, as any queen does.

Karṇa's own imminent death. These examples show that in the battle the Earth is definitely on the side of Arjuna, and hence of *dharma*.

Kṛṣṇa and Śiva

We shall now turn to the role which Kṛṣṇa and Śiva, the two supreme gods in the Epic, play in the war-sacrifice. If the Earth plays an important role at a concrete level by being the recipient of the oblations, her active role in the battle is rather limited. This is far from being the case for Kṛṣṇa and Śiva. The roles of the two Supreme Gods are complementary: Kṛṣṇa plays a major part in the events leading to the war and during the war itself, whereas Śiva's main contribution is to bring the war-sacrifice to an end by his violent intervention. Thus these two gods are made to play a role which has been traditionally theirs since Vedic times. For Viṣṇu (Kṛṣṇa) is always identified with the sacrifice, especially with the positive aspect of the sacrifice, which aims at maintaining the world-order. Śiva-Rudra on the other hand, the ascetic god of the wilderness who is beyond the pale of sacrifice, represents forces which are hostile to the sacrifice, ready to destroy it should anything go wrong. In certain sacrificial ceremonies, Śiva, for propitiation's sake, is given only the 'left-overs' of the oblations, after the other gods have obtained their share.[46]

First of all, Kṛṣṇa's divine nature should be made clear. Though he appears in a human form in the Mahābhārata, yet, as SUKTHANKAR (1975:67) says: "there is [...] not a single passage in the Mahābhārata which does not presuppose the divinity and the cosmic character of Śrī Kṛṣṇa."[47] Kṛṣṇa is one of Viṣṇu's *avatāras*. His present incarnation takes place, as they usually do, in order to restore *dharma* (the cosmic

---

[46] Concerning the respective roles of Viṣṇu and Śiva in the sacrifice, see BIARDEAU (1976a:89-106), and (1989:97). Also ELIADE (1979:214).

[47] And in a very similar vein, see BIARDEAU (2002:145).

as well as social world-order) which is threatened by Evil.[48] Thus Kṛṣṇa tells Arjuna in Bhagavadgītā 4.7-8:

> *yadā yadā hi dharmasya glānir bhavati bhārata /*
> *abhyutthānam adharmasya tadā 'tmānaṃ sṛjāmy aham //*
> *paritrāṇāya sādhūnāṃ vināśāya ca duṣkṛtām /*
> *dharmasaṃsthāpanārthāya sambhavāmi yuge yuge //*
> For whenever the Law languishes, Bhārata, and lawlessness flourishes, I create myself. I take on existence from eon to eon, for the rescue of the good and the destruction of the evil, in order to re-establish the Law. (Transl. VAN BUITENEN 1981).

The *raṇa-yajña* precisely has as its higher aim the destruction of evil-doers and the establishment of *dharma*. That is why Kṛṣṇa strives throughout his career to bring about the war which will have the above-mentioned effects. Indeed, he acts in this sense long before the war itself. Thus he gets rid of various powerful kings, who might have become the allies of the Kauravas in the war.[49] In the Udyogaparvan, during his ambassador's mission to the Kauravas, his behaviour is ambiguous: while officially pleading for peace, he actually plants

48 In this sense, I cannot agree with John D. SMITH (1989:184) who claims that "in the Sanskrit epics, there are stories to explain that the purpose of the incarnation is to resolve a celestial crisis through human conflict", and that "the actions of the gods and 'semidivine' figures [...] are not beneficial to men. Celestial beings propose to provoke and participate in human conflicts, causing enormous human carnage; and their reasons for doing so are purely to avoid trouble in heaven." (1989:183). Finally he concludes (1989:193): "The gods, say the epics, are not averse from mixing in human affairs; but when they do so it is entirely for their own benefit. When trouble threatens them they get rid of it by shifting it to earth through the exercise of their will. Epic heroes – and by extension we ourselves – are the gods' scapegoats: we take on their ills and suffer on their behalf." Smith does not take into account the fact that it is primarily the Earth (and not the heavens) who is suffering in the MBh because she is overpopulated: there is therefore no question of 'shifting trouble to earth', because this is where it started in the first place. He also does not take into account the fact that the crisis here is of a cosmic rather than celestial nature, hence involving and affecting both men and gods. In this respect, I can perceive no dichotomy between men and gods: what is at stake here is the welfare of both – and indeed, of the whole cosmos.

49 Such as Jarāsaṃdha, Śiśupāla and Ekalavya. This is stated by Kṛṣṇa himself in 7.156.

further seeds of hatred in Duryodhana's heart.[50] During the battle itself, Kṛṣṇa often urges Arjuna to take action and to slay certain enemies, even if *adharma* should result from it.[51] Last but certainly not least, the immediate and concrete aim of the recitation of the Bhagavadgītā itself is to promote the battle, since Arjuna refuses to fight; and, likewise, the numerous instances in which Kṛṣṇa consoles and encourages Yudhiṣṭhira, who is repeatedly subjected to crises of 'bad conscience' and threatens at all stages to give up the whole affair and go back to the forest. Thus we see that Kṛṣṇa's attitude is from the start very consistent and that he actively strives to bring about this war, which is his mission on earth.[52] We should remember that in 5.139.29, Kṛṣṇa is said to be the *adhvaryu*-priest of the war-sacrifice. Now the *adhvaryu* is precisely the priest who is in charge of organizing and arranging all the practical details, before and during the sacrifice (measuring the sacrificial ground, lighting the fire, procuring the vessels, cutting the oblations, etc.).

Kṛṣṇa's stance on sacrifice is equally clear. Concerning this topic, we must mainly turn to the Bhagavadgītā. In this text, Kṛṣṇa fully defends the sacrificial life-style (sacrifices of various sorts and at various levels, of course). Thus he says in 4.31: *nāyaṃ loko 'sty ayajñasya kuto 'nyaḥ*: "This world is not of him who fails to sacrifice – could then the higher world be his [...]?" (Transl. VAN BUITENEN 1981). Not only is he in favour of the sacrifice, but, in the ultimate

---

50 For instance, shortly after arriving in Hastināpura, Kṛṣṇa refuses to eat and drink in Duryodhana's *sabhā*, whereas the latter has not yet, at least openly, shown any signs of hostility towards him (5.89). Later, Kṛṣṇa suggests in the assembly that Duryodhana should be imprisoned if he refuses to listen to reason, which of course thoroughly infuriates the latter who had actually planned to make Kṛṣṇa undergo exactly the same fate (5.122-128).

51 Such as Bhīṣma, Karṇa, Bhūriśravas, etc.

52 Kṛṣṇa's responsibility for the war is also indirectly revealed by the curses he incurs after the war: Gāndhārī curses him in Strīparvan (11.25), accusing him of being responsible for the havoc wrought by the war. The sage Uttaṅka threatens to curse him for the same motive, but desists after hearing Kṛṣṇa's reasons for having acted the way he did (14.52-54). For this topic in general, see DEV (1989).

reality, he reveals himself to be the Sacrifice itself (9.16), and, most tellingly, also the Enjoyer and the Lord of all sacrifices: *ahaṃ hi sarvayajñānāṃ bhoktā ca prabhur eva ca* (9.24). That he is the *bhoktṛ* (enjoyer) of the sacrifice is directly and most graphically demonstrated in 11.26-29, where Kṛṣṇa shows himself to Arjuna in his terrible cosmic form, devouring the slain warriors of both armies. Thus, if the Earth, as we have seen above, receives the sacrificial oblations on a concrete level, Kṛṣṇa receives them on the ultimate level.

That he is the *prabhu* (Lord) of the sacrifice is shown by his role in the war. For Kṛṣṇa is Arjuna's charioteer: he thus leads and guides Arjuna throughout the battle.[53] As for Arjuna, he is the champion of the gods and of *dharma*, the greatest warrior of the world, whom neither gods nor demons can defeat, for he knows the *mantra*s of his magic weapons and hence of the sacrifice. He is the one on whom the successful completion of the sacrifice depends to the greatest extent.[54] Finally their chariot, Agni's gift for helping him to burn the Khāṇḍava forest, is actually none else than Agni, the sacrificial fire, himself. For Agni is of course the 'chariot' of the gods, in the sense that he conveys to them their shares of the sacrifice which are poured into himself. Here he takes the shape of an actual chariot to carry the supreme god of the sacrifice and the supreme champion of *dharma*, and thus enable them to perform their sacrificial duties. That the chariot is Agni is also revealed at the end of the war, when, its mission being accomplished, it spontaneously bursts into flames, thus returning to Agni or, better, becoming Agni again (9.61).[55]

---

[53] For Kṛṣṇa's function as charioteer, see BIARDEAU (1981:72, note 1).

[54] BIARDEAU (1976a:132) even goes a step further, and makes Arjuna the *yajamāna* of the *raṇa-yajña,* because, for her, Arjuna represents the figure of the ideal king, and not Yudhiṣṭhira (see BIARDEAU 1978). However, the text of the MBh itself does not seem to support the idea that Arjuna is the *yajamāna*, for if Duryodhana is *dīkṣita* for the war-sacrifice, it follows that he is the *yajamāna,* and we have seen that Arjuna is the *hotṛ*.

[55] Similarly, before going to his last sojourn in the forest (17.1), Arjuna has to surrender his famous Gāṇḍiva bow (also a gift from Agni) into the water (Agni himself

If, up to the Sauptikaparvan, the battle-sacrifice is directed by Kṛṣṇa, another divinity takes over in the last *parvan* of the *yuddha-pañcaka* or the "five *parvan*s of the war", namely Śiva. The Sauptikaparvan, with its striking sacrificial imagery, has been analyzed at depth and in detail by HILTEBEITEL (1976/1991, chapter 12: "Epic Eschatology"). We will therefore deal with it only briefly. HILTEBEITEL makes a thorough comparison between Aśvatthāman's deed, who slays the sleeping army of the Pāṇḍavas during the night following their victory, and the myth of Dakṣa's sacrifice. This parallel is inspired by the text itself: Kṛṣṇa explains to the Pāṇḍavas that it is due to Śiva's grace that Aśvatthāman could accomplish this deed, and proceeds to tell them how Śiva, being the only god who was not invited to Dakṣa's sacrifice, took revenge by destroying the sacrifice with utmost savagery, attacking and variously mutilating the protagonists of the performance (10.18). HILTEBEITEL shows the structural similarities of both deeds: Aśvatthāman was left without his 'share' of the sacrifice (namely Dhṛṣṭadyumna, who had killed his father Droṇa), and likewise, Śiva too had not obtained his share at Dakṣa's sacrifice. Then, Aśvatthāman, after praising Śiva and receiving a sword from him, and, indeed, being 'possessed' by him,[56] proceeds to slaughter the sleeping warriors, but in a peculiar manner, kicking them and mutilating them, "like *paśu*s" (10.8.18 & 122), in the same manner as Śiva at Dakṣa's sacrifice. In the meanwhile, his two accomplices, Kṛpa and Kṛtavarman, to prevent anybody from escaping, set fire to the three gates of the camp: these fires are like the three fires of a sacrifice (10.8). These are the main points of the analogy which directly concern us here.

---

received it from Varuṇa). This gesture represents Arjuna's willing surrender of fighting (the very essence of his *kṣatriya*-hood) and hence of his life.

[56] According to MBh 7.172.82, Aśvatthāman is even born of Śiva.

Now, while HILTEBEITEL's analysis is on the whole very convincing, there is one point which it leaves unexplained. First, if we admit the analogy of Aśvatthāman's deed with Śiva's destruction of Dakṣa's sacrifice, then we should consider the events of the Sauptikaparvan as the destruction (in the sense of rendering it void) of the *raṇa-yajña*. But this, to my knowledge, is nowhere implied in the text. Rather than considering the Sauptikaparvan as the destruction of the sacrifice, I would prefer to see it as its completion, achieved, of course, in Śiva's characteristically 'destructive' fashion. For indeed, Aśvatthāman does get his sacrificial share by performing the slaughter, whereas Śiva in the myth gets his due share only after performing his destructive act and being duly pacified and propitiated by the gods.[57] Moreover, we must note that in the Sauptikaparvan, Śiva himself had no cause to take revenge and destroy the war-sacrifice, for he had by no means been totally excluded from it so far. Thus he is depicted in 7.173 as fighting on the side of Arjuna in the war, and helping the latter, to whom he had moreover given *astras* long before the war (cf. 3.27-41, the Kirāṭa-episode).

Another incident which concurs with the above-mentioned is that Kṛṣṇa very conveniently leaves the camp on the eve of the slaughter, taking only his closest friends with him out of the camp. For this act, he offers only a vague explanation: it is "for the sake of auspiciousness": *maṅgalārthāya*[58] (9.61.35). Later that same night, Kṛṣṇa suddenly declares that he has come to know of Aśvatthāman's evil intentions (9.61.68), but he does nothing concrete to prevent the slaughter. On the whole, his absence at such as crucial moment appears to be highly suspicious,[59] and it seems more probable that he

57 HILTEBEITEL (1976/1991:330) notes this structural inversion himself.

58 Perhaps this is meant as a pun: even today, the last chanting which takes place at the very end of any festive occasion (*pūjā*, music programme, etc.) is called *maṅgalam*.

59 This is HILTEBEITEL's opinion too (1976/1991:314-15).

deliberately left the way free for Śiva's intervention, to allow him thus to 'finish' the sacrifice.[60] This can logically be accounted for by their traditional distribution of roles, which we hinted at above: in certain types of sacrifices, Śiva customarily receives the 'left-overs', in this case, the surviving warriors. Thus the MBh war is not "the nightmarish chaos and ruin caused by sacrifice gone wrong" (HEESTERMAN 1997:52), but it is a sacrificial performance drawn to its full logical conclusion.

The aftermath of the war

Now it remains to be seen why all, or at least nearly all the protagonists of this war had to be killed. The Mahābhārata often stresses the point that the destruction of the whole *kṣatriya* race of the earth was achieved by the war. Therefore, since the war-sacrifice had to be completed in the above-described manner in the Sauptikaparvan, it logically follows that the destruction of all the *kṣatriya*s was somehow a desirable thing. We are here reminded of the episode of the Earth complaining that she is overburdened (and this story is indeed told shortly after the Sauptikaparvan, in Strīparvan 8). It is very probable that the slaughter of the *kṣatriya*s was indeed designed to relieve her of some of her burden. Here one may wonder why the *kṣatriya*s are specifically singled out for such a dubious honour.[61] One answer might simply be that they are the only group in the society which qualifies for such an undertaking as a war-sacrifice, by their up-bringing and training, if not by their very birth. It seems then that as a class, the *kṣatriya*s are scapegoated by the entire society to solve an over-

60 This is already BIARDEAU's opinion (1976b:211).

61 Though there must have been members of other *varṇa*s fighting in the war (we know at least that Droṇa and his son Aśvatthāman are Brahmins), the emphasis is always given to the fact that the *kṣatriya*s have been wiped out.

population problem, and more generally, a problem of imbalance between *dharma* and *adharma* occurring at an end-of-*yuga* period.[62]

But the answer is not quite so simple, and there seem to be more implications to it. In brief, we might discern here traces of the ever-existing rivalry between *kṣatriya*s and Brahmins. It is true that the two *varṇa*s worked hand in hand on most occasions (see Devayānī's words to king Yayāti in MBh 1.76), but the competition between them for supremacy is all too obvious in the Mahābhārata, and is reflected in numerous legends (e.g. that of the same Devayānī, especially in her quarrels with Śarmiṣṭhā, the daughter of the Asura-king), as well as in *dharma*-passages (e.g. in 13.139-142) which insistently stress the superiority of Brahmins over *kṣatriya*s. Indeed, Bhīṣma's last instruction to Yudhiṣṭhira before dying is to show unwavering respect to Brahmins (13.153). For if the *kṣatriya*s wield the political power, the Brahmins have the upper hand in the sacrificial performance, and never let an opportunity go to stress that their power is the highest. As OLIVELLE (1998:11) notes:

> "The relationship between the priestly and royal classes in ancient India was complex. At one level it was symbiotic; the cooperation between these two groups, in whose hands power was concentrated, permitted both to thrive. At another level, the two groups were rivals for power and prestige. The entire Brahmanical ideology of society and the science and practice of ritual were designed, on the one hand, to enhance Kṣatriya power and, on the other, to ensure the recognition by the Kṣatriyas that the source of their power was the Brahmin."

62 We are here reminded to a certain extent of the theory which is central to GIRARD (1977), namely that the basic function of sacrifice is to divert onto a substitute victim the violence which might otherwise engulf the society as a whole in times of crisis: "The surrogate victim dies so that the entire community, threatened by the same fate, can be reborn in a new or renewed cultural order." (1977:255).

This rivalry, or rather, in this case, downright hostility, appears very clearly in another myth, namely that of Rāma Jāmadagnya, later called Paraśurāma, who exterminated the *kṣatriya*-race twenty-one times. The story of Rāma, Bhṛgu's grand-son, is extremely often told in the Mahābhārata. SUKTHANKAR (1936)[63] even claimed that the Bhārgavas, the members of the Bhṛgu family, had to a great extent appropriated the text of the Mahābhārata and added to it a number of stories pertaining to their own family, a thesis which is disputed nowadays.[64] What is especially contestable is SUKTHANKAR's opinion that "the Bhārgavas [...] had strictly speaking no connection whatsoever with the Kuru-Pāñcāla heroes" (1936:44), and that "all this Bhārgava material in our present Mahābhārata is entirely foreign to the plan of the original saga of the Bharatas" (1936:70). It appears on the contrary (and I am not the first to make this point) that the stories pertaining to the Bhārgavas were not always inserted in a totally haphazard manner, and are often quite relevant to the context. For instance, we must note that Rāma's story is often told to Yudhiṣṭhira after the war, and on the latter's own insistence,[65] and it seems indeed that Yudhiṣṭhira considered himself to be the cause of the massacre of all the *kṣatriyas*, just as Rāma had been responsible for it in ancient times. Thus an evident parallel is drawn between both events.[66]

---

63 And following him see also GOLDMAN (1977).

64 See SULLIVAN (1990:19); MINKOWSKI (1991:398-400); HILTEBEITEL (1999) and (2001:105-118).. For a survey of the theories concerning Bhṛguization, see FITZGERALD (2002).

65 For instance, it is told by Kṛṣṇa to Yudhiṣṭhira in 12.48-49. According to SUKTHANKAR (1936:46), "Kṛṣṇa gratuitously volunteers to repeat the whole story of Rāma".

66 To make the analogy even more striking, Rāma's massacre of the *kṣatriyas* is said to have taken place on the Kurukṣetra itself, where five ponds were filled with their blood (12.48), and his deed is also called a sacrifice: *medha* (14.29.18). Moreover, the slaughter is said to have taken place between two *yugas* (the Tretā- and the Dvāparayuga), like the Mahābhārata war. For a very similar line of argumentation, see THOMAS (1996:73-76). We could even postulate that the resemblance between both massacres is the reason why Rāma Jāmadagnya was made into an *avatāra* of Viṣṇu, from the later portions of the Mahābhārata onwards: on the model of Kṛṣṇa who is

Now we must note that Rāma Jāmadagnya, just like Aśvatthāman who is single-handedly responsible for the final massacre of the sleeping army of the Pāṇḍavas, is a Brahmin. Thus it seems to me that we might discern a brahmanical bias in the stories pertaining to the destruction of the *kṣatriya*s, with the implication that too many *kṣatriya*s might be harmful to the world and that their periodical destruction is a desirable thing.[67] In this connection, we might draw a parallel with the snake-sacrifice (*sarpa-sattra*) performed by Janamejaya in the Ādiparvan (1.47 ff.), in which most of the snakes are killed with the express consent of the gods, because they are an extremely numerous, destructive and harmful species (1.34).[68] As we have seen it in a preceding chapter, this sacrifice, which plays a predominant part in the Ādiparvan, can in many ways be said to prefigure the *raṇa-yajña*.[69] Thus ultimately the nearly total destruction of the *kṣatriya*s, like that of the snakes, is viewed as a means of restoring *dharma*.

Let us now examine what is the fate of the dead, and that of the few survivors after the Mahābhārata war. It is a real leitmotiv in this text that "those who are slain will obtain heaven and those who win will enjoy the earth" (see e.g. Bhagavadgītā 2.37). This type of argument,

---

considered as an *avatāra* of Viṣṇu and who is the real instigator of the war (and not, of course, Yudhiṣṭhira) and is therefore to a great extent responsible for the destruction of the *kṣatriya*s.

67 Though not, of course, their complete annihilation, which would be equally dangerous. See for example 12.49. As BIARDEAU (1999:XXIX) says: "les brâhmanes ne demandent rien de plus qu'un *modus vivendi* qui leur permette d'exister... à leur juste place, qui est la première. Jamais ils ne chercheront à détruire l'ennemi dans sa totalité, quelle que soit l'intensité des combats, dont le champ de bataille donne un image effroyable dans les deux épopées. Le *Mahābhārata* remet les *asura*, ces perpétuels ennemis des dieux, à leur place sans les détruire complètement, et le *Rāmāyaṇa* soumet les *rākṣasa* – démons anthropophages quand l'occasion s'en présente, et gardiens minutieux du rituel brahmanique – en les cantonnant à Laṅkā – actuel Sri Lanka – sous un roi *rākṣasa* fidèle à Rāma. L'Inde, au moins en théorie, n'est jamais manichéenne. Il est naturel que les ennemis, créatures de ce monde, aient leur place, à condition que ce soit leur juste place. Les épopées en sont la démonstration."

68 See also the *rākṣasa-sattra* performed by Parāśara for similar reasons of revenge, in 1.172.

69 For this topic, see MINKOWSKI (1991).

calculated to whip up the courage and enthusiasm of the warriors, is widely used throughout the war. Even after the war, the topic keeps on recurring, but mainly as a means to console the living for the death of their relatives. This consolation is often proffered to Dhṛtarāṣṭra, to soften his grief at his sons' death. But the subject continues to torment the old king, so finally Vyāsa grants him, and all those who are present in his hermitage, to see the dead once again. Thus in 15.40-41, all the slain warriors rise out of the Gaṅgā and join the living for one night.

It is of course clear why Dhṛtarāṣṭra is specially worried about his sons' fate in the after-life: in everybody's opinion, including his own, they were evil and therefore certainly do not deserve heaven in the next life. Indeed, some sort of explanation for the fact that all those who die in the battle go to heaven, (however evil they may have been during their life), is even given in a story we have had occasion to refer to previously, that of king Kuru ploughing the Kurukṣetra (9.52). The king asks as a reward for his ploughing (which is said to be a *tapas*) that all those dying in this field should go to heaven. Indra agrees to this, but not unconditionally (for the gods have been reflecting that if impious persons, who did not sacrifice, died there and went to heaven, they (the gods) would lose their share): thus only those starving themselves to death in a sort of religious suicide and warriors slain in a battle, would reach heaven. Therefore, the death of a slain warrior has the same value as a religious suicide.[70] The idea that those who die in a battle go to heaven appears to be very ancient, since it figures already in the Ṛgveda. And in the Ṛgveda too, these warriors are said to deserve this privilege along with ascetics and sacrificers.[71]

---

[70] ELIADE (1964:206) interprets their death as an initiation.

[71] Thus RV 10.154.2-3:

tápasā yé anādhṛṣyā́s tápasā yé súvar yayúḥ /
tápo yé cakriré máhas tā́ṃś cid evā́pi gachatāt [scil. *madhuḥ*] //
yé yúdhyante pradhánesu śū́rāso yé tanūtyájaḥ /
yé vā sahásradakṣiṇās tā́ṃś cid evā́pi gachatāt //10.154.2-3//

In other words, the warriors' death on the battlefield is considered as a self-sacrifice (*ātma-yajña*).[72] We should remember that the *ātma-yajña* is actually the supreme and original form of sacrifice, for the victims (*paśus*) are always considered to be mere substitutes for the offering of the sacrificer's own self.[73] Here again, we are struck by the sacrificial analogy. For the sacrificial victims were considered to go to the gods, and good care was taken that they would not struggle or cry out, but die in silence, to all intent assenting to their fate.[74] In the case of the warriors too, an important precondition for their going to heaven is that they should die '*abhimukha*' (facing the enemy), that is, die a heroic death, and not that of a coward struck in the back while attempting to flee. Thus, they have to fight with courage and resolution, but also with a mental preparedness for death, if it should come. More than that, we even perceive a strong death-wish at places. For instance in 8.33.55-57 in the midst of a furious battle, a sound is suddenly heard in the sky, that of *vimāna*s (celestial chariots) filled with *apsaras*es who come to collect the dead from the battlefield and lead them to heaven. After observing this, the warriors fight with renewed enthusiasm and "with the desire to obtain heaven": *svargalipsayā* (57), in other words, with the wish to die.

Thus, the belief that the warriors slain in battle go to heaven automatically, without regard for their previous deeds, is possible only in the context of a war perceived as a sacrifice wherein their death is seen as a willing and dedicated self-sacrifice, like that of the sacrificial

Those who were unassailable thanks to their *tapas*, those who went to the sunlight thanks to their *tapas*, those who made *tapas* their might, may [the mead] reach them. Those who fight in battles as heroes, those who leave their bodies, or those who offer one thousand *dakṣiṇā*s, may [the mead] reach them.

[72] The ideal of self-sacrifice is prominently seen in the deaths of Bhīṣma and of Droṇa: these two warriors, who virtually cannot be defeated, are finally killed only at the moment when they have mentally resolved to die.

[73] See COOMARASWAMY (1977).

[74] Cf. KEITH (1925:280).

victims.[75] In this connection, we may add that the image of the warriors' *ātma-yajña*, fighting, as their *dharma* demands, with utmost dedication but regardless of the result (that is, without caring whether life or death will be their lot), is amply used by the Bhagavadgītā's *bhakti* ideology, which enjoins the *bhakta* to act according to his prescribed duties, but without being motivated by the fruits of his actions. (See e.g. BhG 2.47).

As for the survivors of the war, how did they 'enjoy the earth'? The answer is of course 'not greatly'. Indeed, in the aftermath of the war, the last *parvan*s, from the Āśramavāsika onwards, come as a great anti-climax. The lordship over the earth, for which the Pāṇḍavas have been striving during their whole life, comes to them finally as a poisonous gift, for which they have had to pay too great a price, for they are dispossessed of most of their friends, allies and family, in brief, all that would have made the possession of the earth enjoyable. Thus a certain *Lebensmüdigkeit* is perceived in all of them, and indeed the last *parvan*s are little more than the description of the successive deaths of the surviving protagonists of the story. Noteworthy is the fact that here again none of these deaths are natural: either they are violent deaths, like those of the Yādavas, and Vṛṣṇis and Andhakas, or they are again in a certain sense *ātma-yajña*s. Thus the elders, Dhṛtarāṣṭra, Gāndhārī and Kuntī let themselves be consumed in a forest-fire from which they do not try to escape. The Pāṇḍavas and Draupadī start climbing the Himālaya-mountain, an obvious metaphor for their willing ascent to heaven.[76]

---

75 In this respect, we can draw an interesting parallel with Northern European mythology. This mythology also knew about a heaven for warriors slain on the battlefield: they were thought to go to Valhalla, Odin's hall. Interestingly, there too, not only those killed in battles, but also those put to death as the willing victims of human sacrifices were said to reach that heaven. (See DAVIDSON 1964:28, 48, 149-153.)

76 Ānandavardhana in his *Dhvanyāloka* 4.5 uses somewhat similar arguments to defend his theory that the overall *rasa* of the Mahābhārata is the *śānta-rasa*: "the great sage who was its author, by furnishing a conclusion that dismays our hearts by the miserable end of the Vṛṣṇis and Pāṇḍavas, shows that the primary aim of his work has

Thus, at least on a superficial level, the pathos and the disgust with life reflected in the last *parvans* of the Mahābhārata are such that one would feel tempted to say that the message of this text (and one which is certainly in keeping with the then-emerging ideal of non-violence) is that battles are not worth fighting, and hence sacrifices not worth performing. And yet, at a deeper level, according to the world-view of the Epic, we know that the world could be saved from total annihilation only by the performance of the great war-sacrifice. As LAINE (1989:162, note 3) remarks:

> "In this light, it is only to humans that war is tragic; to the gods, it is a preordained and necessary process of destruction and renewal. When the human being can submit to this fact, he can find equanimity and become an instrument in the sacrifice of battle."

Conclusions

To conclude, we shall now try to answer some of the questions we posed at the very beginning of this chapter. How are the compounds *raṇa-sattra*, *raṇa-yajña* and *śastra-yajña* to be interpreted? We have two alternatives: a war which *is* a sacrifice, or, a war which is *like* a sacrifice (*raṇa iva yajñaḥ*). We have to decide whether the *karmadhāraya* compound involves a comparison or not, or, in other words, whether to take these expressions in their literal sense, or in a metaphorical sense. It seems to me that the metaphorical interpretation does not hold. For it is not the case that this war bears only some superficial or anecdotal resemblance to a sacrificial performance. On the contrary, if we consider its very essence, function, aims and results, the Mahābhārata war is a full-fledged, albeit peculiar sacrifice, designed to meet and solve the peculiar problems posed by a specific time of crisis.

---

been to produce a disenchantment with the world and that he has intended his primary subject to be liberation (*mokṣa*) from worldly life and the *rasa* of peace." (Transl. by INGALLS et al. 1990:690-691). For the problematic of *śānta-rasa* in the MBh, see TUBB (1991).

Does this mean, then, that in the entire Indian tradition only this war is called a sacrifice? We have seen above that the concept of a war-sacrifice draws its source from some very ancient Indo-European ritual beliefs and customs, so that the concept itself is certainly not an innovation of the Mahābhārata. But, *prima facie*, it seems likely that the Mahābhārata is the only literary work in which this equivalence is worked-out in such a circumstantial and thorough manner. For the sake of comparison, we might here turn to another war which we have ignored so far, namely the war in the Rāmāyaṇa. The Rāmāyaṇa war bears many striking resemblances to that of the Mahābhārata: apart from the fact that it is described in the other great Indian Epic, it also takes place at a time of crisis (though not of end-of-*yuga*), when the *rākṣasas* have acquired supremacy over the world and the world-order is therefore threatened. In the Rāmāyaṇa, we also find an *avatāra* of Viṣṇu, this time Rāma, who incarnates himself to rescue the world by fighting and eliminating the powers of evil. But in spite of these considerable similarities, the Rāmāyaṇa war is only rarely compared to a sacrifice, and the identification is certainly not carried out to such a considerable degree. [77]

What is it, then, that makes this equation necessary in the Mahābhārata, but is lacking in the Rāmāyaṇa? To throw more light on this problem, we might turn to the work of SMITH (1989), especially to Chapter 8: "The Destiny of Vedism". SMITH's argument is that

[77] Concerning the R, BIARDEAU notes that "the idea of the sacrificial war is also quite present though not so well structured as the MBh war." (1997:84, note 13), and "dans l'épopée du *Rāmāyaṇa* [...], comme dans le *Mahābhārata*, on parle du 'sacrifice de la guerre'." (1999:XXXI). She takes up this point again in the notes to the translation (1999:1618-1620), especially underlining the sacrificial symbolism of various fires in the R. She also points out that Rāma arranges his army in the shape of a Garuḍa when he reaches Laṅkā, comparing the Garuḍa shape to the *śyena*-shaped sacrificial altar. Prof. R. Goldman was moreover kind enough to point out to me in a personal communication at least one instance where the comparison between the war and a sacrifice is explicitly made in the R, namely in 6.45.16 (c-d) where the *rākṣasa* general Prahasta vows to sacrifice himself in battle for Rāvaṇa: *tvaṁ paśya māṁ juhūṣantaṁ tvadarthe jīvitaṁ yudhi* / However, the overall evidence concerning a "sacrifice of war" seems much more slender in the R than what we find in the MBh.

"*yajña*, in the history of post-Vedic Indian religions" should be viewed "as a category that acts to provide explanatory power, traditional legitimacy, and canonical authority." (1989:202). Correlatively, therefore, the application of the category of sacrifice in the case of the Mahābhārata war is an explicit reaffirmation of the validity of the ancient Vedic sacrificial world-view. Furthermore, concerning notably the Mahābhārata, SMITH remarks: "Sacrifice, in cases such as these, is called upon to reconcile conflicting Hindu doctrines (*ahiṃsā* and the necessity for kings and warriors to fulfill their duties) through reformulating the new problem as an old answer." (1989:214). But it seems to me that the conflict between the doctrine of *ahiṃsā* and the duties of warriors is too general an explanation to account for the fact that the Mahābhārata war is represented as a sacrifice. For then we might find the same notion in the Rāmāyaṇa, which was composed roughly at the same period. But, as we have seen, the equivalence is only occasionally hinted at in the latter text and is certainly not developed to such a significant extent.

It seems to me that the reason for the war-sacrifice equivalence in the Mahābhārata might be accounted for as follows: the Rāmāyaṇa represents a clear-cut, unambiguous fight between the powers of *dharma* and those of *adharma*: Rāma and his monkey-army are all good, and the *rākṣasa*s, (except Vibhīṣana who conveniently changes camp early on, and survives to take over Rāvaṇa's succession) are all unequivocally bad. Thus our sense of justice is entirely gratified by the issue of the war.[78] This is obviously far from being the case in the Mahābhārata, and this fact has been commented upon far too often for

[78] In the R, things are even carried so far that all the dead monkeys are resurrected after the war by the grace of Indra (6.108). We can contrast this with MBh 10.15: after the war, Aśvatthāman releases his *brahmāstra* into the wombs of the Pāṇḍava-women, thus effectively destroying all future generations of Pāṇḍavas. (Only Parikṣit is saved by Kṛṣṇa's intervention). In the R, the destruction of the good is nullified, whereas in the MBh their destruction is not only allowed to remain, but is even extended with future effect.

us to go into it at length again. Not only are there incarnated gods and *asura*s in either camp, but the war is a morally reprehensible family-feud, in which brothers kill brothers, and *śiṣya*s kill their *guru*s, and nearly everybody is killed in the end, whether 'good' or 'bad'. Therefore we might postulate that the war is represented as a sacrifice in order to legitimatize this very unsatisfactory state of affairs. It is a device used to smooth away these moral dilemmas, which are so numerous in the Mahābhārata. It is not so much violence in general which is reprehensible (killing is after all the *kṣatriya*s' *dharma*), but haphazard, indiscriminate and generalized violence, which uses unstraightforward and morally unjustifiable means to reach its ends. It is in this respect that the war-sacrifice equation is used with its full legitimatizing value: for it is well-known that sacrifice achieves the negation of its own violence.[79]

[79] See ṚV 1.162.21 (addressed to the sacrificial horse):

ná vā́ u etán mriyase ná riṣyasi devā́ṁ íd eṣi pathíbhiḥ sugébhiḥ /

"You do not really die here, nor are you injured. You go to the gods on paths pleasant to go on." (Transl. by BODEWITZ 1999c:24).

And MSmṛ 5.39:

yajñārthaṃ paśavaḥ sṛṣṭāḥ svayam eva svayambhuvā /
yajñasya bhūtyai sarvasya tasmād yajñe vadho 'vadhaḥ //

"The Self-existent one himself created sacrificial animals for sacrifice; sacrifice is for the good of this whole (universe); and therefore killing in a sacrifice is not killing." (Transl. by DONIGER and SMITH 1991).

For the problematic of violence and sacrifice in general, see HOUBEN (1999).

7. Conclusions

Having reached the end of this study, we shall now sum up our most important findings, and especially re-examine some of the common points of all the myths studied separately so far. These points are: the Brahmins' superior status, the parallels between the myths and the central events of the Epics, and the ritual elements of myths. We shall also attempt to draw certain general conclusions as to the persistence of Vedic mythical themes in the Epics. To what extent do the Epics remain faithful to the Vedic representations? In what respects do they innovate? To answer these questions, we shall especially re-evaluate the importance of Vedic gods in the Epics, and the continuation of Vedic mythical thought in the Epics.

The Brahmins' Superior Status

A common theme which keeps on recurring in many of these narratives is the importance and superiority of the Brahmins. More precisely, the predominance of the Brahmins over certain gods on the one hand, and over the *kṣatriya*s on the other hand. (Their predominance over the other *varṇa*s was probably never a matter of dispute). Sometimes, both elements are combined, as in the case of certain gods who have a *kṣatriya*-nature.

This trait is reflected in the following motifs appearing in the epic mythological narratives studied here: in the chapter entitled 'When Agni goes hiding', the Brahmin sage Bhṛgu curses Agni with impunity; Agni does not retaliate, and Brahmā's main concern seems to be to make Bhṛgu's curse come true. The sage Aṅgiras replaces Agni in his functions without the latter's prior knowledge, and Agni is shown to be afraid of the sage's power. In the 'Theft of the Soma', the divine bird Garuḍa is warned not to eat Brahmins, whereas he can eat or kill other people (like the Niṣādas) with impunity; this is also shown by the fact that he asks his father to show him a place where there are no Brahmins to drop the giant branch. Later, Garuḍa pays homage to Indra's *vajra* mainly because the *vajra* is made out of the sage Dadhīca's bones. On the other hand, Garuḍa is shown to be superior to Indra, the *kṣatriya*-god, who is also defeated in the same narrative by the Vālakhilya sages. In 'Indra, the lover of Ahalyā', the sage Gautama curses Indra to lose his testicles, and the god is shown to be absolutely powerless against Gautama. In a closely related narrative, Indra is also severely rebuked by another Brahmin called Vipula when he tries to seduce the wife of Vipula's *guru*. In 'Upamanyu's salvation by the Aśvins', the sage Uttaṅka threatens to curse Kṛṣṇa, who is of course a *kṣatriya*, but also Viṣṇu, the supreme god himself. (But Uttaṅka gives up the idea after seeing Kṛṣṇa's cosmic shape). However, it is in the representation of the Mahābhārata war as a sacrifice that this trait is shown to be exacerbated to the greatest extent. For it appears that the implications of the 'sacrifice of war' are to rid the earth of the supernumerary *kṣatriya*s (which means, in effect, of practically all the *kṣatriya*s of the world). Of course, this attempt is to a certain extent justified by the fact that many Asuras are incarnated as *kṣatriya*s, but this does not seem to explain everything. Comparisons with Janamejaya's *sarpa-sattra* and Parāśara's *rākṣasa-sattra*, as well as with Rāma Jāmadagnya's twenty-one slaughters of all the *kṣatriya*s, tend to show that it is also the *kṣatriya*s in and by themselves who are considered (by the Brahmins) as harmful to the welfare of the world. Thus their population should be limited to a minimum number allowing for the survival and propagation of the group (because the earth has to be governed by a *kṣatriya* king), but not permitting them to become too overbearing and contest the Brahmins' superior power.

The recurring nature of this topic in all the epic versions of the myths studied here (in the MBh as well as in the R) shows that it was one of the fundamental concerns of the epic redactors, who took some pains to make the Brahmins' superiority clear. This trait is indeed all the more striking because the Vedic versions of these same mythical narratives do not seem to contain traces of it.[1] Thus it seems that the redactors of the Epics seized upon these mythological narratives to propagate their message, using the authoritative medium of myth to stress the ideology of *varṇa* hierarchy, and the Brahmins' outstanding position at the top of this hierarchy.[2] We could almost claim that the myths which are mentioned in the ṚV in order to glorify the gods to whom the hymns are addressed, are used in the Epics in order to glorify the Brahmins. This would tend to show (but of course does not prove) that the authors of the Epics were indeed Brahmins, and that at the time when the Epics were composed, the Brahmins, for reasons which I cannot pin-point with any certainty, were specially in need of stressing and justifying their superior position.

Parallels between the myths and the central events of the Epics

We have seen in this work that the mythical tales of the theft of the Soma, Indra's seduction of Ahalyā, and, to a lesser extent, Agni's hiding, can be understood as 'doubles' or 'multiforms' of certain events described in the central epic narratives. Or, to put it differently, the events described in the myths function as 'echoes' of some of the central events of the epic tales. We shall presently summarize these points.

The two clearest cases in this respect are the theft of the *soma* and Indra's seduction of Ahalyā. In the theft of the *soma*, the conflict between the snakes and Garuḍa can be read as a premonition of the

[1] One exception concerns the late Vedic versions of the myth of the *soma*-theft, where the Gāyatrī, which is the Brahmin meter, is the only one who manages to get the *soma*.

[2] This topic is also of paramount importance in an important myth which we have not studied here, namely, the slaying of Vṛtra: in the Epics, Vṛtra is sometimes said to be a Brahmin, and Indra is subsequently overcome by the *brahmahatyā*. In the Ṛgveda on the contrary Vṛtra is the serpent of chaos, and Indra's deed of slaying him is a heroic and cosmogonic act, devoid of all negative implications.

central battle of the MBh, the snakes representing the numerous Kauravas, or the Asuras incarnated as the Kauravas, whereas Garuḍa represents the five Pāṇḍavas, or the gods incarnated as the Pāṇḍavas. Their enmity is thus a variant of the great and eternal battle between gods and demons, or *dharma* and *adharma*, which is one of the most fundamental myths of ancient India. The parallelism is developed with some care: the snakes' mother Kadrū is one-eyed in certain versions of the myth. Likewise Gāndhārī blinds herself. The Kauravas' father is Dhṛtarāṣṭra, which is also the name of a snake-king. Gāndhārī aborts her foetus, a deed which is prefigured in the episode where Vinatā opens Aruṇa's egg before the proper time. In both cases, the abortion is motivated by envy. The Kauravas are exterminated in the 'sacrifice of war', just as the snakes in Janamejaya's *sattra*. This destruction might be motivated by the fact that the Kauravas belong to the lunar dynasty, and the snakes, who cyclically slough their skin, also have affinities with the moon, which decays and grows.

The myth of Indra and Ahalyā functions as a double of one of the most striking events of the R, namely, Rāma's repudiation of Sītā. Just as Gautama condemns, either to invisibility or to exile, his wife Ahalyā,[3] in the same way Rāma repudiates his wife Sītā who is definitely not guilty, but suspected of the same crime as Ahalyā, namely, adultery. This does not mean that Rāma's deed should necessarily be interpreted in a Dumézilian sense as a crime against the third function, reduplicating Indra's sin. In fact, if we look more precisely at the parallelism between the two stories, Rāma's deed of repudiating Sītā is rather a reduplication of Gautama's repudiation of Ahalyā, and Rāvaṇa's deed of abducting Sītā and trying to seduce her would be the reduplication of Indra's seduction of Ahalyā, but with an inversion concerning the respective *varṇa*s of the protagonists.

[3] Ahalyā, unlike Sītā, is guilty in varying degrees: in the second version, she is raped by Indra, but in the first she agrees to sleep with him, even though she has recognized him.

Moreover, Sītā and Ahalyā, as their names show, are so to say 'inverted' figures. Ahalyā, the Brahmin, is 'unploughable', and as such she should not be appropriated by the *kṣatriya*-god Indra. The name Sītā on the other hand means 'furrow': as such, and as a queen, she represents the Earth. In the R, she is said to be the daughter of the goddess Earth. Thus Rāvaṇa's attempt to appropriate her is a variation on the theme of the ever-recurring attempts by the forces of *adharma* to gain supremacy over the earth, which rightfully belongs to the dharmic king, in this particular case, Rāma.

The case of Agni's hiding is a little less straightforward, but is not devoid of echoes in the main events of the MBh: Agni's hiding before resuming his sacrificial duties (sacrificial in various ways) is comparable to the Pāṇḍavas' hiding before the war-sacrifice. In both cases, the residence in a secluded place is comparable to a *dīkṣā* before the sacrifice. On the other hand, Agni's hiding in the waters can also be compared and contrasted with Duryodhana hiding in the Dvaipāyana lake; however, since the lake is masculine, bearing the name of Duryodhana's grandfather, Duryodhana rises out of it to go to his death, whereas Agni rises out the feminine waters to perform his duties successfully.

The case of Upamanyu's salvation by the Aśvins is less clear. I do not think that a direct parallelism can be discerned between this story and the central epic events. However, this tale depicting *śiṣya*s undergoing an initiatory experience, during which they receive the revelation of a new belief or knowledge, and thereby obtain immortality, could be programmatic of the whole MBh, which thereby proclaims that the reward for reciting or listening to the MBh might equally lead to immortality.

In view of the above, and since I believe that the epic redactors rarely, if ever, inserted anything in a haphazard manner, and without keeping in mind the overall significance of the text, I would like to propose that the main function of these Vedic myths on the background of the Epics is that of authority. The Vedic myths represent an authoritative precedent, providing a explanation or a legitimatization of the main epic events, and inscribing them in the line of the ancient tradition.[4]

The ritual elements of myths

On several occasions in the course of this study, we have referred to certain aspects of myth which concern the ritual. We shall presently attempt to summarize these points. Two of the myths studied here (Agni's hiding and the theft of the *soma*) occur in their most complete Ṛgvedic form in *saṃvāda* hymns. These dialogical hymns, at least according to the Indian commentators, do not have a ritual application: this means that they were not recited on the occasion of specific sacrifices. However, both myths have a connection with sacrifice: Agni's disappearance jeopardizes the performance of sacrifices, and the theft of the *soma* allows Manu or mankind to offer the *soma* as a sacrificial oblation. At the time of the later Veda, both myths were used in order to explain certain aspects of the ritual: the myth of Agni's hiding was used by these texts either to explain during what season the *punarādheya* (reinstatement of the fire) had to take place, or to explain why certain types of wood (notably the *aśvattha*) can be used as *saṃbhāra*, or to explain the origin of the *paridhi*s, the three sticks which surround the sacrificial fire, which were previously Agni's elder brothers. The myth of the theft of the *soma* is used in the later Vedic

[4] We may here draw a parallel with a later text, the Kathāsaritsāgara, which in turn frequently refers to epic tales, sometimes precisely to quote a precedent. This happens for instance in 4.21: here Nārada appears to the king Udayana (who is moreover a descendent of Janamejaya: this is one more way of emphasizing the Kathāsaritsāgara's affiliation with the Epic) to warn him against the evil consequences of hunting. As an illustration of his words, he tells him the story of his ancestor Pāṇḍu who was likewise addicted to hunting, and who finally met his doom due to the curse he got by killing an ascetic who had taken on the form of a deer (cf. MBh 1.109). It would be interesting to study more precisely the manner in which textual affiliations function, and how certain bodies of texts invoke some others as authoritative.

texts as a means of explaining the power of speech, especially the *mantra*s uttered during sacrifices, since it is by means of the Gāyatrī meter that the *soma* is won. The myth is also used to legitimize the use of certain *soma*-surrogates. Various plants are shown to be valid substitutes for the *soma*, since they originated either from the fallen *soma*-leaf itself, or from the fallen feather or claw of the *soma*-bringing Gāyatrī.

Are any of these late Vedic ritualistic explanations or interpretations of the myths kept alive in the Epics? In the MBh, the myth of Agni's hiding is not in any way connected with the *punarādheya* ceremony. Neither do we find in the MBh any mention of Agni's three elder brothers, nor *a fortiori* any mention of the three sticks kept around the sacrificial fire which represent them. We still find in the MBh the motif of Agni hiding in the *aśvattha*-tree, but as a means to explain why the wood of this tree can be used to light the fire (although even this can only be inferred rather indirectly), and not to explain why it can be used as a *saṃbhāra* for the sacrifice. On the other hand, the MBh partly preserves the motif that Agni goes hiding because he is afraid to perform his sacrificial duties. This motif was already present in the Ṛgvedic narration, and subsequently in the late Vedic texts. In the MBh it is only preserved explicitly in one version of the myth, whereas in the other versions the reason for his disappearance (when it is mentioned at all) is attributed to Bhṛgu's curse. What is however clearly preserved in the MBh is the distress that Agni's disappearance provokes, and this distress is most importantly caused by the fact that the performance of sacrifices is jeopardized. Besides, many actions for which Agni is retrieved, such as procreation and eating, are interpreted as sacrificial deeds in this text. This shows that, although the epic versions of this myth no longer preserve the purely ritualistic elements of the later Veda, they are nevertheless still principally concerned with the sacrifice.

As far as the myth of the *soma*-theft is concerned, we can note that neither the MBh nor the R preserve the idea that Garuḍa is the Gāyatrī in eagle-shape. Some motifs concerning the ritual still occur in the epic accounts, but their ritual relevance seems to be lost. Thus in the MBh and R, Garuḍa carries the broken branch in his beak and the elephant and tortoise in his claws: this might correspond to the Gāyatrī carrying three *soma*-pressings in some versions of the later Veda. However, in the Epics this connection is no longer explicitly made: indeed, before stealing the 'real' *soma*, Garuḍa himself eats the tortoise and elephant (and the branch is unceremoniously discarded), whereas neither in the ṚV, nor in the later Veda, nor in the Epics does the eagle / Gāyatrī / Garuḍa ever partake of the *soma*. Thus in the Epics this might be a motif carried over from the later Vedic versions, but in effect, the elephant, the tortoise and the branch no longer correspond to *soma*-pressings. In the MBh, the etiologic motif relating to the transformations of the fallen *soma*-leaf is represented by the fact that the *darbha*-grass on which the *amṛta* is kept becomes pure. But the text does not conclude that the *darbha*-grass can therefore be used as a *soma*-substitute. Indeed, a striking characteristic of the epic narrations of the *soma*-theft is the absolute lack of ritual relevance of the *amṛta*, unlike the Vedic *soma* which is obviously of paramount importance for the sacrifice. On the other hand, the story of the *soma*-theft is told at a sacrifice (Śaunaka's twelve-year *sattra*), its frame story is the description of Janamejaya's snake-sacrifice, and it results in the *sarpa-sattra*, which shows that its sacrificial relevance is not entirely lost.

The case of the myth of Indra and Ahalyā is somewhat special, for unlike the other myths studied here, it is not found in the ṚV (except a few motifs which go into the making of this myth, such as Indra as a ram, and the importance of Indra's testicles). The first allusions are found in the later Veda, in the context of the Subrahmaṇyā formula, and it is probably from the conglomeration of the different motifs found in this formula that the more complete tale, such as it is found from the R onwards, was formed. Given such a sacrificial origin, it is not surprising to see that at least in the first version of the myth, the R preserves to a certain extent its ritual relevance. This narrative can be read as an etiologic myth explaining why the *pitṛdeva*s, the gods who bring the sacrifice to the Manes, receive the offerings of gelded rams: the rams are castrated because their testicles were given to Indra, and they are offered to the *pitṛdeva*s as substitutes for Indra, who, had he remained castrated, would himself have fallen into the realm of the *pitṛ*s.

The myth of Upamanyu's salvation by the Aśvins does not seem to have any ritual or sacrificial relevance in any of its versions. In the ṚV, allusions to the saving acts of the Aśvins appear in hymns addressed to the Aśvins, which may or may not have been recited at sacrifices.[5] In any case, the model for these mythical representations was not the ritual or sacrifice, but initiation-ceremonies, a theme which is continued in the Epic. However, what is common to initiation ceremonies and certain types of sacrifices (especially *soma*-sacrifices) is the notion of *dīkṣā*. Constituent elements of the *dīkṣā*, such as seclusion, return to an embryonic stage, etc., are found not only in the myth of Upamanyu's salvation by the Aśvins, where they play a prominent role, but also in the myth of Agni's hiding. The embryonic symbolism of Agni who hides in the waters is especially prominent in the ṚV, but even in the MBh, his hiding preserves the characteristics of an isolation, even a dissolution, similar to a death before his rebirth in the (various) sacrificial deeds he subsequently performs.[6]

On the whole, in the MBh, the sacrificial motifs are most forcefully revealed in the representation of the war as a sacrifice. In the course of

---

[5] The only mention of sacrifice in the Ṛgvedic accounts is that the sage Ṛjrāśva was blinded because he had offered a hundred sheep in sacrifice to a she-wolf.

[6] Even in the theft of the *soma*, some of the deeds Garuḍa performs before flying up to heaven to steal the *soma* (catching and eating the elephant and tortoise, killing the Niṣādas) might have a certain initiatory value. But these are not comparable to a *dīkṣā*: they are rather heroic initiations.

this study, I have said that the chapter entitled '*Raṇa-yajña*' deals with the way in which the sacrifice is 'mythified'. For indeed, it shows how the level of ritual is transferred to the level of myth. We could also say that the sacrificial ritual is 'actualized' or concretely 'worked out' in the representation of the war as a sacrifice.[7] Thus in sacrifices, the ideal victim should be the sacrificer (*yajamāna*) himself: in the MBh war, the *yajamāna* is Duryodhana, who indeed becomes one of the *paśu*s. In sacrifices, the ritual implements are called 'weapons': in the MBh war, they are the real weapons of the war. In sacrifices, certain impure parts of the victim are offered aside to *rākṣasa*s and *piśāca*s, who partake of them as the representatives of the Earth: in the war, these types of demons appear in person to eat the sacrificial offerings, namely, the bodies of the dead, and the Earth herself is also depicted as enjoying these offerings. In sacrifices, the gods Viṣṇu and Śiva have the respective functions of safekeeping the sacrifice, and consuming the left-overs of the sacrificial offerings: in the MBh, Viṣṇu incarnates himself as Kṛṣṇa to prepare and supervise the performance of the war-sacrifice, whereas at the end of the war Śiva 'possesses' Aśvatthāman who kills the warriors who are 'left-over' from the battle. And so on and so forth. Thus is would appear that what is only shown allusively or symbolically in 'real' sacrifices is fully worked out and made explicit on the level of myth.[8] This fact is astonishing, because, *prima facie*, it would seem that sacrifices are 'concrete' and myths are 'symbolic'. But on the contrary, we see that myth sometimes expresses straightforwardly what is only alluded to in the ritual: for it is only on the level of mythical expression that certain deeds can be enacted.

---

[7] Similarly, GEHRTS (1975) shows how the *rājasūya* ritual provides the structure of the Sabhāparvan, and indeed how the action which takes place in this *parvan* is the concrete 'enactment' of this ritual.

[8] In the case of Janamejaya's *sarpa-sattra*, we have seen that it also consists of real snakes poured into the fire, not just, as in the attested ritual, of *soma*-offerings which are in many ways comparable to snakes.

One more token of the importance of sacrifice in the MBh is the fact that Kṛṣṇa, as Viṣṇu's *avatāra*, saves the earth by performing the 'sacrifice of war'. The problematic of *avatāras*, especially the early history of this concept, is somewhat complicated.[9] However, it seems that the oldest attested *avatāra* of Viṣṇu is precisely his *avatāra* as Kṛṣṇa in the MBh. Bhagavadgītā 4.7-8 contains the earliest references to the concept of *avatāra*.[10] Here Kṛṣṇa declares that he "creates himself" *ātmānaṃ sṛjāmi*, which makes his descent on earth different from a mere (involuntary) human incarnation. (See HACKER 1960:48).[11] Now, if we consider all the *avatāras* of Viṣṇu (at least the classical list of ten *avatāras*), it seems that it is only when Viṣṇu 'creates himself' as Kṛṣṇa that he saves the earth by performing a sacrifice: the *raṇa-yajña*.[12] Thus (and I formulate this as a hypothesis, for the topic would deserve further investigation in another paper), the MBh might present an intermediary stage, showing a transition between the view that the sacrifice maintains the world, and the view that the earth is regularly saved from perdition by the grace of the supreme god who incarnates himself to rescue her. Here Viṣṇu

---

[9] Thus is seems that the oldest accounts of the *avatāras* of boar, etc. as they appear in certain Purāṇas were first *avatāras* of Brahmā and not Viṣṇu. For the name Nārāyaṇa was first an appellation of Brahmā which was subsequently transferred to Viṣṇu. In the MBh, Viṣṇu's *avatāra* as a boar is told in a passage inserted by some manuscripts after 3.142, kept in Appendix I.16 of the Crit. Ed.; it is alluded to in the context of the description of the ocean in 1.19.11; Viṣṇu's *avatāras* as boar, man-lion and Vāmana are also related in a passage inserted by certain manuscripts after 3.256.28, kept in Appendix I.27 of the Crit Ed. Thus these accounts are not present in the majority of the manuscripts, and are probably 'later' than the body of the text which represents only Kṛṣṇa as Viṣṇu's *avatāra*. Moreover, in the MBh there are conflicting representations of Kṛṣṇa either as a partial incarnation (*aṃśāvataraṇa*) of Viṣṇu, or as simply identified with Viṣṇu (this representation, according to HACKER (1960:55) being older). Kṛṣṇa is not the only god who is an *aṃśāvataraṇa*. MBh 1.64.ff. narrates how all the gods came down onto the earth as partial incarnations, in order to save the earth.

[10] But as SULLIVAN (1990:69) remarks: "The work *avatāra* seems not to occur in the MBh at all, though many closely related forms [such as *avataraṇa*, *avatartum*, etc.] are used to convey the idea."

[11] The concept of reincarnation does exist in the BhG, see for instance 4.9 and 8.15-16.

[12] Rāma Jāmadagnya might be the only other instance. See chapter 6, note 66.

incarnates himself, but the means he uses to save the earth is still a sacrifice.

What can we conclude from these observations? Scholars generally contend that the Epics refer to sacrificial performances only vaguely, without describing the ritual acts in detail, and often with the implication that these were perhaps no longer actually known or performed. (See RENOU (1960:14) quoted in the Introduction; HOUBEN (2000:529, note 143)).[13] And indeed, we have seen that the Epics do not further deal with some purely ritualistic details which appear in the late Vedic versions of certain myths. However, the Epics are not texts like the Yajur Veda, the Brāhmaṇas, or the Kalpasūtras, whose aim is to explain and describe the sacrificial ritual exhaustively: we cannot therefore conclude that the details and significance of certain rituals were no longer known or understood. Besides, the sacrificial symbolism of the war is elaborated in some detail, which tends to show that the ritual minutiae of sacrifices were not quite unknown to the author(s) of the Epic. And over and above the ritual details, it is indisputable that at least the MBh remains firmly anchored in a sacrificial world-view.

The importance of Vedic gods in the Epics

What importance and significance do the Vedic gods retain in the Epics? Since we have in each case chosen to deal with myths whose protagonists are some of the major Vedic gods, and since in the Epics the same myths obviously deal with the same gods, it would be easy to conclude that these gods maintain their importance in the Epics. But another perhaps surer way to gauge their continued importance is to see which ones of these gods also appear in myths where they do not play

[13] Thus HOUBEN: "While the great epics *Mahābhārata* and *Rāmāyaṇa* discuss some of the ritual aspects of the Aśvamedha in detail, references to the Pravargya are very shallow; [...] Had the Pravargya already become a hollow construct when these epics were composed?".

the main role, and also to examine to what extent the supreme gods in epic times, namely Viṣṇu, Śiva and to a lesser extent Brahmā, interfere in mythical tales in whose Vedic versions they did not play any role.[14]

Agni does not only figure pre-eminently in the myth describing how he hides. He also appears in the story of Indra and Ahalyā, where he intercedes on Indra's behalf with the *pitṛdeva*s, and to a certain extent saves the situation, by seeing to it that Indra will get the substitute testicles of a ram. In the story of the *soma*-theft, not only does Garuḍa exhibit a fire-like nature, Agni is also the only one who knows who is Garuḍa and who tranquillizes the other gods who are unsettled by his threatening appearance. In these two cases, Agni has the role of interceding between certain people and the gods as an undifferentiated group, a role which he probably inherited from his functions as *havyavāhana* or carrier of the sacrificial oblations, which pre-eminently require him to act as a go-between. In both versions of the story of Uttaṅka, Agni helps Uttaṅka to get back his earrings from Takṣaka in the *nāga-loka*, and in a way functions as a teacher and a guide in Uttaṅka's initiatory experience.

Indra plays of course the main role in the story of his seduction of Ahalyā. He plays a very minor role in one version of the story of Agni's hiding (in the Śalyaparvan, the episode of the Agni-*tīrtha)*, where, along with some other gods, he finds the hidden Agni. In the story of the *soma*-theft, he appears as the legitimate possessor of the *soma*, and as such he tries to prevent Garuḍa from stealing the divine drink. He is also the one who gives Garuḍa the boon to have the snakes for his food. In both versions of the story of Uttaṅka, he offers the disguised *amṛta* to Uttaṅka. Thus Indra, except in the story of his adventure with Ahalyā, deserves his continued importance in the myths as the guardian and possessor of the *soma-amṛta*, a role he already has

[14] Viṣṇu and Rudra-Śiva are of course also Ṛgvedic gods. But in Vedic times, they were not yet the supreme gods, unlike in the Epics.

in the Veda (although the Ṛgvedic passages describing the *soma*-theft also show how Indra himself came into the possession of the *soma*). In all the above-cited instances, Indra's most prominent role is either to withhold the *soma*, or else to give it, but often grudgingly and necessarily in a disguised form: Garuḍa gets snakes (which, as we have shown, are equivalent with *soma*), and Uttaṅka gets cow-dung and urine, respectively urine only, which are in each case disguised *amṛta*.

The case of the Soma is somewhat special. In Ṛgvedic times, Soma was considered to be a god. Along with Agni, he is the only 'visible' god, who is present as the *soma*-plant or juice on the sacrificial grounds. This god-like nature of the *soma* is completely lost in epic times. Apart from the myth of the *soma*-theft, the *soma* (or *amṛta*) also appears in the stories of Upamanyu and Uttaṅka. Yet in all these cases, the *soma-amṛta* is represented as a comestible substance, a thing, never as a person. In this, the case of the *soma* is obviously diametrically opposed to that of Agni, who necessarily appears as a god and a person in the Epics, where his personified representation mostly overrides his purely elemental manifestation. In this respect, the representations of Soma and Agni in the Ṛgvedic myths of the *soma*-theft and Agni's hiding respectively may have played a prominent role: for already in the Ṛgvedic narrations of these myths, Agni appears as a person, and *soma* as an object.

Finally, concerning the Aśvins, we can only note that except in the tale of Upamanyu's salvation, they are not even as much as mentioned in the other mythical tales. And in the second narration of Upamanyu's story, their role is even completely dropped. Thus, among the Vedic gods taken in consideration here, the Aśvins are certainly those who have preserved the least importance in the Epics.

We shall now turn to the second question asked above, namely, to what extent do the gods Brahmā, Viṣṇu and Śiva play a role in the epic tales? Brahmā appears in the first version of the myth of Agni's hiding (Bhṛgu's curse): when the gods complain that Agni has disappeared,

Brahmā recalls him by a mere wish, and persuades him to resume his sacrificial duties. In this respect, it seems that Brahmā takes over Varuṇa's role, who also speaks to Agni on behalf of all the gods in ṚV 10.51. In the fifth version (Pārvatī's curse), Brahmā also acts as a mediator: he knows that Agni is the only god who was not affected by Pārvatī's curse and who will therefore be able to generate a son capable of killing the Asura Tāraka, and therefore advises the gods to find him. In these two occurrences of the myth, Brahmā plays a role which is typical for him in epico-purāṇic literature. He is the benevolent creator god, the 'grandfather' to whom the gods and *ṛṣi*s typically turn in situations of distress, and who usually provides a solution to their problems.[15] (See SULLIVAN 1990:82). In the frame story of the second R version of Indra's seduction of Ahalyā,[16] Brahmā reminds Indra how, in ancient times, he had created the living beings, and especially Ahalyā whom he endowed with beauty, and explains to him that his captivity at the hands of the *rākṣasa*s is his just punishment for raping Ahalyā. Here Brahmā functions as the living memory of the world: since he himself created it, he knows events pertaining to the remotest past, and he sees the laws of cause and effect governing the lives of gods as well as men.

Viṣṇu plays a role in the theft of the *soma* (in whose Vedic versions he does not appear), and in the second version of the story of Uttaṅka. The representations of Viṣṇu are quite contradictory in these two stories. In the *soma*-theft, he chooses Garuḍa as his vehicle and gives him the boon of immortality. Viṣṇu in this passage undoubtedly appears as the supreme god: he has the status of a spectator of the troubled, conflict-ridden and on the whole rather violent goings-on, and his position is somewhat detached: unlike Indra, he does not in the

[15] Those problems, however, are often provoked by Brahmā himself, usually because he dispenses boons to people who make a bad use of them (as in the case of Tāraka).

[16] However, none of these three gods plays any role in the story itself.

least worry about the fate of the stolen *amṛta*, and never questions Garuḍa's intentions concerning the divine drink. For indeed, at least in this narrative, Viṣṇu has no use for the *amṛta*: his own immortality, as well as that which he can give to his *bhakta*s, does not depend on it. On the other hand, in the second version of Uttaṅka's adventures, Viṣṇu, attempts to mediate between Uttaṅka and Indra, and to convince Indra to give *amṛta* to Uttaṅka. However, unlike in the *soma*-theft, Viṣṇu does not succeed in his design, and Indra, who sees to it that Uttaṅka does not drink the *amṛta*, wins the day. This is, to my knowledge, one of the rare instances in the Epics where Indra outwits Viṣṇu himself.

In the fifth version of Agni's hiding (Pārvatī's curse), both Śiva and his consort Pārvatī play a role: Pārvatī (unwittingly) makes Agni's reappearance urgent, because, since she cursed the other gods, Agni is the only one who will be able to generate Skanda. Śiva also plays a minor role in this story, because his sperm falls into Agni. However, the presence of Śiva and Pārvatī here is motivated by the fact that Agni's hiding is connected with the story of Skanda's birth. The story of Upamanyu's salvation by the Aśvins is particularly interesting as far as Śiva's role is concerned: the first version, which closely follows Ṛgvedic models, represents the Aśvins as saviours. The second version, which is quite different from the first, and only preserves certain basic motifs, has no mention of the Aśvins: there, instead of praising the Aśvins in *ṛc*es, Upamanyu praises Śiva in *śloka*s.

The continuation of Vedic mythical thought in the Epics

Concerning this topic, we can make the following observations about all the myths we have studied here. Perhaps not surprisingly (for it may well be that this is what all myths are about), we find the topics of death, rebirth and immortality in all of them. In all these cases, immortality is finally dependent on a certain type of food, and the ambivalence of food is a topic which recurs throughout: in the ṚV,

Agni the sacrificial fire vanishes because he is afraid of death, and he agrees to return and act as the *hotṛ* only when he receives the assurance that he will get his share of *soma*, which will make him immortal. In the MBh, Agni hides due to the curse of becoming omnivorous, a fate which he tries to avoid. In turn, he curses others to be eaten or not to eat (i.e., to die), after being retrieved and reinstated in his functions. In the myth of the *soma*-theft, which deals pre-eminently with obtaining immortality, Indra in the ṚV obtains a position of supremacy among the gods because he is able to get the *soma*. In the MBh, Garuḍa is generally described as a voracious eater, but he obtains immortality specifically because he does not partake of the *amṛta*; on the other hand, his arch-enemies, the *nāga*s, are not particularly voracious, but they make the mistake of trying to eat the *amṛta*, which leads to their down-fall: instead of eating the *amṛta* and becoming immortal, they become the ones who are eaten (by Garuḍa). In the stories of Upamanyu and Uttaṅka, the overall pattern is that of an initiation ceremony, thus pre-eminently involving the topics of death, rebirth and immortality. And Upamanyu and Uttaṅka too obtain immortality either because they refuse to eat the false *amṛta*, or on the contrary because they accept to eat the disguised *amṛta*. The connection with food is perhaps less obvious in the myth of Indra and Ahalyā, but it can be discerned in a veiled form even there: Indra, because he seduces (which in mythical language is often equivalent to 'eating') the Brahmin Ahalyā, narrowly escapes in turn becoming 'food' – that is, an offering – to the Manes; at least this is what the fact that he has to be bought off from the *pitṛdeva*s, the gods who bring the oblations to the Manes, suggests.

Thus these mythical narratives in the Epics depict a harsh world of 'eater' and 'eaten', which is strikingly appropriate, especially on the background of the MBh war, where everyone kills or is killed (and mostly both in turn), and which is indeed in direct continuation of the Vedic world-view. As DONIGER and SMITH (1991:XXVII) remark: "The Veda depicts a life where I gain only at your loss, my prosperity entails your ruin, my continued existence depends on your death, my eating requires that you become food." But at the same time these narratives make it clear that one should select one's food with care, and that survival – if not immortality – or death, often depend on one's 'right choice' in nutritional matters.

More than that, many of the underlying meanings of the myths remain the same in the Ṛgveda and in the Epics, even if some of the differences are due to the changed social and religious conditions. Thus the central symbolism of the myth of Agni's hiding is that of the fire as the 'germ of life'. Even though Agni in the Epic has 'grown up' and is no longer represented as a foetus hiding in the waters, his mothers, nevertheless the foetal symbolism is transferred to other typically epic gods, like Skanda, whom Agni engenders in turn. The myth of the theft of the *soma*, in the ṚV as well as in the MBh, mainly illustrates the theme of power relations, and the struggle for the appropriation of power. The Epic, adjusting itself to the changes in mythical history and time, represents Indra as the possessor of the *soma*, from whom the divine drink is in turn stolen by some upstarts, the snakes. In both texts, immortality is considered as the supreme form of power, but in the MBh the ideal of *bhakti* intervenes, and makes the immortality given by the supreme god superior to that obtained by means of the *amṛta*. The myth of Upamanyu's salvation by the Aśvins has strong initiatory undercurrents, both in the ṚV and in the MBh. The resemblances in this case are so striking, with the common themes of blindness, burial, salvation by means of praising with *ṛc*es, and immortality bestowed in the form of gold, that we have to suppose that the author of the epic piece knew very well the Ṛgvedic passages, and more than that, understood their meaning very accurately. This supposition is strengthened by the fact that there are practically no intermediary texts which preserve this mythical motif,[17] and we can therefore reasonably question (unlike for some other myths treated here) whether it was kept alive in the popular tradition during the long lapse of time between the Ṛgveda and the Epic. In fact, concerning these three myths – Agni's hiding, the theft of the Soma and Upamanyu's salvation by the Aśvins – we can observe that their epic representations, and the basic concerns they exemplify, are in general much closer to Ṛgvedic models than to late Vedic ones. Certain motifs which appear in the later Veda do reappear in the Epics, but the late Vedic texts[18] mainly quote myths to explain ritual procedures, an element which the Epics, as we have seen, hardly take into account. In fact, the only myth in which we can really see a fundamental shift of perspective between Vedic and epic times is that of Indra and Ahalyā, and the representation of the god Indra seems to have undergone radical changes between both times: Indra's heroic virility and his magic power

[17] The only late Vedic text in which the story occurs is the Jaiminiyabrāhmaṇa. DONIGER O'FLAHERTY (1985a:117) claims that the JB is a favourite 'stepping-stone' between the ṚV and the MBh, for many myths which occur in these two texts are found 'in between' only in the JB. Can something similar be verified concerning the myths studied here, which are obviously not chosen from the point of view of the JB? Three of our myths occur in the JB (concerning Agni, Indra and the Aśvins), but it is only in the case of the myth representing the Aśvins as saviours that the JB indeed occupies a unique place among all late Vedic texts in mentioning the story: otherwise, there is a gulf between the ṚV and the MBh. However, the JB was probably not the direct model for the epic representation: in the JB the sage Kaṇva is not really blinded, but his eyes are smeared over with a salve by the Asuras, his situation is in no way as desperate and close to death as that of some Ṛgvedic sages, or indeed Upamanyu, who are saved by the Aśvins, and neither does the theme of gold representing immortality appear in the JB. Thus Upamanyu's story is much closer to the Ṛgvedic accounts than to the JB's account of the myth.

[18] The following late Vedic texts contain the greatest amount of material concerning the myths studied here: the Saṃhitās of the Black Yajur Veda contain many references to the myths of Agni's hiding, Indra and Ahalyā, and the theft of the *soma*. On the other hand, the Vājasaneyi Saṃhitā of the White Yajur Veda is conspicuous for its absence. However, one of the texts which contains perhaps the greatest amount of material is the ŚB, which is a precisely a Brāhmaṇa of the White Yajur Veda. Other Brāhmaṇas (KauṣB, TB, ṢaḍvB, AB, TMB) and one Āraṇyaka (the Taittirīya) contain occasional references to one or two of the myths studied here, but their material is not as overwhelming as that of the ŚB.

of metamorphosis have been reinterpreted as despicable lechery in the Epics.

These are the main conclusions and generalizations which can be established on the basis of this study, in which I have attempted to show the continuities and the changes in mythical representations between Vedic and epic times. It should prove very interesting to study along similar lines the other mythical narratives which appear both in the Vedas and in the Epics, and which have not been examined here. This would allow us to verify the above statements on a broader basis, and draw more generally valid conclusions as to the function of Vedic narratives on the background of the Epics, and the continued survival of Vedic (especially Ṛgvedic) thought in the Epics.

The main question which arises is this connection is of course "why?". Why did the composer(s) of the Epics (especially of the MBh) consider it as worthwhile to pursue to such an extent the representation of Vedic myth and ritual in a changing world, where the ritual, the myths and the religion were no longer quite the same as in Vedic times. This is obviously a difficult question, the more so because the historical time of composition of these texts is far from certain. Here BIARDEAU (1999:XXIV-XXXII) and (2002:136-161 & Conclusion) offers one possible answer, namely that the Epics were primarily composed as a reaction to the threat of Buddhism, especially after the conversion of emperor Aśoka, in order to reassert orthodox Brahmanical values. She admits herself that this is not explicitly stated by the Epics themselves, which never even mention the Buddha. However, she explains this coded and veiled mode of expression as being in direct continuation of the Vedic 'esoteric' language. Biardeau's theory certainly has the advantage of explaining why the Epics, especially the MBh, would want to reassert so emphatically the validity of Vedic myths and sacrifice at a time when their importance was undoubtedly waning. As she says: "[La] riposte [de la société brahmanique]... a consisté à mettre en place une "vision" glorieuse, non pas du futur, mais du passé..." (2002:139).

This solution is tempting, though less than fully convincing, mainly because of the very allusiveness of the whole procedure. However, it may well be that the epic composer(s) were indeed reacting to change, and that the very shiftiness and uncertainty of the social and religious conditions around them prompted them to reassert the old Vedic values all the more vigorously.

Bibliography

Secondary Literature, Texts and Translations

BY ALPHABETICAL ORDER OF THE NAMES OF THE AUTHORS / EDITORS

APTE, Vinayak Ganesh. Ed. *Niruktam.* 2 vols. Poona: Ānandāśrama Sanskrit Series, 1921.

BACHELARD, Gaston. *La psychanalyse du feu.* Paris: Gallimard, 1949.

BANDHU, Vishva. Ed. *Atharvaveda with the Pada-pāṭha and Sāyaṇācārya's Commentary.* 4 vols. Hoshiarpur: Vishveshvaranand Vedic Research Institute, 1960.

BASHAM, A.L. *The Wonder that was India.* New York: Evergreen, 1959. First Ed. New York: Grove Press, 1954.

BASU, B.D. (Major) Ed. *Garuḍa Purāṇa (Sāroddhāra).* Transl. into English by Ernest Wood and S.V. Subrahmanyam. The Sacred Books of the Hindus, vol. IX. Allahabad: Pāṇini Office, 1911.

BAWA, Ranbir Singh. Ed. *The Āśvalāyana Śrauta Sūtra with the Commentary of Devatrāta.* 2 vols. Hoshiarpur: Vishveshvaranand Vishva Bandhu Institute of Sanskrit and Indological Studies, 1986.

BEDEKAR, V.M. "Kārttikeya (Skanda) in Sanskrit Literature, with Special Reference to the Mahābhārata: From a Folk spirit to the Chief War-God", in *Annals of the Bhandarkar Oriental Institute* LVI (1975): 141-177.

BENVENISTE, Emile & RENOU, Louis. *Vṛtra et Vṛθragna: Etudes de mythologie Indo-Aryenne.* Paris: Cahiers de la Société Asiatique, 1934.

BHATT, Govindlal Hargovind, et al. Ed. *The Vālmīki-Rāmāyaṇa.* 7 vols. Baroda: Oriental Institute, 1960-1975.

BHATTACHARJI, Sukumari. *The Indian Theogony. A Comparative Study of Indian Mythology from the* Vedas *to the* Purāṇas. Cambridge: Cambridge University Press, 1970.

BHATTACHARYA, Chintamani. Ed. *Gobhilagṛhyasūtram. With Bhaṭṭanārāyaṇa's Commentary.* The Calcutta Sanskrit Series XVII. Calcutta: Metropolitan Printing and Publishing House Ltd, 1936.

BIARDEAU, Madeleine. "Le Sacrifice dans l'Hindouisme", in *Le sacrifice dans l'Inde ancienne* (M. Biardeau and C. Malamoud): 7-154. Paris: Presses Universitaires de France, 1976a.

— "Etudes de Mythologie Hindoue, IV", in *Bulletin de l'Ecole Française d'Extrême-Orient* 63 (1976b): 112-263.

— "Etudes de mythologie hindoue, V", in *Bulletin de l'Ecole Française d'Extrême-Orient* 65 (1978): 87-238.

— *Etudes de Mythologie Hindoue. Tome 1. Cosmogonies Purāṇiques*. Paris: Ecole Française d'Extrême Orient, 1981. 1st ed. in *Bulletin de l'Ecole Française d'Extrême Orient* LIV (1968): 19-54; LV (1969): 59-105; and LVIII (1971):17-89.

— *Hinduism: The Anthropology of a Civilisation*. Delhi: Oxford University Press, 1989. (Transl. of *L'hindouisme: Anthropologie d'une civilisation*. Paris, 1981).

— "Some Remarks on the Links between the Epics, the Purāṇas and their Vedic Sources", in *Studies in Hinduism. Vedism and*

Hinduism. Ed. Gerhard Oberhammer. Wien: Verlag der Oesterreichischen Akademie der Wissenschaften, 1997.

—— et al. *Le Rāmāyaṇa*. (Transl.) Paris: Gallimard (Bibliothèque de la Pléiade), 1999.

—— *Le Mahābhārata. Un récit fondateur du brahmanisme et son interprétation*. 2 vols. Paris: Editions du Seuil, 2002.

BIGGER, Andreas. "Wege und Umwege zum Himmel". Die Pilgerfahrten im Mahābhārata. *Journal Asiatique* 289.1 (2001): 147-166.

BLOOMFIELD, Maurice. "Contributions to the Interpretation of the Veda" (I. The legend of Soma and the Eagle.), in *Journal of the American Oriental Society* 16 (1894-96): 1-24.

—— *Hymns of the Atharva-Veda*. Transl. Sacred Books of the East. Ed. by F. Max Müller. Oxford: Oxford University Press, 1897. Repr. Delhi: Motilal Banarsidass, 1992.

—— *A Vedic Concordance*. Cambridge, Mass.: Harvard Oriental Series 10, 1906. Repr. Delhi: Motilal Banarsidass, 1964.

BODEWITZ, Henk W. "Yonder World in the Atharvaveda", in *Indo-Iranian Journal* 42 (1999a): 107-120.

—— "Pits, Pitfalls and the Underworld in the Veda", in *Indo-Iranian Journal* 42 (1999b): 211-226.

—— "Hindu *ahiṃsā* and its roots", in *Violence Denied. Violence, Non-Violence and the Rationalization of Violence in South Asian Cultural History*. (17-44). Ed. Jan E.M Houben and Karel R. van Kooij. Leiden: Brill, 1999c.

—— "Distance and Death in the Veda", in *Asiatische Studien / Etudes Asiatiques* LIV. 1 (2000): 103-117.

BOLLEE, W.B. *Ṣaḍviṃśa-Brāhmaṇa*. (Transl.) Utrecht: Storm, 1956.

BOSCH, F.D.K. *The Golden Germ. An Introduction to Indian Symbolism*. Delhi: Munshiram Manoharlal, 1994. 1st ed. 's-Gravenhage: Mouton & Co., 1960.

BRANDON, S.G.F. "The Significance of Time in Some Ancient Initiatory Rituals", in *Initiation*. (40-48). Ed. C.J. Bleeker. Leiden: Brill, 1965.

BROCKHAUS, Hermann. Ed. *Katha Sarit Sagara. Die Mährchensammlung des Sri Somadeva Bhatta aus Kaschmir*. 2 vols. Sanskrit and German. Leipzig & Paris: Brockhaus, 1839.

BROCKINGTON, John L. *The Sacred Thread: Hinduism in its Continuity and Diversity*. Edinburgh: Edinburgh University Press, 1981.

—— *The Sanskrit Epics*. Leiden: Brill, 1998.

—— "Indra in the Epics", in *Vidyārṇavavandanam. Essays in Honour of Asko Parpola*. (67-82). Ed. Klaus Karttunen and Petteri Koskikallio. Helsinki: Studia Orientalia, 2001.

BRONKHORST, Johannes. "Veda", in *Annals of the Bhandarkar Oriental Research Institute* 70 (1989[1990]): 125-135.

—— *The Two Sources of Indian Asceticism*. Bern: Peter Lang, 1993.

—— "The origin of Mīmāṃsā as a school of thought: a hypothesis", in *Vidyārṇavavandanam. Essays in Honour of Asko Parpola*. (83-103). Ed. Klaus Karttunen and Petteri Koskikallio. Helsinki: Studia Orientalia, 2001.

CALAND, Willem. Ed. *The Baudhāyana Śrauta Sūtra*. 3 vols. Delhi: Munshiram Manoharlal, 1982. 1st ed. Calcutta: Asiatic Society, 1904-1913.

— *Das Jaiminīya-Brāhmaṇa in Auswahl*. (Transl.) Wiesbaden: Sändig, 1970. 1st ed. Amsterdam, 1919.

— *Pañcaviṃśa-Brāhmaṇa*. Calcutta: Asiatic Society of Bengal, 1931.

CARNOY, A. "Les mythes indiens de Mātariśvan-Agni et ceux d'Ulysse en Grèce", in *Le Muséon* 44 (1931): 319-334.

CHARPENTIER Jarl. *Die Suparṇasage*. Uppsala: A.-B. Akademiska Bokhandeln, 1920.

COOMARASWAMY, Ananda Kentish. "Measures of Fire". In *Selected Papers 2: Metaphysics*. Ed. R. Lipsey. Bollingen Series 89. (159-165). Princeton: Princeton University Press, 1977.

— "Ātmayajña: Self-Sacrifice", in *Selected Papers 2: Metaphysics*. Ed. Roger Lipsey. Bollingen Series 89. (107-147). Princeton: Princeton University Press, 1977. 1st ed. *Harvard Journal of Asiatic Studies* VI.

DANDEKAR, R.N. *Vedic Bibliography*. vol. 1. Bombay: Karnatak Publishing House, 1946; vol. 2. Poona: Bhandarkar Oriental Research Institute, 1978. 1st ed. 1961; vol. 3. Poona: Bhankarkar Oriental Research Institute, 1973; vol. 4. Poona: Bhankarkar Oriental Research Institute, 1985.

— "Rudra in the Veda", in *Journal of the University of Poona*. Humanities Section 1. (94-148). Poona: 1953.

DANGE, Sadashiv Ambadas. *Legends in the Mahābhārata*. Delhi: Motilal Banarsidass, 1969.

—— *Sexual Symbolism from the Vedic Ritual*. Delhi: Ajanta Publications, 1979.

DAVE, J.H. Ed. *Manusmṛtiḥ* (with nine commentaries). 6 vols. Bombay: Bharatiya Vidya Bhavan, 1972-1984.

DAVIDSON, H.R. Ellis. *Gods and Myths of Northern Europe*. Harmondsworth: Penguin, 1964.

DEFOURNY, Michel: "L'initiation, mythe et rituel. Commentaires sur un épisode du Mahābhārata", in *Les rites d'initiation*. (269-282). Ed. J. Ries et H. Limet. Louvain-la-Neuve: Centre d'Histoire des Religions, 1986.

DEPPERT, Joachim. *Rudras Geburt*. Wiesbaden: Franz Steiner Verlag, 1977.

DEV, Amiya. "La guerre de Kurukṣetra n'aura pas lieu: Udyoga Reconsidered", in *Moral Dilemmas in the Mahābhārata*. (77-88). Ed. B.K. Matilal. Delhi: Motilal Banarsidass, 1989.

DONIGER O'FLAHERTY, Wendy. "The Post-Vedic History of the Soma Plant." "Part Two" of Robert Gordon WASSON. *Soma, Divine Mushroom of Immortality*. (95-147). The Hague: Mouton, 1968.

—— *Asceticism and Eroticism in the Mythology of Śiva*. London: Oxford University Press, 1973.

—— *Hindu Myths*. Harmondsworth: Penguin Books, 1975.

—— *The Origins of Evil in Hindu Mythology*. Berkeley: University of California Press, 1980. 1st ed. 1976.

—— *Women, Androgynes and Other Mythical Beasts*. Chicago: The University of Chicago Press, 1980.

—— *The Rig Veda, An Anthology*. Harmondsworth: Penguin, 1981.

—— *Dreams, Illusion and Other Realities.* Chicago: The University of Chicago Press, 1984.

—— *Tales of Sex and Violence: Folklore, Sacrifice and Danger in the* Jaiminīya Brāhmaṇa. Delhi: Motilal Banarsidass, 1985a. 1st ed: University of Chicago Press, 1984.

—— "The case of the stallion's wife: Indra and Vṛṣaṇaśva in the *Ṛg Veda* and the *Brāhmaṇas*". *Journal of the American Oriental Society* 105.3 (1985b): 485-498.

—— *Other Peoples' Myths. The Cave of Echoes.* New York: Macmillan, 1988.

DONIGER, Wendy and Brian K. SMITH. *The Laws of Manu.* Harmondsworth: Penguin, 1991.

DONIGER, Wendy. "Minimyths and Maximyths and Political Points of View", in *Myth and Method.* (109-127). Ed. Laurie L. Patton and Wendy Doniger. Charlottesville and London: The University Press of Virginia, 1996.

—— *The Implied Spider. Politics and Theology in Myth.* New York: Columbia University Press, 1998.

—— *Splitting the Difference. Gender and Myth in Ancient Greece and India.* Chicago: The University of Chicago Press, 1999.

DOUGLAS, Mary. "Children Consumed and Child Cannibals: Robertson Smith's Attack on the Science of Mythology", in *Myth and Method.* (29-51). Ed. Laurie L. Patton and Wendy Doniger. Charlottesville and London: The University Press of Virginia, 1996.

DUBUISSON, Daniel. *La légende royale dans l'Inde ancienne. Rāma et le Rāmāyaṇa.* Paris: Economica, 1986.

DUMEZIL, Georges. *Le festin d'immortalité.* Paris: Annales du Musée Guimet Tome 34, 1924.

—— *Mythe et Epopée*. Paris: Gallimard, 1968. (4th ed.)

—— *Heur et malheur du guerrier*. Paris: Flammarion, 1985.

DUNDES, Alan. "Madness in Method, plus a Plea for Projective Inversion in Myth", in *Myth and Method*. (147-159). Ed. Laurie L. Patton and Wendy Doniger. Charlottesville and London: The University Press of Virginia, 1996.

EGGELING, Julius. (Transl.) *The Śatapathabrāhmaṇa According to the Text of the Mādhyandina School*. 5 vols. Sacred Books of the East. Oxford: Clarendon Press, 1885. Reprint Delhi: Motilal Banarsidass, 1963.

ELIADE, Mircea. *Traité d'histoire des religions*. Paris: Payot, 1949.

—— *Patterns in Comparative Religions*. (Transl. of the preceding by Rosemary Sheed). New York: Sheed & Ward, 1958.

—— *Initiation, rites, sociétés secrètes. Naissances mystiques*. Paris: Gallimard, 1959. First published in English under the title *Birth and Rebirth*. New York: Harper, 1958.

—— *Myths, Dreams and Mysteries*. (Transl. from the French.) London: Harvill Press, 1960.

—— *Shamanism, Archaic Techniques of Ectasy*. (Transl. from the French.) Bollingen Series LXXVI. Princeton: Princeton University Press, 1964.

—— *A History of Religious Ideas, Vol.1: From the Stone Age to the Eleusinian Mysteries*. (Transl. from the French by Willard R. Trask). Chicago: The University of Chicago Press, 1979.

ELIZARENKOVA, Tatiana. "An Approach to the Description of the Contents of the Ṛgveda", in *Mélanges d'Indianisme*. (255-268). Paris: E. de Boccard, 1968.

FALK, Harry. "Soma I and II." *Bulletin of the School of Oriental and African Studies* 52 (1989): 77-90.

FELDHAUS, Anne. *Water and Womanhood.* New York: Oxford University Press, 1995.

FELLER, Danielle. *The Seasons in Mahākāvya Literature.* Delhi: Eastern Book Linkers, 1995.

FELLER JATAVALLABHULA, Danielle. "Raṇa-yajña: The Mahābhārata War as a Sacrifice", in *Violence Denied: Violence, Non-Violence and the Rationalization of Violence in South Asian Cultural History.* (69-103). Ed. Jan E.M. Houben and Karel R. Van Kooij. Leiden: Brill, 1999 a.

— "The Theft of the Soma", in *Composing a Tradition: Concepts, Techniques and Relationships.* (199-225). Proceedings of the First Dubrovnik International Conference on the Sanskrit Epics and Purāṇas. August 1997. Ed. Mary Brockington & Peter Schreiner. Zagreb: Croatian Academy of Sciences and Arts, 1999 b.

FINDLY, Ellison Banks. "Jātavedas in the Ṛgveda: The God of Generations", in *Zeitschrift der Deutschen Morgenländischen Gesellschaft* 131 (1981): 347-373.

FITZGERALD, James L. "India's Fifth Veda: The Mahābhārata's Presentation of Itself", in *Essays on the Mahābhārata.* (150-170). Ed. Arvind Sharma. Leiden: Brill, 1991.

— "The Rāma Jāmadagnya 'Thread' of the Mahābhārata: a new survey of Rāma Jāmadagnya in the Pune text", in *Stages and Transitions: temporal and historical frameworks in epic and purāṇic literature.* (89-132). Proceedings of the Second Dubrovnik International Conference on the Sanskrit Epics and Purāṇas. August 1999. Ed. by Mary Brockington. Zagreb: Croatian Academy of Sciences and Arts, 2002.

FRAZER James George. *The Fall of Man*. Repr. from *Folklore in the Old Testament*. London: 1918.

—— *Mythes sur l'origine du feu*. (Traduit de l'anglais par G.M. Michel Drucker). Paris: Payot, 1931. 1st ed. *Myths of the Origin of Fire*. London: Macmillan, 1930.

FREUD, Sigmund. "Zur Gewinnung des Feuers", in Gesammelte Werke, Sechzehnter Band: *Werke aus den Jahren 1932-39*. (3-9). London: Imago, 1950.

GANGULI, Kisari Mohan. *The Mahabharata of Krishna-Dwaipayana Vyasa*. (Transl.) 12 vols. Delhi: Munshiram Manoharlal, 1970. (Reed. 1998). 1st ed. (100 fascicles): Calcutta: Pratap Chandra Roy, 1883-1896.

GARBE, Richard. Ed. *The Śrauta Sūtra of Āpastamba*. 3 vols. Delhi: Munshiram Manoharlal, 1983. 1st ed. Calcutta: Bibliotheca Indica, 1882-1902.

GEHRTS, Heino. *Mahābhārata. Das Geschehen und seine Bedeutung*. Abhandlungen zur Kunst-, Musik- und Literaturwissenschaft, Band 178. Bonn: Bouvier Verlag Herbert Grundmann, 1975.

GEIB, Ruprecht. "Agní Kravyā́d das Fleisch fressende Feuer im Ṛg- und Atharvaveda", in *KZ* (*Zeitschrift für vergleichende Sprachforschung auf dem Gebiete der Indogermanischen Sprachen*) 89, 2 (1976): 198-220.

GELDNER, Karl Friedrich. *Der Rig-Veda aus dem Sanskrit ins Deutsche übersetzt und mit einem laufenden Kommentar versehen*. 4 vols. Harvard Oriental Series, vols. 33-36. Cambridge, Mass.: Harvard University Press, 1951-57.

GERLITZ, Peter. "Das Fasten als Initiationsritus", in *Initiation*. (271-286). Ed. C.J. Bleeker. Leiden: Brill, 1965.

GIRARD, René. *Violence and the Sacred*. (Transl. from the French by Patrick Gregory.) Baltimore: The Johns Hopkins University Press, 1977.

GITOMER, David L. "Rākṣasa Bhīma: Wolfbelly among Ogres and Brahmans in the Sanskrit *Mahābhārata* and the *Veṇīsaṃhāra*", in *Essays on the Mahābhārata*. (296-323). Ed. Arvind Sharma. Leiden: Brill, 1991.

GODBOLE, N. Śāstrī. Ed. *Taittirīya-Brāhmaṇam with Sāyaṇa's Commentary*. 3 vols. Poona: Ānandāśrama Sanskrit Series 37, 1934-1938.

GOLDMAN, Robert P. *Gods, Priests and Warriors. The Bhṛgus of the Mahābhārata*. New York: Columbia University Press, 1977.

—— "Fathers, Sons and Gurus: Oedipal Conflict in the Sanskrit Epics", in *Journal of Indian Philosophy* 6 (1978): 325-392.

—— Ed. *The Rāmāyaṇa of Vālmīki. An Epic of Ancient India*. Vol. 1: Bālakāṇḍa. Transl. by Robert P. Goldman. Princeton: Princeton University Press, 1984; vol. 2: Ayodhyākāṇḍa. Transl. by Sheldon I. Pollock. 1986; vol. 3: Araṇyakāṇḍa. Transl. by Sheldon I. Pollock, 1991; vol. 4: Kiṣkindhākāṇḍa. Transl. by Rosalind Lefeber, 1994.

—— "Vālmīki and Vyāsa: Their Contribution to India's Discourse on Ethnicity", in *Journal of the Oriental Institute, M.S. University of Baroda* 46, 1-2 (1996): 1-14.

GONDA, Jan. *Aspects of Early Viṣṇuism*. Utrecht: N.V.A. Oosthoek's uitgevers mij, 1954.

—— *The Vision of the Vedic Poets*. The Hague: Mouton & Co., 1963.

—— *Change and Continuity in Indian Religion*. The Hague: Mouton & Co, 1965.

—— *Vedic Literature*. A History of Indian Literature, vol. 1. Wiesbaden: Harrassowitz, 1975.

—— *Hymns of the Ṛgveda not Employed in the Solemn Ritual*. Amsterdam: North-Holland Publishing Company, 1978.

—— "All-India Oriental Conference, Poona, 1978. General President's Address", in *Selected Studies*, vol. VI, Part 2 (1-16). Leiden: E.J. Brill, 1991.

GONZALEZ-REIMANN, Luis. *The Mahābhārata and the Yugas. India's Great Epic Poem and the Hindu System of World Ages*. New York: Peter Lang, 2002.

GOPAL, Ram. "The Veda and the Mahāhārata", in *Golden Jubilee Volume*. (232-240). Ed. T.N. Dharmadhikari. Poona: Vaidika Saṃśodhana Maṇḍala, 1982.

GRASSMANN, Hermann. *Wörterbuch zum Rig-Veda*. (6., überarbeitete und ergänzte Auflage von Maria Kozianka.) Wiesbaden: Harrassowitz, 1996.

HACKER, Paul. "Zur Entwicklung der Avatāralehre", in *Wiener Zeitschrift für die Kunde Süd- und Ostasiens und Archiv für Indische Philosophie* IV (1960): 47-70.

HAUG, Martin. Ed. and transl. *The Aitareya Brahmanam of the Rigveda*. 2 vols. Repr. Delhi: Bharatiya Publishing House, 1976.

HAYAKAWA, Atsushi. "Three Steps to Heaven", in *Asiatische Studien / Etudes Asiatiques* LIV.1 (2000) : 209-247.

—— "Descent of Fire", in *Asiatische Studien / Etudes Asiatiques* LV.2 (2001): 291-320.

HEESTERMAN, Jan C. "Other Folk's Fire", in *Agni*, vol. 2. (76-94). Ed. Frits Staal. Berkeley: Asian Humanities Press, 1983.

—— *The Broken World of Sacrifice. An Essay in Ancient Indian Ritual*. Chicago: The University of Chicago Press, 1993.

—— "Vedism and Hinduism", in *Studies in Hinduism. Vedism and Hinduism*. (43-68). Ed. Gerhard Oberhammer. Wien: Verlag der Oesterreichischen Akademie der Wissenschaften, 1997.

—— "Rituel et Rationalité", in *La Rationalité en Asie. Rationality in Asia*. (153-164). Ed. Johannes Bronkhorst. Lausanne: *Etudes de Lettres*, 2001/3.

HERTEL, Johannes. *Das Indogermanische Neujahrsopfer im Veda*. Leipzig: S. Hirzel, 1938.

HILLEBRANDT, Alfred. *Vedic Mythology*. 2 vols. Delhi: Motilal Banarsidass, 1980. Transl. into English by Sreeramula Rajeswara Sarma of the 2nd revised ed. of *Vedische Mythologie*. 2 vols. Breslau: Marcus, 1927 & 1929. 1st ed. 3 vols. Breslau, 1891, 1899, 1902.

HILTEBEITEL, Alf. *The Ritual of Battle: Krishna in the Mahābhārata*. Ithaca: Cornell University Press, 1976. 2nd ed.: Delhi: Sri Satguru Publications, 1991.

—— "The Burning of the Forest Myth", in *Hinduism: New Essays in the History of Religions*. Ed. Bardwell L. Smith. Leiden: Brill, 1976. Repr. 1982.

—— "Draupadī's Garments", in *Indo-Iranian Journal* 22 (1980): 97-112.

—— "Brothers, Friends, and Charioteers: Parallel Episodes in the Irish and Indian Epics", in *Homage to Georges Dumézil*. (85-112). Ed. Edgar Polomé. Journal of Indo-European Studies, Monograph 3, 1982.

—— *The Cult of Draupadī, vol. 1: Mythologies: From Gingee to Kurukṣetra*. Chicago and London: The University of Chicago Press, 1988.

—— "Reconsidering Bhṛguization", in *Composing a Tradition: Concepts, Techniques and Relationships.* (155-168). Proceedings of the First Dubrovnik International Conference on the Sanskrit Epics and Purāṇas. August 1997. Ed. Mary Brockington & Peter Schreiner. Zagreb: Croatian Academy of Sciences and Arts, 1999.

—— "Review of John Brockington. *The Sanskrit Epics*", in *Indo-Iranian Journal* 43 (2000): 161-169.

—— *Rethinking the Mahābhārata. A Reader's Guide to the Education of the Dharma King.* Chicago: The University of Chicago Press, 2001.

HOLTZMANN, Adolf. *Agni nach den Vorstellungen des Mahābhārata.* Strassburg: Karl J. Trübner, 1878.

—— *Grammatisches aus dem Mahabharata.* Leipzig: Breitkopf & Härtel, 1884.

HOPKINS, E. Washburn. *Epic Mythology.* Strassburg: Karl J. Trübner, 1915. Repr. Delhi: Motilal Banarsidass, 1974.

—— *The Great Epic of India. Its Character and Origin.* New Haven: Yale University Press, 1920.

HOUBEN, Jan E.M. "To kill or not to kill the sacrificial animal (*yajña-paśu*)? Arguments and perspectives in Brahminical ethical philosophy", in *Violence Denied. Violence, Non-Violence and the Rationalization of Violence in South Asian Cultural History.* (105-183). Ed. Jan E.M. Houben & Karel R. van Kooij. Leiden: Brill, 1999.

—— "The Ritual Pragmatics of a Vedic Hymn: The 'Riddle Hymn' and the Pravargya Ritual", in *Journal of the American Oriental Society* 120 (2000): 499-536.

INGALLS, Daniel H.H., Jeffrey Moussaieff MASSON and M.V. PATWARDHAN. *The Dhvanyāloka of Anandavardhana*. (Transl.) Cambridge, Mass.: Harward University Press, 1990.

JAMISON, Stephanie W. "Natural History Notes on the Rigvedic "Frog" Hymn", in *Annals of the Bhandarkar Oriental Research Institute* 72-73 (Amṛtamahotsava) (1991-92): 137-144.

— *The Ravenous Hyenas and the Wounded Sun: Myth and Ritual in Ancient India*. Ithaca: Cornell University Press, 1991.

JEZIC, Mislav. "The *Bāṣkalamantra-Upaniṣad* and the *Bhagavadgītā*", in *Stages and Transitions: temporal and historical frameworks in epic and purāṇic literature*. (35-54). Proceedings of the Second Dubrovnik International Conference on the Sanskrit Epics and Purāṇas. August 1999. Ed. by Mary Brockington. Zagreb: Croatian Academy of Sciences and Arts, 2002.

KARVE, Iravati. *Yugānta: the End of an Epoch*. New Delhi: Sangam Books, 1974.

KEITH, Arthur Berriedale. Ed. *The Veda of the Black Yajus School entitled Taittiriya Sanhita*. 2 vols. Cambridge, Mass.: Harvard Oriental Series 18-19, 1915. Repr. Delhi: Motilal Banarsidass.

— *Rigveda Brahmanas. The Aitareya and Kauṣītaki Brāhmaṇas of the Rigveda*. (Transl.) Cambridge, Mass.: Harvard Oriental Series 25, 1920. Repr. Delhi: Motilal Banarsidass, 1971.

— *The Religion and Philosophy of the Veda and Upanishads*. 2 vols. Harvard Oriental Series 31-32. Cambridge, Mass.: Harvard University Press, 1925. Repr. Delhi: Motilal Banarsidass, 1971.

KINJAWADEKAR, Ramchandrashastri. Ed. *Mahābhāratam with the Commentary of Nīlakaṇṭha*. (7 vols.) Poona: Chitrashala Press, 1929-1936.

KNIPE, David M. "The Heroic Theft: Myths from Ṛgveda IV and the Ancient Near East", in *History of Religions* 6 (1966-67): 328-360.

— *In the Image of Fire. Vedic Experiences of Heat.* Delhi: Motilal Banarsidass, 1975.

KOSKIKALLIO Petteri: "When time turns: Yugas, ideologies, sacrifices", in *Studia Orientalia* (Helsinki: The Finnish Oriental Society) 73 (1994): 253-271.

KRICK, Hertha. *Das Ritual der Feuergründung (Agnyādheya).* Ed. Gerhard Oberhammer. Wien: Verlag der Oesterreichischen Akademie der Wissenschaften, 1982.

KUHN, Adalbert. *Die Herabkunft des Feuers und des Göttertranks.* Berlin: Ferd. Dümmler's Verlagsbuchhandlung, 1859.

KUIPER, Franciscus Bernardus Jacobus. "An Indian Prometheus?", in *Etudes Asiatiques* 25 (1971): 85-98.

— *Ancient Indian Cosmogony.* Delhi: Vikas Publishing House, 1983.

LA FONTAINE, Jean S. *Initiation. Ritual Drama and Secret Knowledge Across the World.* Harmondsworth: Penguin Books, 1985.

LAINE, James W. *Visions of God. Narratives of Theophany in the Mahābhārata.* Publications of the De Nobili Research Library. Ed. G. Oberhammer. Vienna: Gerold, 1989.

LEVI, Sylvain. *Le théâtre indien.* Paris: E. Bouillon, 1890.

LEVI-STRAUSS, Claude. *Le Cru et le Cuit. Mythologiques 1.* Paris: Plon, 1964.

— *L'Homme Nu. Mythologiques 4.* Paris: Plon, 1971.

— *The Naked Man. Introduction to a Science of Mythology: 4.* London: Harper and Row, 1981. (Transl. of the preceding.)

LIMAYE, P.V. & R.D. VADEKAR. *Eighteen Principal Upaniṣads*. Vol. 1. Poona: Vaidika Saṃśodhana Maṇḍala, *śāke* 1880 (= 1958?).

LINCOLN, Bruce. *Myth, Cosmos and Society*. Cambridge Mass.: Harvard University Press, 1986.

— *Discourse and the Construction of Society. Comparative Studies of Myth, Ritual, and Classification*. New York: Oxford University Press, 1989.

— "Mythic Narrative and Cultural Diversity in American Society", in *Myth and Method*. (163-176). Ed. Laurie L. Patton and Wendy Doniger. Charlottesville and London: The University Press of Virginia, 1996.

LONG, J. Bruce. "Life out of Death. A Structural Analysis of the Myth of the 'Churning of the Ocean of Milk'", in *Hinduism. New Essays in the History of Religions*. Ed. Bardwell L. Smith. Leiden: Brill, 1976. Repr. 1982.

MACDONELL, A.A. *Vedic Mythology*. Strassburg: Walter De Gruyter & Co., 1898. Repr. Delhi: Motilal Banarsidass, 1974.

— *The Bṛhaddevatā*. (Ed. and transl.) 2 vols. Harvard Oriental Series 5-6. Cambridge, Mass.: Harvard University Press, 1904.

MACDONELL, A.A. & A.B. KEITH. *Vedic Index of Names and Subjects*. 2 vols. Delhi: Motilal Banarsidass, 1958. 1st ed. London, 1912.

MANI, Vettam. *Purāṇic Encyclopaedia*. Delhi: Motilal Banarsidass, 1975.

MEHTA, Mahesh. "The Evolution of the Suparṇa Saga in the Mahābhārata", in *Journal of the Oriental Institute of Baroda* 21, 1-2 (1971): 41-65.

MINKOWSKI, Christopher Z. "Janamejaya's *sattra* and Ritual Structure", in *Journal of the American Oriental Society* 109 (1989): 401-420.

—— "Snakes, *Sattras* and the Mahābhārata", in *Essays on the Mahābhārata*. (384-400). Ed. Arvind Sharma. Leiden: Brill, 1991.

MONIER-WILLIAMS, Sir Monier. *A Sanskrit-English Dictionary, Etymologically and Philologically Arranged, with Special Reference to Cognate Indo-European Languages*. Oxford: Oxford University Press, 1979. 1st ed. 1899.

MUKHOPADHYAY, Manmatha. "Some Notes on Skanda-Karttikeya", in *The Indian Historical Quarterly* VII (1931): 309-318. Repr. 1985.

MYLIUS, Klaus. *Geschichte der Altindischen Literatur*. Leipzig: Scherz, 1988.

—— Ed. *Älteste indische Dichtung und Prosa. Vedische Hymnen, Legenden, Zauberlieder, philosophische und ritualistische Lehren*. Leipzig: Erata, 2002. 1st ed. Leipzig: Philipp Reklam jun., 1978.

NATU, Ganapatarao Yadavarao. Ed. *Taittirīyāraṇyakam*. 2 vols. Poona: Ānandāśrama Sanskrit Series 36-37, 1967.

OBERLIES, Thomas. "Die Aśvin. Götter der Zwischenbereiche", in *Studien zur Indologie und Iranistik* 18 (1993): 169-189.

—— *Die Religion des Ṛgveda. Erster Teil. Das Religiöse System des Ṛgveda*. Publications of the de Nobili Research Library, vol. XXVI. Ed. G. Oberhammer. Wien: Gerold, 1998.

—— *Die Religion des Ṛgveda. Zweiter Teil. Kompositionsanalyse der Soma-Hymnen des Ṛgveda*. Publications of the de Nobili Research Library, vol. XXVII. Ed. G. Oberhammer. Wien: Gerold, 1999.

OERTEL, Hanns. "On the legend of Indra's visit to Medhātithi, Sāyaṇa on RV i.51.1", in *Proceedings of the American Oriental Society*, 1895, *Journal of the American Oriental Society* 16, p. CCXL. Repr. in *Hanns Oertel Kleine Schriften,* Teil 1. Ed. Heinrich Hettrich & Thomas Oberlies. (24-25). Stuttgart: Franz Steiner Verlag, 1994.

O'FLAHERTY (see under DONIGER O'FLAHERTY).

OLDENBERG, Hermann. "Das altindische Ākhyâna, mit besondrer Rücksicht auf das Suparṇâkhyâna", in *Zeitschrift der Deutschen Morgenländischen Gesellschaft* 37 (1883): 54-86.

—— "Ākhyāna-Hymnen im Ṛgveda", in *Zeitschrift der Deutschen Morgenländischen Gesellschaft* 39 (1885): 52-90.

—— *The Gṛhya-sūtras. Rules of Vedic Domestic Ceremonies.* Part II. (Transl.) Sacred Books of the East, vol. XXX. Ed. F. Max Müller. Oxford: Oxford University Press, 1892. Repr. Delhi: Motilal Banarsidass, 1964.

—— *Die Religion des Veda.* Berlin: Verlag von Wilhelm Hertz, 1894.

OLIVELLE, Patrick. *The Early Upaniṣads.* Annotated Text and Translation. New York: Oxford University Press, 1998.

OOSTEN, Jarich, G. *The War of the Gods: The Social Code in Indo-European Mythology.* London: Routledge & Kegan Paul, 1985.

PARKER H.W. & A. BELLAIRS. *Les amphibiens et les reptiles.* Lausanne: Editions Rencontre, 1971.

PARPOLA, Asko. *Deciphering the Indus Script.* Cambridge: Cambridge University Press, 1994.

PATTON, Laurie L. *Myth as Argument. The Bṛhaddevatā as Canonical Commentary.* Religionsgeschichtliche Versuche und Vorarbeiten. Band 41. Berlin: Walter de Gruyter, 1996.

—— "Myth and Money: The Exchange of Words and Wealth in Vedic Commentary", in *Myth and Method*. (208-244). Ed. Laurie L. Patton and Wendy Doniger. Charlottesville and London: The University Press of Virginia, 1996.

PATTON, Laurie L. and Wendy DONIGER. Ed. *Myth and Method*. Charlottesville and London: The University Press of Virginia, 1996.

PIOVANO, Irma. "Some Reflections about False Witness in Ancient Indian Law", in *Professor Gregory M. Bongard-Levin Felicitation Volume. Indologica Taurinensia* XXIII-XXIV (1997-98): 645-652.

PISCHEL, Richard & Karl Friedrich GELDNER. *Vedische Studien. Erster Band*. Stuttgart: Verlag von W. Kohlhammer, 1889.

POTDAR, K.R. *Sacrifice in the Ṛgveda*. Bombay: Bharatiya Vidya Bhavan, 1953.

RAMANUJAN, A.K. "Three Hundred Rāmāyaṇas: Five Examples and Three Thoughts on Translation", in *Many Rāmāyaṇas. The Diversity of a Narrative Tradition in South Asia*. (22-49). Ed. Paula Richman. Berkeley: University of California Press, 1991.

RANADE, H.G. Ed. and transl. *Lāṭyāyana-Śrauta-Sūtra*. 3 vols. Delhi: Indira Gandhi National Centre for the Arts & Motilal Banarsidass Publishers, 1998.

RAVEN, Ellen M. *Gupta Coins with a Garuḍa-Banner*. 2 vols. Gonda Indological Studies, vol. 1. Groningen: Egbert Forsten, 1994.

RENOU, Louis & Jean FILLIOZAT. *L'Inde Classique. Manuel des études indiennes*. 2 vols. Paris: Payot, 1947-49. Repr. Paris: Librairie d'Amérique et d'Orient, 1985.

RENOU, Louis. "L'hymne aux Aśvin de l'Ādiparvan", in *Louis Renou. Choix d'études indiennes réunies par Nalini Balbir et Georges-Jean Pinault*. (763-773). 2 vols. Paris: Ecole Française d'Extrême-

Orient, 1997. First published in *A Volume of Eastern and Indian Studies in Honour of F.W. Thomas.* (177-187). Bombay, 1939.

— *Littérature sanskrite.* Glossaires de l'hindouisme, Fascicule V. Paris: A. Maisonneuve, 1945.

— "La composition du dixième Maṇḍala", in *Etudes védiques et pāṇinéennes II.* (1-30). Paris: E. de Boccard, 1956a.

— *Bāṣkala-Mantra-Upaniṣad.* (Transl.). Paris: Librairie d'Amérique et d'Orient, 1956b.

— "Le destin du Véda dans l'Inde", in *Etudes Védiques et Pāṇinéennes VI.* Paris: E. de Boccard, 1960.

SARMA, E.R. Sreekrishna. Ed. *Kauṣītaki-Brāhmaṇa.* Wiesbaden: Franz Steiner Verlag, 1968.

SASTRY, Alladi Mahadeva. (Transl.) *The Bhagavad Gita.* Madras: Samata Books, 1979.

ŚASTRI, A. Chinnasvāmi (Pandit). Ed. *The Tāṇḍyamahābrāhmaṇa Belonging to the Sāmaveda with the Commentary of Sāyaṇācārya.* Kashi Sanskrit Series 105. Varanasi: Chowkhamba Sanskrit Series Office, 1935-1936.

— *Śuklayajurvedīyamādhyandinīyaṃ Śatapathabrāhmaṇam.* 2 vols. Kâshî Sanskrit Series 127. Varanasi: Chaukhamba Sanskrit Series Office, 1950.

SCHEUER, Jacques. *Śiva dans le Mahābhārata.* Paris: Presses Universitaires de France, 1982.

SCHMIDT, Hanns-Peter. "Die Kobra im Ṛgveda", in *KZ* (*Zeitschrift für vergleichende Sprachforschung auf dem Gebiete der Indogermanischen Sprachen*) 78 (1963): 296-304.

SCHNEIDER, Ulrich. "Die Geschichte von den beiden Jaratkāru", in *Wiener Zeitschrift für die Kunde Süd- und Ostasiens* III (1959): 1-11.

—— *Der Somaraub des Manu. Mythus und Ritual*. Wiesbaden: Harrassowitz, 1971.

SCHREINER, Peter. "Gewaltlosigkeit und Tötungsverbot im Hinduismus", in *Angst und Gewalt. Ihre Präsenz und ihre Bewältigung in den Religionen*. (287-308). Ed. Heinrich von Stietencron. Düsseldorf: Patmos Verlag, 1979.

—— "Fire – Its Literary Perception in the *Mahābhārata*", in *The Perception of the Elements in the Hindu Traditions*. (113-144). Ed. Maya Burger & Peter Schreiner. Studia Religiosa Helvetica. Vol. 4/5. Bern: Peter Lang, 1999.

SEGAL, Robert A. "Does Myth Have a Future?", in *Myth and Method*. (82-106). Ed. Laurie L. Patton and Wendy Doniger. Charlottesville and London: The University Press of Virginia, 1996.

SEN, Chitrabhanu. *A Dictionary of the Vedic Rituals. Based on the Śrauta and Gṛhya Sūtras*. Delhi: Concept Publishing Company, 1978.

SENART, Emile. *Chāndogya Upaniṣad*. (Traduite et annotée par). Paris: Les Belles Lettres, 1930.

SHARMA, Arvind. "Of Śūdras, Sūtas and Ślokas: Why is the Mahābhārata Preeminently in the Anuṣṭubh metre?", in *Indo-Iranian Journal* 43 (2000): 225-278.

SHARMA, Bellikoth Ramachandra. Ed. *Ṣaḍviṃśa Brāhmaṇa with Vedārthaprakāśa of Sāyaṇa*. Tirupathi: Kendriya Sanskrit Vidyapeetha, 1967.

—— Ed. *Drāhyāyana Śrauta Sūtram*. (With the commentary of Dhanvin). Ganganatha Jha Kendriya Sanskrit Vidyapeetha Text Series 6. Allabhabad: Rashtriya Sanskrit Sansthan, 1983.

SHASTRI, J.L. Ed. *The Garuḍa Purāṇa*. 3 vols. Ancient Indian Tradition & Mythology, vol. 12. Delhi: Motilal Banarsidass, 1978.

SHUKLA, K.S. Ed. *Āryabhaṭīya of Āryabhaṭa with the Commentary of Bhāskara I and Someśvara*. New Delhi: Indian National Science Academy, 1976.

SIEG, Emil. "Die Sagenstoffe des Ṛgveda und die indische Itihāsatradition 1. (Itihāsa zum Ṛgveda)", in *Kleine Schriften*. (91-243). Ed. Klaus Ludwig Janert. Stuttgart: Franz Steiner Verlag, 1991a. 1st ed. Stuttgart: Kohlhammer, 1902.

— "Indra und der Somaraub nach dem Ṛgveda", in *Kleine Schriften*. (347-358). Ed. Klaus Ludwig Janert. Stuttgart: Franz Steiner Verlag, 1991b. 1st ed. in *Beiträge zur Literaturwissenschaft und Geistesgeschichte Indiens. Festgabe für Hermann Jacobi*. (228-239). 1926.

— "Bhṛgu", in *Encyclopaedia of Religion and Ethics*. (558-560). Ed. James Hastings. Edinburgh: Clarke, 1909. Reed. in *Kleine Schriften*. (318-320). Ed. Klaus Ludwig Janert. Stuttgart: Franz Steiner Verlag, 1991c.

SIMON, J.G.: "Initiation et espace sacré. A propos d'Eliade et de Bettelheim", in *Les rites d'initiation*. (107-127). Ed. J. Ries et H. Limet. Louvain-la-Neuve: Centre d'Histoire des Religions, 1986.

SIMSON, Georg von. "The Mythic Background of the Mahābhārata", in *Indologica Taurinensia* XII (1984): 191-223.

— "Remarks on the Suparṇa/Garuḍa Myth (Later Vedic Period)", in *Indologica Taurinensia* XV-XVI (1989-90): 353-360.

SMITH, Brian K. *Reflexions on Resemblance, Ritual, and Religion*. New York: Oxford University Press, 1989.

— "Classifying Animals and Humans in Ancient India", in *MAN* 26 (1991): 527-548.

—— *Classifying the Universe. The Ancient Indian* Varṇa *System and the Origins of Caste.* New York: Oxford University Press, 1994.

SMITH, John D. "Scapegoats of the Gods: The Ideology of the Indian Epics", in *Oral Epics in India.* (176-194). Ed. Stuart H. Blackburn, Peter J. Claus, Joyce B. Flueckiger, and Susan S. Wadley. Berkeley: University of California Press, 1989.

SNOEK, Johannes Augustinus Maria. *Initiations.* Pijnacker: Dutch Efficiency Bureau, 1987.

SÖHNEN-THIEME, Renate. "The Ahalyā Story through the Ages", in *Myth and Mythmaking. Continuous Evolution in Indian Tradition.* (39-62). Ed. Julia Leslie. Richmond: Curzon Press, 1996.

STAAL, Frits. *Agni. The Vedic Ritual of the Fire Altar.* 2 vols. Berkeley: Asian Humanities Press, 1983.

STIETENCRON, Heinrich von, et al. *Epic and Purāṇic Bibliography (up to 1985) annotated and with indexes.* 2 vols. Wiesbaden: Harrossowitz, 1992.

STRENSKI, Ivan. *Four Theories of Myth in Twentieth-Century History. Cassirer, Eliade, Lévi-Strauss and Malinowski.* London: The Macmillan Press, 1987.

—— "The Rise of Ritual and the Hegemony of Myth: Sylvain Lévi, the Durkheimians, and Max Müller", in *Myth and Method.* (52-81). Ed. Laurie L. Patton and Wendy Doniger. Charlottesville and London: The University Press of Virginia, 1996.

SUKTHANKAR, Vishnu Sitaram, et al. *The Mahābhārata for the First Time Critically Edited.* 19 vols. Poona: Bhandarkar Oriental Research Institute, 1933-59.

—— "Epic Studies VI. The Bhṛgus and the Bhārata: A Text-Historical Study", in *Annals of the Bhandarkar Oriental Research Intstitute* 18 (1936): 1-76.

—— *On the Meaning of the Mahābhārata*. Bombay: Asiatic Society of Bombay, 1975.

SULLIVAN, Bruce M. *Kṛṣṇa Dvaipāyana Vyāsa and the Mahābhārata: A New Interpretation*. Leiden: Brill, 1990.

TARKALANKARA, M.C. Ed. *Karmapradīpa*. Calcutta: Asiatic Society of Bengal, 1909.

THAPAR, Romila. *The Past and Prejudice*. Delhi: National Book Trust, 1975.

—— "Society and Historical Consciousness: The Itihāsa-Purāṇa Tradition". Chapter 6 of *Interpreting Early India*. (137-173). Delhi: Oxford University Press, 1993.

THOMAS, Lynn. "Paraśurāma and Time", in *Myth and Mythmaking. Continuous Evolution in Indian Tradition*. (63-86). Ed. Julia Leslie. Richmond: Curzon Press, 1996.

TOKUNAGA, Muneo. *The Bṛhaddevatā*. Kyoto: Rinsen Book Co., 1997.

TUBB, Gary A. "*Śāntarasa* in the *Mahābhārata*", in *Essays on the Mahābhārata*. (171-203). Ed. Arvind Sharma. Leiden: Brill, 1991.

VAN BUITENEN, Jakobus Adrianus Bernardus. *The Mahābhārata*. (Transl. & edited by). vol. 1: "The Book of the Beginning". Chicago: The University of Chicago Press, 1973; vol. 2: "The Book of the Assembly Hall. The Book of the Forest", 1975; vol. 3: "The Book of Virāṭa; The Book of the Effort", 1978.

—— *The Bhagavadgītā in the Mahābhārata: A Bilingual Edition*. (Transl. and ed.) Chicago: Chicago University Press, 1981.

VAN GENNEP, Arnold. *Les rites de passage*. Editions Picard: Paris, 1981. 1st ed. Paris: Emile Nourry, 1909).

VAN NOOTEN, Barend A. & Gary B. HOLLAND. Ed. *Rig Veda. A Metrically Restored Text with an Introduction and Notes.* Harvard Oriental Series 50. Cambridge, Mass.: Harvard University Press, 1994.

VASSILKOV, Yaroslav. "Kālavāda (the doctrine of Cyclical Time) in the Mahābhārata and the concept of Heroic Didactics", in *Composing a Tradition: Concepts, Techniques and Relationships.* (17-33). Proceedings of the First Dubrovnik International Conference on the Sanskrit Epics and Purāṇas. August 1997. Ed. Mary Brockington & Peter Schreiner. Zagreb: Croatian Academy of Sciences and Arts, 1999.

VIRA, Raghu. Ed. *Kapiṣṭhala-Kaṭha-Saṃhitā*. Delhi: Meharchand Lachhmandas, 1968.

VIRA, Raghu and Lokesh CHANDRA. Ed. *Jaiminīya Brāhmaṇa of the Sāmaveda.* Delhi: Motilal Banarsidass, 1986. 1st ed. Nagpur, 1954.

VOGEL, J. Ph. *The Indian Serpent-Lore*. London: Probsthain & Co., 1926.

VON SCHROEDER, Leopold. *Mysterium und Mimus im Rigveda.* Leipzig: H. Haessel Verlag, 1908.

—— Ed. *Maitrāyaṇī Saṃhitā. Die Saṃhitā der Maitrāyaṇīya-Śākhā*. 4 vols. Wiesbaden: Franz Steiner Verlag, 1970-72.

—— Ed. *Kāṭhaka. Die Saṃhitā der Kaṭha-Śākhā*. 4 vols. Wiesbaden: Franz Steiner Verlag, 1970-72.

WEBER, Albrecht. Ed. *The Śatapatha-brāhmaṇa in the Mādhyandina-çākhā*. Varanasi: The Chowkhamba Sanskrit Series 96, 1964. 1st ed. Berlin-London: 1855.

—— *The Śrautasūtra of Kātyāyana*. Varanasi: Chowkhamba Sanskrit Series 104, 1972. 1st ed. 1856 (?).

—— "Analyse der in Anquetil du Perron's Uebersetzung enthaltenen Upanishad", in *Indische Studien*, vol. IX. (1-173). Leipzig: Brockhaus, 1865.

—— Ed. *Die Taittirîya-Saṃhitâ*. Indische Studien 11-12. Leipzig: Brockhaus, 1871-72.

—— Ed. *The Vājasaneyi-Saṃhitā in the Mādhyandina and the Kāṇva-Śākhā with the Commentary of Mahidhara*. Varanasi: Chowkhamba Sanskrit Series 103, 1972.

WEBER-BROSAMER, Bernhard. *Annam. Untersuchungen zur Bedeutung des Essens und der Speise im vedischen Ritual*. Religionswissenschaft und Theologien 3. Rheinfelden: Schäuble Verlag, 1988.

WILHELM, Friedrich. *Prüfung und Initiation im Buche Pauṣya und in der Biographie des Nāropa*. Münchener Indologische Studien, Band 3. Wiesbaden: Harrassowitz, 1965.

WINTERNITZ, Moriz. "Der Sarpabali, ein altindischer Schlangenkult", in *Kleine Schriften*, Teil 1. (5-47). Ed. Horst Brinkhaus. Stuttgart: Franz Steiner Verlag, 1991a. 1st ed. in *Mitteilungen der Anthropologischen Gesellschaft in Wien* 18, N.F. 8, (1888): 25-52 & 250-264.

—— "Das Schlangenopfer des Mahābhārata", in *Kleine Schriften*, Teil 1. (373-385). Ed. Horst Brinkhaus. Stuttgart: Franz Steiner Verlag, 1991b. 1st ed. in *Kulturgeschichtliches aus der Tierwelt. Festschrift des Vereins für Volkskunde und Linguistik*. (68-80). Prag, 1904.

—— *A History of Indian Literature*. 2 vols. 1st ed.: University of Calcutta, 1927. 2nd edition: Delhi: Munshiram Manoharlal, 1972.

WITZEL, Michael. "Tracing the Vedic Dialects", in *Dialectes dans les littératures indo-aryennes*. (97-265). Ed. Colette Caillat. Paris: de Boccard, 1989.

ZELLER, Gabriele. *Die vedischen Zwillingsgötter. Untersuchung zur Genese ihres Kultes*. Wiesbaden: Harrassowitz, 1990.

Texts and Translations

BY SANSKRIT ALPHABETICAL ORDER OF THE NAMES OF THE TEXTS

Atharvaveda Saṃhitā

Atharvaveda with the Pada-pāṭha and Sāyaṇācārya's Commentary. Ed. Vishva BANDHU. 4 vols. Hoshiarpur: Vishveshvaranand Vedic Research Institute, 1960.

Hymns of the Atharva-Veda. Transl. by Maurice BLOOMFIELD. Sacred Books of the East. Ed. by F. Max Müller. Oxford: Oxford University Press, 1897. Repr. Delhi: Motilal Banarsidass, 1992.

Āraṇyakas

Taittirīyāraṇyakam. Ed. Ganapatarao Yadavarao NATU. 2 vols. Poona: Ānandāśrama Sanskrit Series 36-37, 1967.

Upaniṣads

Eighteen Principal Upaniṣads. Ed. P.V. LIMAYE & R.D. VADEKAR. Vol. 1. Poona: Vaidika Saṃśodhana Maṇḍala, *śāke* 1880 (= 1958?).

The Early Upaniṣads. Annotated Text and Translation by Patrick OLIVELLE. New York: Oxford University Press, 1998.

Chāndogya Upaniṣad. Transl. by Emile SENART. Paris: Les Belles Lettres, 1930.

Bāṣkala-Mantra-Upaniṣad. Transl. and ed. by Louis RENOU. Paris: Librairie d'Amérique et d'Orient, 1956b.

Ṛgveda Saṃhitā

Ṛgveda-Saṃhitā with the Commentary of Sāyaṇācārya. 5 vols. Poona: Vaidika Saṃśodhana Maṇḍala, 1972.

Rig Veda. A Metrically Restored Text With an Introduction and Notes. Ed. Barend A. VAN NOOTEN and Gary B. HOLLAND. Harvard Oriental Series 50. Cambridge, Mass.: Harvard University Press, 1994.

Der Rig-Veda aus dem Sanskrit ins Deutsche übersetzt und mit einem laufenden Kommentar versehen. Karl Friedrich GELDNER. 4 vols. Harvard Oriental Series, vols. 33-36. Cambridge, Mass.: Harvard University Press, 1951-57.

Kathāsaritsāgara

Katha Sarit Sagara. Die Mährchensammlung des Sri Somadeva Bhatta aus Kaschmir. 2 vols. Ed. Hermann BROCKHAUS. Sanskrit and German. Leipzig & Paris: Brockhaus, 1839.

Karmapradīpa

Karmapradīpa. Ed. M.C. TARKALANKARA. Calcutta: Asiatic Society of Bengal, 1909.

Garuḍapurāṇa

The Garuḍa Purāṇa. Ed. J.L. SHASTRI. 3 vols. Ancient Indian Tradition & Mythology, vol. 12. Delhi: Motilal Banarsidass, 1978.

Garuḍa Purāṇa (Sāroddhāra). Ed. Major B.D. BASU. Transl. into English by Ernest Wood and S.V. Subrahmanyam. The Sacred Books of the Hindus, vol. IX. Allahabad: Pāṇini Office, 1911.

Gṛhyasūtras

Gobhilagṛhyasūtram. With Bhaṭṭanārāyaṇa's Commentary. Ed. Chintamani BHATTACHARYA. The Calcutta Sanskrit Series XVII. Calcutta: Metropolitan Printing and Publishing House Ltd, 1936.

The Gṛhya-sūtras. Rules of Vedic Domestic Ceremonies. Transl. by Hermann OLDENBERG. Part II. Sacred Books of the East, vol. XXX. Ed. F. Max Müller. Oxford: Oxford University Press, 1892. Repr. Delhi: Motilal Banarsidass, 1964.

Dhvanyāloka

The Dhvanyāloka of Ānandavardhana. Transl. by Daniel H.H. INGALLS, Jeffrey Moussaieff MASSON and M.V. PATWARDHAN. Cambridge, Mass.: Harward University Press, 1990.

Nirukta

Niruktam. Ed. Vinayak Ganesh APTE. 2 vols. Poona: Ānandāśrama Sanskrit Series, 1921.

Bṛhaddevatā

The Bṛhaddevatā. Ed. and transl. by A.A. MACDONELL. 2 vols. Harvard Oriental Series 5-6. Cambridge, Mass.: Harvard University Press, 1904.

The Bṛhaddevatā. Ed. by Muneo TOKUNAGA. Kyoto: Rinsen Book Co., 1997.

Brāhmaṇas

The Aitareya Brahmanam of the Rigveda. Ed. and transl. by Martin HAUG. 2 vols. Repr. Delhi: Bharatiya Publishing House, 1976.

Rigveda Brahmanas. The Aitareya and Kauṣītaki Brāhmaṇas of the Rigveda. Transl. by A.B. KEITH. Harvard Oriental Series 25. Cambridge, Mass.: Harvard University Press, 1920. Repr. Delhi: Motilal Banarsidass, 1971.

Kauṣītaki-Brāhmaṇa. Ed. E.R. Sreekrishna SARMA. Wiesbaden: Franz Steiner Verlag, 1968.

Jaiminīya Brāhmaṇa of the Sāmaveda. Ed. Raghu VIRA and Lokesh CHANDRA. Delhi: Motilal Banarsidass, 1986. 1st ed. Nagpur, 1954.

Das Jaiminīya-Brāhmaṇa in Auswahl. Transl. by Willem CALAND. Wiesbaden: Sändig, 1970. 1st ed. Amsterdam, 1919.

The Tāṇḍyamahābrāhmaṇa Belonging to the Sāmaveda with the Commentary of Sāyaṇācārya. Ed. Pandit A. Chinnaswami ŚASTRI. Kashi Sanskrit Series 105. Varanasi: Chowkhamba Sanskrit Series Office, 1935-1936.

Taittirīya-Brāhmaṇam. Ed. with Sāyaṇa's Commentary by N. Śāstrī GODBOLE. 3 vols. Poona: Ānandāśrama Sanskrit Series 37, 1934-1938.

Pañcaviṃśa-Brāhmaṇa. Ed. W. CALAND. Calcutta: Asiatic Society of Bengal, 1931.

The Śatapatha-brāhmaṇa in the Mādhyandina-çākhā. Ed. Albrecht WEBER. Varanasi: The Chowkhamba Sanskrit Series 96, 1964. 1st ed. Berlin-London: 1855.

The Śatapathabrāhmaṇa According to the Text of the Mādhyandina School. 5 vols. Transl. by Julius EGGELING. Sacred Books of the East. Oxford: Clarendon Press, 1885. Reprint Delhi: Motilal Banarsidass, 1963.

Śuklayajurvedīyamādhyandinīyaṃ Śatapathabrāhmaṇam. Ed. Pandit A. Chinnasvāmi ŚASTRI. 2 vols. Kâshî Sanskrit Series 127. Varanasi: Chaukhamba Sanskrit Series, 1950.

Ṣaḍviṃśa Brāhmaṇa with Vedārthaprakāśa of Sāyaṇa. Ed. Bellikoth Ramachandra SHARMA. Tirupathi: Kendriya Sanskrit Vidyapeetha, 1967.

Ṣaḍviṃśa-Brāhmaṇa. Transl. by W.B. BOLLEE. Utrecht: Storm, 1956.

Bhagavadgītā

The Bhagavad Gita. Transl. by Alladi Mahadeva SASTRY. Madras: Samata Books, 1979.

The Bhagavadgītā in the Mahābhārata: A Bilingual Edition. Transl. and ed. by Jakobus Adrianus Bernardus VAN BUITENEN. Chicago: Chicago University Press, 1981.

Manusmṛti

Manusmṛtiḥ (with nine commentaries). Ed. J.H. DAVE. 6 vols. Bombay: Bharatiya Vidya Bhavan, 1972-1984.

The Laws of Manu. Transl. by Wendy DONIGER and Brian K. SMITH. Harmondsworth: Penguin Books, 1991.

Mahābhārata

The Mahābhārata for the First Time Critically Edited, by Vishnu Sitaram SUKTHANKAR, et al. 19 vols. Poona: Bhandarkar Oriental Research Insitute, 1933-1959.

Mahābhāratam with the Commentary of Nīlakaṇṭha. 7 vols. Ed. Ramchandrashastri KINJAWADEKAR. Poona: Chitrashala Press, 1929-1936.

The Mahābhārata. Transl. & ed. by Jakobus Adrianus Bernardus VAN BUITENEN. vol. 1: "The Book of the Beginning". Chicago: The University of Chicago Press, 1973; vol. 2: "The Book of the Assembly Hall. The Book of the Forest", 1975; vol. 3: "The Book of Virāṭa; The Book of the Effort", 1978.

The Mahabharata of Krishna-Dwaipayana Vyasa. Transl. by Kisari Mohan GANGULI. 12 vols. Delhi: Munshiram Manoharlal, 1970. (Reed. 1998). First Publ. (100 fascicles): Calcutta: Pratap Chandra Roy, 1883-1896.

Yajur Veda Saṃhitās

Kapiṣṭhala-Kaṭha-Saṃhitā. Ed. Raghu VIRA. Delhi: Meharchand Lachhmandas, 1968.

Kāṭhaka. Die Saṃhitā der Kaṭha-Śākhā. Ed. Leopold VON SCHROEDER. 4 vols. Wiesbaden: Franz Steiner Verlag, 1970-72.

Die Taittirîya-Saṃhitâ. Ed. Albrecht WEBER. Indische Studien 11-12. Leipzig: Brockhaus, 1871-72.

The Veda of the Black Yajus School entitled Taittiriya Sanhita. 2 vols. Transl. by Arthur Berriedale KEITH. Cambridge, Mass.: Harvard Oriental Series 18-19, 1914. Repr. Delhi: Motilal Banarsidass.

Maitrāyaṇī Saṃhitā. Die Saṃhitā der Maitrāyaṇīya-Śākhā. Ed. Leopold VON SCHROEDER. 4 vols. Wiesbaden: Franz Steiner Verlag, 1970-72.

The Vājasaneyi-Saṃhitā in the Mādhyandina and the Kāṇva-Śākhā with the Commentary of Mahidhara. Ed. A. WEBER. Varanasi: Chowkhamba Sanskrit Series 103, 1972.

Rāmāyaṇa

The Vālmīki-Rāmāyaṇa. 7 vols. Ed. Govindlal Hargovind BHATT, et al. Baroda: Oriental Institute, 1960-1975.

Śrīmadvālmīkīyarāmāyaṇam. Gorakhpur: Gītā Press, 2017 (Vikrama era).

The Rāmāyaṇa of Vālmīki. An Epic of Ancient India. Vol. 1: Bālakāṇḍa. Transl. by Robert P. GOLDMAN. Princeton: Princeton University Press, 1984. vol. 2: Ayodhyākāṇḍa. Transl. by Sheldon I. Pollock. 1986; vol. 3: Araṇyakāṇḍa. Transl. by Sheldon I. Pollock, 1991; vol. 4: Kiṣkindhākāṇḍa. Transl. by Rosalind Lefeber, 1994.

Le Rāmāyaṇa. Transl. by Madeleine BIARDEAU, et al. Paris: Gallimard (Bibliothèque de la Pléiade), 1999.

Śrautasūtras

The Śrauta Sūtra of Āpastamba. Ed. Richard GARBE. 3 vols. Delhi: Munshiram Manoharlal, 1983. 1st ed. Calcutta: Bibliotheca Indica, 1882-1902.

The Āśvalāyana Śrauta Sūtra with the Commentary of Devatrāta. Ed. Ranbir Singh BAWA. 2 vols. Hoshiarpur: Vishveshvaranand Vishva Bandhu Institute of Sanskrit and Indological Studies, 1986.

The Śrautasūtra of Kātyāyana. Ed. Albrecht WEBER. Varanasi: Chowkhamba Sanskrit Series 104, 1972. 1st ed. 1856 (?).

Drāhyāyana Śrauta Sūtram. (With the commentary of Dhanvin). Ed. B.R. SHARMA. Ganganatha Jha Kendriya Sanskrit Vidyapeetha Text Series 6. Allabhabad: Rashtriya Sanskrit Sansthan, 1983.

The Baudhāyana Śrauta Sūtra. Ed. W. CALAND. 3 vols. Delhi: Munshiram Manoharlal, 1982. 1st ed. Calcutta: Asiatic Society, 1904-1913.

Lāṭyāyana-Śrauta-Sūtra. Critically edited and translated by H.G. RANADE. 3 vols. Delhi: Indira Gandhi National Centre for the Arts & Motilal Banarsidass Publishers, 1998.

General Index

By English Alphabetical Order

For letters with diacritical marks, see under the corresponding letter without diacritics